THE JUST

The Just

how six unlikely heroes
saved thousands of Jews
from the Holocaust

JAN BROKKEN

translated by David McKay

SCRIBE

Melbourne · London

Scribe Publications
18–20 Edward St, Brunswick, Victoria 3056, Australia
2 John St, Clerkenwell, London, WC1N 2ES, United Kingdom
3754 Pleasant Ave, Suite 100, Minneapolis, Minnesota 55409, USA

First published in Dutch as *De rechtvaardigen* by Atlas Contact 2018
Published by Scribe 2021

This publication has been made possible with financial support from the Dutch
Foundation for Literature.

N ederlands
letterenfonds
dutch foundation
for literature

Typeset in Dante MT by J&M Typesetting
Printed and bound in the UK by CPI Group (UK) Ltd, Croydon CR0 4YY

Scribe Publications is committed to the sustainable use of natural resources and the use
of paper products made responsibly from those resources.

9781925849295 (Australian edition)
9781912854219 (UK edition)
9781950354566 (US edition)
9781925938722 (ebook)

Catalogue records for this book are available from the National Library of Australia and
the British Library.

scribepublications.com.au
scribepublications.co.uk
scribepublications.com

Contents

Author's note

The Talmud tells of the *khasidei umót ha'olám*, the Righteous Among the Nations. According to legend, there are thirty-six such people at any moment in world history. In 1940 there were two in Kaunas, Lithuania; one in Riga, Latvia; one in Stockholm, Sweden; and two in Japan – one in Kobe, and one in Tokyo.

This is, at its heart, the story of Dutch consul Jan Zwartendijk in Kaunas. I have reconstructed it with the help of his children, drawing on documents and personal testimonies. But no one succeeds alone. It is also the story of three other consuls and two ambassadors, all equally unknown. Together, they set up one of the greatest rescue operations of the twentieth century. Thanks to their children, I can now recount their historic acts.

Ach, töten könnt ihr,
aber nicht lebendig machen.
Oh, you can kill,
but not bring to life.
– Friedrich Hölderlin

Inscription on the memorial plaque for Louis Aletrino in
Mauthausen concentration camp

I

Mister Radio Philips

Everything important begins unexpectedly and makes you suspicious. You may be confronted with an impossible choice and have only a split second to decide. You're not yet sure what to do, but already you sense that the rest of your life may depend on your decision. How will you respond? I can't answer that question for myself, and that may explain why I've burrowed into this story like a mole.

Jan Zwartendijk heard the telephone ring. He was already outside with his bag under his arm and a key in his hand. He had just locked up the office and the showroom. It was almost 6.00 p.m., Eastern European Summer Time. The sun was shining through the treetops along Laisvės Alėja, 'Freedom Avenue', the longest, widest boulevard in Kaunas. The radios gleamed in the display window; their emblems – four stars and three waves – looked like silver. 'Mister Radio Philips', the people of Kaunas called him, always with a hint of admiration, as if he had screwed the sets together himself and equipped them with electron tubes and loudspeakers. In Lithuania, more than in the West, radios were seen as heralds of the modern age.

Kaunas (sometimes still called by the pre-war name of Kovno) had shaken off its provincial backwardness many years earlier. But the complete telephone book was still a slim volume. Something told him that if he didn't answer the phone there would be consequences. The date raced through his mind like a warning: 29 May 1940. Although he was just an ordinary businessman – forty-three years old, married, with three children – he was also a foreigner, and in Lithuania he never knew exactly who to trust. Whenever he could, he kept a safe distance. If he unlocked the door, walked back to his desk, and picked up the receiver, he would let in all the dangers of a city teetering on the brink of war.

He was not a born hero. He lacked ambition. What he really wanted to do was hurry home for an idle hour in the garden with Erni and the children before dinner. It was his third year in Kaunas, and he knew you had to savor the warm summer nights. Otherwise you'd never make it through the long winter. Under the apple trees, the unhinged world would dwindle into a cloud on the far horizon. He couldn't help hiding away from reality sometimes, even though it had become absurd to believe in peace.

All afternoon at the office, he'd felt the tension. On the surface, nothing was out of the ordinary, aside from the overflowing ashtrays. No customers, no orders. A grim quiet. He had sent De Haan and Van Prattenburg home at five-thirty. De Haan, the manager of the radio-assembly plant, now frittered away his days at the office. Since production had been halted, he made only a brief appearance at the factory each morning, to show the few remaining employees he hadn't vanished from the face of the earth. Van Prattenburg kept the books and was the financial director. His one brief spurt of activity came at the end of the week when they paid the wages. The three nerve-wracked men had not done much that day except smoke cigarettes and glance outside every other minute. Everyone in town was expecting the Red Army. Maschewski had stuck around for a while, until he'd spotted a woman in a much too skimpy summer dress standing in front of the showroom window. He'd approached her as if she were a potential customer, and struck up a conversation in German, Lithuanian, Polish, or Russian – Zwartendijk couldn't hear. But he was sure Maschewski had gone outside mainly to steady his nerves.

The city was in the calm before the storm. At any moment, tanks might roll down the hills and take their positions at the bridges over

Jan Zwartendijk

the Neris and Nemunas (or Neman) Rivers. He could already picture Russian soldiers marching down the two-kilometre-long Laisvės Alėja, which – oh, the irony – had been built in the tsarist period to enhance the glory of military parades. It could happen today or tomorrow. From that time on, there would be no more free, independent Lithuania. The country would be incorporated into the Soviet Union; there was no question about that.

The telephone went on ringing. All week it had not rung once. Was this, at long last, a customer? The threat of war meant zero sales for them. Times were just as hard as in the Great Depression, which had dragged on in Lithuania until 1937 or 1938. He'd had to send fifteen factory workers home, and the other twenty were sitting idle. In the whole month of May, they hadn't sold a single radio. The last remaining employees loitered around the empty assembly tables, waiting to find out what was going to happen. They were listening to every station they could find on the short-wave radio, searching for news. De Haan said they turned up the volume whenever they heard Hitler.

A customer calling to place an order? No. Who would call around 6.00 p.m. on a weekday to buy a brand-new radio? Nor was it Philips headquarters in Eindhoven; they did everything in writing, because an international call was as expensive as a railway ticket to Berlin. It had to be something else, something that couldn't wait.

Bad news, no doubt. He hoped it wasn't Piet. His bond with his identical twin was so strong that when Piet caught a cold, two thousand kilometres away, Jan started sneezing. He hadn't heard from his brother in a month. Had Piet been in Rotterdam on 14 May, during the German bombing? If Jan didn't pick up the phone, he would spend all evening and all night wondering whether something had happened to his brother.

Or was the call somehow connected to the precarious political situation? And supposing it was, what kind of chump would pretend he didn't hear it? He turned the key in the lock, pushed open the door, sprinted through the showroom, rushed up the stairs to the office on the second floor, lifted the receiver from the Bakelite telephone, and panted, 'Hello … Lietuvos Philips …'

'Zwartendijk?'

The voice was Dutch, with a rolling southern r. Jan made an affirmative grunt as his free hand loosened his necktie – he had brought the heat in with him.

'De Decker speaking.'

The name meant nothing at first.

'Dutch legation in Riga.'

Oh. That De Decker.

'Your Excellency —'

'No need for all that, under the circumstances.'

He had met De Decker only once, at the reception in the presidential palace when the ambassador had come to present his credentials. At that stage, the Baltic countries had still been independent. It was some time in the spring of 1939, a few months before Hitler and Stalin made their infernal pact, dividing Poland and the Baltic states between themselves as if playing Monopoly. De Decker had been appointed the Dutch ambassador to Latvia, Estonia, and Lithuania. In each of the three countries, he'd had to present himself to the president and the parliamentary leader. Though still in his fifties, he looked old before his time, worn down by life. Shortly after his arrival in Riga, his wife had died. No children. How must that feel, in a country where you don't know a soul?

As the director of one of the few Dutch companies in the region, Zwartendijk had felt an obligation to show his face at the event, even though he hated receptions.

Bald. Long face, crooked nose, sunken cheeks. At the reception, Zwartendijk was surprised to learn that De Decker had been born in Belgium, because he certainly didn't glow with southern European *joie de vivre*. Apparently, he was something of a homebody, and he never walked away from negotiations until he got results.

He was also a man of few words. After the two of them were introduced at the reception, he had mumbled, 'Ah, Philips … How many countries have you been assigned to?'

Zwartendijk tried to keep his answer short: 'I worked in Prague for a long time … then in Hamburg.' He'd worked for a different company back then, but what did that matter?

'Hamburg? I just finished a seven-year stint as consul general in Düsseldorf. Nice country, Germany. Did you have a good time there, too? Or did you get a little tired of all those outstretched arms?'

He had asked the question in a serious tone. Zwartendijk liked that.

After the Dutch capitulation, which came much sooner than expected, De Decker had stayed in his post. The Kingdom of the Netherlands had not yet been subjugated completely – they still had the Indies, Curaçao, and Suriname – and the queen and government had not resigned, but gone into exile. A few days after the surrender, the ambassador had sent a telegram asking whether Philips would keep its Lithuanian branch open. Zwartendijk had telegraphed back, 'No instructions to close from Eindhoven.'

They'd never talked on the telephone before.

'I'd better cut to the chase, Zwartendijk. I'm in sore need of a consul in Kaunas.'

He said nothing. Then, 'We have Tillmanns, don't we?'

'A German. After the invasion and capitulation, I'd have to be crazy to let our country be represented by *Herr Doktor* Tillmanns. And he's not just any German! You know —'

'That's his wife, more than him. She'd stand in line to welcome Hitler here tomorrow with a bunch of flowers. Tillmanns is not so bad, I think. He's been living in Lithuania a long time.'

'All German speakers in Lithuania are Nazi sympathisers – you know that better than I do. Anyway, it's beside the point. I didn't have to give Tillmanns the boot. He tendered his resignation the very day of the German invasion, the tenth of May. Have to give him credit for that. I haven't officially accepted his resignation yet, but I can't put it off much longer. I need an acting consul tout de suite. You're the obvious choice.'

'Goodness gracious, what an honour.'

Zwartendijk wondered whether his words had sounded ironic enough.

'This way we'll have an office there, you see ...'

Ah, that explained it.

'... since we're no longer welcome under Tillmanns's roof. We have to clear out of there right away. Your shop would make a fine consulate.'

'You're assuming Eindhoven will approve?'

'All the top Philips managers are in London now, with our government and Her Majesty the Queen.'

'All except Frits Philips and Guépin, who stayed at work in

Eindhoven. Guépin is my direct supervisor. Yesterday I received a message from him to all the foreign branches.'

'And?'

'Keep a cool head and carry on as usual.'

'Sounds like a fantasy to me, Zwartendijk. Philips is under German supervision now, like all major Dutch companies. But if I'm not mistaken, you, as the director of the Lithuanian office, run an autonomous enterprise and have a fairly free hand.'

'Your information is correct, Mr De Decker.'

'I need to fill this vacancy as fast as possible, you understand?'

'I don't mean to be difficult, Mr Ambassador —'

'Envoy. The Kingdom of the Netherlands has envoys, not ambassadors.'

'What's the difference?'

'Lesser powers have envoys; great powers have ambassadors. Since the Congress of Vienna in 1815, the Netherlands has been classed as a lesser power. An ambassador outranks an envoy. It's called *préséance*. I have to defer to the German, French, and British ambassadors.'

'You see, I don't know the first thing about this stuff.'

'Just call me ambassador. It makes no difference. That's what everyone does around here.'

'I wish I could help you, Mr De Decker, but when it comes to diplomacy and consular affairs, I'm an ignoramus. I don't have a clue about the field or the work involved.'

'There's practically none. Now and then, our fellow Dutch nationals may need a passport renewed … or a little advice and assistance while travelling abroad. A Dutch company might ask you to act on its behalf. Nothing too demanding.'

The ambassador coughed, as if he were only too well aware of the gap between this rosy picture and the actual work involved.

'The thing is, Zwartendijk, the Netherlands needs a representative in Lithuania. If we close the consulate, we'll lose our foothold in the region. Now, I've managed to keep the consulate open in Tallinn, and the legation in Riga … but I sometimes feel like the captain of a sinking ship. I need help. I can't handle this on my own. There's too much trouble on the way: the nationalisations, the refugees. Everyone in the region has come adrift. I am asking you to be our man in Kaunas.'

'All well and good, Your Excellency, but I don't see how I can help you with those kinds of problems ... What exactly would I have to do —'

'Tillmanns will hand over the official papers and seals, as well as the files. I'll send you the consular handbook and further instructions by mail. Any time you're in a bind, you can call me – collect. I don't mean to sound melodramatic, but for God's sake, help me out here. Terrible things are about to happen.'

'Sure, war is coming.'

'Not just war. This is ...'

'Apocalypse.'

'Exactly. Zwartendijk, we have to prepare for the worst.'

'You can count on me.'

'Are you saying what I think you're saying?'

'I can hardly imagine what I'm getting myself into, and, to be honest, I'd rather not try.'

'Splendid, Zwartendijk, splendid. I hereby appoint you acting consul of the Kingdom of the Netherlands in Lithuania. In a moment, I'll swear you in. Then I'll ask the government in London to approve the appointment and report the news to the transitional authorities in Lithuania. Go to Tillmanns tomorrow and pick up all the official papers.'

'One question, though ... My wife's native language is German. She was born on the border of Poland and Czechoslovakia in a little town that was part of the Austrian Empire. How do you know she can be trusted? My children go to a German school, my eldest is at a German secondary academy. What makes you think I can be trusted?'

A curt laugh. 'I know people, Zwartendijk. One look at you was enough.'

Was that the gist of their conversation?

Seventy-six years later, I'm in Kaunas, at 29 Laisvės Alėja, peering through the window of the building where Jan Zwartendijk answered the phone.

His daughter, Edith, is next to me. She was thirteen years old then; now she's eighty-nine. She holds on to my arm to keep her balance, and says in a steady voice that it all started here on that fateful evening in May. Her father had just locked up the showroom when he heard the telephone ringing. Inside the store, nothing has changed, Edith tells me: the same light-brown panelling, the same wooden stairs from the showroom to the upper floor. I picture Jan Zwartendijk standing there with the Bakelite receiver in his hand. Edith makes the scene even more vivid.

'Pa had great confidence in De Decker right from the start. It was mutual. Later, when the situation became truly explosive, the two of them talked often on the phone – usually in the evening, after he came home exhausted. The phone was mounted on the wall of the corridor. He would make fierce gestures and kick the wall. After a few minutes, you would see him calm down.'

2

One last breath of peace

For the second time, Zwartendijk closed the showroom. He looked a mess. Before opening the door of the Buick and taking a seat behind the wheel, he straightened his tie. He hated pomp and pretension, but he dressed like a gentleman. In the summer, he wore a lightweight suit, a white shirt, a waistcoat, a light-grey tie, and a white handkerchief in his breast pocket. His impeccable grooming reflected his upbringing as the scion of an elite Rotterdam family. His parents were determined never to let their standards slip, especially not when their business – a tobacco factory – ran into trouble. Zwartendijk removed his jacket only on Sundays. His necktie stayed on.

It also had to do with England. At the age of seventeen and eighteen, he'd attended a boys' boarding school in Reading, a stone's throw from Oxford. Apart from good English, he hadn't learned much there, but he'd become more aware of how he looked and dressed. According to his English schoolmasters, sloppiness was a sign of a weak character. School uniforms were mandatory in Reading, and you stuck out like a sore thumb if your hair was uncombed, or if the cuffs of your trousers were turned improperly.

He started the engine, and the car began jolting and jerking its way home. It was a massive four-door with a running board and a high roof. Two spare tyres, behind the front wings, against the bonnet. Three windows on each side, and a double rear window.

Jan Zwartendijk with his son, Robbie. On proud display in the background is
the Buick Roadmaster. Kaunas, 1940.

The Buick Roadmaster had been left for Zwartendijk when his
predecessor, Edward van Breda, was ordered back to Eindhoven
because of his Nazi sympathies – a legacy of his time in Austria, where
he had headed the Philips Radio sales department from 1928 to 1933.

Like Zwartendijk, Edward van Breda came from Rotterdam, but
Eddy, as he was called, was more of a show-off. He wanted the biggest,
most expensive car on Laisvės Alėja – which was no great feat, since
even on a busy Saturday there were no more than four cars parked on
the boulevard. He had the only American car in town, and the only
one with two spare tyres and a mahogany dashboard.

It was absurdly expensive; King Farouk of Egypt had himself driven around in the same model. The first time Zwartendijk stepped into the Buick, the interior still smelled of leather, and it had barely 8,000 kilometres on the clock. Eddy had used it for only a few months before his transfer – which happened so unexpectedly that he thought the head office must have made some mistake.

It had come as an even greater shock to his wife, who had always behaved as if she'd married not Eddy, but the head of the whole Philips organisation. Mrs Van Breda, in her extravagant fur coats, was the talk of the town. She looked down on Erna Zwartendijk, seeing her as no real German. And she was right: Erna, called Erni by everyone in her family, was not entirely German, Polish, Czech, or Austrian. Erni came from Central Europe, and that meant you were a little of everything.

Zwartendijk had never had any quarrel with Van Breda, or even the slightest friction. They were so different from one another that they had naturally kept their distance. Van Breda had said that Zwartendijk was 'not really a salesman', and told head office to appoint Maschewski as his successor, 'just the kind of wheeler-dealer we need around here'. Zwartendijk hadn't heard about that until later, more than a year after Van Breda was told to pack his bags. Fortunately, Philips wanted to appoint a Dutchman, so Maschewski was out. Wheeler-dealers had no place in the corporate culture; electronics had a touch of class, thank God.

The Philips directors had begun to have doubts about Van Breda after the columnist for the liberal daily newspaper in Kaunas wrote a letter, dated 5 November 1934, to the company's director, Dr Anton Philips. The Lithuanian journalist complained of the strong tendency toward 'Hitlerism' shown by 'Herr Brede [sic]', and of his fanatical anti-Jewish views. He claimed that Van Breda spent more time in the capital's cafés than he did at work, and that the assembly plant was in a deplorable state. Poor ventilation led to a build-up of toxic fumes, and while the workers laboured under these life-threatening conditions,

Jan and Erni Zwartendijk. Erni has a folding camera.

Van Breda led a life of leisure in coffee houses and restaurants. Dressed in a fur coat (which he later declared as a business expense), he made long speeches about the political situation in the country, bellowing forth his pro-Hitler views and proclaiming his contempt for Jews. According to the journalist, who wrote to Anton Philips in excellent German but closed his letter with an illegible signature, Van Breda had inspired horror in Lithuania's Jewish community. He made no secret of his belief that the Jews should be 'exterminated'.

This letter has been preserved in the Philips archives in Eindhoven, with a note from Anton pencilled in the margin: 'Check if it's true'. The president-director, who had turned sixty on 14 March 1934 and been with Philips for forty years, was known for his careful attention to both the big picture and any little threat to the company's reputation.

Almost nothing escaped his attention. To an international corporation with thirty thousand employees in 1934, such a letter was little more than village gossip, but Anton had a sixth sense for alarming details. He would lead the company until 1939, and as the war approached, he took ever-stricter steps to keep it free of anti-Semitic statements and actions – perhaps because of his Jewish ancestors, who had left Germany in the mid-nineteenth century (and were related to Karl Marx, a secret he closely guarded). Seven years before the outbreak of the Second World War, Anton began to transfer Jewish senior managers to Philips offices in the Americas. He helped Dr Meinhardt, the Jewish director of the Osram light bulb factory – a Siemens subsidiary in which Philips was a minority shareholder – to escape to London. And he sidelined Van Breda, along with other managers whose political views were too outspoken or Nazist.

In 1939, the former director of Philips in Lithuania found himself assigned to a desk job in the commercial department of the Eindhoven headquarters. In the summer of 1941, Van Breda was sent to Sofia, at the recommendation of the company's German administrator, as a sales manager and an assistant to the Philips director in Bulgaria. After the liberation of Eindhoven in 1944, his employment was terminated with immediate effect. A brief post-war evaluation of the management in Bulgaria states, under the heading of ATTITUDE OF E. VAN BREDA: 'Is a member of the Dutch Nazi party and in every way unfit to represent the company internationally.' Van Breda returned to the Netherlands, destitute, and died of stomach cancer in 1947, at the age of forty-three.

The engine was roaring, the gears grinding. Zwartendijk had never learned to drive smoothly – he had no feeling for it. He'd had a driver in Prague, and in Hamburg he had chosen to live three stops from the Exchange so that he could take the tram. Not until after the age of forty had he taken the wheel. He couldn't do much harm in Kaunas, with so little motor traffic. Still, the streets were far from vacant. He had to keep a constant lookout for the trams that trundled through the city centre and seemed to have no brakes, for the countless horse carts, always carrying a much too heavy load, and, of course, for the crowd of pedestrians who crossed the boulevards diagonally. Yet, despite its population of 120,000, Kaunas had a provincial quality. Vilnius, the historical capital, had been captured by Poland after Lithuania declared independence in 1918, and Kaunas had become the seat of government and parliament. But the Lithuanians still called Kaunas the *laikinoji sostinė*, 'temporary capital', and all its grandeur and economic activity did seem ephemeral in nature.

Zwartendijk would pass the Church of St Michael the Archangel at a slow crawl, and every day he enjoyed the sight of the beautiful building, especially when the evening sun raked the light-blue domes. It had been a garrison church for Russian Orthodox soldiers in the late nineteenth century, had served as a Lutheran church for German soldiers in the First World War, and finally, after Lithuania declared its independence, had become a Roman Catholic church for Lithuanian soldiers.

Getting a grip on Lithuanian history had been a major challenge for him. The country, a grand duchy in the fifteenth century, had for centuries been tossed back and forth between the great powers: Germany, Sweden, Russia, and Poland. Driving by the pavement cafés, and seeing the men and women with their tankards of beer, you might imagine yourself in Germany. The food there was heavy and greasy – again, German. It took a little longer to notice the differences. Lithuanian women, like those in Poland, tended to have jet-black hair and dark eyes. And like the Polish, Lithuanians were fervent Catholics who practised their faith with great devotion, lying on the ground with their arms outstretched before the altar, instead of kneeling

Lithuanian Jews were equally pious. Half the population of Vilnius was Jewish. The number of Jews living in Kaunas was smaller, but there were at least thirty thousand. The most often heard language in the shopping streets was Yiddish. Every day, Zwartendijk had a sandwich in a Jewish bakery or a pastry in a Jewish tearoom. Most of his business associates were Jewish shopkeepers and Jewish radio repairmen.

If you focused on the buildings and the mix of wooden and masonry houses, Kaunas looked very Russian. The city had the Russians to thank for all its splendours: the sprawling city park, the snow-white concert hall, the main church, and the railway station, an impressive building despite having only one platform.

He double-clutched and shifted back into second gear. The gears grated. If little Jan had been sitting next to him, he would have been furious with his father for releasing the clutch too quickly again. Jan had reached the age when he wanted his father to be a man's man, capable of anything.

Jan, Jan, Jan … He'd had no choice but to call his eldest son Jan. He'd heard it was a tradition among the Dutch urban elite – in any case, it was well established in his family. He'd been called Jan because he'd arrived ten minutes before his brother, Piet.

The road wound uphill in wide curves. The centre of Kaunas formed a triangle where two rivers converged. Its most fashionable neighbourhood was on the highest hills – on the Green Hill, as they said in Kaunas. It was a steep climb. In the winter, tall, skinny Edith and little Jan would ski down the slope, hurtling around the curves and making giant leaps. Sometimes more than a metre of snow fell in one night.

When he reached the top, he took a right onto Perkūno Alėja. On either side of the avenue, the plum trees were in blossom. Most of his neighbours were sitting in the front gardens of their large, detached wooden houses. It was a green part of town, with tall trees along the avenues, bushes lining the broad pavements, and many flowers around the houses – although late in the winter it became a slushy mess, like the rest of the city.

At number 15, he turned into the driveway. Edith and Jan rushed out to meet him. That was always the way: whenever you saw Edith, Jan was sure to follow two seconds later. Or vice versa. The bond between them was as strong as his own connection to his twin brother. He had thought they would grow apart when Edith started secondary school and Jan was left behind in the *Grundschule*. But, by

Jan Zwartendijk with Edith and Jan junior in Kaunas, 1940.

happy chance, the two schools shared one building, so they could still walk down the stairs to the city centre side by side each morning.

Edith had been born in Prague, attended nursery school in Hamburg, begun primary school in the Kralingen district of Rotterdam, and gone on to other primary schools in Rotterdam's Schiebroek district and later in Eindhoven. She had completed *Grundschule* in Kaunas and enrolled in the classical grammar school there. Any other child would have lost their mind, but Edith was overjoyed whenever they moved to a new place or a new country. She said that for her it was like always being on vacation. She was so cheerful that he sometimes wondered if she really had the same personality as her mother, or was only pretending. In any case, she certainly was enterprising. And she always gained the highest grades at school, whether the lessons were in German or in Dutch.

Jan never complained either when they moved to a new house or a new city. He loved Rotterdam and Kaunas equally. Not to mention Prague, which he was most familiar with from holiday trips. Every summer, Erni would take the children to Czechoslovakia to spend time with her family, while her husband travelled the Mediterranean on a freighter. He was a true son of Rotterdam, and the chance to see and smell the sea for a few weeks was what kept him sane for the rest of the year in the heart of Europe.

He had hardly stepped out of the car when Jan jumped on his shoulders. He shook the boy off, kissed Erni, and gave Robbie a hug.

Robbie had been born in Kaunas – and had even been conceived there, in the Metropolis Hotel. Less than a week after Zwartendijk's appointment in Kaunas, he had travelled ahead to start work right away and look for a house. At Christmas, Erni had come to visit. He was then staying at the Metropolis on Laisvės Alėja, less than fifty metres from his office. A few months later, he had been joined by the pregnant Erni and their children.

Robbie had the most striking eyes of the three siblings, the same shade of blue as his mother's. But he also had a problem: his beet-red nose. A clown nose, Jan and Edith would joke. They learned it was a frequent skin condition among newborns: a strawberry mark. Four months after the delivery, Dr Rabinowitz had recommended radiation therapy for the baby. The treatment wasn't available in the Kaunas hospital, where most of the equipment was antiquated. Erni's mind was soon made up: she would take Robbie to the Netherlands for treatment once a month. It was quite a journey for her: first the night train to Berlin, then the day train to Utrecht, more than twelve hours of travel in total – with a baby whose diapers needed changing

Erni with Robbie in front of the house in Kaunas, spring 1940.

once every four hours. But when Erni had said to Jan, 'Ach, mensch ...',
he had realised that no argument could stop her.

On the first trip, in January 1940, Erni had stopped for the night in
Berlin, in the hotel in Unter den Linden where she stayed whenever
she passed through the city. But the atmosphere in Berlin no longer
appealed to her: too much bluff and bravado.

In February, she had gone straight on to Utrecht without staying
in Berlin. Her husband's cousin, who worked as a pathologist in
the Utrecht hospital, had organised the treatment in the radiology
department. She stayed with the cousin, and boarded the train back to
Berlin with Robbie the next morning. Then they went on, by way of
Königsberg, to Kaunas.

She had never uttered a word of complaint about this routine, and would surely have continued if Robbie had not received an excessive dose of X-rays in March, which burned his entire nose. Dr Rabinowitz's advice was to put the treatment on hold. If she hadn't agreed to this, she would have been in Utrecht with Robbie when the Germans invaded the Netherlands.

Every evening after work and before dinner, it was football time, at least in the summer. Young Jan could not sit still – a condition he had inherited from his father. During his time at the boarding school in Reading, he had begged his parents, in letter after letter, for new football shoes. He didn't get them right away; they told him he had to improve his marks first. This incentive worked, and by the end of the school year he was able to buy both football and tennis shoes.

Jan was ready, with the ball under his arm. It was a spacious garden, even though part of the land had been sold and a house was starting to be built on the south side. A few days earlier, Edith had asked Jan why only women worked in Lithuania, and it had certainly been strange to see that not one man was involved in the construction of the house. Even though the communist era was still in the future, Kaunas resembled Moscow: women operated the concrete mixers, laid the bricks, and installed the roof trusses. Likewise, there were more women than men working at the radio-assembly plant. De Haan said they knew what they were doing and were meticulous.

Zwartendijk's homecoming tended to be a playful interlude. He would carry Robbie around the garden, listen to the latest tune that Edith had learned to play on the piano, or stop Jan from grabbing his violin and stepping out into the roof gutter. The boy could scratch away on that thing for hours at a time. His father had once spoken to him about it, and since then he'd gone out on the roof to play his gypsy melodies, to the delight of the whole neighbourhood.

At seven o'clock, he called out, 'Time to eat!' He didn't have many principles, but he did expect his dinner on time. In the summer, that meant seven o'clock.

The house was so large that they could have made do with half the space. The owner, a professor of Lithuanian language and literature, lived on the ground floor with his daughter and his wife, who was a schoolteacher. The Zwartendijks had the run of the rest of the house: the first floor and the attic rooms. The first-floor dining room was the size of a ballroom.

Petrite, their Lithuanian maid, served the food. She couldn't cook – Erni did that – but she liked to serve the food, like a waiter in a restaurant. Edith and Jan would try to make her laugh. They'd been trying for two years, but had never yet succeeded.

When Petrite returned to the kitchen, Zwartendijk made an offhand remark about being appointed as consul.

'You're replacing Tillmanns?' Erni asked, not surprised in the least.

He gave a slow nod.

'You're doing the right thing.'

It was exactly the response that he had expected from her. He never asked for her opinion before making a decision. Long before he'd met Erni, he'd grown used to taking care of his own business. He had been thirty years old when they married; she was twenty-one. Still, he never made a decision without wondering what Erni would think of it. If he had the faintest suspicion she might disapprove, he wouldn't do it. His guesses about what she would think were usually right, or at least she had never said she utterly disagreed with him.

'You may be called an honorary consul, but it's not an honorary position,' he muttered.

'You'll have a diplomatic passport, right?'

'You think the Ivans will have much respect for that?'

'Russians have no respect for anything.'

'And Jerries even less …'

'Tillmanns had to go,' Erni blurted. 'That man was an embarrassment to the Netherlands, and to the free world. I'm glad you said yes.'

'I hope you still feel that way in a couple of months.'

'Will Mamma smell like Mrs Sugihara now?' Edith asked.

He chuckled. 'How so? What does she smell like?'

'Paris.'

On their way to school, along Perkūno Alėja and Vaižganto Gatvė, Edith and Jan would often run into the Japanese consul's wife. The Japanese consulate was at Vaižganto 30, in an ordinary house. They could never resist following her, just a few steps behind, to enjoy the cloud of perfume she gave off. Perfume from Paris.

'You may be right,' Jan senior said with a nod. 'Consul Sugihara came to Kaunas by way of Paris.'

'And she brought the most beautiful clothes with her, too.'

'And high-heeled shoes,' young Jan added.

Sometimes Mrs Sugihara would stop for a moment, turn her head, and smile at Edith and Jan. She was the only Asian woman in Kaunas, and enjoyed the attention. In the spring, she wore a kimono; in the summer, she hid her face in the shade of a parasol. As Edith remembers her, she was 'always as pretty as a picture'.

What Edith didn't tell her parents was that she would imitate Mrs Sugihara's walk. Jan would always double over laughing and beg his sister to 'do it again'.

Mrs Sugihara could not have been much older than thirty. She was fairly tall for a Japanese woman. Edith would swing her hips like Mrs Sugihara and study the woman's pinned-up hair. She sighed to her mother that she could never wear her own hair that way, with a knot and a thin stick through it. Young Jan only had eyes for her shoes. No other woman in Kaunas walked on such high heels.

'Your Mamma will still be the same as ever,' Zwartendijk said, 'and so will your Pa. Nothing will change.'

'If the war comes, it'll change everything,' young Jan said, in an insistent, adult tone. 'Everyone at school is talking about the war.'

'And tomorrow,' said Edith, 'I'll tell Irka and Manjuha that my papa is now the Dutch consul.'

Irka and Manjuha Opasnova were her Russian friends at the German school. Edith made friends easily – in that respect, she was just like her mother. Erni had made dozens of friends in Neutitschein, the town where she had grown up, and later in Prague, where she had worked – and all close friends, too.

Edith and I are riding up the hill that she raced down seventy-six years ago on skis. Rob is driving, and Jan junior is with us in spirit.

There can be few siblings so firmly bonded by shared experience as the three Zwartendijk children. Jan, who died in 2014, left behind a typed memoir in English; he had spent most of his life in Canada and the United States. But the Zwartendijks maintained a connection that bridged the distance between them. As Jan lay dying in his home in Tucson, Arizona, Rob sat on his bed beside him, and Edith talked to him for hours on Skype. They often reminisced about their years in Lithuania. 'I can smell Kaunas again,' Jan whispered to his sister through the screen, not long before he let out his last breath. 'The smell of the spring. Or the dry, cold air as we rushed down the hill on our skis.'

Edith effortlessly directs us to the house.

'Take a right. That's the shop where Jan and I would eat sour cream with sugar. Back then it was more of a shack. Sour cream never tasted so good anywhere else …'

And those steps there?

'We took those when we went to school. Two hundred steps – we counted. On the way home, we ran up the steps almost as fast as we'd run down them. The school day was finally over, and we could go ice skating at the rink at the end of our street. Or if fresh snow had fallen, we could ski …'

A hundred metres on: 'Look, the Japanese consul's house. That's where his wife would sashay down the street. She was so beautiful, and looked so strong. The kind of woman you couldn't ignore. Like my mother. I don't know if she influenced the consul. But I can hardly imagine she didn't. After this house became a museum, she returned to Kaunas to see all the things she remembered. She planted three saplings in front of the house, Japanese cherry trees, and look – they're full-grown now.'

Another hundred metres further: 'Here's Perkūno Al. *Al* is short for *Alėja*, Avenue. There's our house – it's still there. With the same plum tree in front of it … Only the house number has changed: it's 59 now, but it was 15 then.'

We get out of the car. I offer my arm, and she goes on with her stories. I feel like I'm touching the past, breathing in the scents of yesteryear.

Edith may be 'so old it's ridiculous', as she puts it, but she claps her hands like a schoolgirl and cries, 'Ab-so-lute-ly nothing has changed.' Nothing about the house, nothing about the garden, nothing about the street. And the plum blossom is as white as ever.

We're staying in a hotel two houses up the street. In 1940, Edith used to play with the mother of the current owner. The mother is still alive, and lives in the neighbourhood. The owner drives off to fetch her. A quarter of an hour later, Edith and Gygaja are face to face. They clasp hands and take a long look at each other, as if they can barely believe that they're both still alive. Edith is the first to find words. Ever since the war, Gygaja has spoken nothing but Lithuanian and Russian. But then the German words well up inside her, too, and that's when the two old women finally embrace, tears rolling down their cheeks.

3

Losing your company

Zwartendijk was not well acquainted with the former Dutch consul, though he had shaken Dr Tillmanns' hand three or four times. Herbert Tillmanns was a young man, in his early thirties, born and educated in Berlin. But he had spent his childhood in Kaunas, and soon after his medical studies he had returned to Lithuania to work in his father's company. His father, Dr Richard Tillmanns, owned a machine works, a cardboard factory, a chocolate factory, and a few other businesses. With two thousand employees, the machine works was the largest employer in Kaunas. About five hundred people worked at the other companies.

Richard Tillmanns had a reputation as a philanthropist and a patron of the arts. He made large donations to the German secondary school, the Evangelical Church, and the Čiurlionis Museum. The museum, a mausoleum-sized building, had been founded to commemorate the pride of the Lithuanian nation, the painter and composer Mikalojus Konstantinas Čiurlionis. It exhibited many works from the Tillmanns collection. Čiurlionis was much admired in Germany; his work vaguely resembles the landscapes of Caspar David Friedrich.

Richard's son, Herbert, succeeded him as director of the cardboard factory, and was appointed at a young age to the board of the Deutsche Commerzbank, in which his father held a majority interest. One of the bank managers' offices for had been furnished for him, but he preferred to meet at Laisvės Alėja 42, in the same building as the consular office. He felt that he could conduct his business more freely there.

His father had become an honorary consul in the 1920s, first for Sweden and later for both Sweden and the Netherlands. In the 1930s, Richard had involved Herbert in his consular work. At one time – probably 1937 or 1938 – he had stepped down, and his son had taken over his duties.

'I know what they're saying about me,' Tillmanns explained, after Zwartendijk had sat down opposite him. His voice betrayed his emotion. 'But what can I do? I believed in that man [Hitler]. A true leader.'

He told his successor the whole story. In a couple of days, the Red Army would invade the country. Then Lithuania would become a Soviet Republic, and all its companies would be nationalised. His family would be left with nothing – except maybe a kick in the pants. He had hoped that Hitler would take both Poland and the Baltic states. That was what all German Lithuanians had hoped, in their own financial interests. The trouble had started in March 1939, when Hitler had secured the transfer of the Memel Territory to Germany. But less than five months later, he had made a pact with Stalin and the communists. That made strategic sense, since the *Führer* could not wage war in the west and the east at the same time. So he'd played for time by negotiating an agreement with the Soviet Union. But the German Lithuanians felt betrayed, as if they were just another minority instead of a *Brudervolk*. One thing was certain: they had lost everything. Their homes, their businesses, their possessions, everything ... Hitler had at least offered the Memel Germans a helping hand, but not the German-speaking Lithuanians with German nationality. They – the Germans of the *Reich* – were not worth the trouble, being only 3 or 4 per cent of the population. Yes, they could return to Germany – but penniless.

Zwartendijk said nothing. No doubt, the Lithuanian branch of Philips would be nationalised by the Soviets, too, but it wasn't his family property, and he could count on assistance from headquarters.

But Tillmanns's fate was sealed. Still, it was the man's own fault for dancing to Hitler's tune.

The former consul shook his head, as if he could no longer make any sense of the changes in the world. He told Zwartendijk how horrified and sorry he was that the Netherlands, a country he'd represented with so much pride and pleasure, had been trampled on and occupied ...

Zwartendijk broke in, unable to contain himself. He said he was sorry, too— sorry his old hometown of Rotterdam had been demolished by German bombs. He held everyone who sympathised with Hitler personally responsible for the choice of Rotterdam as a target. There hadn't been any news yet from his brother, Piet, but he was almost certain the house where the two of them were born had been wiped off the face of the earth – along with their family business in Middensteiger, right in the heart of Rotterdam.

As he thought back to that large street lined with elegant shops and businesses, he recalled the scent of tobacco leaves drying in the factory and the smell of tea in the house next door, which had a roof that sagged in the middle and a long corridor that led to another street, Pompenburgsingel.

It had been an old and respectable business: the Zwartendijk Brothers Tobacco Factory and Tea Company (Gebroeders Zwartendijk Tabaksfabriek en Theehandel), established in 1808. Around seventy people worked in the tobacco factory, and ten in the tea company. He remembered the company's hundredth anniversary, when he was twelve. Six years later, the Great War broke out. The Netherlands remained neutral in that conflict, but Jan and Piet were called up for military duty and mobilised. They remained in service for two years. By then, the factory was on its last legs; the supply of tobacco leaves was dwindling, and they could no longer export their wares. Their father saw the bankruptcy coming, and his heart failed him. He died in 1918. Jan and Piet took over the business in 1919, but they had to sell it four years later to a larger company, Van Rossem's, with greater capital reserves.

Middensteiger 28 in Rotterdam. The building with the turret housed the
Zwartendijk family tobacco and tea company. The entire Middensteiger
was blasted from the face of the earth in May 1940.

He could still see the old advertisements and the pictures on the
packages. Skipper's Tobacco was the name of Zwartendijk's best-
known brand, 'robust in flavour'. Van Rossem's Consolation was
milder. They had sold those two brands side by side for many years.
They also had Best Bird's Eye and Black Lion for the British market and
Yellow Short Filler for customers on a tight budget. Oh, well, what did
it matter anyhow ... He was meeting with Dr Tillmanns to collect the
stamps with the logo of the Kingdom of the Netherlands, not to mourn
the decline and fall of the Zwartendijk Brothers Tobacco Factory.

Losing a company ... Tillmanns might be shedding hot tears,
but it had happened to Zwartendijk not once, but twice. Not long

Poster advertising the Zwartendijk tobacco factory.

before the sale of the tobacco factory, he had boarded a ship to South America. Argentina was his first stop, then Paraguay; he had hoped to buy good tobacco and save the factory. He had never found his feet in Buenos Aires, but in Paraguay he had practically become a cowboy at Estancia Belen-cue. After an attack of malaria and a snake bite, he decided to pack his bags. He returned to Rotterdam, leaving behind a few illusions, but bringing home a monkey on his shoulder – which ended up in the Rotterdam zoo.

Second try: Prague, selling oil and grease for the Rotterdam firm of Van der Hoeven. He was more successful there, until the stock market crash of 1929 – 24 October, Black Thursday. The panic swept Prague

– and was even worse in Rotterdam, where the goods in stock were suddenly as good as worthless. Huge volumes of vegetable oil had to be written off at 0.0 per cent of their former value. He should have packed his bags in February 1930. After Prague, he gave it another try in Hamburg, still working for Van der Hoeven. But he was swimming against the tide.

In 1932, he'd returned to Rotterdam with his family. Unemployed. That had gone on until 1936. For four years, he'd done the housekeeping – washed the windows, vacuumed. He'd found it soothing. The drone of the vacuum cleaner turned the mind to higher things. He'd never had an ambitious nature, but he had a family, and he had to put food on the table one way or another.

Later, he couldn't remember if he'd sent a lot of job applications, but he did know that Philips was the first company to invite him to an interview. They asked him to start right away, because of his international experience. He had one condition: a job for his twin brother. To his surprise, they agreed. That was after Piet and Jan each paid a visit to Mr Anton. Anton Philips never hired a man without a two-minute meeting. When the two minutes were up, if he nodded, you were hired. Otherwise he'd stand up without a word and leave the room.

Ever since getting the nod from Mr Anton, Zwartendijk had felt like a real Philips man, which was odd, since he hadn't joined the company until the age of forty. He'd even had to move to Eindhoven, a city one hundred kilometres too far from the sea. But he soon started to feel like any attack on Philips was an attack on him. It was the same way he felt about his twin brother; the two of them fought like cat and dog, but woe betide anyone who said anything bad about Piet. Once Zwartendijk made a commitment, his loyalty was unshakeable. He had a brother, a sister, a wife, and a friend, and he would walk through fire for any of them. Likewise, he had no intention of ever leaving Philips.

Piet was still working in Eindhoven. His brother was his exact opposite. Piet didn't like travelling or foreign countries. He hadn't

In the Stoffel family's market garden.
Left to right: Koen de Haan and his wife, Edith; Jan Zwartendijk holding
Robbie; Robert van Prattenburg and his wife.

gone to boarding school in Reading, but in Haarlem. He had married a real Rotterdam girl, and considered even the move to Eindhoven a hell of a distance. Yet Piet, like Jan, saw Philips as his family.

Tillmanns was about to start moaning again, when Zwartendijk interrupted him with a question: 'So, issuing a visa, how does that work?' Yes, it was rude, but he wanted out of this conversation as soon as possible. Of course, Tillmanns was living through the end of an era and would soon be going through difficult times, although he undoubtedly had a tidy sum in a Swiss bank account. What annoyed

Zwartendijk was that the man's fear of the future had scared him into supporting Hitler. What was the next step? Wearing a uniform? Volunteering for the SS?

Tillmanns realised he was trying his successor's patience. After a brief explanation of a consul's duties, he handed over the paraphernalia. Fifteen minutes later, Zwartendijk was back outside. To get to his own office on Laisvės Alėja, all he had to do was cut diagonally across the street.

'We'll have a sign next to the door,' he said to De Haan and Van Prattenburg. 'Consulate of the Kingdom of the Netherlands. With a lion and everything. I'm sure you'll like it.' They were too surprised to respond at first.

Koen de Haan, twenty-nine years old, was married and had a son Robbie's age. Robert van Prattenburg, who had just turned thirty, was also married, but so far had only his cacti to care for. He had an apartment full of succulents in the city centre. But that would soon change; his wife was expecting a child in August.

'They won't be happy about this at the plant,' De Haan predicted. The assembly plant was crawling with Nazi sympathisers. Zwartendijk had suspended the worst rabble-rousers, in consultation with De Haan, but there was still a great deal of support for the Nazis among the workers, most of whom were German Lithuanians.

Maschewski feared that Lietuvos Philips would be branded a foreign company, much more than it ever had been. After the Soviet occupation, the new regime's first move would be to nationalise foreign companies. Maschewski feared that the sales force would panic. If the company was rapidly nationalised, they'd be the first to go; a planned economy had no use for travelling salesmen.

Lietuvos Philips really was a Lithuanian company. To avoid high import duties, Philips had set up independent firms all over the world and built assembly plants. Most parts came from the parent company in Eindhoven, but the radios, gramophones, transmitters, and medical equipment were assembled locally. Different models of radios and gramophones were sold in each country: the Germans preferred dark oak for the case; the Lithuanians, light-brown walnut. The Lithuanian branch was relatively small, while the Polish and Hungarian branches were medium-sized, like the Swedish and German ones. They made different product ranges; the Lithuanian subsidiary assembled only radios and gramophones and ordered its light bulbs from the Polish Philips factory. Each company had a degree of autonomy. The directors didn't have to obtain permission from headquarters for every little thing, but all over the world, the employees – some 45,000 in 1940 – worked for the international Philips conglomerate. For a company like this, with offices in almost seventy countries, the world war posed painful dilemmas.

It had been company policy since 1919 for each international subsidiary to be integrated as fully as possible into its national economy. There were licensing agreements with RCA in the United States and Telefunken in Germany for the production and sale of vacuum tubes. That was not a problem in peace time, but Hitler's expansionism had clogged the channels of international trade.

The next day, Zwartendijk met with his sales force. Maschewski was right: they disliked the idea of a consular office in the same building, which would emphasise the company's Dutch character. He downplayed the duties of the consul, just as De Decker had on the phone, and told the salesmen that Lietuvos Philips would be nationalised in any case when the Soviet Union annexed the country. What difference would an extra sign next to the door make then? But he predicted that the Soviets would proceed with care, because they would want the company to manufacture good radios for them without too much delay. The salesmen seemed a little calmer by the time they left, if not entirely convinced.

Zwartendijk waited exactly two weeks before he informed head office in Eindhoven. On 14 June, he sent a brief report:

> The mood in the office is very tense, because of differences of opinion and everything they entail. Unfortunately, this situation makes it impossible for me to plan a visit to Eindhoven for the time being, and

in any case, I would be unable to travel there. As far as work goes, we have enough for the next few months. Only the factory is idle at the moment; I had to let twenty men go there.

… The envoy in Riga has asked me to perform consular duties, and I have agreed. The consul here, who was not a Dutchman, got a case of nerves after the invasion of Holland and bowed out.

He had briefly entertained the idea of asking head office for permission to act as consul. Then he remembered what De Decker had said: Philips had been placed under German administration. He no longer had any way of knowing who would receive his reports. Anthony Guépin or Jan Schaafsma, his longstanding contacts? Or some Dutch fascist, or, worse still, the German administrator?

The letter took an unusually long time to arrive, almost three weeks. The copy in the Philips archives is marked 'received 5/7'. By then, the situation in Lithuania had grown dramatically worse.

4

Scales and cacti

That Friday, 31 May, Jan Zwartendijk could feel how tense he was after his meeting with the sales force, and hoped he could shake it off by focusing all his attention on his family. He left the office much earlier than usual, at four-fifteen, to pick up Edith from her piano lesson. Although he'd never done this before, it suddenly seemed only natural that he would. She had a weekly lesson right after school on Fridays.

Her strict Russian teacher lived entirely *für die Musik* – or so it had seemed until Edith began coming home with more colourful tales. The woman was always overheated, gave piano lessons in her slip with her legs spread wide, and smoked one cigarette after another, sighing, '*Ach, Kind,* can't you tell it doesn't sound good …' When Edith played her scales too slowly, she would get a rap on the knuckles. Whenever that happened, she would respond the same way: '*Liebe Frau Lehrerin,* I can't learn that way.'

The door was ajar. He hesitantly pushed it open and entered the house, guided by the sound of the piano. With a tentative cough, he said, 'I thought I'd pick up my daughter myself for once today. Tensions are running high in the city.'

'There's no denying it, *Herr Direktor*. War is coming.'

And sure enough, there she was in her white silk slip, seated on a straight-backed chair beside Edith, who was struggling to believe that

Edith in a school photograph taken in Eindhoven, 1938.

her father had come just for her. The shoulder bands were halfway down her upper arms.

'As a Russian,' he said, 'you don't have much to fear …'

'Ach, Herr Zwartendijk, do you really believe that? True, I would have nothing to fear if I were a Bolshevik. But a Russian who fled to Lithuania? Your daughter needs to play more at home, Herr Zwartendijk. Practise, practise, practise. Every week, I tell her she'll never get anywhere if she doesn't master those scales first.'

'I'll make sure she does. But now I'd like to take her out for ice cream.'

'Just as I suspected, you spoil the girl. But *ach lieber Gott*, I have such fond memories of the two or three times my father pampered me. So go on, but I warn you, I will charge full price for the lesson.'

He had to chuckle at that.

'Dad, is something wrong with Mam?' Edith asked in the car.

'No, sweetheart, don't you worry. I wanted to surprise you, and the city is in such confusion. No one at the office is acting normal anymore.'

'Are we really going for ice cream?'

'What do you think of the place next to the pastry shop?'

'Be careful, Dad. You'll be in plain sight of your office.'

'How was school?'

She shrugged. She tried to say as little as possible about the German school, so that her parents wouldn't worry. They would think it was much too strict. Whenever a teacher entered the room, the students had to close their desks, jump to their feet, stand at attention, and clearly say, *'Guten Morgen, Herr Lehrer.'* They might has well have been in the army, except that they weren't *quite* expected to salute.

They had school uniforms. The girls wore white blouses under pinafore dresses with dark-blue georgette skirts, smooth at the waist and pleated. Their peaked caps were royal blue with silver edging. Edith thought they were gorgeous, and would have chosen the German school for the uniforms alone. But her father had said, 'I preferred the way you looked in Kralingen, in your regular clothes.'

Gymnastics meant drilling. In the schoolyard, they had to take off their shoes and skirts, and march in circles in the pouring rain, freezing cold, or snow – barefoot, in their underpants. She didn't mind that either; five minutes of marching warmed you up. When she told her mother, Mammie said, 'What a bunch of thugs!', even though Mammie – she often spoke German to her mother, but never called her *Mutti* – had gone to a German school herself.

Most of the students were Prussian Lithuanians, *Volksdeutsche*. When she visited one of her classmates, she was shocked to see that her small wooden house was on the verge of collapse. The interior was full of statuettes of saints, but unfurnished except for a table, a wooden bench, and a sideboard. There were also a couple of wealthy German children at the school. They didn't want anything to do with the *Volksdeutsche*, who were looked down on by everyone in Lithuania.

Edith (seated) with her Russian friends, Kaunas, 1940.

The other foreign students, like her Russian friends and the Swedish girl in her class, had no more trouble at school than Jan and Edith. Their nationality was never an issue. The Jewish children had been taken out of the school by their parents. They no longer felt at home in that German-speaking environment.

Her father obviously had no idea what he was doing; first he took her to the ice cream parlour next to the pastry shop, and then to the terrace of the Metropolis Hotel for more ice cream, served in a glass dish.

'Aren't you spoiling me, Pa? It's only Friday.' As far as she knew, Friday was not a day for goodies. They didn't get sweet treats until

Saturday, and of course on Sunday, when they would visit the Stoffels and wolf down one piece of apple pie after another.

The Stoffels lived next to their market garden in Kaunas; but eight kilometres out of town, in the village of Dainava, they had a second home with a large orchard around it. In the summer months, they would rent a farm on the banks of the Memel River (now the Neman) for Saturday afternoon and Sunday, and the farmer and his wife would spend the night in the hayshed. On Sunday evening, they would hurry home, because they couldn't leave their garden and orchard untended for more than a day and a half.

Lenie Stoffel was seventeen years younger than Kees. They had three children: Anneke and Alice and one boy, Pieter, who had red hair and a protruding chin. He was a rather unusual boy, in Edith and Jan's opinion. He always wore a sailor suit and a military cap that concealed his red hair. If anyone knocked the cap off his head, he would scream and shout. The girls wore Lithuanian dress.

Kees's family was in Deventer, and had always traded in wood. Kees himself had begun his career as a forester in Archangelsk. By 1920, when he had to leave the Soviet Union, he had been married to the Latvian Lenie Barnehl for just over a year. Lenie's father was an Anabaptist preacher from a village near Riga. Kees returned to the Netherlands with Lenie, but couldn't adjust to the country of his birth. He used his inheritance to buy land in Kaunas, and started a market garden. Aside from cucumbers, not many vegetables were available in Lithuania. Kees introduced spinach, endive, chicory, Brussels sprouts, and peas to the market, supplying all of Kaunas.

Besides her native German, Lenie also spoke Latvian, Lithuanian, Polish, and Russian, and could get by in Yiddish. She was a charming woman who made friends easily and liked to have lots of people around.

Kees liked to help Dutch families who settled in Lithuania. 'We were so naïve in those days,' Edith recalls. 'We didn't know a thing about the situation in the country, and just took it all as it came.'

Robert van Prattenburg had more insight into the real state of affairs. He followed political developments from day to day. Twenty-five years after the war, he could still paint such a detailed picture in the Philips employee periodical that it sounds like an eyewitness account written at the time:

Events surged forward at a dizzying pace. The Germans felt confined by their borders and longed for *Lebensraum*. The first to fall prey were the Czechs. Chamberlain set out to Munich, but his umbrella of peace did not provide the protection he had hoped. In March 1939, the Memel Territory adjoining Lithuania was reunited with Germany. Germany also wanted a free hand in Danzig, but the Poles refused, supported by England and France. Germany and Italy forged a military alliance, and on 23 August the foreign ministers of Germany and Russia, Joachim von Ribbentrop and Vyacheslav Molotov, made a pact of non-aggression between the two countries. On 1 September 1939, German forces invaded Poland. Two days later, England and France declared war on Hitler's Germany. On 17 September the Russians, deciding to play it safe, occupied the east of Poland. Ten days later, Warsaw fell into German hands. Lithuania found itself in an awkward position, sandwiched between two totalitarian powers. It had always been faced with the fallout of war: Russian refugees from 1917 to 1920 and then multitudes of *Volksdeutsche* from the impoverished post-war Reich. Now Polish Jews on the run from the German armies were fleeing into the country. As the large neighbouring countries changed their positions on the Baltic states, there were corresponding shifts within Lithuania. At first, Russia limited its ambitions to Finland, Latvia, and Estonia, allowing the Germans to cast a covetous eye on Lithuania's territory. As a result, the Reich citizens living in the country were soon parading around in brown Nazi uniforms. As the German war machine rolled on, the Russians developed a new interest in Lithuania. When they made treaties with the three Baltic states, the Germans living there started to keep a slightly lower profile.

As a boy, Robert had dreamed of being a radio sportscaster and covering the Amsterdam Olympics of 1928. Instead of a radio reporter, he became a radio salesman; but in the article above, you can hear an echo of his early enthusiasm. Robert devoured the news, sitting by the radio night after night, and passed on what he'd learned to Zwartendijk and De Haan. A report from the Philips personnel department describes him as 'very calm, very cooperative, and very compassionate'. After the war, he managed the company's Norwegian branch for twenty-seven years, becoming 'a Norwegian among Norwegians' and, according to that same report, the 'father figure of the Norwegian organisation'. He identified so strongly with the Norwegians that he eventually took Norwegian nationality. He already possessed all those qualities in Lithuania, and immersed himself in the society around him. The only difference was that he grew cacti in Kaunas and orchids in Norway.

De Haan – who would become the manager of the Philips car-radio factory in Tessenderlo, Belgium, in the 1960s – had a practical nature. His first question was always, *What do we need to do?* Then Zwartendijk would have to come up with an answer.

The three of them made a good team. Under Zwartendijk's leadership, they formed a 'small but militant organisation' (as Van Prattenburg put it) in Lithuania. The two ambitious young men at the start of their careers were given plenty of room to grow by Zwartendijk, who had ten years of international experience under his belt and saw good management as mainly a question of good listening. Even before he became a consul, Zwartendijk was something of a diplomat.

Kees and Lenie Stoffel kept pointing out to the Philips men that there was just as much hatred of the Poles in Lithuania as there was of the Russians. In 1918, on the eve of Lithuania's independence, Poland had snatched a quarter of its land and occupied the historic capital of Vilnius. At first, the desperate Lithuanians looked around for a strongman to lead them. The coup of 1926 smothered parliamentary democracy

The last summer afternoon with the Stoffels. Standing (l to r): Koen de Haan,
Pieter Stoffel, Robert van Prattenburg, Jan Zwartendijk holding Robbie, Kees
Stoffel. Seated in the middle row: Lenie Stoffel with Jan Junior and Erni to her
right and Mrs De Haan, Edith, and Mrs Van Prattenburg to her left.

and paved the way for the dictatorship of president Antanas Smetona.
When even he could not turn the tide, the Nazis were seen as the great
hope. But their popularity was short-lived. After Hitler annexed the
Memel Territory, the Lithuanians no longer trusted the Führer.

The Stoffels must have explained that Lithuanian anti-Semitism
was born not of any desire for racial purity, but out of the envy and
frustration inflamed by the extreme right-wing party Iron Wolf. In
the late eighteenth century, Russia had sent its poorest Jews, by the
millions, to Lithuania, Latvia, and Poland. In all three countries, they
served as cheap labour in the manufacturing and textile industries.
In Lithuania, they specialised in processing fur, and a few tried their
hands at farming, to the irritation of the Lithuanian farmers, who
were unable to earn a decent living.

The Lithuanians wanted to be rid of the Jews – the sooner, the better. But not entirely, because then they would have to harvest their own potatoes, close most of their textile factories, and tear down whole districts of Vilnius and Kaunas, full of small businesses, sweatshops, and other workplaces. 'It can't have escaped you,' Stoffel said to the Philips men, 'that Lithuania is the only country in the region that still has open borders for Jewish refugees from Poland and Czechoslovakia.' Yes, Van Prattenburg said, it was a striking contradiction.

Once they had covered the Eastern Europe situation, it was time to relax. Zwartendijk and Jan swam across the Memel while Erni and Edith watched from the bank. Edith wanted to join them; she wanted to do everything her father and brother did. But she didn't dare. And she didn't blame anyone but herself for that. The Memel had a strong current. Jan senior had swum in the Rotte and Maas Rivers throughout his childhood, sometimes going against the current for several kilometres. Little Jan swam like an otter. And by the time he finally returned to dry land, he would be panting like a steam engine.

Jan dried off in the sun and picked up his violin. This was when the adults decided it was time for a beer. Jan tucked the violin under his chin and played a gypsy tune. Edith was the only one who really listened.

5

Erni Christianus

Erni was happy in Kaunas. Their home, built in 1938, still smelled like fresh paint. Their garden was so full of trees that you could always find a shady spot. Thanks to its location on a hilltop, it was cooled by a constant, gentle breeze, even in the heat of summer. Erni would often lounge on a deck chair in the garden, with Robbie on her lap, daydreaming. After hours of this, she might suddenly become outgoing and energetic. Her extroversion came from her mother, and her contemplative side from her father.

The Sundays she spent in the countryside, on the banks of the Memel with the Stoffels, reminded her of summers from her childhood when her father was still alive. Her summers in the woods. If the war hadn't broken out, she could have stayed in Lithuania for years without ever becoming too homesick for the Netherlands. Besides German, she could also speak fluent Polish and more than a little Russian, and she had a good feel for the different mentalities of the country's ethnic groups. Her father's ancestors had lived in the Baltics.

She had a Swedish surname: Christianus. Her great-grandfather had migrated from Sweden to Estonia, and her grandfather had gone on to Latvia and points south, ending up deep in the heart of Poland. Her father had been born in Bielsko, Silesia, not far from the border with Czechoslovakia.

Bielsko was part of the twin city of Bielsko-Biała, divided by the

Biała River (Polish for 'white'). A divided city: for centuries, the two parts were in different duchies – Bielitz (the German name for Bielsko) in the Duchy of Teschen and Biała in the Duchy of Auschwitz – and, later, even in two different countries, Bielitz in Austria and Biała in Poland. On top of that, the city was a linguistic enclave: most of the population spoke German, while Polish was spoken all around the city. Likewise in religion: most of the city's people were Lutherans, including the Christianus family.

Erni's father spent most of his childhood in Bielitz. After high school, he worked as a bookkeeper for a number of Kraków businesses. At the age of twenty-two, he left to seek his fortune in Neutitschein, one hundred kilometres to the west, where in just a few years he rose to become the director of the Hückel hat factory. There was no need for him to change his nationality, since the whole region was part of the Austro-Hungarian Empire.

Ernst Moritz Christianus waited until he had a good job and a good income before marrying Sophie Skijba. Eight years younger, Sophie came from Lipník (Leibnik in German) in Moravia (Mähren, also Austrian territory then) and had grown up in nearby Hohenstadt (Zábřeh in Czech). Erna Marie was born on 13 July 1905 in that same city of Hohenstadt. She was Ernst and Sophie's third daughter, with Austrian nationality. Sophie liked to give birth in her mother's home; her eldest children, Gretl and Ille, had also been born in Hohenstadt.

The girls grew up in Neutitschein, at the foot of the Carpathians. Through every window, they could see mountains looming on the horizon. Closer to home, the hat factory puffed white clouds into the sky. Hückel had the first steam-powered hat factory in the vast Austrian Empire. From Prague to Budapest to Vienna, gentlemen's bowlers, fedoras, and top hats almost invariably came from Hückel. At the turn of the century the company began manufacturing ladies' hats, which were also a great success.

The factory is still running – after major renovation, of course. Even so, it defies all logic that a manufacturer of such an old-fashioned product as hats has survived two world wars, five economic crises,

Neutitschein/Nový Jičín, 1932.

the transition from capitalism to communism and vice versa, and the transition from communism to a free-market economy. After nationalisation, the company was renamed TONAK. It still has more than seven hundred employees. In 1905, it had twice that number.

As the youngest daughter of the city's largest employer, Erni was born with a silver spoon in her mouth. She could hardly suppress the feeling that the sun rose every day as a special favour to her, and some hint of that feeling would linger for most of her life. She was always cheerful, dressed as if she might be invited to dinner at any moment, courteous but firm in her opinions and preferences, and perpetually confident that everything would work out for the best.

Neutitschein looked like a German town, judging by a postcard from 1932 that Erni always carried in her purse, and which her daughter gave me. *Stadtplatz mit Rathaus*, it says, main square with city hall. Arcades, town houses in a classical style, Renaissance buildings. The tower of the city hall, with the silhouette of a Baroque church tower barely visible. All the towns at the foot of the Carpathians and in the

former duchies of Teschen and Auschwitz looked German, with a
strong Jewish influence. The postcard shows the stalls on market day
and the vendors – Jewish, no doubt. Neutitschein's Jewish community
went as far back as the fourteenth century; by the sixteenth century,
there were forty-six houses in the Jewish ghetto. In 1848 the Jews there
were granted full civil rights, in 1875 they established a cemetery, and
in 1908 they opened a synagogue.

They worked as merchants, vendors, and retailers, in the textile
industry, and at Hückel, where Ernst Moritz Christianus was pleased
to employ them, because they tended to work with such precision.
Erni's best friends were Jewish and Czech girls, and it was the same
for her sisters, Gretl and Ille. As she later insisted, 'With the Polish and
German girls, you could cry, and with the Czech and Jewish girls, you
could laugh.'

Erni's pleasant, carefree life lasted until three months after the
outbreak of the First World War, when her father's lungs failed him
and he was confined to bed with tuberculosis. He died in 1916, not
long before his forty-eighth birthday.

In those days, widows and orphans could not count on a decent
pension, and Ernst left his wife and daughters in dire financial straits.
The only thing they could count on was their home – a stately house.
But the little money their father had left them almost all went to the
maintenance of the building.

Erni was eleven years old at the time. Her mother and the
three daughters lived on the vegetables from their garden, the
wild mushrooms they gathered in the surrounding forests, and
the needlework her mother had taken on right away to meet their
most pressing needs. From a young age, Erni and her sister Ille, who
was only one year older, had to provide for their family. After a crash
course in touch typing and shorthand, they went to Prague to find
secretarial work.

Gretl's heart condition made her incapable of any form of physical
labour – the slightest exertion, and her lips turned blue. But she found
an office job so that she could contribute to the household expenses.

Until her mother's death, she would remain in the house in Nový Jičín, as Neutitschein was called after the collapse of the Austro-Hungarian Empire. The house had a forecourt and a long corridor. Erni and Ille returned home every weekend to bring their mother and Gretl what they'd earned in Prague.

They didn't think of their lives as tragic – difficult at times, to be sure, but that kept things exciting. In any event, their childhood was out of the ordinary. They enjoyed Prague and their early freedom, and soon found better jobs selling encyclopaedias door to door, or address books to businessmen. That led to invitations from good-looking young men to dance halls or the amusement park near Prague Castle.

Every Friday, Ille and Erni took the steam train home. They had to change trains in the middle of the night. By the time they arrived in Nový Jičín on Saturday morning, they were black with the soot that blew in through the open windows.

Erni in Prague at the age of twenty.

6

Between Prague and Rotterdam

In the 1920s, Erni and Ille Christianus could often be found in Josefov, the former Jewish ghetto and the quarter where most of Prague's fifty thousand Jews lived. In its cluttered cafés, you could have a full meal and sip white wine for next to nothing. And you could chat, debate, or quarrel about the issues that interested people in their twenties, at least if you weren't one of those who saw rigid nationalism as the solution to every trauma affecting the countries of Central Europe.

It was in Josefov that Ille got to know the journalist Bert Komma and first laughed at his name, assuming it must be a flashy pseudonym for a professional writer. But no, it was his real name. Albert Komma had been born and raised in Prague. When he and Ille first met, he was working for the German-language newspaper *Prager Montagsblatt*. He became the Prague correspondent for the *Berliner Börsen-Zeitung* soon after they married in 1930, and also for the *Frankfurter Zeitung*, a forerunner of the *Frankfurter Allgemeine Zeitung,* from 1935 onwards. He would go on working for the *Frankfurter* until Hitler banned the newspaper in May 1943.

Bert formed the hub of a circle of young intellectuals who spent evening after evening discussing the fast-changing political situation, especially in nearby Weimar. Most of them were Jewish, and Ille thought at first that Bert was Jewish, too. Who knew, maybe he had some distant Jewish ancestry, but the main reason he kept coming to

Josefov was that he was a social democrat to the core, and many Jews were like-minded.

'He's so clever,' the love-struck Ille said to Erni. 'And good-hearted. And optimistic. And never angry or upset.'

He would sit quietly and smoke his pipe, a mug of beer in hand, waiting for just the right moment to make some witty remark. Bert could say a lot in a few words; he was more concise in conversation than in his writing. Ille, on the other hand, was lively, animated, energetic, and always intent on having the last word – she undertook, understood, and organised everything.

In Josefov, Erni befriended Gertrude Polak. She saw in Trude the woman she would have liked to be: a stunning blonde, intellectually gifted, quick thinking, athletic, and artistic, whose German was as musical as her Czech. They became friends for life, and in the mid-twentieth century, that was nothing short of a miracle.

Trude, who had not known she was Jewish until the age of twelve, would barely survive Theresienstadt. Just after the war, she would become a newsreader for the Czech department of the BBC. And eventually, in an ironic twist of fate, she would find herself unable to return to Prague because she belonged to the German-speaking Jewish minority. As Erni would tell her daughter, Edith, 'They became anti-Semites in Prague in 1945 to wipe out the traces of Judaism that the Nazis had overlooked.' If Kafka had been alive after the war, he too would have been sent away.

Trude, whose husband had been murdered in a different concentration camp, remained in London for twenty years, was remarried to a distant cousin from Prague, and moved to Cologne. Erni then picked up the thread of their friendship, visiting four or five times a year. Ille and Bert, who didn't live far from Cologne, would also come by to relive the old days in Prague.

I believe many people in the thirties and early forties didn't want to open their eyes to the impending Holocaust. They let all the fragments of information pass by like so much debris on a fast-flowing river. Don't worry – the water's still clean enough. When they heard rumours, they would turn away or focus on something more agreeable. Even the ones who were close to the centre of power averted their eyes and plugged their ears. But Erni did just the opposite, keeping the windows of her conscience wide open. She and her sisters and friends knew perfectly well what was going on and what might lie ahead.

At the same time, Erni and Ille were young, and they celebrated that fact every day in their turbulent city, which after the First World War and the fall of the Austro-Hungarian Empire was coming into its own as never before. Prague flourished in the 1920s as if in a hothouse. Erni would always remain nostalgic for the twisting Baroque streets, the dance halls, the cafés, the beer and wine cellars, and the casual, open-hearted atmosphere of the Czech capital as it woke from slumber.

They spoke Czech in the countryside and at home in Nový Jičín – at least, that was how Ille and Erni remembered it. In Prague, the language was German. They didn't look down on Czech at all – it was their second language, which they'd learned to write in primary school – but in Prague they had hardly any need for it.

Jan Zwartendijk and his twin brother, Piet, earned most of their money by selling address books, knocking on the doors of Czech and Polish businessmen. Once business took off, they also went to trade fairs and tried to arrange meetings with foreign representatives based in Prague.

After the sale of their tobacco factory, Jan Zwartendijk and Piet went to work for the international wholesaler Van der Hoeven. Jan became the company's Prague representative, and Piet, who hated travelling and would have most liked to stay in Rotterdam all his life, organised the transport of the orders from the Netherlands, generally by rail: tank wagons full of palm oil, and goods wagons laden with other vegetable oils.

One afternoon, Erni Christianus stepped into Jan's office in Staré Město (the Old Town) and sold him an address book in two minutes flat. She put him down for an annual subscription, but he wouldn't let

Jan and Erni Zwartendijk in Prague, 1926.

her go until she'd agreed to go out on a date with him.

That night, they had dinner in the eatery around the corner, and danced until the first glimmer of dawn. Erni was Austrian enough, she confessed to Jan, that you could wake her up for a waltz any time, day or night. Jan didn't care what kind of dance it was, as long as he could see her in action in her chiffon dress decorated with lace and beads, so short and modern it took his breath away.

From day one, Erni saw Jan as a perfect gentleman – his conduct, his bearing, even the way he dressed. Sure, he had a serious nature – maybe even a little too serious – but he was bursting with *joie de vivre*. She made Jan laugh until he cried – he took great pleasure in her personality, and wanted to go out with her night after night.

You could never tire of a man like this, Erni thought. She had always worried about marrying some crashing bore, the kind of fellow who read the newspaper twice over dinner, the second time so he wouldn't have to talk. *I'll never get tired of a woman like her*, Jan told himself. He had chased plenty of women in Prague but never met another Erni.

She couldn't keep her eyes off him, so different from the Bohemians with their beer bellies and short legs. He was tall, slender, well-dressed – *always* well-dressed, even on weekdays, when he made the rounds of the Prague shops with his oils and seeds. He had a thick, dark forelock and expressive eyes. You meet a man like that only once in a lifetime, she would later tell her children.

To Jan, Erni's round face looked typically Central European. Her clear blue eyes held the perpetual promise of a smile. The dimple in her chin accentuated her cheerful expression. And he liked her funny habit of wearing a white blouse and necktie. She had light-brown hair with a part in the middle, and amazing legs.

In photo portraits of the two of them, their faces are never far apart, and their young love leaps out at you.

Jan wanted to introduce Erni to his twin brother, Piet, and his sister, Didi, who was seven years older than Jan and had been like a mother to him. He wasn't too concerned about what Piet would think; the two brothers practically always disagreed – with a passion. Piet always took it lightly; if Jan gave the least hint of taking his side, he would ask if his brother was ill. But their clashes were never about fundamental values, on which they always agreed. Piet had been married for almost two years, to Mary, who – though she'd been born in Leiden – loved Rotterdam even more than her husband. They were expecting a second child. Piet wished his brother the same happiness.

But their sister, Didi, was a different story – highly critical, holding them to the highest moral standards. If Didi had shown the least sign of scepticism or disapproval, Jan would have put any notion of marrying Erni out of his head.

Didi's influence over Jan was strong and ran deep. Her long letters had restored his courage when he considered returning to Rotterdam from Paraguay, disillusioned with life in South America, which had done nothing for him but dent his self-confidence. After

Jan, Jo (Didi), and Piet Zwartendijk.

several months in Buenos Aires, he had left for Asunción as a 'tobacco dealer', hoping to save the family business in Rotterdam by making good purchasing decisions. But he met with bad luck at every turn, and on 23 March 1923, after weeks of delay, he heard that his brother, Piet, had been forced by circumstances to sell their tobacco company to the competition, Van Rossem. Jan had found work on an *estancia*, but the wages were low, corruption was rife, and in fact he had known from the start that his future did not lie on that continent.

The only reason he'd lasted eight months in Paraguay was Didi. His sister had sent him letter after letter telling him it would be unwise to return so soon. 'The malaise here is still very deep; life is expensive, and all the taxes you've just escaped as a non-resident would have to be paid after all, in part or in full.' More generally, Didi warned him that the intellectual climate in Europe was becoming impoverished and bleak. Ever since Jan had admitted that he wished he had studied philosophy instead of going into business, every letter from Didi referred to thinkers and scholars who predicted the decline of the West. For example, she quoted Professor Johan Huizinga, the renowned historian and author of *Autumntide of the Middle Ages*, who in an essay called 'Our Time' had written, 'The place of humanity has been taken by the masses. Ideas have given way to objectives, symbols to programmes, quality to quantity, depth to breadth.'

Yet in December 1923, Jan decided to return home, even though he hated the thought of coming home to Rotterdam as a failure. He had considered travelling north instead, as Didi had recommended: 'If you can't find your feet in South America, then try North America.' While pondering this choice, or maybe just waiting for a ship, he spent a few days in Curaçao; then a mail boat for the Rotterdamsche Lloyd shipping company took him back to his city of birth. At the wharf, Didi was waiting. She clasped him in her arms and said, 'Good to have you back. I missed you every day.'

By then, Didi was a well-known art critic. As an editor for the *Nieuwe Rotterdamsche Courant* (*NRC*) newspaper, she helped to shape its public image. She had strong political convictions and an unerring sense of moral character.

Alida Josina Zwartendijk didn't write under a pseudonym but used the nickname 'Jo'. This clipped byline matched her writing style and razor-sharp judgements. She was the intellectual in the family. Her physical handicap – not just a hunchback, but a severe back deformity from rickets – had never kept her off her feet for even a day. She possessed the keen curiosity and enormous appetite for work and life of a person who never forgets that every day could be her last. She had gone on from a modern grammar school for girls to study art history at l'Ecole du Louvre in Paris. Back in Rotterdam, she was appointed curator of contemporary prints and drawings at Museum Boijmans Van Beuningen.

She soon switched to journalism, and her impassioned arguments shook up the *NRC*'s sleepy staff of art critics. She introduced the work of Picasso and Braque to the Netherlands, and became a driving force in the city's artistic life, organising exhibitions for young local painters and sculptors. Her outlook was so progressive that the old guard of Rotterdam artists rose up in protest, giving Jo Zwartendijk the mocking name of *Juffrouw Zwartekijk*, Miss Dimview. Anonymous slanderers sneered she would rather exhibit one of Picasso's rags than the work of an experienced, widely respected Rotterdam painter. Because she was always surrounded by other women, she was rumoured to be a feminist and a lesbian. Childish rhymes in those anonymous pamphlets, made with cut-and-pasted letters from newspapers, accused her of having eight breasts and being a hermaphrodite. Jo didn't let it bother her. As the criticism grew louder, she made her writing even better and more incisive, commanding the respect of truly significant artists and of the writer Top Naeff, who became a close friend.

Didi's reviews and critical pieces were often extraordinarily harsh. The family sent me scrapbooks full of them, and I was surprised to see what trouble she stirred up in the staid 1930s. She firmly rejected the principle of art for art's sake; as she saw it, art was always in dialogue with society, correcting its errors, resisting its wrongs, trying to make it more beautiful, or revealing its vile underbelly. Any other ideal was servile and bourgeois. She saw great tragedies ahead and, at an early stage, fought the rise of fascism. German vengefulness after the humiliating conclusion of the First World War could not count on any sympathy from her. Ever since 1923, when Hitler had shown his true colours in his failed Beer Hall Putsch in Munich, she had been his sworn enemy. And she became ever more radical. She looked at Germany in much the same way as the satirical, apocalyptic artist George Grosz, about whom she wrote: 'He sees the world as grim and terrible, he accuses, he puts pen to paper and points out the patches of rot; he sees people in their weakest moments; he is the artist of vivisection, with no notion of mild pity; his caricatures are pure satire, mockery, scorn, piercing shrieks in the void.'

In 1926, when Didi shook Erna Christianus's hand at Rotterdam Maas railway station, she would have preferred to speak to her future sister-in-law in French – that's how anti-German she was. Jan had written long letters assuring Didi that his future wife was a Bohemian at heart, and not at all the kind of German-speaking, German-thinking person despised by Didi.

It didn't take Didi long to discover how true that was. After a couple of long conversations, she gave Jan a curt nod, indicating her approval of the marriage. A nice, lively girl, she called Erni, quick and intelligent. 'Not the type to fall for cheap tricks – Hitler doesn't stand a chance with her,' she wrote in a letter to her brother.

Jan and Erni had a civil wedding on 19 July 1926; seven-and-a-half months later, their first child was born. 'I obviously arrived too early,' Edith would later say, with the same laughing eyes as her mother.

Didi was Jan's witness at the ceremony in Prague, where in the course of the 1920s she visited Jan and Erni many times. To her, the city seemed a perfect expression of everything that frightened and impressed her in Kafka's writing. Meanwhile, she was working on her own first novel, which would be entitled *De overlaat* (*The Overflow Dam*).

Jan wanted a church wedding in Rotterdam. He'd had a difficult relationship with his parents – first his father and, after his father's early death, with his mother. His reason for freely choosing to go to boarding school in England at the age of seventeen was the tense situation at home. He was a difficult adolescent and just couldn't get along with his father. But after his mother's death, in 1921, he had begun to harbour regrets, which grew in the course of his South American adventures. In the letters Jan wrote to Didi from Argentina and Paraguay, he repeatedly expressed his feelings of guilt, saying that he had not been the son his parents had hoped for, that he had severed his ties with his family and tradition by running off to Reading. In England, he had felt contented with his life for the first time.

But after Jan married Erni, he felt a sudden need to be part of a tradition. The Zwartendijk family had never really gone in for religion. The only one who had ever called on her Dear Lord or tried to teach the boys a prayer was their nanny, a woman they called Juffie. Juffie didn't have much authority; Jan and Piet would kick her until she was blue in the shins. On Sundays, the boys would spend time outdoors with Pa or, as he put it, they would follow their nose. They had a sailing canoe tied up in Hillegersberg, and would row down the Rotte

River or cross the nearby ponds. Once they were a little older, they would row up the Maas River every Sunday, even in the pouring rain. They would take turns swimming after the boat, not stopping until they got cramps. They never saw the inside of a church.

But the family tradition, going back more than a century, was that a scion of Rotterdam's elite Zwartendijk family belonged to the Remonstrant faith and married in the Remonstrant Church. That was fine with Erni; her father had been Lutheran, her mother Catholic. She had Christmas memories of walking through the snow to church for midnight mass. Religion, to her, was a soft crunching sound underfoot and carols around the Christmas tree. That was far from the worst part of her childhood, and when she folded her hands together in prayer, she felt no inner protest.

Even so, they must never have had a Remonstrant wedding in Rotterdam. The register of marriages of the city's Remonstrant congregation does not list Jan and Erna Zwartendijk. I learned at the city archives that, while Zwartendijk was originally registered as a Remonstrant, his stated religious affiliation when he returned to Rotterdam in 1931 was 'None'. So was Erni's.

After they were married, the young couple remained in Prague for four more years. On 9 March 1927, Edith was born. Didi visited two months later to dote on the baby and attend her baptism. Even after Jan junior was born, in 1929, they had him baptised in Prague. It was a curious thing: Erni was so scared of the Russians that she insisted on having her children baptised, so that they would be listed in a baptismal register. In her nightmarish visions, their names could be scraped or rubbed out of the civil records; the state could not be trusted for a moment. In Kaunas, she demanded that Robbie be baptised – it didn't matter in what church, as long as he was registered somewhere.

Didi could not entirely understand this fear, but she loved playing godmother to Edith and baby Jan, holding them in her arms at the baptismal font. Day in and day out, she would sit with one of the children on her lap in the large garden of the house on Cukrovarnická, Sugar Street, among the villas of Ořechovka, a garden suburb west of

Didi Zwartendijk with Edith on her lap. Prague, summer 1928.

the Moldau (Vltava) River. When evening fell, they would walk to the nearby Villa Muller, designed by the Viennese architect Adolf Loos, which they saw as a breathtaking pinnacle of modernism. As far as Didi was concerned, Jan and Erni could have stayed in Prague forever.

On 24 October 1929, Black Thursday, share prices on Wall Street went into a free fall that would continue until the summer of 1932. Jan's employer, the vegetable oil company, felt the squeeze right away; overnight, their reserves became worthless. The crash brought an abrupt end to the Zwartendijks' prosperous Czech years.

Zwartendijk didn't want to return to the Netherlands – in his mind, that would mean the second defeat of his young life. After some back-

and-forth by post with his employer and a long conversation with Piet, who had come to Prague for Christmas, he decided to try his luck in Hamburg, still representing the same company.

In Hamburg, the Zwartendijks lived in Johnsallee near the Alster River, in a house with a roofed-over rock garden that Edith thought was a little creepy. But what really shocked her was a trip with her father, in 1932, to a Nazi rally in Rathausmarkt, the city's main square.

Three-quarters of a century later, she's still angry. 'He should have known in advance what kind of mass hysteria we would run into there, but he wanted to see for himself. Pa dived headfirst into everything.'

What Edith witnessed there was a terrifying throng of people, whipped into a fury by inflammatory speakers, venting their anger on anyone who was not in the same frenzy. The people of Hamburg seemed to be boiling over with rage. They pressed forward, screaming and bellowing themselves hoarse, and performing the Hitler salute so many times that the whole crowd seemed to be one outstretched arm. It took Zwartendijk two hours to leave City Hall against the current of people in the square, with Edith on his back.

When he heard his turnover was disappointing and the Van der Hoeven company would have to let him go, Zwartendijk did not spend much time lamenting his loss. During his two years in Hamburg, he had come to loathe Germany, the Germans, and their language. He went on speaking German to the children, but used Dutch with Erni. Erni always responded in German, until she had learned enough Dutch from the children.

After the rally, Zwartendijk no longer felt like going out in Hamburg. Instead of visiting the cabarets and dance halls, he would wander along the harbours and the Elbe river. He let Erni do as she liked; she was twenty-six or twenty-seven, and loved to dance. Zwartendijk was pleased to see Carel de Neeve, a boy under twenty who worked in his office, step in as her dancing partner. Carel had special dancing shoes, black and white with smooth soles. In Prague, too, Erni had found a dancing partner: Louis Aletrino, Jan's best friend. Jan was never childish about it.

'As long as you're not getting bored,' he told Erni.

Edith had one other memory of Hamburg. Her father would often take her to the zoo – without her brother. Jan was still too young. In Hagenbeck Zoo, the animals weren't behind bars but, as far as possible, in their natural habitats. This made it more exciting than a traditional zoo. But it wasn't the lions and bears that made Edith shiver, even when they jumped from boulder to boulder or hid behind thick tree trunks. On every visit, they had to pass a sculpture near the entrance. It was large and grey and glistened in the rain, which made all the sculpted snakes look like slithering, living creatures. She remembered that as they approached that sculpture, her father always flinched. Then he would shrug his broad shoulders and walk on.

Erni had a hard time when they move to Rotterdam. She saw the Netherlands as old-fashioned. Polite. Well-behaved. Boring. People never talked to each other heart to heart; they just complained about everything under the sun, to no one in particular. Everything there moved slowly, a smile seemed to cost a hundred guilders, and hospitality began and ended with weak coffee and a biscuit so thin it shattered at first bite.

She couldn't help but laugh about Didi's maid, who patrolled her sister-in-law's beautifully decorated home, enforcing order and cleanliness. Someone had to, because Didi was a slob. She had also taken in a maiden aunt from her mother's side, Aunt Cootje. The maid's name was Marie, but she soon made it clear that she was nobody's little Marietje, and that her full name was Marie van Lambalgen van de Walle. When Erni was in a good mood, this brought a smile to her face, but in a bad mood, she saw it as petty middle-class pretentiousness.

The one thing she loved about her new home was Didi. Didi had long, beautiful hair that she always pinned up, but she was in a constant hurry and never took the time to look after herself properly. Instead of washing her hair with water and soap, a time-consuming

Edith and Erni in Prague, 1934.

chore, she would use petrol, because it evaporated right away, so she didn't have to wait for it to dry.

'What a horrible thing to do,' the ever-anxious Marie would complain to Erni. 'How irresponsible.'

Erni thought, *Finally, someone has the nerve to do something crazy.*

A couple of times a year, she would take Edith and little Jan to visit friends and family in Prague and Neutitschein. Bohemia still felt like home, and she missed it terribly at first in the Netherlands. Erni, her mother, and her two sisters all adored each other.

After the death of *Grossmaman*, as Edith called her grandmother, Erni was sick with grief for months. She didn't get over the loss until she moved to Lithuania.

Zwartendijk had evidently made an awfully good living in Prague – at least enough to support a family for years on end with no income and skimpy unemployment benefits. Didi would make occasional contributions, but Piet was jobless, too, and she couldn't keep three households afloat. In 1934, Jan had to give up his rented home in Kralingen, which had become too expensive for him. His family moved to Schiebroek, another district of Rotterdam – not a run-down urban area, but more like a village grafted onto the city. Even then, finding a new job was not a priority for Jan. Edith had the impression that her father was quite happy to potter about the house. He whistled while doing the housework – dusting, polishing, and vacuuming as if it were all he had ever done. He would pick Edith and Jan up from school and go for long walks around the city with them. Their financial situation cannot have been too precarious; the family could still afford to go on holiday with Piet and Mary and their three daughters, choosing the Zeeland town of Zoutelande for its beautiful sea views, and Erni spent every Christmas with her sisters in Bohemia. Maybe Jan, Piet, and Didi had received a good price for the tobacco factory and invested the money well, because even Piet didn't seem to be in any great hurry to find a job.

The fact that both of them were hired by Philips after four years of unemployment is remarkable. They didn't come from the Dutch province of North Brabant – 'the nest', as it was called at Philips, with the implication that it was the natural breeding ground for new employees. They weren't Catholic, and hadn't gone to business school. Philips was an international corporate group, but it was also very provincial. Its leaders were all connected to Eindhoven and had all joined the company early in life, not at the age of forty.

In 1936, Jan Zwartendijk began work in the commercial department at headquarters, serving Country Group B, the less-important countries. In 1938, he shifted to Country Group B II and III, the countries of Central and Eastern Europe. A few months later, he was sent to Kaunas as assistant director of Philips in Lithuania.

On 27 April 1938, Didi died at the age of fifty-one. After the funeral in Rotterdam, as Jan Zwartendijk boarded the train to Berlin, he resolved that he would finally start taking his career seriously. By the end of the year, he was the general director of the Lithuanian office. This was his way of paying his last respects to his sister, who had always told him that sooner or later you have to face up to your responsibilities, however slight or however great they may be.

7

Aletrino

For all those years, Louis Aletrino was his only friend. They had met in Prague and lived in the same block of flats, Zwartendijk on the fourth floor and Aletrino on the seventh. They would see each other every morning as they both ran down the stairs to work and every evening when they went out for dinner somewhere in town. He had never called Louis anything but Aletrino, just as Aletrino usually addressed him as Zwartendijk. When he was in a tearing hurry, which was often, he would just say 'Dijk'.

Aletrino was four years older than Zwartendijk. The differences in their knowledge and interests were much greater. Aletrino followed political developments in Eastern Europe from day to day, was a keen observer, and served as an example to Zwartendijk of how to base your views on the facts as carefully as possible. When Jan was fence-sitting, Aletrino would challenge him: 'Don't you have an opinion, then?'

Aletrino wandered the city daily, got to know every street in the old centre, and was fascinated by Kafka's novels, which had just been posthumously published: *The Trial* in 1925, *The Castle* in 1926, and *Amerika* in 1927. He also acquainted himself with the music of Bohemia and Moravia. He swept up Zwartendijk in his enthusiasms, rushing him from one thing to the next.

It was thanks to Aletrino that Zwartendijk became part of Prague life. Otherwise, he would merely have wandered around doing business; Aletrino drew his attention to many other facets of the city, telling him you either had to learn to identify with the place where you lived or else move on. He would toss out remarks like that casually as he leaned over the baize-covered table in the billiard room of Café Louvre in Národní Avenue. Later in the evening, they would sit by one of the tall windows and order goulash, which tasted better there than anywhere else.

Aletrino introduced him to all the attractive women in town, or at least Zwartendijk had that impression. Jan hadn't met Erni yet; Aletrino had married two years earlier, but that didn't stop him from flirting with other women.

Zwartendijk hadn't had much of a childhood. When he was eighteen years old, the First World War broke out and, although the Netherlands was neutral, he was drafted into military service for two full years. By the time he returned home, Rotterdam had become a city where almost nothing was going on. English girls had struck him as surly; in Buenos Aires, he had met a Frenchwoman who lent him her room in a pension in Asunción for three months, but she left for Brazil.

In Prague, he made up for lost time. They went out night after night. For Aletrino, it was not purely recreational; he heard more news in the dance halls than he could read in the telex messages. He had a sixth sense for people who knew just a little more than everyone else, and would pick them out like diamonds in gravel.

Aletrino was a journalist for the NRC, the respected Rotterdam newspaper where Didi worked. She had given Jan his address when he left for Prague. 'Go see Louis, he knows everyone and everything in Czechoslovakia.' He had become the NRC correspondent in Prague in 1921 and would remain in the job until 1939.

At first, he told Jan very little about his Jewish background. It didn't come up until later, when Erni introduced him to her Jewish women friends. He avoided talking about his family. Aletrino was related to Arnold Aletrino, a physician and author who was always lumped together with the writers Lodewijk van Deyssel and Frederik van Eeden. Arnold's novels were 'so gloomy', Louis said, 'that you

Jan and Erni's wedding in Prague on 19 July 1926. To Jan and Erni's right are
Piet Zwartendijk, Louis Aletrino, Eliska Eckstein, and Ille Christianus. Far left:
Didi Zwartendijk and Gretl Christianus.

won't be surprised to hear he's turned to morphine to ease the pain
of life.' Because Uncle Arnold (whose real name was Aaron) was
so widely read, it was public knowledge that the Aletrinos had a
Sephardic background. In the early eighteenth century, the family had
migrated from Italy to Amsterdam, and from there they fanned out
to Suriname and the West Indies. Louis's father, David, had been born
in Paramaribo and spent his childhood in Suriname. After studying
medicine in Amsterdam, he had decided to stay in the Dutch capital,
where he became a well-known and well-liked physician – much like
Arnold, who wrote his novels only on Sundays, and on weekdays
practised medicine in the impoverished Amsterdam districts of Kadijk
and Kattenburg. Louis had planned to follow in his footsteps, also
enrolling as a medical student at the University of Amsterdam. But
after four years, he abandoned his studies.

During the First World War, he worked as an editor at the *Nieuws van den Dag*, a popular newspaper that opposed Dutch neutrality and promoted the Allied cause, a minority view in 1915. In the early years of that war, many Dutch people – even the strongest advocates of neutrality – had felt more sympathetic to Germany than to France and England. Aletrino was anti-German, a good ideological fit for the *Nieuws van den Dag*.

When peace came, many readers cancelled their subscriptions, compelling the newspaper to lay off some editors. The last hired were the first fired, and that included Aletrino. In 1918, he took a job at the *Deventer Dagblad* and moved to the eastern Dutch province of Overijssel – first Gorssel, then Deventer. 'A city where you wouldn't want to be found dead,' he later said to Zwartendijk. 'One of the most miserable places in the world.' Not until they got to know each other better did Aletrino explain why he so detested the place; a brief affair with a woman named Martha Lader had cast a dark shadow over his memories.

Martha had divorced in December 1917, told Aletrino she loved him three weeks later, and moved from Amsterdam to be with him in Deventer. On the next-to-last day of May 1919, their child had come into the world, stillborn. They did not name it. The death certificate issued by the city of Deventer reads 'nn Aletrino': *nomen nescio*, name unknown. To Aletrino, there was something dreadful about that, as if the child had never been meant to exist. Martha returned to Amsterdam, and Aletrino took off for Prague with no more than a vague assurance that he could work for the *NRC* as a correspondent. His sudden departure looked a lot like an escape.

In 1923, he had married Gertrude Josefa Kisch, who came from a Bohemian Jewish family. Her father, like Aletrino's, was a physician. She was a magnificent actress, who smoked cigarettes in a long, thin ivory-holder, spoke in a musical voice, and swung her legs high in the air when she danced the Charleston. But she wanted to start a family, and after his Deventer experience, Aletrino had lost interest in that. Their marriage was dissolved in the very month and year that Jan and Erni married.

Aletrino would have two later marriages, to Eliska Eckstein and to Bertha Haase, both ending in divorce. Zwartendijk sometimes wondered if Aletrino was really the bohemian he pretended to be, or whether deep inside he was frightfully anxious about the future. His refusal to have children sank all three of his marriages; he called it 'criminal' to bring children into the world 'in the present era'. But most of his friends and fellow journalists saw him mainly as a carefree hedonist.

Thinking back on Aletrino's wives, Zwartendijk could see hardly any difference between them. They all wore elegant, light-coloured hats, and were all tall, slender, athletic, articulate, and cosmopolitan; all three were Jewish, and each had a little dog. The second Mrs Aletrino's dog had been white, and so had the third's. The difference was that Bertha's dog followed her on a lead, and Eliska's dog had to be carried. 'That was a bad dog,' Edith recalled. 'A real nuisance.'

After Aletrino told his first wife he wanted a separation, she threw up all sorts of obstacles. She loved sour pickles, which she made herself. One evening, Aletrino opened the jars, urinated into them, and shut them again. Edith heard the story from her father, who couldn't stop laughing. But she didn't quite know what to think. 'Well, what if she never noticed?'

Aletrino worked like a horse. Besides his columns for the NRC, he also wrote for another Dutch newspaper, the *Algemeen Handelsblad*, and for the *New York Times*, the *New York Evening Journal*, and a press agency, the International News Service. His English was as good as his Dutch, and he translated Czech literature. His greatest accomplishment was the Dutch edition of Ivan Olbracht's *Nikola the Outlaw* (in Czech: *Nikola Šuhaj loupežník*). In 1937, he completed the translation: an intense novel, as intense as Aletrino himself. The defiant tale of a Czech rogue who stole from the rich to help the poor in the chaotic years of 1917 and 1918, it was socialist in tenor – 'not quite communist,' Aletrino claimed. But Zwartendijk, the businessman, saw it as a frontal assault on capitalism. Yet their friendship remained as close as ever. Perhaps

I should mention that Aletrino also translated a travel guide into Dutch for Czech Railways. Not everything about him was larger than life; he earned more from the travel guide than from his journalistic scribblings.

In the summer, he would entertain his friend's children. While Zwartendijk sailed the Mediterranean, Aletrino would take Edith and Jan on the funicular to the amusement park on Petřín Hill, almost every day. Aletrino was always excited to see 'the boys' again (to him, Edith was one of the boys). He spoiled them rotten: nothing was too expensive, and after the second pickle he was happy to buy them a third, or else ice cream.

Every evening, he would go dancing with Erni. They had always got along well, and he sometimes grew tired of his cosmopolitan ladies in their little hats. They made no secret of these outings, and Jan was glad that Erni enjoyed herself. Aletrino would also accompany her to the dentist. Erni said the dentists in Prague were much better than their Dutch counterparts, much friendlier, and much cheaper, too.

After Zwartendijk left Prague, he kept in touch with Aletrino. They corresponded – Aletrino's letters were three times as long as his – and saw each other at least once a year. Aletrino would stay with him in Rotterdam when summoned for a face-to-face meeting with the NRC editors. Aletrino would always bring his wife; Jan and Erni would pick them up from Maas Station. Aletrino remained a regular guest even after the Zwartendijks moved to Eindhoven.

Over the years, Aletrino became more politically radical and more religious. It was the latter, more than the former, that made Zwartendijk uncomfortable. When they had first met, Aletrino had seen religion more or less as humanity's biggest mistake. That was a great source of amusement to Zwartendijk, who felt roughly the same way. They both saw religion as a thing of the distant past, and for Jan it also had something vague to do with family tradition. Still, you had to be old and sick to go to a synagogue or a church every week. While Aletrino's father was Jewish, his mother was Protestant,

Jan Zwartendijk, the stationmaster, and Bertha Haase (the third Mrs Aletrino)
at Maasstation in Rotterdam.

or at least had been raised that way. But his parents had given him a
completely irreligious upbringing.

It was his first marriage, to Trude Kisch, that sparked his interest
in Judaism. Each following marriage strengthened it. It even began to
look as if he insisted on Orthodox Jewish wives. He went to synagogue
more and more often on Saturday, the Jewish sabbath. As he put it,
'It's like when you decide to join a party: you hang the poster in your
window.'

Edith and little Jan's jaws would drop when they heard their father
discuss Hitler with Aletrino. It was a unique opportunity for them to
enrich their vocabulary of curses and profanities. They relished those
discussions, without understanding much of what was said.

Aletrino's intensity and engagement also made him a favourite of
their Aunt Didi. The feeling was mutual; even when they thoroughly
disagreed, Aletrino felt that Didi's opinions deserved serious thought.
'Didi,' he said, 'is the very model of sound thinking.'

Immediately after the German occupation of Czechoslovakia,
Aletrino was picked up by the Gestapo. On 16 March 1939, when

Hitler came to Prague to proclaim the German protectorate of Bohemia and Moravia, Aletrino was locked in a cell. Three days later, he was interrogated; the Gestapo knew all about him, and the officers kept calling him *der Jude Aletrino* ('the Jew Aletrino'). He was released, not because of his Dutch nationality or the freedom of the press, but because of a diplomatic row with the United States. At this stage, the Gestapo did not yet have the confidence to eliminate the correspondent for the *New York Times*, but they sent a clear message to Aletrino that he was under close surveillance and would be better off packing his bags. Aletrino understood and returned to the Netherlands, where he stayed in The Hague until October 1939.

Aletrino and Zwartendijk wrote each other postcards full of abbreviations. Aletrino thought about going to see him in Lithuania for a couple of weeks, but decided against it after the Germans occupied Poland. He sent his longer letters by way of Piet, who would slip the pages into his own letters to his brother. That was how Jan learned that Aletrino, from his new home in The Hague, was in touch with the politician Hubert Ripka, a member of the Czech government in exile who had fled to Paris.

After meeting with Ripka, Aletrino travelled on to Romania in November 1939, with Dutch and American press cards in his pocket. From the Balkans, he would report on the situation in Central and Eastern Europe for the *NRC* and the *New York Times*.

A month after arriving in Bucharest, Aletrino sent a Christmas card to Kaunas – with a funny message, as usual. That was the last Zwartendijk would hear from him. Erni thought Aletrino would land on his feet. Zwartendijk wasn't so sure.

8

Stalin in the shop windows

On Thursday 13 June 1940, De Decker called him at home. Later on, Zwartendijk could never recall the exact time, but he remembered thinking it was strange to hear the telephone ring at such a late hour. First, he heard De Decker's voice, somewhat crackly, saying, 'The government in exile will soon officially appoint you consul. It's a matter of days.'

On 22 June, Queen Wilhelmina signed the decision in London. By Royal Decree, the two consuls in Kaunas, Dr R. and Dr H. Tillmanns, were granted an honourable discharge. The Dutch foreign ministry had evidently never realised that the elder Tillmanns had withdrawn from consular affairs years earlier. But that said more about the situation than about the ministry officials – when they fled to London, they had brought along only the most essential documents from The Hague.

It would take another two weeks before De Decker received confirmation of the honourable discharge in Riga. In the meantime, Zwartendijk was already known as 'the acting consul in Kaunas', and in fact his appointment as consul had already taken place. As prospective consul, to be exact – this was his first consular post, and according to the hierarchical rules of the Dutch foreign service, he would remain 'prospective' for the next three years.

Jan Zwartendijk himself, when acting as consul, always signed documents and papers as *consul a.i,* short for *ad interim.*

De Decker did not send the proposal to appoint Zwartendijk to the foreign minister until 19 June. The letter arrived at the Dutch foreign ministry in London on 26 July. By that time, Zwartendijk had been writing visas for days.

But the appointment was a mere formality. De Decker obviously had another reason for calling: to find out what his brand-new consul could tell him about the tense situation in Kaunas.

'Tense is a euphemism,' Zwartendijk said, after a hurried puff on his cigarette. 'We're all nervous wrecks.'

It was around then that he started smoking like a chimney: one cigarette after another, at work and at home. His peaceful days of filling a pipe were over.

'Here in Riga, there's a constant stream of lorries coming and going,' De Decker said. 'The Latvians are being picked up by the hundreds.'

The detainees were being taken to the nearest station and sent on freight wagons to Siberia. A year later, the Russians deported all supposed anti-Soviet elements. On 13–14 June 1941, 15,424 men, women, and children were arrested in Riga and deported – in a single night.

'And there? Any signs of a Russian invasion?' De Decker asked.

'Everyone's talking about it. Everyone's holding their breath. Everyone's nerves are frazzled. It's like watching at a deathbed.'

That was no exaggeration. In the diary of Rose Shoshana-Kahan, a Jewish refugee from Poland staying with relatives in Vilnius, I found these words: '14 June 1940 ... Smoke is felt in the air ... The whole day Soviet tanks ride by. Something is going to happen and we poor refugees tremble.'

But not a single tank had yet reached Kaunas.

De Decker kept raising his voice, as if afraid the one person he could still talk to would be unable to hear him. 'The days ahead are crucial, Zwartendijk. Here and in Lithuania. Keep a cool head. If things are about to go wrong, don't hesitate to pick up the phone.'

After Zwartendijk placed the receiver back in its cradle, he said to his wife, 'That man is so alone.'

Jan Zwartendijk on the banks of the Memel, 15 June 1940.

On 15 June, a Saturday, the Zwartendijk family spent the day on the banks of the Memel with Kees and Lenie Stoffel. It was unseasonably hot, and they took hourly dips in the river to cool off. For once, Jan senior was wearing shorts and a short-sleeved shirt, both white. He was photographed in that outfit by the river, and the little photo, the size of a contact print, was preserved. Even with a magnifying glass, all I can see of Zwartendijk's face is a vague smile. If he was tense that day (and there's every reason to assume he was), he hid it well.

On the evening of that same Saturday, 15 June, what everyone had been expecting happened. A long column of Russian tanks, hundreds at once, drove into Kaunas. Sources disagree about the exact time: 'around dinner time', by most accounts, which makes sense if 'dinner' refers to the evening meal. The tanks reached the city centre between seven and eight in the evening, soon after the Zwartendijks returned from their trip to the Memel.

President Smetona told his ministers he was in bed ill, escaped the presidential palace through a back door, hurried to the station in Kaunas, and left the country by rail. From Germany, he travelled on to Switzerland. A week earlier, Smetona had proposed mobilising the Lithuanian army. But parliament, fearing the measure would give the Soviet Union a pretext for armed intervention, had voted it down. Now it was clear the Russians needed no pretext; their tanks rolled into Lithuania unopposed. Independence was over.

The other Baltic countries suffered the same fate; Estonia and most of Latvia were occupied two days later, on 17 June. Since 13 June, Riga had been under the control of the Red Army.

The owner of 15 Perkūno Alėja, Professor Malinauskas, came to the house in tears to tell them he was soon to be banished to Siberia. Edith stared wide-eyed; she had never seen a man her father's age crying. 'All the thinking people have to go, all the people who speak our language.'

The actual occupation of Kaunas took place on 16 June. That day had been chosen with care; all of the Soviets' political opponents, the 'thinking people', were at home then. Around midday, Edith watched Professor Malinauskas leave with his wife and child and one small suitcase. He was a professor of Lithuanian language and literature at Kaunas University; his wife was a teacher. The three of them made their way to the intersection with the major road leading down the hill. Edith followed, staying one hundred metres behind them.

At the crossroads, they stopped. Meek and quiet. Not smoking one cigarette after another, not gesticulating, not upset or angry. Around fifteen minutes later, a drab-green lorry picked them up. Russian soldiers opened the back and helped Professor Malinauskas climb in. He turned away from his wife and daughter, as if he couldn't bring himself to say goodbye. As the lorry drove off, the professor hid among the other men. His wife and daughter seemed stunned. They were picked up a little later by a second lorry. That one was crammed

15 June 1940: Soviet troops driving into Vilnius.

with women and children only, most without coats.

Edith clapped her hands to her face. She couldn't believe that people would let themselves be taken away so easily. Their destination was no secret to her. Her mother had often told her that the Russians sent disobedient or freethinking people to Siberia, where they were locked up in camps and died of cold and starvation.

She would always remember Professor Malinauskas as a sweet man who, every time he saw her, would teach her a word of Lithuanian. Edith never forgot those words.

Telling me this story, seventy-five years later, she claps her hands to her face again. A few days later, we hear from a former neighbour of Professor Malinauskas that he survived the gulag. Long after the war, he returned from Siberia and emigrated to the United States. We couldn't find out anything about what had happened to his wife and daughter.

I'm not even sure the neighbour was talking about the same professor; Malinauskas is a common name in Lithuania. But Edith seems relieved. Even at the age of sixty, she still has nightmares about that morning in Kaunas. 'I would see him being carried off in the army lorry, and then I was his wife instead of the little girl looking on.'

Edith and Jan stayed home from school that Monday. Her mother said she was sure the school administrators wouldn't take the risk of opening the doors.

At the end of Perkūno Alėja was a large park, which is still there today. When Edith and Jan passed near it, they heard that all the tall trees had been used for hanging Lithuanians: intellectuals, organisers of the Resistance against the Soviets, and, for the most part, innocent men and women.

'Go home,' said a neighbour they knew by sight. 'This is much too terrible for children to see.'

The way his voice wobbled was so strange that they took him at his word and returned home fast.

Or did they?

Half a century later, when I asked Jan about his scariest memory of Kaunas, he said, 'There wasn't a tree without someone hanging from it.'

Edith can't remember. She assumes she looked away, or kept her eyes fixed to the ground.

At home, they found their father. That morning, as life in the city ground to a halt, he'd gone to work just like any other day. There wasn't a normal person in sight, only tanks and Russian soldiers.

Pa was in the garden with Robbie on his knees. 'That's right, little boy,' they heard him say, 'you were born at the wrong time in history. Your life won't be easy.' They laughed to hear him.

The next morning, Edith and Jan promised to stay home, but as their mother was cleaning Robbie's diapers they slipped out of the house and went down the stairs to the city centre. Their mother was right – school was closed. But a sign on the door said it would reopen the next day. This must have been an act of resistance by the administrators; instead of rolling over without a fight, they had decided to press on with teaching in German. The Russification of the educational system would not begin until that autumn.

From the German grammar school, they walked to their father's office. It wasn't far – the school and the office were both in the city centre, less than a kilometre apart. Their father had decided to go to work after all that morning, even if he had nothing to do there. Staying at home makes you look frightened, he said, and, after all, the office was also a consulate now.

Jan drank in all the unusual sights; Edith thought the atmosphere in town was creepy. All the roads, streets, and pavements had been crushed when the tanks rolled over them. A brief rain the night before had turned the city centre into a muddy mess.

The strangest transformation that they saw was in the two-kilometre shopping street, Laisvės Alėja. All the merchandise had been removed from the shop windows: no more shoes, no more clothes, no more glasses or flowers or books, no more bread or any other food. Instead, each display window was draped with a red cloth. Against the rear wall hung portraits of Lenin and Stalin. Each one was the same: Lenin on the left, Stalin on the right.

From one day to the next, the free market had made way for a command economy. The portraits of Lenin and Stalin must have been distributed by the occupiers, but the fact that the shopkeepers had cleared out their display windows without the least fuss and draped them with red cloths showed that most people had resigned themselves to the new situation.

'I can't treat you two to ice cream anymore,' Zwartendijk said when he saw his children walk into the showroom. They went upstairs to the office and plopped into their father's chairs.

De Haan kept watch at the assembly plant to stop the Russians from commandeering the machines or carrying off the parts. Van Prattenburg interrogated the children about whether they'd noticed anything strange on the way there. Jan junior couldn't wait to tell the story:

'All the shop windows are empty, except for two photos and red cloths. All the roads have been smashed by tanks. But I didn't hear a single shot. Not one!'

He kept quiet about the hangings.

In the mid-afternoon, Zwartendijk drove the children home. Erni had called him with alarming news. Lithuanians were being arrested and taken away all over the neighbourhood, and even before they had left their houses, Russian soldiers had started moving in.

The Red Army troops looked like sixteen-year-old boys. Erni had pictured the Russians as savage Cossacks. They turned out to be children, most of them from far beyond the Urals.

The Philips employee Maschewski, who also lived in Perkūno Alėja, had ten Russians quartered in his home, farmboys who had never before in their lives seen a big city. They didn't know what a toilet was for, and guessed it was a basin for washing your feet. They would relieve themselves behind a tree in the garden, stick their feet in the toilet bowl, and flush. What a lovely, cool feeling, that water between your toes.

Six days after the occupation, on 21 June 1940, Zwartendijk sent his second report to Eindhoven. He chose his words with great care:

'enormous concentrations' instead of 'Soviet occupation' or 'invasion by the Red Army'. The terms 'Russians', 'Soviets', and 'Soviet Union' are nowhere to be found; he clearly realised that the report would come into the hands of the German occupiers and the German Philips administrator:

Since this past Saturday [15 June] quite a lot has changed here, for it is clear that the enormous concentrations have had repercussions in every possible area. By this time, we have a new government here; the banks are closed, so business has more or less come to a halt. Many political prisoners have been released now, of course, and with all the rumours circulating, the general mood is fairly anxious.

The next few weeks are looking a little bleak; we don't yet know exactly what will happen, but I'm almost certain it will no longer involve an independent Lithuania. Just to let you know that we're 'present and accounted for' business-wise, no matter how things develop from here. The only possibilities are bad or still worse.

The letter arrived in Eindhoven on 30 June.

Left-wing political prisoners had been released, as Zwartendijk wrote, and nationalists arrested. In the first wave of arrests, it was mainly the politically active patriots who were picked up. Soon after the Russian occupation, two thousand Lithuanians were deported to Siberia. A year later, it was open season on all 'anti-Soviet elements'. This meant every kind of instructor, from nursery-school teachers to university professors, as well as writers, journalists, judges, lawyers, and politicians – in short, everyone who spoke and wrote Lithuanian.

Owen Norem, the chief of the United States diplomatic mission in Kaunas, noted in his diary on 25 July 1940, 'Arrests are being made consistently and so silently, usually under cover of night, that a veritable pall has descended over the country.'

The first case to reach the new Dutch consul was the disappearance

Lithuanian nationalists being deported to Siberian camps.

of a Dutch priest in Kaunas. Edith recalls: 'All of a sudden that very young, friendly priest was nowhere to be found, and everyone in town was very worried. All I remember is that his name was Jan, and people were afraid he had got into trouble with the Russians.'

He had protested to the Soviet authorities about the arrest of numerous men, women, and children in his parish.

The Stoffels raised the alarm. They had invited the priest, like the Philips employees, into their home on several occasions, and for the same reasons: out of sheer friendliness, and to hear Dutch spoken again. Kees Stoffel contacted the consul.

When the rumour persisted that the priest had been deported to Siberia, Zwartendijk called De Decker.

'I'll issue an official protest,' came the reply from Riga, 'but it won't make much of an impression. What does an envoy amount to these days? Maybe you could try talking to the military commanders, or at least to some high-ranking Russian officer. There's no point in threatening these people. Say something about good relations and your concerns about this nice young man who wouldn't hurt a fly and has a Dutch passport.'

After hanging up the phone, Zwartendijk realised he'd spoken to

De Decker on informal terms, as if they'd been working together for years.

His meeting with the Red Army officer, whose name, rank, and duties Zwartendijk never learned, lasted exactly two minutes. Holding court in the city hall, the officer refused to discuss the case, saying only – in remarkably crisp German – that all the churches, monasteries, and convents were to be closed. So were the consulates – first the American consulate, followed by its British, Swedish, Dutch, and Japanese counterparts.

'You will be informed of the definitive closing date.'

However inexperienced Zwartendijk was as a diplomat, he had no intention of being brushed off like a fly.

'I did not ask you,' he replied, raising his voice slightly, 'when you plan to cut off diplomatic ties – that decision is not for you to make, but for your government. I asked about the disappearance of a Dutch priest. That *is* your responsibility.'

The officer pretended not to have heard, wheeled around, and left.

The young, idealistic priest would never be heard from again; Zwartendijk was already pretty sure of that. In the best case, he was in a freight wagon bound for Siberia; otherwise, he was out in the woods somewhere, under the soil, shot in the chest – and then in the head to put him out of his misery. Either way, his consul could do precious little to help him. It weighed on Zwartendijk – he told himself he should have put up more of a protest.

In the months that followed, seventy-eight priests disappeared in Lithuania. Sixteen of them were found murdered. The others vanished without a trace.

I suspect the Dutch priest was Jan Peeperkorn, even though I lack decisive evidence from any church records. The Dutch episcopal archives are hardly in working order anymore, and the archives of the Jesuit order remain closed for at least one hundred years – no exceptions for martyrs. But I did find a report in a mission newsletter about Jan Peeperkorn, a Jesuit in Lithuania, and there can't have been so many Jans working there. In 1941, he turned up in Latvia.

Had he escaped, or had the Russians released him after a few months?

In 1942, he was spotted providing pastoral care in a hospital in Minsk. After that, the trail goes dead. Did he die during wartime negotiations? Or was he banished to Siberia, where his life ended in the gulag?

9

Peppy Sternheim Lewin

Peppy Sternheim Lewin was the first refugee to go to consul Zwartendijk for help; Nathan Gutwirth was the second. Peppy came to the consulate one morning; Nathan showed up that very afternoon. The two of them had been living in Lithuania for some time, and both told Zwartendijk they had never been scared of the Soviets, who at least offered protection from German expansionism. That was until the Soviets actually occupied the Baltic states and right away started closing churches, monasteries, synagogues, and other religious institutions and arresting the clergy. Peppy's husband was a rabbi and a legal scholar, and Peppy had studied Hebrew. Nathan was a student at an advanced Talmud school. They had begun to fear for their future.

Peppy and Nathan's experiences were so similar they seem almost interchangeable. Each of them later claimed to have given the Dutch consul a brilliant idea; each took credit for coming up with the magic word 'Curaçao' that would guarantee them a safe escape route.

Peppy Sternheim came from Amsterdam. According to her relatives, her full personal name was Pessla; the name on her Dutch naturalisation papers was Penla. In Amsterdam's civil registry, she is listed as Pessla. Everyone called her Peppy.

From the age of eleven to eighteen, she lived in Amsterdam; her first address was Andreas Bonnstraat 24, a street between the

Peppy Sternheim Lewin with her son, Nathan.

old Weesperpoortstation and Oosterpark, where many Polish and German refugees had rented the second floor. Later in that early Amsterdam period, she moved to the upper floor of Sarphatistraat 175, and still later to Sarphatipark 115. From the age of twenty-two to twenty-six, Peppy lived in the Dutch capital again, this time at Jan van Eijckstraat 26, a side street of Beethovenstraat in the Amsterdam-Zuid district. So many different homes – what a restless youth she'd had!

She was born, according to her immigration papers, in Baligród, Poland, on 17 December 1911. Her mother, Rachel Lieber, came from the same village. Rachel married Naftali Sternheim, who came from Łańcut, not far from Baligród, in the south-east of Poland. Naftali was almost seventeen years old when he left for the Netherlands in 1902. In the early twentieth century, his new home, Scheveningen, had a Polish-Jewish community that was starting to grow. Rachel, the same age as Naftali, was married off to him at the age of eighteen, but remained in Poland. The two of them often took the train to see each other.

In 1905, Naftali moved from Scheveningen to Amsterdam to start his own business as a textile wholesaler. Every time he visited Rachel in Poland, he would stock up on fabric and clothing there. Even after Pessla's birth, Rachel remained in Poland. She did not move to Amsterdam until 1920. That same year, her son, Levie, was born; in the Netherlands, he was called Leo.

In the summer of 1927, the Sternheim family was granted Dutch nationality, but the three of them continued moving between countries. In the late 1920s, Naftali visited Palestine to learn about Zionism; by then, Peppy was completing her secondary education at a Jewish boarding school in Switzerland.

In 1929, the family moved to Berlin so that Peppy could study Hebrew at the university. That was not the only reason, as we can see from a note in the Amsterdam civil registry. Under 'Sarphatipark 115', it reads, 'House Burned Down'. The fire must have left the family no choice but to move on.

In Berlin, the Sternheims were surprised by the hostile climate. Even as late as 1929, the city was not known for being anti-Semitic. Hannah Arendt wrote, in letters to her mother, that Berlin was the best and safest place to live in all of Europe – especially for Jewish intellectuals. Arendt finished secondary school in Berlin and, in 1924, began studying philosophy there, at the same university where Pessla Sternheim was later enrolled.

In early 1933, when Hitler came to power and immediately expelled all Jews from the civil service, the Sternheims feared for their future there and returned to the Netherlands. They started out in The Hague, because of their old ties to the Polish-Jewish community in Scheveningen, and a few months later moved to Amsterdam.

Two years later, Peppy met her future husband. Rabbi Isaac Lewin had come from Poland to Amsterdam to crown his studies with an academic degree. He soon became a doctor of Jewish law.

Her parents must have put a little pressure on her to accept this suitor's proposal; Dr Isaac Lewin was a good catch. He had a spotless reputation, and was neither too Orthodox nor too Liberal in his beliefs for Mr and Mrs Sternheim.

In 1935, shortly after marrying Peppy, Dr Lewin returned to Poland. There he soon became a university instructor, and at the age of thirty he joined the Łódź municipal council.

Peppy did not look forward to leaving Amsterdam. It wasn't that Poland was an unfamiliar country – after all, both her parents had been born there, and she had lived there until the age of nine. But the future for Jews looked more treacherous in Łódź than in Amsterdam. Yet there was no denying that Łódź was a prosperous city with a thriving clothing and textile industry. It had more or less the same population as Amsterdam, around 650,000. One in three inhabitants was Jewish, an even higher proportion than in Amsterdam. But anti-Jewish hatred was rising to disturbing new heights there.

At first, Peppy was happier in Łódź than she had expected. She found a city abuzz with cultural activity, and soon became a regular theatregoer. They lived in a large house that Isaac had inherited from his parents, in a suburb that vaguely reminded her of Amsterdam-Zuid. In 1936, she gave birth to a son, Nathan.

The situation became alarming when a twenty-three-year-old Jewish man was stabbed to death in the street for no reason at all. Isaac Lewin protested in a city council meeting, crying out from the podium, 'In the streets of our city, we will not permit an innocent Jew to be murdered.' The responses from the other councillors were shocking. According to the minutes, Councillor Czernik of the National Radical Camp said, without batting an eyelid, 'It is necessary to kill all the Jews. Your days are numbered.' Councillor Kowalski added, 'We have to evict the Jews from their dwellings and give the apartments to the Poles.' Councillor Makuch, also of the National Radical Camp, shouted, 'To Palestine, you choleric.' At the same time, Czernik shouted, 'Jews, your days are numbered in Poland.' When another councillor screamed at Lewin, 'Jew, don't speak any more, because if you do not stop, we will throw you down from the rostrum,' the president intervened and rang the bell.

But in 1938, Isaac Lewin was re-elected to the city council. He could go on speaking freely. The economy was recovering; life in the textile city was good.

On 1 September 1939, the Nazi army invaded Poland. Though not entirely unexpected, this still came as a shock. After the Treaty of Munich and the Molotov–Ribbentrop Pact, most Poles and most Europeans had justified their passivity by telling themselves that the status quo would be maintained for the time being.

When the war broke out, Peppy's parents and her brother, Levie, were visiting Łódź. Her father flew back to Amsterdam by way of Warsaw to attend to the interests of his textile business. He made it out of Poland just in time; Warsaw had not yet been captured by the German army, and the Battle of Łódź did not take place until a few days later. Not that he had escaped the Nazis once and for all; three years later, on 26 September 1942, Sternheim was murdered in the gas chambers of Auschwitz. In the summer of 1942, he had attempted to flee from Amsterdam. With diamonds sewn into the lining of his coat, he had tried to reach Switzerland. But he was removed from the train in France, and sent first to the Drancy internment camp and later to Auschwitz, where he was murdered on arrival.

Diamonds had been his reason for flying from Łódź to Amsterdam. In 1939, only statesmen, captains of industry, and film stars travelled by air; it was too expensive even for the wealthy. But Naftali Sternheim had converted his savings to diamonds, and he was bound and determined to get his hands on them so that he could go on providing for himself. He'd been clever enough not to put his money in the bank or invest it in foreign currency; the first thing the Nazis did in occupied countries was freeze the bank accounts and put a stop to currency trading. In Germany, Jews had been forbidden to withdraw their savings and foreign currency since the mid-1930s, and if they left the country, they forfeited their home and belongings. The main reason that relatively few Jews tried to escape between 1933 and 1939 was that they knew the Nazi regime would rob and plunder them as they left. Not only was there almost no country willing to take them in, but as soon as they crossed the border, they were penniless.

Naftali Sternheim's last years in the Netherlands were difficult. At his last address, Sarphatistraat 141, he was registered as a 'rag merchant' – in other words, a rag-and-bone man – having previously been listed in the civil register as a 'draperies merchant'.

By the time he tried to flee, it was too late. Controls had been tightened in 1941, and he couldn't use his diamonds as bribes, as he had hoped. In the summer of 1942, Gestapo agents pulled him off the train and pocketed the gems.

After the victory of the Nazi army, Łódź was renamed Litzmannstadt, and one working-class neighbourhood became the Jewish ghetto. In just a few weeks, all Jewish households were moved there. Regardless of their occupation or background, men had to do forced labour in the Nazi war industry. Litzmannstadt became the main supplier of munitions and uniforms to Poland.

Isaac and Peppy Lewin escaped this fate by fleeing. Along with their three-year-old son, and Peppy's mother, and brother Isaac, and Rachel Sternheim, they arranged to be smuggled into Lithuania. It was a fairly smooth process, once you reached the Lithuanian zone; at that stage, Lithuania was neutral, and it was the only country in the region still accepting refugees. The dangers were on the Polish side of the border; large areas there were under Russian control, and other zones had become a no-man's-land where soldiers, bandits, and human traffickers enforced the law of the jungle. In the dead of night, they fled. To keep little Nathan quiet, they warned him, 'If you cry, we'll be eaten by wolves.' It would be his one memory of Poland and their flight; the whole time, he was as quiet as a mouse.

The Lewin and Sternheim families were not the only ones to cross the border. A few days later, a full-scale exodus began, and before the year was out, more than thirty thousand Jews would seek refuge in Lithuania. But for those who had entered the ghettos of Łódź, Warsaw, Kraków, and many other Polish towns and cities, there was no escape. The decision to flee had to be made in a matter of weeks or, in many cases, days.

Polish refugees at a Zionist shelter in Vilnius, 1940.

In Vilnius, the Lewins and the Sternheims believed themselves safe for months. Vilnius was under Polish control, and they stayed with relatives of Isaac. The situation became worrisome for them again only when the Red Army occupied both Vilnius and the rest of Lithuania. The Soviets were not anti-Semitic, at least not systematically, but they distrusted Zionists, political activists, rabbis, rabbinical students, and supporters of the Bund – that is, the social-democratic General Jewish Labour Bund, which they saw as a bunch of half-Trotskyites.

Peppy sought help from the Dutch consul. It took a while before she found him. She happened to hear that the consul's name was Zwartendijk and that she could find him in Kaunas, one hundred kilometres from Vilnius, at the Philips branch office.

Later, Zwartendijk couldn't remember whether Peppy was the first of his compatriots to visit the consulate. He thought it had been Nathan Gutwirth, a man he'd known since 1938.

On the way from Vilnius to Kaunas, Peppy had been stopped five times by the occupying forces, and when she was finally face to face with the consul, she got straight down to business. Zwartendijk didn't have the time or the opportunity to form a clear impression of her. She explained to him that her mother and her brother were Dutch citizens and that she, too, had held Dutch nationality before she married. She asked if he would provide exit visas for her and her husband, mother, brother, and young son, with a final destination of Java or Sumatra in the Dutch East Indies.

'I'd like to help you,' he replied, 'but I have no idea how to do that.'

'Well, who *would* know, then?' she snapped, infuriated by this display of amateurism.

'The Dutch envoy in Riga.'

She nodded curtly, stood, and left the consulate.

From Vilnius, Peppy wrote a letter to envoy L.P.J. de Decker. War is a strange kind of chaos; despite the Soviet occupation, the Baltic countries maintained a working postal system, not just for a few weeks or even a few months, but for at least a year and a half. Express letters – even to neighbouring countries – took no more than two days.

De Decker replied by return of post that he had no choice but to reject her application for a visa for Java or Sumatra.

Peppy wrote to De Decker again, and asked him if he could help her family any other way, since they were Dutch citizens.

In his reply, the envoy pointed out that the Netherlands Antilles, 'including Curaçao and Suriname', were destinations without a visa requirement. De Decker was wrong about Suriname; although it was a Dutch colony at the time, it was not part of the Netherlands Antilles. (In 1940, those were the islands of Curaçao, Aruba, Bonaire, Saba, and Sint Eustatius and the Dutch half of Sint Maarten.) He firmly believed that the governor of Curaçao could grant permission to anyone who arrived there by ship to stay on the island indefinitely; that was not true either. The governor of the Netherlands Antilles (not Curaçao) represented the head of state of the Kingdom of the Netherlands, and defended the interests of that kingdom.

De Decker was bluffing or telling tall tales to make the refugees' hopeless circumstances easier to bear. He seems to have thought that once they escaped Europe, they would have some chance of survival.

Peppy immediately wrote to him again to ask whether he could note the exception for Curaçao and Suriname in her Polish passport, which was still valid. And she urged the ambassador to leave out the phrase 'with permission from the governor of Curaçao'. She wasn't asking him to lie, but to withhold a salient detail. After all, she wrote, 'we really do not plan to go to Curaçao or Suriname'. De Decker's response was brief and businesslike: 'Send me your passport.' So she did.

On 11 July 1940, De Decker wrote in her passport in French:

> The Consulate of the Netherlands in Riga declares that, for admission to Suriname, Curaçao, and other Dutch possessions in North and South America, no visa is required.

Peppy made the trip from Vilnius to Kaunas again, this time accompanied by her husband, Isaac Lewin, and showed Zwartendijk what the ambassador had written in her passport. She asked him to copy it word for word into her husband's *leidimas*, the temporary travel document issued by the Lithuanian government specifically to Polish refugees. She also asked him to add the same note to her mother and brother's Dutch passports.

It was 22 July 1940.

Zwartendijk was willing. He added De Decker's note to the travel documents of Peppy and Isaac Lewin, and Rachel and Leo Sternheim, changing 'Riga' to 'Kaunas' and 'North and South America' to 'the Americas [Amérique]':

> Le Consulat des Pays-Bas à Kaunas déclare par la présente que pour l'admission d'étrangers au Surinam, au Curaçao et autres possessions néerlandaises en Amérique un visa d'entrée n'est pas requis.
> Stamp. Date of issue. Signature. And title: 'Consul des Pays-Bas a.i.'.

Zwartendijk could not imagine that the Soviets would accept this procedure without question. By adding that he was merely the interim

Peppy Sternheim Lewin's visa, bearing the name of Isaac Lewin.

consul ('a.i.'), he left an opening for himself to use his inexperience as an excuse if the Soviet authorities decided to interrogate him.

This was anything but paranoid. In April 2015, I was permitted – by rare exception and thanks to the intercession of the deputy minister of foreign affairs, Mantvydas Bekešius – to study all the documents about consul Zwartendijk that have been preserved in the Lithuanian National Archives. There I found a KGB report that subjected the newly appointed consul to intense scrutiny. It included everything: his years at boarding school in Reading, his activities in Prague, Hamburg, and Eindhoven, his duties and responsibilities at Philips, his city of birth, the childhood and activities of his wife, Erna, and the name, age, and school of his children. The investigation had overlooked nothing – neither his political views nor his attitude in the 1930s ('anti-German'). The only thing the KGB failed to note was the one-and-a-half years he had spent in South America. But if they wanted to arrest or blackmail him, they had all the information they needed.

One other note was added to Peppy and Isaac Lewin's travel document: '1 child'. No name, no age.

Women and children travelled on the same document as the male head of household. So the three members of the Lewin family could flee on a single visa.

In fact, 'visa' is not the right word. It was a note stating that no visa was required. But the consular stamp made it look like a bona fide travel document.

'And now?' Zwartendijk asked.

From the Lithuanian port of Klaipėda, it was almost impossible to reach Sweden; Germany had closed off the entire Baltic coast. Travelling south or west was equally impossible. There was only one route: straight across Russia, taking the Trans-Siberian Railway and then a boat to Japan, in the hope that from there they could travel on to Australia, New Zealand, or the United States. A journey around the world. It was worth a try.

'Then we'll need a transit visa for Japan,' Peppy said.

'You're in luck – the Japanese consulate in Kaunas is still open. The consul's name is Sugihara. He lives in the upper city. The consulate isn't far from where I live. I'll drive you there.'

Zwartendijk dropped them off in front of Sugihara's home.

'Call or write me if it all works out.'

He wanted to know if the escape route via Japan was a real option, and whether Sugihara would make things difficult.

Day after day, he heard nothing. This was because, at Sugihara's doorstep, Peppy and Isaac had changed their minds. They had decided that, before applying for the transit visa, they would work out whether they could pay for the trip. They had no idea how much a ticket on the Trans-Siberian Railway cost, or whether all five of them could afford the crossing from Vladivostok to Japan. They also had to persuade Peppy's mother and brother to go with them; this, in particular, must have taken quite a few days of talking and arguing. Knowing that her husband had returned to Amsterdam, Rachel Sternheim must have wanted to join him there. This would not have been impossible; although the journey through Poland would have taken days, her Dutch passport would have got her there. But she would have been walking into a trap, because she would never have been allowed to leave the Netherlands again. Leo Sternheim, too, was confronted with a very different future from the one he had hoped for. Having always been expected to take over his father's business, he balked at the idea of a journey to Japan. He knew nothing about the country, except that the capital was called Tokyo.

For the time being, money was no obstacle. Since the Soviet occupation on 15 June 1940, the Lithuanian banks had stopped issuing foreign currency. Fortunately, Peppy and Isaac Lewin had brought dollars with them to Lithuania; Isaac had withdrawn the money a few months before the German invasion, just in case.

The question was whether they dared to set out on a journey of many weeks with an uncertain outcome. By then, they had learned they could spend two weeks at most in Japan before the transit visa expired. Where could they go from there? The United States had announced well before then, in 1939, that it would not accept Jewish refugees. Or could Isaac Lewin count on help from his brother, who lived in Washington? Maybe he could reach him from Japan.

After four days of weighing up the pros and cons, they decided to risk it. Peppy and Isaac, this time accompanied by Rachel and Leo Sternheim, returned to Kaunas. They rang the doorbell of the Japanese consulate.

Behind his heavy oak desk, Chiune Sugihara murmured the French words of Zwartendijk's note a few times and nodded. He wore a black suit, a white shirt, and a dark-blue tie. His black hair, parted on the right, shone like silk. With clean-shaven cheeks and neatly trimmed eyebrows, he looked impeccable – and young, younger than you'd expect a man of forty to look.

He was visibly pleased that the French note met worldwide consular standards. It was a formula he could work with, inside the framework of international law. If the final destination had no entry

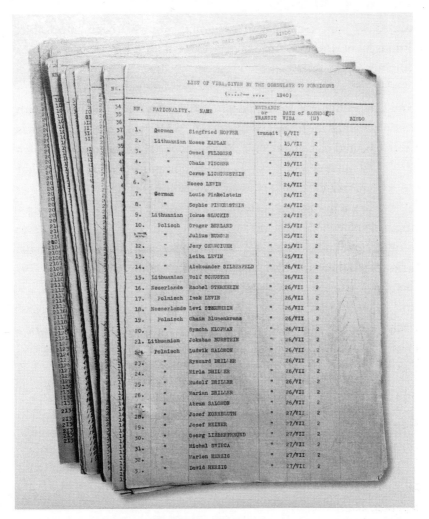

The list of transit visas that Sugihara kept in Kaunas. No. 16 was issued to
Rachel Sternheim; no. 17 to Isaac Lewin.

visa requirement, then he had the power to issue a transit visa.

Emboldened by Zwartendijk's signature, consul Sugihara agreed,
on 26 July 1940, to issue a transit visa for Japan to Isaac and Pessla
Lewin, and to Rachel and Leo Sternheim, as part of their supposed
trip to Curaçao.

Chiune Sugihara took up his brush and wrote the text in each travel document – six short lines of calligraphy. It took him many minutes. When Isaac reached out for his document, Sugihara shook his head severely – the ink hadn't dried yet.

The Japanese consul kept a list with the names of the people to whom he had issued transit visas. While the ink was drying, he would type the full name and nationality on a tall Underwood with a Polish keyboard.

Oddly, Rachel Sternheim is number 16 on the list; Isaac Lewin is 17. Peppy and their son, Nathan, travelled on Isaac's document. Leo Sternheim is number 18, listed as Levi; he had given his true name at the consulate in Kaunas.

But how could fifteen others have preceded them: two German Jews, six Lithuanian Jews, and five Polish Jews? After Peppy's visit, had the Dutch consul put the idea to use right away, copying the text into fifteen other travel documents? Probably, because right after Peppy's visit, Nathan Gutwirth had turned up at the consulate.

10

Nathan Gutwirth

Twenty-three-year-old Nathan Gutwirth, a student at the advanced yeshiva (Talmud school) in the Lithuanian town of Telšiai, had known Zwartendijk since late 1938, and paid him regular visits when in Kaunas. In later years, he always claimed that he and Zwartendijk had mapped out the Curaçao route together – a story no more or less plausible than Peppy's version of events.

When Nathan told other yeshiva students that they could obtain visas – or something very similar – on Laisvės Alėja in Kaunas, the run on the Dutch consulate began.

Although Nathan had been born in Antwerp, he had Dutch nationality. His parents had fled Antwerp late in the First World War. Like most Antwerp Jews, they had Austrian nationality. Since the Austrian Empire was allied with the Germans, life in Belgium during the First World War was difficult for the family. They had decided to move to Scheveningen, a striking coincidence; Peppy Sternheim's father had gone to that same coastal village near The Hague.

After the war, most Austrian Jews returned to Antwerp, but Nathan's father did not. He traded in diamonds, spending the first part of the week at the diamond market in Amsterdam and the second part at the one in Antwerp. On Thursday, he came home to Gentsestraat 34 in Scheveningen, and the first thing he did was take his children for a long walk by the sea. On the beach, he would fill his lungs with clean air. This was vital to his health, he explained to the children, because the diamond market in Antwerp was near a candle factory that belched out filthy, toxic smoke.

In mid-1933, the Gutwirths hosted Mr and Mrs Birnbaum, Jewish refugees from Berlin. Mrs Birnbaum was seen as something of a curiosity in Gentsestraat, because she was so broad, tall, and fat. Besides Mrs Birnbaum, who soon became chronically ill, and her husband, the Gutwirths took in many other Jewish refugees from Germany, pampering and financially supporting them. Quite a few of their guests were medical doctors, who were being consulted by other refugees. The Gutwirth home was a loud, messy, welcoming place. The Gutwirth children had gone to a public school in The Hague. Now, at Nathan's modern grammar school, he focused on literature and economics, passing his final exams by the skin of his teeth.

After the Gutwirth daughters, Chana and Esther, were married, the family returned to Antwerp. Nathan went to Lithuania to study at the illustrious yeshiva in Telšiai (Telz or Telshe in Yiddish). This institution of higher learning was no boarding school. Nathan shared a room with his friend Nusen Weiser in the home of Rabbi Shmuel Schiff, a Talmud scholar and businessman, and the owner of the town's largest grocery. Nusen Weiser also came from Antwerp, and outside of school hours he and Nathan enjoyed speaking Dutch to each other.

The educational programme was divided into four *shiurim*, or cycles: the first and third took four semesters; the second and fourth, five. The youngest students were eighteen years old; the oldest, twenty-five to thirty. In a photograph of the class of 1938, Nathan Gutwirth is one of thirteen young men wearing severe suits and fedoras.

The yeshiva drove its students hard: they learned by debating every moral, theological, and philosophical question raised in the Talmud, arguing themselves blue in the face. That left little time to keep up with developments outside the school and the shtetl of Telz – until the autumn of 1939, when thousands of Jews poured out of Poland and into Lithuania. Most were men, who firmly believed that only

Polish refugees on their way to Lithuania, 1939.

men were in danger, because a civilised state like Germany would never hurt women or children.

Nathan saw that the refugees were welcomed with open arms by the Lithuanian people and that the Jewish men felt safe in Lithuania's towns and cities. He would later put this in writing, as if to correct a wrong impression. Yes, there had been anti-Semitism in Lithuania; yes, it had been fierce and bloodthirsty; but at that time, in 1939, it had not yet arrived. At least not as far as Nathan saw or heard. Or wanted to hear or see – Nathan was a born optimist. He loved Lithuania, and felt at home in his fiancée Nechama's family, and in her village, where Yiddish was heard as often as Lithuanian.

Everything changed when the Red Army invaded. Right away, the occupiers shut down all religious institutions: churches, monasteries, yeshivas, and synagogues.

Nathan wanted to leave and was looking for a route to the United States, or somewhere in that general area. As a Dutchman, he knew about his country's colonies and wondered: Was Curaçao a possibility?

Or the other islands in the Netherlands Antilles? Or maybe Suriname? His fiancée, Nechama, had a cousin living in Curaçao.

From this point on, his story strongly resembles Peppy's, so strongly I can't help but think that one of them may have borrowed it from the other. Peppy could have heard something about a relative in Curaçao – not from Nathan himself, but in Telz, from one of the many rabbis from Vilnius who visited the home of Rabbi Shmuel Schiff.

Nathan describes taking exactly the same steps as Peppy. He wrote a letter to De Decker, the Dutch ambassador in Riga, to ask whether a visa was required for Curaçao, Suriname, or the other islands of the Netherlands Antilles. The ambassador replied that no special permission was required to enter Curaçao and stay on the island, but doubted the Russians would grant someone with a Dutch passport a transit visa, since the Netherlands had not yet recognised the Soviet Union.

Nathan wrote again and asked him if, even so, he might be willing to issue ten to fifteen visas to his friends, who were mostly Lithuanian citizens hoping to leave the country for religious reasons.

De Decker responded that no visa was required for Curaçao, but only a residence permit from the governor – which he doubted would be granted, considering Curaçao's strategic importance. He did not explain what made the island so important, but it was true: the Shell refinery in Curaçao fuelled the American and British air force, and was vital to the conduct of the war.

Nathan wrote yet another letter, asking the ambassador to note in his passport that no visa was required for Curaçao, leaving out any mention that the governor's permission was required.

De Decker wrote back, telling him to see consul Zwartendijk in Kaunas, who would write the note in his passport.

For the rest of Nathan Gutwirth's life, it would remain a mystery to him why ambassador De Decker, after his initial reserve, had suddenly agreed to his plan and referred him to consul Zwartendijk. In the twelve pages of memoirs he typed for his children some fifty years later, he speculates that De Decker assumed it would be impossible for anyone to leave Russia by way of Siberia. In other words, De Decker may have thought he was sending Nathan on a wild-goose chase.

If that is true, the envoy in Riga did not go to the trouble of responding to his requests seriously. I am 99 per cent certain that the idea of the escape route was first presented to De Decker by either Peppy or Nathan. Nathan's version is much more informative, but lacks one crucial detail: the note in French.

When Nathan showed up at the consulate in Laisvės Alėja, Zwartendijk simply added the note to his passport.

Back in Vilnius, Nathan told a Polish refugee, Zorach Warhaftig, how he had received a visa, or something much like a visa. Warhaftig had fled Warsaw with his wife and child. He was a well-known lawyer and a leader of the Mizrahim, or Oriental Jews, in Poland.

Warhaftig was uninterested until Nathan told him that the Japanese consul was cooperating by issuing transit visas. Then, all at once, he thought of the hundreds of rabbinical students in Lithuania, who Nathan believed should be the first to go because they were in the greatest danger. Warhaftig asked whether the Dutch consul would be willing to issue large numbers of visas. Nathan promised to ask.

He returned to Kaunas, and went to see Zwartendijk:

I had met Mr Zwartendijk on various occasions before he became consul. Once as I was walking down a large, upscale shopping street in Kaunas – it must have been in 1938 or early '39 – I noticed the Philips Radio logo. I went into the showroom and chatted with the director, a Dutchman like me, and we hit it off right away. We remained in contact. Mr Zwartendijk sent me the *Nieuwe Rotterdamsche Courant* twice a week and the *Haagsche Post* once a week. There was no more than a smattering of Dutch people in Lithuania, so we soon developed a kind of bond.

They also kept up with Dutch football, tearing through the sports section of the Monday newspaper.

Nathan told the consul about Zorach Warhaftig's request and the plight of the Polish refugees. After thinking about this for a couple of minutes, Zwartendijk said, 'The ambassador didn't place any restrictions on me, so I'll grant a Curaçao visa to anyone who wants one.'

The next day, dozens of Jewish refugees were waiting in front of the consulate. That was partly because the Red Army had eliminated the border between Kaunas and Vilnius. When the Socialist Soviet Republic of Lithuania was founded in August 1940, Vilnius would be restored to its old status of capital; the border was no longer needed.

In his weekly report to Philips Eindhoven, Jan Zwartendijk wrote:

> My door is being beaten down by Dutch people in various kinds of trouble. As consul, I must strive to help them. That creates a lot of work, and unfortunately not in the business.
>
> It is not unthinkable that you will soon see my wife and children in Eindhoven, not on holiday, but for good – or should I say, for the foreseeable future. You see, peculiar things are happening here, things you may not hear much about there. It is also possible that I will send back the furniture before it is too late. I will remain here myself, of course, as long I possibly can. There is no point in stubbornly refusing to see the consequences of what is expected to happen. Those consequences will not be pretty, and while I will not return for my own pleasure, there are some things against which one is powerless. Would you be so kind as to share the above information in the appropriate place? It will be understood that there were reasons I did not write immediately.
>
> All this notwithstanding, it may of course take some time for my expectations to become a reality, but I would rather be a month too early than a day too late.

As in his earlier messages to the occupied Netherlands, he avoided giving too much detail. He wrote that the people beating down his door were Dutch nationals in trouble, not Polish-Jewish refugees.

When he wrote of 'peculiar things' happening in Lithuania, he was referring to the Russian occupation and the plans announced by the Soviets to nationalise all the businesses in the country. Zwartendijk expected a communist supervisor to take over his job at any moment and kick him out of the country, with or without his furniture. But he did not directly refer to the Russians or the Soviet Union, and avoided the word 'nationalisation'.

The letter was posted on 26 June, and was received at Philips headquarters in Eindhoven on 5 July. And that's odd.

The visa that ambassador De Decker sent to Peppy Sternheim was dated 11 July 1940. The note that consul Zwartendijk copied into her husband's, Isaac Lewin's, travel document was dated 22 July 1940. Peppy and Isaac each held onto the lifesaving visa, having a photo taken of the original. I can read the dates clearly: 11 July and 22 July.

But as early as 26 June, Zwartendijk wrote that his door was being beaten down by Dutch people in need. His letter has been preserved in the Philips archives; again, no misunderstanding is possible.

Or did Zwartendijk, in his haste, write the wrong date: 26/6 instead of 26/7?

Nathan Gutwirth's story does not include exact dates. Yet my vague, lingering suspicion is that the first refugees found their way to the Dutch consulate earlier than the letters and documents tell us, and that envoy De Decker and consul Zwartendijk started looking for ways to help refugees leave Lithuania right after the Russian occupation on 15 June. In that case, their lifesaving operation must have started earlier. But there's no evidence of this, aside from the fifteen visas written by the Japanese consul before Peppy's visit.

When Nathan Gutwirth returned to Kaunas, he neglected to visit the consul. Zwartendijk understood why. When a Dutch woman came to pick up a visa, Zwartendijk remarked, 'I heard Gutwirth was in Kaunas. He didn't come to visit. He must be in shock about what he set in motion.'

Zwartendijk was right. Nathan feared the consul would shower him with abuse. After his conversation with Warhaftig, the news had spread like wildfire: a certain Mr Radio Philips in Kaunas was issuing visas to all, without hesitation. In just a few days, the queue of applicants grew to many dozens, and then to many hundreds.

Yet not all the refugees rushed to Zwartendijk's door. Many saw no immediate need to leave Lithuania. The Russians were leaving the vast majority of them alone. The Red Army forces were hunting Lithuanian nationalists, not Jews. While it was true that some Jewish political activists had been arrested in Vilnius, they were being held in the Vilnius prison. In the freight wagons headed for Siberia, not a word of Yiddish was heard. So why leave?

Zorach Warhaftig travelled throughout Lithuania, going from city to city and village to village, to impress upon Jewish refugees that this was their last chance to escape the coming storm. 'It is a question of months, not years, before the Nazis toss the non-aggression pact in the bin and invade the Baltic states,' he warned.

He would soon be proved right. But in July 1940, plenty of people refused to believe him. Many Jews imagined that in Lithuania they were safe, that the Red Army would protect them. The Soviet security service, the NKVD (the forerunner of the KGB), arrested only political activists and hard-core Zionists. The vast majority of Jews saw no reason to flee. Although Bund members had their disagreements with Bolsheviks, they were all part of the same socialist movement. And, more importantly, they had a common enemy: the Nazis.

Warhaftig visited all the yeshivas in Lithuania, and contacted as many groups as possible that could play a role in organising and managing the stream of refugees. He pleaded with refugees and foreign students to seize the opportunity presented by the Curaçao visas and Japanese transit visas. 'You will get this chance once, not twice,' he kept telling them. The *roshe yeshivot* – heads of the Talmudical academies – and the rabbis disapproved. 'You're scaring off our students,' they told him, or, 'You're waking sleeping dogs and just asking for a response from the Russians.'

Nathan Gutwirth described the attitude of the academy directors and the rabbis as *Shev ve'al ta'ase*, stay put and do nothing. The persuasive power of Zorach Warhaftig, the lawyer from Warsaw, eventually prevailed. He insisted, again and again, that the Nazis would invade the Soviet Union, driven by their burning hatred of communists, and that Lithuania would be overrun by German troops. He also pointed out – perhaps his best argument – that applying for a visa did not commit you to leaving right away. For example, Nathan Gutwirth did not leave Lithuania until 8 December 1940, more than four months after consul Zwartendijk signed the French note in his passport, straight across the stamp of the Dutch consulate in Kaunas.

I I

Not a chance in hell. But who knows?

Zwartendijk wrote the visas with his fountain pen, one after another without interruption, never pausing or looking up. When his hand became too sore to continue, he ordered a stamp with the French text. The ink was green, because that was the only inkpad available in a large-enough size. Using the stamp, Zwartendijk could work much faster, but he still had to handwrite the name of the applicant and the date of issue, and sign the document. Reducing 'J. Zwartendijk' to a quick scribble was not an option. He dotted the i's and j's on every single visa.

He sat at his desk from seven in the morning to six in the evening. Sometimes, by late afternoon there was such a long line that he stayed till after dark. One evening, he received a visit from a Russian officer, who ordered four or five soldiers to block the sidewalk and posted a corporal at the door. In a few German words, he said that Zwartendijk was posing a threat to public safety. The officer threatened to close the consulate, effective at once. Zwartendijk calmed him down by giving him a Philishave, the revolutionary electric razor introduced in late 1939, which he'd begun selling in April. He had planned an advertising campaign with posters on kiosks and newspaper ads, but the threat of war had intervened. The officer, thrilled with the gift, had only one question: was it designed for 110 volts, or 220? Jan demonstrated the razor in the showroom.

'*Kakoe chudo!*' the officer exclaimed. Later that evening, Maschewski, who stayed around to assist and prevent misunderstandings, translated this outcry: 'What a miracle!'

To avoid further trouble, Zwartendijk made sure to stop working by 7.00 p.m. from then on, or seven-thirty at the latest. But he never paused, even for a minute. He ate nothing all day long, drank only cold coffee, and barely took the time to light his cigarettes. The number of visas became an obsession. Forty more today than yesterday. Fifty more. Sixty. He was so intent on his work that on 29 July he forgot his own birthday. Erni and the children shared his constant preoccupation, so they forgot, too. It wasn't until that night, as Erni was getting into bed, that she said – with a blend of surprise and regret – 'Oh my goodness, Jan, you turned forty-four today!'

Zwartendijk's laconic reply was, 'We'll celebrate next year, if we're still alive.'

When Wilek Frankel joined the line in front of the consulate on Laisvės Alėja, he found 'maybe a thousand people' there. He had to wait for hours in the scorching July heat. When he finally reached the consul's office, he requested six visas for his immediate family. Wilek had fled Cracow with his wife, Perla, his brother, David, his brother-in-law, Berl Schor, his two sisters, and his aunt. Their original destination had been Romania, but a long, circuitous route had instead brought them to Vilnius. Along the way, they had been separated from his sister, Brenda, born two years after him. He feared he would never see her again. So by the time he went to see consul Zwartendijk, Wilek was fed up, and determined to lead the rest of his family to safety however he could.

'Six?' Zwartendijk said. 'I don't have time for that. Here …'

He wrote the words of the visa in Wilek's passport.

'Can you write in French?'

Wilek nodded, even though he spoke only Polish and German.

'Sit down over there and copy that into the other passports.'

Wilek pulled up a chair to an adjacent desk, and followed

The Lietuvos Philips building containing the office and showroom.
Now no. 29 Laisvės Alėja, formerly no. 17.

Zwartendijk's instructions, sweating over every word. It took him
more than two hours. After checking the results, the consul signed
and stamped the passports.

'Nice work,' he mumbled in German. 'Didn't miss a single accent.'

The only mistakes were made by the consul himself. Instead of
'Frankel,' he wrote 'Frenkiel' on his own list of visas issued:

Frenkiel Josef
Frenkiel Perla
Frenkiel Schabse
Frenkiel Szarlota

He spelled the name of Wilek's brother-in-law, 'Schor Berl', correctly. But he forgot to add the applicant himself, Wilek Frankel, to the list.

Zwartendijk had no time to learn more about the men who came to him. He would ask for their countries of origin and nationalities, and write their family names and personal names in their visas – which sounds simpler than it was. Polish names were especially complicated, and he often left out an accent. Many of these names were quite long: Czerwonogóra Szloma, Dobekirer Jechil, Fajwuszowicz Szmul, Międzylewski Dawid. He was constantly hesitating between 'v' and 'w'.

The German-Jewish names and the English ones were easiest. He issued a visa to David Sidney, but it was a mystery to him how the man had ended up in 'Kovno', as Kaunas was then known in English. A name like 'Friedlander, Alfred' gave him a reassuring sense of saving time.

He numbered each visa and, after writing a name, would copy it onto a slip of paper that he handed to Van Prattenburg or De Haan. On the same slip he would note the nationality – most often Polish, but sometimes German, Czech, British, Dutch, or Hungarian. Van Prattenburg would type the name and nationality on the list.

He had no way of checking who these people were. After a hurried glance at the applicant's face, he would ask for the name or read it in the passport, and start writing. He saw the fingers handing him the document – sometimes trembling, sometimes calm. He saw a hand, perhaps old and wrinkled, perhaps young. He heard a voice – deep, or high-pitched, or scratchy – saying 'Ja' and 'Nein', or 'Yes' and 'No'. Many refugees spoke English to him, imagining the consul of a Nazi-occupied country would hate the German language. That was also why they called him *Mister* Radio Philips.

As the days passed, the waiting throng grew ever more restless, and crowd control became a difficult job for Van Prattenburg and De Haan. More and more often, they had to shout to keep the line moving in the right direction, up the stairs. It was at the foot of the stairs that most fights tended to break out, when people tired of waiting all day tried to press forward, shoving other applicants off the staircase. Then the air would fill with shouts, insults, and curses.

Every day, Erni came to watch, with Edith and little Jan at her side, and Robbie in her arms. It was frightening, Edith recalled. The line of applicants stretched far outside the consulate – all men, of all ages, but most of them fairly young. Their wives and children had stayed behind in the Kaunas or Vilnius ghetto; it was very rare for a woman to accompany her husband to the Dutch or Japanese consulate. The men sometimes stood in line for days in the burning sun, exhausted, hungry, and thirsty, clamoring for water. Fights kept breaking out. Once the men were inside, they became more aggressive, especially when closing time approached and they started to worry they wouldn't reach the head of the line that day. Edith could still picture the whole scene:

> I remember that De Haan and Van Prattenburg helped to keep the crowd under control from early in the morning till late in the evening. Pa was full of praise for the way they organised things so that he could go on writing as many visas as possible.

In the afternoon, Van Prattenburg and De Haan carried wooden clubs, hoping the sight would deter violence. They shared Zwartendijk's fear of any disturbances that might develop beyond a brief shoving match or fistfight. Any rioting, and the Soviets were bound to close the consulate at once and nail the door shut.

Edith told me she still had nightmares years later about the scenes she'd witnessed there. She feared that something would happen to her father, that he would be beaten or maybe even lynched. She did understand that her father's death wasn't in the refugees' interest, since a dead man couldn't help them. But at the same time, she was aware that the people who came to see her father were desperate and at their wits' end, no longer capable of thinking clearly about the consequences of their actions.

Zwartendijk understood how tense their situation was. He remained calm – eyewitnesses say his composure was exemplary. When it all became too much for him, he would light a cigarette, but after a single puff would return to writing, with perseverance and growing haste:

Cukier Abram
Zilber Icek
Piekarz Mordka
Gutgeshalt Marrem
Rozencwajg Chil
Ornstein Ernst
Winograd Srul
Krysztal Hawa Laja

Sometimes a story slipped out, compressed into a few brief statements, a story that gave him the strength to go on and strengthened his conviction that he was doing the right thing.

'Your name and your nationality?'

'My name is Abram Marber. I come from Turek, which is near Kalisz, in Poland. I was on the road for weeks. I walked until I wore out my shoes, and went on with rags wrapped around my feet. I was attacked, beaten, and chased away. I hid in the woods in the daytime and walked on at night. Once in a while, in a village, a peasant would give me something to drink. I lived on raw potatoes I dug up with my bare hands. I wasn't much more than skin and bone by the time I reached Vilne [Vilnius]. The Lithuanian Red Cross gave me clothes and shoes. In Vilne, I heard about Mister Radio Philips and the Japanese consul. It took me five days to walk to Kaunas.'

He told his story in a steely voice, emphasising every word. When

Zwartendijk handed him the passport with the visa for Curaçao, Abram Marber said, 'Danke sehr, Heer Konsul. Ich weisz, ich werde überleben.' Thank you, Mr Consul. I know I will survive.

Abram Marber had an unconquerable will to live. He found his way to an American aid organisation that paid for his one-way ticket to Vladivostok on the Trans-Siberian Express. From Vladivostok, he took the Osaka Shosen steamship company's Amakusa Maru to Tsuruga, Japan. As the coast drew near, he saw snow-capped mountains. Like most Jewish refugees, he took the train to Kobe, where he was placed in a camp not far from the harbour. He remained there till late 1941. After the Japanese attack on Pearl Harbor and the American declaration of war, Marber and all the other Jewish refugees in Kobe were sent to Shanghai.

On my desk is a yellowed card that I was given by Asher Sarfati, Abram Marber's grandson. The letter is addressed to Jewisch [sic] Community, Kobe (Japan). Under the name of the city is für [for] A. Marber. There is no writing on the card, apart from the name and address of the sender: Ch. Marber Warszawa. Miła 13/17 Above this is a square red stamp: Judenrat Warschau [Jewish Council, Warsaw]. Under it is another red stamp, this one rounded: the words Ortskommando im Warschau [German army headquarters in Warsaw] with the eagle and swastika below them. There are two postal-date stamps, both for 15 IV 41.

The Marber family sent the card from the Warsaw ghetto to Abram, the only family member who had managed to escape from Poland, to show him that the rest of the family was still alive. We do not know how much longer that was the case. This was the last sign of life that Abram received from them. He kept the card in his wallet every day of his life, wearing it over his heart. None of the family members who remained in Poland would survive the war.

I carefully slide the card back into the folder of documents, not as an item of evidence, but as the final testimony of people murdered in an extermination camp – one we can no longer even identify.

Not everyone with a visa was safe. Oskar Schenker and his brother, Alfred, were allowed to leave Lithuania, but when their mother, their wives, and their children went from Kaunas to Vilnius with Curaçao visas in their handbags, they were taken into custody by Russian soldiers and sent to a camp in Siberia. Oskar's son, Alexander, is known to have been held captive from 1940 to 1942 and to have worked in the Soviet Union from 1942 to 1946. I was unable to trace the movements of the other family members, and it remains a mystery why the women and children were arrested. Maybe there were no consistent criteria, and it was a simple case of bad luck.

For a long time, Zwartendijk believed that most of the refugees would make it no farther than Irkutsk, and that only a scattered few would slip through the net. Or, no, Edith tells me, actually it wasn't that simple. One day, he might think they all would make it. The next day, he'd say it would be almost impossible for them to travel straight across the Soviet Union and reach Japan. 'Impossible,' he'd cry. 'Not a chance in hell.' Then he'd add, 'But who knows?'

One morning, at quarter past six – the city was already heating up in the bright sunshine – Zwartendijk muttered over breakfast, 'I have to do something, because I can't do nothing. But there are so many of them … If only I'm granted the time. Time, time, that's what it comes down to.' He looked up and saw not only his wife, at the counter, staring at him, but also Edith next to her. He bolted down his tea, stood up, pulled on his jacket as he headed out to the car, and drove off to another long day at the office.

By five in the morning, a long line had already formed in front of the consulate. By seven, Laisvės Alėja was mobbed.

What was officially a remark in a travel document that no visa was required for Curaçao and Suriname soon became known as a Curaçao visa. Refugees with Curaçao visas could go to the Japanese consulate. There they had to stand in line again, usually for days on end, waiting for the transit visa provided by Japanese consul Chiune Sugihara.

As incredible as it may seem, the Dutch and Japanese consuls never met. Nor did they ever make joint arrangements or discuss what procedures to follow, even though they did talk on the phone.

'They had an unspoken understanding, and were in cahoots,' Edith told me. 'When Sugihara saw a visa my father had issued for Curaçao, he would fill in the transit visa for Japan next to it. He figured out right away what was going on. And he was willing to take risks.

'I was there once when Pa received a call from Sugihara, who complained about his cramped fingers. He had to write six columns of Japanese characters in each passport, using a dip pen or a brush. He had practically stopped eating, was skipping meals, and sat at his desk eighteen to twenty hours a day, with terrible cramp in his fingers. He had called my father to ask whether many more refugees would be coming his way.'

The only interview Zwartendijk ever gave refers to *several* phone conversations with consul Sugihara. In the *Leeuwarder Courant* of December 27, 1963, he said:

> The only bright note in that dark time was supplied by the Japanese consul. He had to brush the transit visas into the passports in black ink. He called me several times in a panic, begging me to slow down, because he couldn't brush fast enough to keep up. The street outside his office was full of people waiting ...

12

The manual for consular officials

Before writing the first visas, Zwartendijk asked De Decker in Riga for permission to do so. After issuing a travel document to Nathan Gutwirth, he never asked again. Throughout the war, De Decker was unaware that hundreds of students from Talmud schools in Lithuania were making their way to the Dutch consulate in Kaunas. Nor did he have the slightest suspicion that the escape route would be used by so many men, women, and children. But Zwartendijk did talk to De Decker on the phone, telling him it was 'very busy' at the consulate, and the envoy concluded, correctly, that writing a note in the passports was a brilliant idea that was enabling many Jews to escape. Later, De Decker would re-use the same note, but he never found out the full scale of the rescue operation until after the war.

After an uneasy start, Zwartendijk set aside his qualms and acted on his own initiative, partly to shield De Decker from later criticism and disapproval. Zwartendijk was not paid a penny for his work. An honorary consulship was a voluntary position that, aside from prestige, brought nothing but responsibilities. On the other hand, if he was sacked, he ran no risk of unemployment or being reduced to beggary. De Decker did.

The envoy and the consul talked on the phone about ten times. Half a word, or a cough, often told them all they needed to know. They realised the NKVD was listening in on their calls – or, at least,

De Decker knew for certain, and Zwartendijk must have suspected, because he was always prepared for the possibility that he would be arrested by the Russians. The two of them must have proceeded with caution, responding sometimes with a grunt or a sniff instead of yes or no. Their actions were not the product of careful planning. They adapted to the situation from day to day. When the Japanese consul proved willing to cooperate, the operation could begin in earnest. Without a Japanese transit visa, a Curaçao visa had no value whatsoever.

Only one portrait of De Decker has been preserved. Judging by that likeness, he was a nervous wreck, a sourpuss, a gastric patient, or maybe all three. And don't forget his chronic fatigue, which had started in Yokohama and continued in Singapore and Tehran. Even before war broke out, De Decker was exhausted.

But his beady, piercing eyes reveal more about the man: vigilant, and shrewd when he had to be. An expert in slipping through the holes in the net of international law. His long consular experience had taught him all the tricks of the trade.

Seventy years after his death, it was hard to reconstruct his life. Each new puzzle piece presented me with a new riddle. For example, how could a Belgian become an 'envoy extraordinary and minister plenipotentiary' of the Netherlands?

We know that Leendert Pieter Johan de Decker was born in Berchem in 1884, in a grand building by the Antwerp harbour, the second son of Cornelis de Decker and Wilhelmina Frederica de Beuse. Yet, despite those good Flemish names, his parents belonged to the Dutch Reformed Church – Protestants in a fashionable Antwerp suburb, Calvinists who had remained faithful to the Dutch church. Half a century after Belgian independence, it's a strange anomaly. I couldn't make sense of it.

First clue: Mr De Decker came from a family of shipowners. In the early nineteenth century, the De Decker–Cassiers shipping company had owned ten three-masters that sailed to Mexico and South America,

Leendert de Decker.

but by century's end the fleet was reduced to seven barques and brigs. The company offices were in Venusstraat in Antwerp.

Second: De Decker–Cassiers had a bad reputation in the city. Nineteenth-century Belgium was an overwhelmingly Catholic country, yet *haute commerce* in Antwerp was controlled mainly by families of foreign origin who were anticlerical, or had remained Protestant after the Belgian secession from the Netherlands in 1830 and made a point of boasting about their pro-Dutch sentiments.

The De Decker family had been wealthy; the son of the company founder bought the Hof van Brabant, a castle in Hoboken. This wealth had lasted a century, and ended because De Decker and Cassiers were late in switching from sailing ships to steamships – a mistake made by many Belgian and Dutch shipowners. So in 1890, the company had to be 'wound up', liquidated. By then, Leendert was six years old. The family was not immediately plunged into poverty; they even managed to stay in the stately home in Berchem a while longer. But the children no longer had a prosperous future laid out for them.

Both at home and at school, Leendert had a bilingual upbringing: French and Dutch. He completed secondary school in Belgium and left for Nijmegen, in the south of the Netherlands, in 1902, staying with his sister, Eva. Eva, two years older than Leendert, was a schoolteacher. On 31 May 1905, the daily newspaper *Het Volk* announced that L.P.J. de Decker had passed the exam for certification as a mercantile clerk. This may not sound like the start of a glamorous career, but in a sense, he was following in the footsteps of his forefathers; the De Decker–Cassiers shipping company had always traded in the goods carried by its ships. Trade turned out to be in the boy's blood; before the year was out, he found a job at an export office in Hamburg.

A nomadic period followed: two years in one country, three in another. Leendert stayed longest in Romania, where love and work kept him for seven years. He became involved with a Romanian woman, Eufrosina Savulescu. When she gave birth to a daughter, the couple married. On the official papers, 'relationship' was crossed out and replaced with 'marriage'.

In 1909, he and a Dutch business partner had established a firm in the Romanian capital, importing and exporting textiles. But the two of them could not make the company turn a profit. The Second Balkan War had brought trade to a standstill; in 1913, their firm had to shut down. The day after it was liquidated, De Decker became a junior member of the consular service in Bucharest. Seven months later, he was appointed as prospective vice-consul in Düsseldorf, with an annual salary of 1,200 guilders. The merchant had become a consular officer, not honorary but salaried.

To join the Dutch diplomatic service, you had to have Dutch nationality. The Lists of Naturalisations from 1850 to 1934 do not include L.P.J. de Decker. Nor do we find the name of his brother, Ludovicus Johannes – a professional soldier and a major in the Dutch field artillery branch – or his sister, Eva. This tells us that the De Decker children possessed Dutch nationality from birth. Apparently, when Belgium became independent, their grandfather had opted to remain Dutch. This solves the riddle of the family's Dutch Reformed faith.

De Decker spent most of the First World War in Germany. After Düsseldorf, he worked at the Dutch consulates in Berlin and Hamburg. Then he had a more restful interlude as a deputy vice-consul in Tangiers, where he arrived in June 1919. The city had strong Jewish, French, Spanish, and Islamic influences that attracted painters and poets, as well as adventurers and shady dealers. Tangiers made a deep impression on everyone who came to the city; life was good there. But in October 1920, De Decker had to move on again, this time to Japan.

His new post was Yokohama. But he spent just as much time at the consulate in Kobe, four hundred miles away, another port city often visited by Dutch ships, and the base of a lively trade with Java and Sumatra. The Dutch consulate in Kobe was one of the longest-established in Asia, and was an efficiently run trading post and a well-oiled organisation. It can hardly be a coincidence that almost all the refugees who received Curaçao visas in 1940 and 1941 travelled to Kobe. And if not Kobe, they ended up in Yokohama. But I found no proof that De Decker mapped out that route for them.

In Japan, De Decker was five weeks by ship from the Netherlands. When his daughter, Yvonne, died in a hospice in Hilversum, he had no way of getting there in time for the funeral. She died just before her tenth birthday.

Born in 1911, Yvonne had accompanied her father to all his posts except Tangiers and Yokohama. By that time she was ill, probably suffering from tuberculosis. The two official witnesses of Yvonne's death were not relatives; one was an undertaker, and the other a Hilversum city employee. Yvonne was staying in a hospice at Middenweg 2 run by two unmarried women schoolteachers. The death notice in *De Gooien Eemlander* was signed only by E. Savulescu, her mother, and not by De Decker. Not long before the girl's death, her parents had separated.

Eufrosina left Japan a year before Leendert was assigned to his following post. She took a ship to Istanbul; the last short leg of her journey was by train, to Bucharest. In a yellowed copy of *De Gooien Eemlander*, I found a second notice, thanking those who had expressed their sympathies on the death of 'my young daughter'. Again, it was signed only by E. Savulescu.

De Decker remained in Asia. In late 1922, he moved into the Singapore consulate general's white country house. At a reception, he shook the hand of the great Dutch novelist Louis Couperus. The writer, who was staying in the Europe Hotel and working on a series of reports for the *Haagsche Post*, was impressed with the diplomat's wife – his German bride, the second Mrs De Decker.

Couperus thought Jenny Heyer charming, courteous, and intriguing, with a hint of sensuality. She had taken Eufrosina's place with speed and apparent ease. Jenny Mathilde Christine Cornelia Heyer, born in Hamburg, was a year younger than De Decker. It remains unknown where and when the diplomat first met her. If it was in Hamburg, where De Decker had served as consul from the middle of the First World War, then they had known each other for around six years.

Like Zwartendijk, De Decker had married a German-speaking woman, although Jenny's mother was Danish in origin.

In late 1923, De Decker went to Hong Kong with Jenny to become deputy consul general there. One posting was swiftly followed by another; in June 1924, he became deputy envoy in Bangkok.

On 21 August 1925, four years after Yvonne's death, he was finally granted extended leave. The De Deckers travelled by boat to the Netherlands, where, after a brief holiday, he was put to work at the foreign ministry in The Hague. De Decker was instructed to revise the *Manual for Dutch Consular Officials*. This guide to the consular service dated from 1908, and many new rules had been made since then, partly because of the founding of the League of Nations.

In The Hague, they already saw De Decker as such a dyed-in-the-wool consular official that he seemed the obvious choice to update the guidelines. It took him almost two years, and by the time he had finished, he knew what a consul was and was not supposed to do,

The manual revised by Leendert de Decker and the letter appointing Jan
Zwartendijk as consul.

down to the finest details, and how to evade the rules in a way that
was formally correct – if not entirely bona fide.

Consular work was disdained by any *real* diplomat – and before
the Second World War that typically meant an aristocrat with a law
degree and impeccable French. A diplomat kept his government
apprised of the political situation in a country, and tried to mediate
whenever conflicts arose. A consul, on the other hand, had closer
ties to the host culture, and provided real assistance to individuals in
trouble. De Decker knew more about how to do that in practice than
anyone else in the Dutch foreign service.

The ministry was grateful to him for his labours. In 1927, he made a
huge leap up the career ladder, becoming a *chargé d'affaires* in Teheran.

There he spent three years negotiating a treaty of amity between the Netherlands and Persia, which he signed on behalf of Her Majesty in 1930. By this time, he wore the decorations of an officer in the Order of Orange-Nassau. From his humble origins as a certified clerk from a family of merchants, his career had taken off like a rocket.

In 1930, he was assigned to Düsseldorf, an important consular mission for the Netherlands. He served an unusually long term as consul general there, until December 1937, witnessing both the Nazi rise to power and the *Gleichschaltung*, the establishment of a totalitarian state. He saw the stream of refugees begin, but could offer little or no assistance, because of the Dutch government's ever-stricter admission policy.

In the course of the 1930s, some 30,000 German, Polish, and Austrian Jews tried to flee to the Netherlands. Some travelled on to the United States or Palestine, but most, after arriving in the Netherlands, wanted to remain there. This influx of refugees, which began after Hitler took power in 1933, soon grew so large that in 1934 the Dutch government took measures to restrict the flow. German Jews were admitted and granted visas only for a limited time. Polish Jews who had come to the Netherlands earlier were required to return to their own country. New Polish refugees and stateless people were no longer admitted unless their lives were in danger. In May 1938, these restrictions were tightened even further. No longer was there any exception for German Jews; the Netherlands no longer admitted a single refugee. During his final years as a consul in Düsseldorf, De Decker had constantly had to say no.

Did this trouble him? Considering his actions in Riga and later in Stockholm, I'm inclined to say it must have, but De Decker was enough of a diplomat not to leave any written record of his objections or to express them openly. Another real possibility is that in 1940–1945 he was trying to make up for his serious failure to act in the 1930s. Unfortunately, De Decker had no surviving children who could tell us more; his second marriage remained childless. If he felt remorse, he did not leave behind any written evidence of it.

ONZE NIEUWE GEZANT IN LETLAND

DE NIEUWE NEDERLANDSCHE GEZANT TE RIGA, Z. Exc. L. P. J. de Decker, heeft enkele dagen geleden zijn opwachting gemaakt bij president Ulmanis en dezen zijn geloofs-brieven overhandigd. De gezant (in het midden links naast een Letlandschen functionaris) verlaat het presidentspaleis.

Leendert de Decker presenting his credentials to President Ulmanis of Latvia.
From the Dutch newspaper *Algemeen Handelsblad*, 25 March 1939.

Be that as it may, De Decker must have accepted his transfer to the Baltic countries with some relief. He could put the refugee crisis behind him – at least, for a time. On 1 January 1938, he was appointed the temporary Dutch *chargé d'affaires* in Riga, and his promotion soon followed, on 20 February 1939, to envoy extraordinary and minister plenipotentiary and *chargé d'affaires* for Estonia, Latvia, and Lithuania.

After presenting his credentials to the Latvian president, Karlis Ulmanis, he made a speech reported in the regional Dutch newspaper

De Gooien Eemlander on 24 March 1939. De Decker pointed out that Latvia and the Netherlands had similar political objectives: staying out of conflicts between third powers, maintaining strict neutrality, and devoting serious energy to preserving peace.

Whether he personally believed in strict neutrality remains a mystery. During his years in Germany, he had seen at first hand that the Nazis would violate any treaty and did not respect a single written agreement or informal arrangement. It is hard to believe he did not conclude that the neutrality so sacred to the Dutch government was a persistent denial of reality. But the L.P.J. de Decker I found in the files of the foreign ministry was an obedient diplomat who followed his government's lead.

De Decker was fifty-five years old when he moved into the official residence in Riga. The house overlooked the city, but he is unlikely to have spent much time enjoying the panoramic view. His wife was already seriously ill by the time he arrived in Latvia. Jenny died on 23 January 1939.

Until he left Riga, the envoy shared the official residence with a cook and a servant. De Decker had become a solitary man in a solitary place. Maybe it no longer mattered so much to him whether everything that went on at the consulates falling under his legation was strictly correct. If he could save a few lives, so much the better.

Audacity and personal initiative were not prized qualities in the Dutch diplomatic corps – a conservative organisation, cautious to the point of cowardice and compliant to authority. Even so, it was a Dutch envoy and a Dutch consul who took prompt action to help large numbers of Jewish refugees.

After the war, a few refugees who had reached Los Angeles after many wanderings gave Jan Zwartendijk an honorary title: The Angel of Curaçao. The first time he heard about this, in 1963, he told the editor of the *Leeuwarder Courant*, 'If anyone deserves that title, then it's De Decker, who gave me the successful wording for the pseudo-visas.'

13

The white ship with the black hull

In 1939, every newspaper reader in the Americas and Western Europe followed the journey of the *St. Louis* from day to day. This 'Voyage of the Damned', as the British and American papers styled it, would, many people believed, determine the direction of the near future. Would a few countries be willing to accept large groups of Jewish refugees whose lives had been in danger in Hitler's Germany? And, above all, how would the United States respond?

The ship, part of the Hamburg-America Line, was referred to in all the newspapers as white. But that wasn't entirely true; it had a white superstructure and a greyish-black hull. On 13 May 1939, the *St. Louis* left the port of Hamburg with 907 Jewish passengers on board. Their backgrounds were very diverse. They included Orthodox Jews who ate only kosher food, Liberal Jews who rarely saw the inside of a synagogue, Jews who chose to lead secular lives, and so-called Jews who had been unaware of their Jewish ancestry until their passports were stamped with a red 'J'. Most passengers came from the middle class, and, although their native language was German, they expected to find work in law, medicine, and business in the United States. In Cherbourg, another thirty Jews boarded. With 937 passengers, a full German crew, and a German captain, the ship set a course for Havana.

Passengers on the *St. Louis* arriving in Cuba, 26 May 1939.

All the passengers had valid papers for disembarking in Cuba, 'passports' purchased from a Cuban businessman for $1,000 each. The refugees had coughed up $1 million in total for access to Cuba. They were confident that in Havana they could lay their hands on visas for the United States without much difficulty.

On 26 May, the ship entered Havana Harbour. It was moored to a buoy, because the authorities denied the captain permission to dock. The *St. Louis* was soon surrounded by sloops and boats filled with the American relatives of the passengers. They whistled and called out through megaphones to their nieces, nephews, uncles, aunts, and cousins who were leaning over the rails, feeling as if they were already close to becoming part of the New World. Relatives exchanged the latest news, but not one of the passengers was allowed on land.

The Cuban authorities refused to admit the refugees, afraid that the country would be overrun by Jews. They regarded the passports as forgeries; the crooked businessman turned out to be an enemy of the corrupt president. President Brú feared that if he admitted 900 Jews, he'd be punished for it in the next elections. And, in fact, he would lose those elections, to General Batista. Both presidential candidates were out to earn money any way they could – and that included selling visas to refugees. To begin with, the price was raised to $2,800 per visa; then conflicting interests led to a stalemate.

On the ship, the tension became unbearable. One of the passengers slit his wrists, and three hours later another passenger – a doctor from Munich, travelling alone – was drifting between life and death after an overdose of insulin. After two more suicide attempts, the passengers could no longer sleep, and spent the night on deck, talking, praying, or quarrelling.

The negotiations between the captain and the authorities went on for days, but only a few passengers were allowed to leave the ship, and only after explicitly declaring that they were of the Christian and not the Jewish faith.

After five days in Havana harbour, the *St. Louis* was instructed to leave and return to Europe. Captain Schröder was able to postpone their departure one more day. He put on his civvies, went on land, and knocked on the door of the Cuban president, who said he 'regrettably' had to attend an important meeting and could not see the captain. Meanwhile, desperate passengers were storming the gangway; two women were seriously hurt and had to be taken to a hospital in Havana (a lifesaver, because it permitted them to stay in Cuba).

The letters of protest sent to the Cuban president – around two thousand from around the world – did not help. Captain Schröder received no more than a few extra hours to buy provisions and drinking water for the nine hundred passengers. He said to his officers, 'It won't be an easy voyage. But keep in mind that it's hardest on our passengers. Be polite and attentive to their needs; they are our guests. If they want to know where we're bound, refer them to the bulletins posted around the ship.'

The captain and crew had left Hamburg as Nazi sympathisers. But as the voyage went on, they had come to understand their passengers better. Still, they sometimes had to lie and deceive to prevent mutiny. Under the pretext that all the passengers would be allowed to disembark in New York, the *St. Louis* left Havana harbour and headed

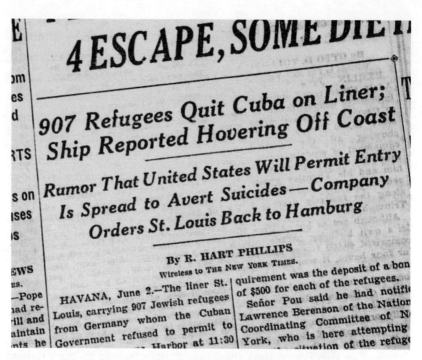

Headline announcing the start of the return voyage.

north. Off the coast of Florida, Captain Schröder gave orders to stop the engines. Three hundred passengers had said they wanted to make for the coast in boats and sloops, and hope for the best. Two United States Coast Guard vessels rushed to the scene and prevented the illegal landing. The coast guard signalled to the *St. Louis*, 'Know all about passengers. Sorry.'

From early 1939 onwards, the United States kept its borders firmly closed to Jewish refugees. President Roosevelt pointed apologetically at his country's high unemployment rate. The thinking was that if you let in a thousand, a million more would come. This fear was shared by a majority in Roosevelt's party, the Democrats, and by three-quarters of Republicans.

The ship received telexes claiming that the passengers could disembark on the Isla de Pinos, just south of Cuba. So they sailed back to the Caribbean. But the story proved false. Another telex reported that the passengers would be allowed to land in the Dominican Republic. But nothing came of that, because the country's dictator, Rafael Trujillo, was negotiating with the Gestapo in Berlin to accept 100,000 Jews for $500 each. The $50 million to be made in that transaction overshadowed whatever money could be squeezed from the St. Louis passengers. Incidentally, the deal with the Gestapo led nowhere.

The St. Louis had to take the passengers back to Europe. As the ship sped across the ocean and the passengers sent word that they were headed for their doom, representatives of the French, British, Belgian, and Dutch governments held frenzied talks, the outcome of which was that France agreed to accept 224 passengers, Britain 288, Belgium 214, and the Netherlands 181.

On 17 June 1939, the St. Louis docked at the port of Antwerp. The passengers admitted to the Netherlands were transferred to the Heijplaat quarantine station. They included the twelve-year-old Hannelore Klein, who would become the mother of the well-known Dutch author Arnon Grunberg. After six weeks, they were moved to the Lloyd Hotel on Oostelijke Handelskade in Amsterdam, where they were confined for a year. As soon as the country was occupied by the Germans, they were sent to Westerbork transit camp, established in 1939 with funds from Jewish aid organisations, and originally meant to hold Jewish refugees from Germany.

Hannelore Klein, like many other passengers from the St. Louis, would be sent on to Auschwitz-Birkenau. She survived the war. But 254 of the passengers would die in the concentration camps.

The way the refugees on the St. Louis were kicked back and forth across the Atlantic made many people angry. Jan de Hartog, then a more-or-less unknown sailor and writer working on a Dutch sea tug, heard his captain say, 'If that had been my ship, I would never in my life have brought those people back.' As a reflection on this thought, De Hartog wrote the novel Schipper naast God, which he completed in the spring of 1940. During the war, he adapted the book into an English-language

Passengers on the *St. Louis*.

play, *Skipper next to God*, which in 1945 had full houses in London and New York crying their eyes out or shouting in rage.

The captain of Jan de Hartog's fictional ship refuses to return to Europe. Going on to one South American port after another, he hawks his Jewish refugees. Captain Joris Kuiper is caught between the Bible and Calvin on the one hand, and his salty seaman's ways on the other. He fights an inner battle between ruthless greed and the demands of his faith. The outcome is a correction of what happened to the passengers on the *St. Louis*.

Peppy Sternheim and Nathan Gutwirth knew the details of the fruitless landing attempt in Cuba. The name of the ship was burned into the memory of Jan Zwartendijk, Leendert, and every consul.

Corruption-riddled Cuba was clearly not a viable destination. Nor were Florida or the Dominican Republic. But Curaçao was a Dutch island. Besides, it had a second advantage: almost no one had ever heard of it – and that was certainly true of soldiers and border guards in Lithuania, the Soviet Union, and Japan.

By naming Curaçao as the final destination of the visa applicants, the consul of the Kingdom of the Netherlands in Kaunas created the impression that he knew just what he was doing. The pathetic *St. Louis* debacle had inspired a much larger-scale rescue operation, with Curaçao as its endpoint.

But what would have happened if the refugees had actually taken a ship there?

Dr Piet Kasteel was an Engelandvaarder, one of the Dutch men and women who became well known for escaping the Netherlands by sailing across the North Sea. He had made it onto one of the last ships in May 1940. After arriving in London, he had immediately offered his services to the Dutch government in exile. There was no need for introductions; for years, Kasteel had been a reporter for two Roman Catholic newspapers, *De Tijd* and later *De Maasbode*, covering the Dutch parliament. Everyone in the political circles of The Hague knew that, although he was a devout Catholic who had received his doctoral degree from the very Catholic university in Leuven, Belgium, his thesis topic had been the Dutch Reformed leader Abraham Kuyper. He was not only fascinated with orthodox, strait-laced Calvinists, but also acted just as if he were one. Furthermore, he detested Nazism just as much as they did.

In London, he became the principal private secretary to the Dutch prime minister, Pieter Sjoerds Gerbrandy, who was as Frisian, and as strictly Reformed, as they came. The two men debated theology daily, honing their arguments for their opposing views. Gerbrandy was so taken with the well-spoken journalist that he wanted to make him finance minister in the government in exile. But that was a step too far for the other ministers; Kasteel's mastery of theology was equalled by his ignorance of public finance. Queen Wilhelmina brought his lightning career to an end with a lateral promotion to Curaçao. As governor of the Netherlands Antilles, he couldn't do much harm.

On 16 July 1943, Dr P.A. Kasteel moved into the Governor's Palace in Willemstad, a neoclassical building that was part of a fort, right beside the harbour entrance. He would remain there until 1 July 1948, going on to become an ambassador in Chili, Ireland, and – from 1964 onwards – Israel.

When asked by an Israeli newspaper in 1967 whether, as governor of Curaçao, he would have admitted a ship to the island with hundreds of Jews on board, and whether he would have granted the passengers political asylum, he replied, 'No way. I would have sent the ship back to the ocean, like the Cuban and American authorities did with the *St. Louis*.'

14

The independent-minded Sugihara

Unlike envoy De Decker and consul Zwartendijk, who left the Dutch government in exile out of the loop, Chiune Sugihara kept his government informed about the long queue of refugees in front of his consulate waiting for visas. In a telegram sent on 28 July 1940, he asked the Japanese foreign minister what exactly he should do with the 'socialists, Bundists, Zionists, and other Jews' at his door who wanted 'to travel to the US by way of Japan'. Should he grant them transit visas? Amid the confusion of the global political situation, Sugihara hoped that his government would say yes.

On 25 November 1938, Japan had concluded the Anti-Comintern Pact with Nazi Germany. Fascist Italy joined the pact in 1937; Mussolini envisaged one axis running straight through Europe from Rome to Berlin, and another from Berlin to Tokyo. The Japanese Empire, Nazi Germany, and the Kingdom of Italy were the Axis powers, whose main objective was to form a united front against the Soviet Union.

When Berlin signed a non-aggression treaty with Moscow, Japan felt betrayed, and withdrew from the Anti-Comintern Pact in indignation. The Japanese government saw the Molotov–Ribbentrop Pact as a stab in the back, proof that Hitler could not be trusted. But the German conquest of western Europe in May and June 1940 made the European colonies in South-east Asia – especially the French, British, and Dutch possessions – easy prey for Japan. So it decided to

The Japanese consul Chiune Sugihara at his desk.

renew its friendship, and its alliance, with Germany. The Axis powers decided to work together from that moment on to defeat France and the United Kingdom.

It was during this period that Sugihara asked his government whether he could issue visas to refugees. At first, the proposal was rejected by the Japanese foreign minister, who sent the consul a telegram forbidding him to issue transit visas to people whose papers were not in order or who had no papers. By return telegram, Sugihara suggested that those refugees could simply be turned away at the Japanese border. He was nothing if not bold.

Because of a change of government, there was no response from Japan for days. The newly appointed foreign minister, Yosuke Matsuoka, had a reputation for being a strict, dogmatic politician with militant nationalist views, but he had begun his career as the head of the South Manchuria Railway Company and, in that capacity, worked with the local Jewish community. He felt no animosity towards Jews, and decided to leave the visa question in Sugihara's hands.

The Soviet Union required everyone with a transit visa for Japan to cross the border into Japan. In the end, Tokyo would allow this to happen, without any further written instructions or comments in telegrams.

Chiune Sugihara would pay the price later, after the war, when he was informed that it would be best for him to leave the Japanese diplomatic corps. He had charted his own political course, in conflict with the guidelines from the foreign office, and the officials in Tokyo had never forgotten. Lesson one for any diplomat: obey your government, and don't show personal initiative. But Sugihara was independent-minded, even obstinate, and had not shown enough sensitivity to authority.

'The incident in Lithuania,' as his wife, Yukiko, called it in her memoirs, had cost him his job.

Sugihara could hardly believe it.

'The dismissal came as an incredible shock,' his eldest son, Hiroki, said a quarter century later. 'My father had expected recognition for his deeds – he had done it for Japan. He had upheld his country's reputation.' And contempt was his reward.

But that was not all. Soon rumours were circulating among senior officials in Tokyo that Sugihara had accepted bribes from wealthy Jews in exchange for visas. When he heard this story, Sugihara felt utterly humiliated. He was so outraged that from then on, he refused to talk about his time in Lithuania. Even in the family circle, his eldest son says, the subject became taboo.

By the late 1940s, Japan's most illustrious consul was selling light bulbs door to door to support his family. When that failed to provide a decent living, he spent sixteen years performing the most miserable jobs in the Soviet Union, and sent the hard-earned money to his family in Japan.

Chiune Sugihara was born on 1 January 1900 – the exceptionally cold first day of the new century – in the village of Mino, near Yaotsu, in the mountainous centre of Japan's largest island, Honshu. In Japanese mythology, a child who comes into the world on a freezing, cold night is blessed with special qualities, and will lead a different kind of life from ordinary mortals. In Chiune Sugihara's case, this turned out to be quite true.

He came from a humble family, but soon proved to have a good head on his shoulders. So his father, a lowly tax collector, wanted him to become a doctor. This didn't appeal to Chiune, who was most interested in foreign languages, but his father felt that studying languages would be a waste of money. Chiune went to Tokyo, and flunked the admission exam for the medical programme at Waseda University – one of Japan's three best universities then and now – by turning in a blank sheet of paper with nothing but his name on it. Then he signed up to study English at that same university.

He did all sorts of odd jobs to put food on his plate. As a young man, he must have been searching for something. He joined Yu Ai Gakusha, the Brotherly Love Learning Association, a Christian fraternity founded by a Baptist missionary in Japan named Harry Baxter Benninghoff – to perfect his English, he claimed, but in fact it was his first step towards Christianity.

One day, he saw a newspaper advertisement placed by the foreign ministry. Students of foreign languages could receive a scholarship covering the whole cost of their studies, after a selection procedure and admission exam, if they made a commitment to work for the ministry afterwards. Chiune was admitted. For the next seven years, he devoted himself to English, German, and Russian, interrupting his studies only for his compulsory military service in Korea, then a Japanese colony.

Chiune studied in Harbin, a major city in Manchuria, in northeastern China. The city was still young, having been founded by the Russians in 1898. After the Russo-Japanese War of 1904–1905, Harbin had come under Japanese administration. Not until 1946 would Manchuria become part of China again. Relations between ethnic groups – the Russians, the Japanese, and the Chinese – were tense. In some ways, Manchuria resembled Lithuania, and for Sugihara it was a valuable experience.

In the early 1920s, many White Russians (meaning not Belarusians, but anti-revolutionary émigrés) had settled in Harbin, along with many Jews who had fled the October Revolution and the civil war. Among the White Russians was Klaudia Semionova Apollonova, aged nineteen, who became Sugihara's wife. In order to propose to her, he converted to Christianity and joined the Russian Orthodox Church. He changed his personal name to Pavlo Sergeivich, and spoke Russian at home.

Sugihara met his obligations to the foreign ministry. For years, he served the Japanese government in Manchuria, negotiated with the Russians on a railway from Manchuria to Siberia, and carried out several secret missions. His greatest strength was always his fluency in Russian. But Manchuria was too close to home for his taste, and too Asian. His enduring hope was that one day he would be sent to the Japanese embassy in Moscow, so that he and Klaudia could live in the Russian capital. He seems to have been driven in substantial part by his passion for Russian literature, Dostoyevsky and Tolstoy in particular. This fact, combined with his conversion to Russian Orthodoxy, suggests that Sugihara was a Slavophile – not the type they were looking for in the Soviet Union.

A Japanese proposal to station him in Moscow as a diplomat was rejected by the Soviet Union as 'not terribly advisable'. This must have been due in part to his marriage to a White Russian. Furthermore, he had often opposed Soviet plans in the negotiations on the North Manchuria Railway. He had been just as critical of his own government, but this didn't impress the Soviets.

In fact, that had been Sugihara's first show of courage; he had requested a transfer because he could not reconcile himself to the way the Japanese authorities treated the Chinese population in Manchuria. This principled stance came at the expense of his career; back in Japan, he was assigned to a low-level job at the foreign ministry.

Many years later, he did have the chance to leave for Moscow and work at the embassy – but as a translator, not as a diplomat. That posting came too late for Klaudia; by then, Sugihara had divorced her and married a Japanese woman, Yukiko Kikuchi.

Even so, Chiune remained in touch with Klaudia all his life. In his old age, he revealed that the marriage failed because they had remained childless. Klaudia emigrated to Australia, and died at the age of ninety-three in a Sydney hotel operated by Russians. She never lived anywhere else in Australia but in that Russian hotel.

Yukiko seemed to have two sides: one European and one Japanese. She adored classical music, especially Mozart, as well as Japanese modern art. In her school days, she posed for a photograph as a sailor, with her hair tucked under a cap. She did not start wearing a kimono until she was married to Chiune. Yukiko was thirteen years younger, and the two of them would have four sons together. The eldest had already been born by the time the family moved to Moscow.

Sugihara didn't have the chance to stay in Moscow long. After not much more than a year, he was transferred to Helsinki in the role of consul. In Finland, he worked for both the Japanese government and the Polish intelligence service, reporting to Warsaw on troop movements in western Russia and the Baltic states. Sugihara had become a consul and a spy.

After Finland, he was appointed as consul in Kaunas, where he moved in 1939 after short stays in Paris and Berlin.

Chiune Sugihara arrived in Kaunas by train in the company of his wife, her sister, his eldest son, Hiroki, and his second son, Chiaki, who was still a baby, cradled in Yukiko's arms. The first thing that struck him was that the station was large but had only one, short platform.

Housing in Kaunas was hard to come by. It took months for the new consul to find a suitable home. In the meantime, he and his family stayed at the Metropolis, the same hotel where Zwartendijk had spent a few months after arriving in Lithuania. Then Sugihara rented a house at Vaižganto Gatvė 30, which he set up to serve both as the consulate and as his private home. Japan had never before been

Chiune Sugihara and his wife, Yukiko, in Kaunas.

represented in Lithuania; Sugihara was a pioneer. The consulate opened on 23 November 1939.

The house in Vaižganto Gatvė also accommodated two Lithuanian students. Sugihara agreed with the owner that they could remain there. One was a young man who soon moved on; the young woman, Jadvyga Ulvidai, remained, and witnessed all the events of the war years through her window. She would go on living at that address for the rest of her life.

A flagpole was placed next to the front door. Sugihara maintained a strict schedule, raising the Japanese flag fifteen minutes before sunrise, and lowering it fifteen minutes before sunset.

The first months were tranquil. Sugihara set to work at the consulate, contacted the Lithuanian government, and investigated the political situation in the Baltic region. He devoted a lot of time to his family, spending the weekends with his wife and children in the countryside. His life in Kaunas was very similar to Zwartendijk's; he liked his new surroundings and enjoyed being a father, with a third child on the way. When the boy was born, he had a medical problem, just like little Robbie Zwartendijk. He refused his mother's milk, and Yukiko had to look for a wet nurse. The woman she found was a Lithuanian peasant – not a Jewish refugee, as shown in *Persona Non Grata*, the Japanese feature film released in 2015 about the consul's life in Kaunas. The film's suggestion that Sugihara acted out of gratitude is incorrect. Personal motives did not play a role.

Sugihara's eldest son, a boy of nearly five, later recalled that during their Saturdays and Sundays in the countryside, his father would sometimes disappear. Those trips took them to various parts of the country, but always near one border or another, whether with Poland, Latvia, the Memel Territory, or Königsberg.

In other words, Sugihara continued his espionage in Lithuania. He no longer worked for the government in Warsaw, since Hitler's army had invaded Poland, but for the Polish government in exile and the Polish Resistance. Shortly after arriving in Kaunas, he'd been approached by Polish partisans. He had offered to use his diplomatic channels to send messages to their government, which was in the French city of Angers at first, and later, after the German invasion of France, in London.

For a long while, it remained unclear to me why Sugihara went to such lengths for the Polish cause. He had never been to Warsaw and didn't speak a word of Polish. No other people despised the Russians as much as the Poles, and Sugihara did not feel the same antipathy. Did he do it simply because he opposed communism? I now believe Sugihara was not anti-Soviet so much as he was a Slavophile. The Soviets reached the same conclusion, judging by a note I found in the Lithuanian NKVD/KGB archives – a stroke of luck for Sugihara, and most of all for the Jews to whom he issued transit visas. The Soviets were wary of the Japanese, considering their humiliating defeat in the Russo-Japanese War of 1904–1905, but they expected *less* trouble

Chiune Sugihara near his house in Kaunas, 1939 or 1940.

from Sugihara than from the average official of the Japanese Empire.

At first, I thought Sugihara had spied for the Poles for money – a welcome supplement to his small salary as Japanese consul in Kaunas. But I had no evidence, and could find no mention of payment in any Polish archives. Another flaw in my theory was that Sugihara had never before been motivated by money, personal gain, or professional ambition. His criteria were almost always humanitarian, although he undeniably had a certain thirst for adventure. He enjoyed novel experiences and chance encounters that brought him new insights. Sugihara had an ever-inquiring mind.

It seems more probable that he was spying for Poland in exchange for information he sent to Tokyo. The Japanese government wanted daily updates on troop movements in the region. Rather than reporting to the Japanese embassy for the Baltic states in Riga, consul Sugihara was expected to send all the intelligence he gathered directly to Tokyo.

Kaunas was crawling with spies; from his first day there, Sugihara was watched by secret agents of Lithuania, the Soviet Union, and undoubtedly Nazi Germany as well. Although in the spring of 1940 he distanced himself somewhat from the Polish Resistance, he did not let his actions be dictated by any intelligence service. He went his own way.

One dark afternoon in December 1939, Chiune Sugihara stepped into a shop to buy sweets for his children. On his way out, he bumped into a little boy whose long face suggested he had lost all joy in life forever. The ambassador smiled at the youngster, who seemed too downcast to even burst into tears. 'What's wrong?' he asked in German. Oh, nothing, the boy said. Actually, Hanukkah, the festival of lights, was coming up, and he hadn't saved any money for sweets. No problem, the consul replied, as he fished for a couple of quarters in his pocket. The boy, an eleven-year-old named Solly Ganor, said he wasn't allowed to take money or gifts from strangers. Sugihara smiled again and said, 'Now we've talked, we know each other, and we've become friends, so I can give you some money for sweets.' The boy mulled it over for a second, nodded, and said there was one condition: his new friend would have to come and celebrate Hanukkah at his house with his parents and all his relatives. He gave Sugihara the address, and three days later the consul called on the surprised Ganor family.

Sugihara stayed for the whole celebration: the candle-lighting, the singing, the mouth-watering delicacies. It made a deep impression on him. He told them he had met Jews before, but had never been invited into their homes, let alone celebrated with them.

By the end of the evening, he is said to have told them (though it does sound a bit like a legend): 'This was my first visit to a Jewish family, and I hope it will not be the last.'

In the spring of 1940, Solly Ganor visited the consul again to ask for a couple of cancelled Japanese stamps for his stamp collection. Sugihara urged the boy to tell his father not to hesitate to ask for help if the situation in Lithuania became too dangerous for them and they considered leaving.

Solly's father cannot be found on any list of visas granted, neither under Ganor nor under his original name of Genkind. Yet he did receive a visa from Sugihara. Did the consul leave him off the list? And did Mr Ganor neglect to apply for a Curaçao visa, in which case Sugihara's visa would have been useless to him?

In the early 1990s, Solly was tracked down. He was then dividing his time between Israel and California. He wrote his memoirs in 1995, and published them under the title of *Light One Candle*. His true story turns out to be far more interesting than the anecdote above. It shows that even if you had a visa, it wasn't so easy to leave Lithuania, especially not if you were a successful businessman like Solly's father.

You see, Solly was anything but a poor Jewish urchin with no money for candy. He had been saving for Hanukkah, and had received ten *litai* in total from uncles and aunts. That was equivalent to twenty euros today. But a collection was then being held by Jewish women for children whose parents had fled Poland, were starving, and had no blankets, and, on impulse, Solly had donated the ten *litai*. He regretted it at once, and the very next day begged his parents for at least a little money for Hanukkah. His mother wanted to give him some, but his father said he had shown a noble heart. He shouldn't spoil it by acting petty, but should remain true to his principles.

In the cinema, a Laurel and Hardy film was playing. Solly wanted to see Stan and Ollie, but knew there was no point in asking his father, or even his mother, for the price of the ticket, because he would just get another lecture about moral constancy. So, in a funk, he went to see his aunt, who owned a sweet shop in a little street in the centre of Kaunas – the kind of aunt any boy would love to have. He wasn't afraid to ask her. When he entered the store, she was talking to a distinguished, well-dressed man with a strange look on his face. At least, that's how Solly felt; the boy had never seen a Japanese person before, and was startled at first by his Asian eyes. The man understood and gave him a reassuring smile. His aunt told him not to gawk, and introduced the stranger as 'His Excellency Mr Sugihara'. The man gave another smile, which put Solly at ease. He had a friendly way about him, a goodness that seemed unforced. Then Solly came out and told his aunt that he wanted to see Stan and Ollie. 'Oh, so that's why you're here,' she said, and shuffled over to the cash register. Before she could fetch him some change, consul Sugihara pulled a few small coins out of his pocket and said, 'Well, well, my boy, time off from school and a trip to the cinema. As long as you're on holiday, let me be your uncle.' Solly, caught by surprise, said the first thing that came to mind: 'If you're my uncle, you should come to our Hanukkah party on Saturday.' And Sugihara said, very calmly, as if he were the same age as Solly: 'Sure, that sounds like a lot of fun.'

It was a big party with around thirty guests. Sugihara brought his wife, Yukiko, who would not soon forget that evening. In her memoirs, she would write that the Japanese don't dare to say no, and that the aunties there had plied her with so much pastry and cake that, back at home, she spent all night kneeling in front of the toilet. She had never thrown up so much or for so long before. Still, like her husband, she had enjoyed the Yiddish songs and the rituals, which were unfamiliar yet reminded her of Japan: the attention to detail and the lighting of the candles.

Sugihara had mostly listened to Solly's father and uncles, and to Mr Rozenblat, who had fled Poland with his little girl and been taken into the Ganor home – to the dismay of Solly, who'd had to give up his bedroom and share a room with his brother ...

Rozenblat talked about the German invasion of Poland. About the ghettos established all over the country in October and November 1939. About the young men in Warsaw seized indiscriminately and executed by firing squads. About the men, women, and children driven together into a synagogue and shot dead – in their own shul, in front of the Aron Hakodesh, the ark with the Torah scrolls.

For the first time, Sugihara heard in detail what had happened to the Polish Jews. He decided that he would return to see the Ganor family again. Mr Rozenblat had given him exact information. Rozenblat had fled Warsaw when a German bomb demolished his home, killing his wife and two of his three children. These things happen in wartime, Rozenblat remarked with surprising stoicism. But what he couldn't accept was that a German officer walked into a shop and, because he didn't like the looks of the Jew behind the counter, murdered him with a shot to the head. That wiped out a thousand years of civilisation.

Solly recalled that not only the consul, but also Mrs Sugihara spoke good German. The two families remained in touch, and even went to the countryside together.

The story of the stamps is accurate, but less peculiar than it seems, since Solly often dropped in on the Sugiharas. Maybe, like little Jan Zwartendijk, he had a secret crush on Mrs Sugihara. He himself claimed that he enjoyed playing with the toddlers, but that would be unusual for an eleven-year-old. Sugihara's two youngest children couldn't even stand up on their own. But I can imagine how much he would have enjoyed Sugihara's stories of Japan, prompted by the images on his stamps. And how surprised he must have been when the consul told him that Solly would soon see Japan for himself. Sugihara impressed the boy with the importance of urging his father to apply for a visa as soon as possible.

The consul had spoken to Ganor and Rozenblat about it: Don't wait too long! Leave now! Ganor's brother and sister, who lived in the United States, had the financial means to act as guarantors for him, his wife, and his four children. Once they had left Kaunas, everything would turn out for the best, Sugihara assured him. But Ganor wasn't so sure.

In Ganor's factory in the Memel Territory, the mood had shifted in the early 1930s; the locals had developed a hatred of the Jews.

He had sold the factory and left for Kaunas, where he had started a new company. By working day and night again, he had got the new business off the ground. But now he found himself unable to sell it; potential buyers offered him nothing, or a pittance, for it. They knew he was a Jew and eager to leave, so they thought he would accept any price, even the lowest.

Sometimes he was tempted to take the offer, but then his wife would protest. She had her parents nearby and didn't really want to leave Kaunas. A month later, the situation was reversed; his wife became nervous, but he thought to himself, *Do I really have to give up everything I own and start over, empty-handed, on the other side of the world?*

Other objections followed: the language, their age. Were they capable of building a new life from the ground up in a new country? But then new refugees from Poland came to visit them, with new horror stories, and Ganor said, 'Enough. We cannot stay here.'

In the second week of July 1940, Sugihara insisted, 'You have to do it now; in a couple of weeks the consulate will close. If I were you, I wouldn't worry so much about your business. Forget the money and think of the lives you'll save – your children, your wife, and yourself.'

Ganor was about to leave when he received an offer for his business. Someone wanted to buy it for 20 per cent of its value. He was ready to sign the contract, except for one thing: the buyer couldn't pay for another six weeks. And Ganor thought, *Oh, well, what difference does six weeks make; in six weeks, nothing too terrible could happen …*

He had his mind set on leaving with his wife, his two sons, and his two daughters, as well as Rozenblat and his little girl. His decision was prompted in part by his meeting with Nathan Gutwirth, a Dutch national who was in touch with the Dutch consul – 'I say consul,' Solly added in a somewhat disparaging tone in 2005, 'but really there wasn't a Dutch consul in Kaunas anymore, just a man known as Mr Radio Philips who had received the stamps from the previous consul.' Gutwirth and Mr Radio Philips had a good plan: issuing visas that named Curaçao as a final destination, with Sugihara then providing a transit visa for Japan … Gutwirth discussed the idea with Rozenblat and Ganor, and the three of them went to see Sugihara. The Japanese consul told them, 'This is a good plan. I can work with this. I needed a final destination; otherwise I can't issue a transit visa. But now I have Curaçao. This is the solution …'

Ganor organised his papers, and told his wife and children to prepare for departure. They left for the station, where a train to Moscow was waiting. On the platform, an NKVD agent and a Russian soldier stopped a refugee with a Polish passport, a Curaçao visa, and a transit visa for Japan. The man and his family were allowed to board. The next man they stopped had a Lithuanian passport. He and his whole family were arrested. Ganor thought, *We have to get out of here. This won't work for us – we have Lithuanian passports.*

A few days earlier, Lithuanian Jews had become Soviet citizens, so, unlike Polish Jews, they had nothing to fear – or so the Russians claimed. Ganor signalled to his wife and children to turn back. But maybe he was also influenced by the thought that he could claim the 20 per cent for his business if he stayed in Kaunas just a couple of weeks longer.

Rozenblat, in contrast, took the consul's advice and left with his daughter. On 3 August, Sugihara brushed the visas into their Polish passports: Dawid and Zofia Rozenblat, numbers 949 and 950 on the Sugihara list. Earlier, the consul had issued visas to two other Rozenblats: Stanislaw and Mara Rozenblat (numbers 71 and 72 on the list). But they were a young couple. If a woman wasn't registered in her husband's passport but had her own, she had to apply for a separate visa.

Rozenblat, instead of Rosenblatt or Rosenblat, is not a misspelling. Sugihara always used the Polish spelling: Rozental, Rozenbaum, Rozenblat.

So Ganor and his family remained in Kaunas. Life under the Russians didn't seem so bad; the early months of 1941 went by without incident. Then his eldest son, who was twenty years old and friends with a few

Russian officers, brought news of plans to deport Ganor and his wife and children to Siberia.

Ganor had spent his childhood in Russia and, like many other young Jewish men, had joined the Bund. He had never made any secret of his admiration for Trotsky, born Lev Davidovich Bronstein to a Jewish family in Ukraine. Trotsky, who had joined the Bolsheviks just before the 1917 revolution, fell out of favour under Stalin, and Bund members such as Ganor were blacklisted.

The family waited all night to be arrested, but the Russians never turned up. In the early morning, Solly noticed German aircraft landing in Kaunas. It was 24 June 1941. Two days earlier, Operation Barbarossa had begun; Nazi Germany had invaded Lithuania, and German forces were advancing towards the Soviet Union.

Mr Ganor shouted, 'To the station!' The six of them made a dash for it, hoping to jump aboard the last train to Moscow. But the station was empty, without a single eastbound train.

A Jewish man was leaving the city on a horse-drawn wagon. For a huge sum, Mr Ganor bought places in the wagon for his wife, his two daughters, and Solly. He and his eldest son followed on foot. For days on end, they were part of a long column of Jewish refugees, Lithuanian communists, and Russian soldiers in retreat with some leftover materiel: a tank and a lorry. The column was under frequent fire from German fighter aircraft. When at last they reached the Russian border, they learned it had been closed by the Wehrmacht. They had to make a U-turn, back to Kaunas.

Along the way, the Jewish refugees were attacked by Lithuanian civilians. Hundreds of men, women, and children were stabbed with pitchforks, or shot with hunting rifles by the roadside. Others were taken to the Ninth Fort near Kaunas, where Lithuanian militias carried out a more systematic genocide. They made their victims stand against the ramparts in rows of twelve for execution. Each new group had to clear away the last twelve bodies, dragging them into a mass grave.

Only a few hundred Jewish refugees, including Solly and his

father and eldest brother, reached Kaunas. When they saw another group of Lithuanians approaching, Mr Ganor went up to a couple of German officers and requested their protection in polished German. 'Of course,' they said, 'naturally.' The officers called the Lithuanians' methods 'filthy', and offered the family a lift to Kaunas.

Mrs Ganor and the two daughters also survived the ordeal. It came as a great relief to them to be sent to Stutthof concentration camp, thirty kilometres from Danzig. In Kaunas, rape had almost become the norm. Women and girls were stripped naked, sent out into the street, and violated by countless men. Later, when these crimes were denied, photos were produced as proof. Until late 1943, Stutthof was not an extermination camp and had no gas chambers. The large-scale murder did not begin there until a year before the end of the war.

Likewise, Mr Ganor and his two sons counted themselves lucky to be granted a place in the Nazi-controlled Kaunas ghetto. There, at least, they were safe from the Lithuanians who were venting their pent-up hatred of the Jews by staining the countryside and the streets of Kaunas with blood.

Ganor became a forced labourer at a factory for anti-tank weapons. Solly was made a galley boy in the ghetto kitchen. That gave him access to adequate food, not only for himself but also for his father. The anti-tank weapons were manufactured in a bunker under five metres of concrete.

One day, Solly's elder brother vanished. He and his father had spent almost three years in the ghetto. Six months before the end of the war, they were transferred to Dachau, where in April 1945 they were liberated by American troops.

But as Mr Ganor would often tell his son, 'We would have suffered ten thousand times less if we had seized the opportunity offered by Sugihara without delay.'

When, after the war, Sugihara was asked the reason for his actions, his answer was always the same:

In the end, I made my decision as a *human being*. I thought it through all night long. What I did might have been wrong as a diplomat. Still, I couldn't abandon those thousands of people depending on me. I did not do anything special – I just did what I had to do.

Those could just as well have been the words of Jan Zwartendijk.

Every time Sugihara brushed the six or seven columns of calligraphy into a travel document – the length varied a little, but there were usually seven short columns – he would hand over the visa, look the applicant straight in the eyes, smile, and wish him happiness. He did that 2,139 times, without forgetting once.

Every two or three hours, his wife would have to massage his cramped right hand and fingers. Even so, there was a limit to how many visas Sugihara could issue per day. The queue kept growing, and sometimes the people who reached the front of it had been waiting for more than forty hours.

The queue consisted almost entirely of Polish Jews. According to the Soviet authorities, Lithuanian Jews were in no danger at all. Even with the visas issued by Zwartendijk and Sugihara, the refugees needed permits from the NKVD to cross the Soviet Union. The NKVD refused to issue such permits to Lithuanian Jews, making it impossible – or at least tremendously difficult – for them to flee.

The former Japanese consulate in Kaunas, now the Sugihara Museum, has a photo of Louis Finkelstein on display. He received one of the first visas from consul Sugihara: visa number 7. Finkelstein was a Jewish businessman from the port of Klaipėda – in Lithuania. He and his wife and three-year-old daughter reached Yokohama in December 1940, and eventually found their way to San Francisco.

The list of Curaçao visas included 109 Lithuanian Jews. That's not many compared to the 1,943 Polish Jews on the list. But it was not completely impossible for Lithuanian Jews to leave the country; especially not if they were well off, like Louis Finkelstein, and could pay for the journey themselves.

It is unclear if the Jews with Polish travel documents all really came

Jewish refugees in front of the Japanese consulate in Kaunas.

from Poland. In any case, Vilnius was part of Poland from 1920 to 1940, so any Jew from the Vilnius ghetto had a Polish *leidimas*. The list of Curaçao visas does not state the places of birth. I am certain the list of 'Polish' Jews includes dozens of Lithuanian Jews who had spent much of their life in Vilnius.

The list also includes 51 Jews from Germany, three from Canada, one from the United States, ten from Great Britain, fourteen from Czechoslovakia, three from Luxembourg, three from the Netherlands, and two with dual nationality: Lithuania and the USSR. They were all allowed to leave. But most Jews born and bred in Kaunas itself were headed for a gruesome fate.

15

The yard of the Lietūkis garage

The Ninth Fort is just outside Kaunas. From July 1941 to the end of the war, it was a concentration camp. No one stayed there longer than a few days before being executed in the long trench behind the walls of the fort. The bullet holes are still visible, so many that they must have been made by machine guns. To the west of the fort is the mass grave, a slight bulge stretching for kilometres.

This is where the Lithuanian Jews who were not saved by consul Zwartendijk and consul Sugihara ended up. Most of the thirty thousand Jews in Kaunas ended their lives here, if they weren't slaughtered by the locals first.

Before German troops reached the city, members of the Lithuanian Activist Front (LAF) – a fascist and highly anti-Semitic paramilitary organisation – went on a killing rampage in Vilijampolė, Kaunas's Jewish quarter. During the night of 25 to 26 June 1941, they killed 1,500 Jews, and during the night of 26 to 27 June, 2,300.

These events are summarised in a museum near the fort. Fifteen hundred. Twenty-three hundred. I tend to skim over figures like that, loath to face their full horror. An armed gang that murdered 1,500 people one night and 2,300 the next. It remains inconceivable.

In the yard of the Lietūkis garage, crime took on its most revolting form, becoming a spectacle. Around one hundred Jewish men were driven together there, near a garage and filling station on Vytautas

The 'Death Dealer' of the Lietūkis garage.

Boulevard in the city centre. One photograph, now notorious, shows a blond Lithuanian around twenty-five years old, with a contented smile on his face, standing among the bodies with an iron rod in his hand. Egged on by a crowd, he went from one Jew to the next, smashing in their skulls. When he killed his victim with a single blow, the crowd would cheer; when it took more than one, they booed him. Children were lifted onto their fathers' shoulders for a better view of the bloodbath. That young man killed eighty-six Jews without assistance. The German colonel Lothar von Bischoffshausen, who arrived in Kaunas in the late afternoon of 27 June 1941, declared after the war that it was the most horrifying event he had witnessed in the course of *two* world wars.

The massacre at the Lietūkis garage.

The Jews from Kaunas who escaped this bloodbath died in the Ninth Fort, mown down by Einsatzkommando 3, a death squad commanded by Standartenführer Karl Jäger. In Lithuania as a whole, the Nazi death squads carried out 137,346 executions. In 1944, they declared the country 'Jew free'.

Twenty-seven thousand of their victims were tossed into the mass grave around the fort. Also lying just under the grass of that kilometres-long field are some three thousand Jews transferred to the fort from Berlin, Munich, Vienna, and the French camp of Drancy.

I walk over the burial ground with Edith on my arm. Rob, overwhelmed by all the information about the genocide, is sitting on a bench, shaking his head, under the only tree in this windy field.

The men who marched into the Jewish quarter carrying iron rods were the fathers of Edith's classmates.

I have spent six days touring Edith's past with her; this is day seven. I no longer dare to ask her any questions, afraid that something inside her will snap. I can see on her face that this chapter of Lithuanian history still baffles and frightens her.

A cold wind blows across the field. On one side of the mass grave is the dim outline of Kaunas in the distance; on the other, a recent luxury development. A few crows take to the air.

'It has to hit very close to home,' Edith says softly, though I haven't asked her anything. 'Father heard all sorts of rumours. He saw hatred flaring up. It hit close to home. That's when he made decisions.'

She sniffs.

'He was a down-to-earth man. He had no interest in playing the hero. He was as scared as everyone else was in those days. But the hate and the violence hit close to home. Then he stopped looking the other way, stopped searching for excuses, and made the decisions he had to make. Like Sugihara.'

'Exceptional.'

'I'm sure that word never entered his mind.'

'Did he ever reveal anything to you, his children, about his motivations?'

'One evening, when he was very tired and strained, he told me and Jan, "I have to help those people. Otherwise they face certain death."'

'How could he be so sure?'

'My father did what his conscience told him he had to. He believed you should be true to your chosen values. If you messed with those, that was the last straw.'

'The last straw?'

'Then you were no longer a decent human being. And here you see the consequences of that. This place is intolerable. This place never should have existed.'

I think back to a conversation I had a few weeks earlier with an elderly Belgian woman.

Arlette Pollet lived in Kaunas from July 1925, when she was two years old, to July 1944. Her father was an engineer at the Belgian company that built and ran the electrical plant in Kaunas. Like Edith Zwartendijk, she went to the German secondary school, but Arlette was four years older, and the two women don't remember each other. The other difference was that Arlette remained in Kaunas until almost the end of the war.

'One summer day in 1941, our maid Stepa came in, pale as a sheet,' she told me in her home on Rooseveltlaan in Amsterdam. 'Her legs were shaking. Stepa had caught a glimpse of something ghastly. "Next to a garage ..." she whimpered, "dozens of people ... killed with ..." My mother cut in. "Stop. I don't want to hear this. And certainly not in front of the children." That was the general feeling back then. Don't talk about it; don't listen ...'

But Arlette was eighteen years old, not really a child anymore. I asked her if she had seen it coming – that unbridled anti-Jewish hatred. 'One sweltering summer day in 1937, I saw my classmate Hannir Sandmeyer sitting inside. I went to the window and asked why she wasn't playing outside with the other girls in our class. She said, "It's better for me and better for you this way."'

The girl had made a sensible choice: silent exclusion instead of open hatred. Sensible, but tragic.

'A year later, a boy I was sweet on, Leo Assiran, pedalled away from me on his bicycle at top speed. I rode after him and could just barely catch up. When I asked why he'd done it, he looked at me in surprise and said, "Don't you know why?" That was all ...'

I shut my eyes for a moment, and can picture the scene.

'A few months later, I was ill. Nothing serious – a bad case of flu with bronchitis. Ingrid, a girl from the Reich, came to visit me. I showed her photos. She asked me, "*Warum hast du so viel jüdische Freunde?*" ["Why do you have so many Jewish friends?"] When I returned to school, all the Jewish children were gone.'

'They went to —'

'— Lithuanian schools, or stayed at home. There was a militant, violent group that felt intense hatred. Most other Lithuanians were like my mother. They didn't want to hear about it.'

16

Comrade Nina

Solly Ganor saw Nathan Gutwirth visit the Japanese consul and explain to him that the Dutch consul could write visas for Curaçao as a final destination. Sugihara was overjoyed – this was the missing piece. But before he started issuing transit visas, he phoned the Russian consul. Solly had seen the Russian in question in Sugihara's house before, in January or February 1940: blond-haired and red-faced, not young but definitely not old. This was the man Sugihara called. After about ten minutes, he put the receiver down, nodded, and said, 'It's OK.' The Russian consul obviously had a good deal of influence. Without his go-ahead, Solly told me, it would never have been possible to organise the rescue operation.

I don't know if every detail of what Solly told me, half a century later, is reliable. But the record shows that the Soviet authorities let Zwartendijk and Sugihara go on for weeks. Sugihara had apparently managed to strike a deal with the Russians.

It remains unclear what he thought of his own government, which had friendly relations with both Hitler and Mussolini.

In early August, Rabbi Eliezer Portnoy took a seat opposite Sugihara at his desk. Still a young man, thirty-three years of age, he would receive visa no. 1,099. When the consul finished his calligraphy, he walked the rabbi to the door, shook his hand, and said, 'The world says that America is civilised.' He paused. Then: 'I will show the world that Japan is more civilised.'

Rabbi Portnoy didn't know what to think. Was he serious? Even the consul's smile left room for doubt. Either he was a man with a mission, or he saw himself as a *mashiah*, an anointed one, a messiah.

The refugees needed permits from the NKVD to travel through the Soviet Union. The procedure for obtaining them was nerve-wracking. The NKVD tried to recruit agents and informers among the refugees. But those who declined were not shown the door right away. Instead, the recruitment of agents seemed to be just one tactic in a broader programme of intimidation.

Some applicants had only a five-minute interview at the NKVD offices; others were held there all day. Students from the Talmudic academies found it especially hard to believe that the secret police would issue hundreds of permits unless it was part of some diabolical plan. Many put off applying for their exit visas for a long time, not daring to enter the headquarters of the security service until they had heard that the first group of students had reached Vladivostok without any trouble.

Many applicants had to spend whole days and nights waiting before they were interviewed. In the crowded corridors of the NKVD building, everyone was required to stand. Anyone who had the gall to sit on the floor – or, still worse, to lie down – was sent outside and had to go to the back of the queue. Before an applicant's interview with the NKVD agent began, he had to fill in a questionnaire and write a personal statement explaining why he wanted to leave the Soviet Union.

Joseph Mlotek was a devoted Bund member and had worked for the Yiddish daily *Folksstaytung*, which staunchly supported the Bund. Fearing immediate arrest if he told the truth, he wrote that he was a textile manufacturer whose company had been torched. Even more than the capitalists, the Soviets despised the social democrats and Bund members, whom they saw as traitorous Trotskyites. Maybe the NKVD in Kaunas lacked the budget for background checks; in any case, Mlotek was granted his exit visa, and a few weeks later reached Vladivostok safe and sound.

Rabbi David Lifszyc wrote frankly in his personal statement, 'I am not qualified for any other job, because I have dedicated my whole life to rabbinical education and the performance of rabbinical duties. That is why I am unable to settle here.' He, his wife, and their five-year-old daughter received an exit visa, and were able to travel by way of Japan to San Francisco.

The exit visas were not issued right away. Instead, the applicants had to check the daily lists posted on a large noticeboard in the main hall of the NKVD office in Kaunas or Vilnius – in much the same way students in those days checked the results of their final exams. It sometimes took three weeks before an applicant's name was posted on the board. There was no point in protesting or pleading, especially not in Kaunas. The office was run by Nina, who had a face of stone and a voice that issued from an internal megaphone. Her decisions were dictated purely by personal whim, but it was said she never changed her mind. Even her subordinates trembled when they spoke of her.

After three weeks, Wilek Frankel found his name on the list. His wife was listed there, too, but not her younger brother, Bercik. 'Tovarishch [Comrade] Nina,' he begged, 'surely we can't abandon a twelve-year-old boy? How can we leave without him? Won't you please do your best to arrange a permit for him?' He flashed his sweetest smile; Wilek was a real charmer. But Nina didn't bat an eyelid. Wilek returned to Vilnius. The next day, he heard from an acquaintance that Bercik was on the NKVD list in Kaunas. Two days later, Wilek was back in Kaunas. No sooner did he enter the office of the secret police than he heard, from the far end of the corridor, the booming voice of Comrade Nina. 'Where were you? You beg for an exit visa, it's been waiting here for you for days, and you can't even be bothered to pick it up.' He said he'd been ill and unable to pick it up, but that he was eternally grateful. 'Well, I hope you're feeling better now,' she snarled, throwing the visa down in front of him.

Intourist poster, 1940.

Soon after, Wilek learned that Bercik had accidentally been put on the NKVD list in Vilnius, too. He picked up the second exit visa, had it altered by an experienced forger, and gave it to a friend from Poland. Bercik's second visa saved Asher Wiener's life.

I tracked down Asher Wiener's family by placing a classified ad in a Jewish weekly in Australia. His daughter Deborah, a barrister in Melbourne, responded. Her father had travelled from Vladivostok to Kobe, and from Kobe to New Zealand.

The only plausible explanation for this story is that the NKVD officials in Kaunas and Vilnius had instructions from their higher-ups to make the exodus as fast and efficient as possible.

The journey was organised by Intourist, the travel agency established by Stalin in 1929, which had always worked hand in hand with the NKVD. Tickets cost $400 per refugee, five times the usual price. This sum had to be paid in American dollars, a striking departure from official Soviet ideology. In the Soviet Union, possessing even one dollar was a crime punishable by ten years in the gulag. But the Russians decided to turn a blind eye when it came to a one-way trip to Vladivostok.

It was almost impossible for the Polish refugees to get their hands on American currency. In many cases, Vaad Hatzalah supplied the dollars. This Orthodox lobbying group based in the United States was allowed to offer assistance and send currency because President Roosevelt had broken his promise, made just before the outbreak of the Second World War, to issue five thousand visas to Jewish refugees. Even more often, the American Jewish Joint Distribution Committee bankrolled families that could not afford all their tickets. The JDC was a non-governmental aid organisation with its European head office in Lisbon.

Moses Beckelman was its representative in Kaunas. After the war, he said he had worked in close coordination with Jan Zwartendijk. The Dutch consul put refugees in touch with Beckelman. As Zwartendijk put his signature under the consular stamp of the Netherlands, he would say, 'For an exit visa, you need to go to the NKVD. For a train ticket, Intourist. And for dollars, the Joint Distribution Committee across the street.' Beckelman worked out of the Metropolis Hotel. Zwartendijk never mentioned that he had done this, not even to his wife and children.

Moses Beckelman was also in touch with Chiune Sugihara, and

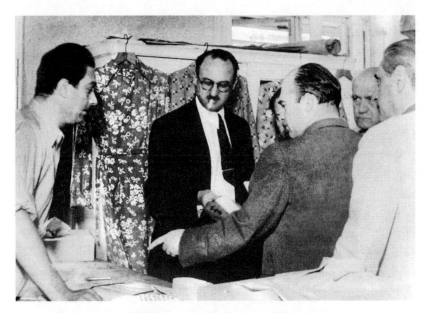

Moses Beckelman of the American Jewish Joint Distribution Committee
handing out clothes in Lithuania.

informed the US ambassador in Moscow of the stream of refugees who
were on their way, not all at once but in large numbers. Ambassador
Laurence A. Steinhardt, in turn, warned Washington that the Dutch
consul in Kaunas had issued 'nonsensical visas', and that at least two
thousand refugees were en route to Japan. Steinhardt feared they
would go to the Moscow embassy to apply for visas for the United
States. This fear proved groundless; most refugees were in a hurry to
leave the Soviet Union. Not until they reached Japan did they look
into their options for travelling onwards.

Moses Beckelman remained in Lithuania until February 1941. He
could have been a key source of behind-the-scenes information on
the rescue operation but, unfortunately, he had no time to write his
memoirs. He died of heart failure in New York in 1955, at the age of
forty-nine.

Beckelman soon realised the Soviets were willing to do business,
as long as there were dollars on the table. Considering the exorbitant

ticket price, a hunger for foreign currency seems to be the most plausible explanation of the Russians' cooperative attitude. In the rush to equip its army with modern weaponry, the USSR was in urgent need of dollars for placing orders with foreign arms-dealers.

Perhaps strangest of all, the journey to Vladivostok was comfortable. 'Because the Russians wanted dollars, we were treated like ordinary tourists, not like refugees,' Jan Krukowski remembers.

First, the train went from Kaunas to Moscow, where an Intourist guide picked up the groups of foreigners and took them to the Novomoskovskaya, one of the capital's finest hotels, normally reserved for Russian officers and diplomats. The Mir Yeshiva students could not believe their eyes when they were served freshly squeezed orange juice at breakfast in February. The next day, they were taken sightseeing. To the Frankel family, who had trekked from Kraków to the Lithuanian border while under constant fire from German fighters, the whole experience seemed so absurd that they suspected a Russian trick. The bus was sure to take the Polish Jews straight to a camp or a ghetto – or so they thought. But instead, they found themselves visiting Red Square, Lenin's Mausoleum, the Volga, the Bolshoi Theatre ...

'After everything we'd been through in Poland, we were suddenly on holiday. And all for free,' Wilek Frankel said with a chuckle.

On board the Trans-Siberian Express, the menu included Russian champagne and caviar. Few of them could afford it, but the very fact that it was available seemed festive to the travellers.

The journey took twice as long as usual because of westward troop movements. Before the war, the Kaunas-Moscow-Vladivostok itinerary took twelve days; in the autumn and winter of 1940, the travellers were en route for at least sixteen days, and in the spring of 1941, it took almost three weeks. Long stretches of the 9,287-kilometre Trans-Siberian Railway were single track; the passenger trains sometimes had to wait half a day, or all night, while goods trains passed in the opposite direction.

Some Japanese accounts of these events, including a feature film, describe refugees on the train to Vladivostok being robbed of their money and jewellery. Professional researchers working for the Sugihara Foundation have never heard this type of story from survivors. Nor have I; in all the first-hand testimonies I've tracked down, I've never seen a single account of a robbery. Refugees' children can't remember their parents ever having talked about any such incidents.

The oppressive thing was the uncertainty. There were rumours that the train was crawling with secret agents, and that foreigners and suspect individuals were being pulled off the train at the intermediate stops. And they were all scared that in Vladivostok they might be sent back, that the whole plan would prove to be based on a misunderstanding. Beyond this point, the future looked even more perilous. As Polish and Yiddish speakers, how would they get by in Japan?

17

The fiat: the party leader and
the influential dwarf

The Soviets permitted thousands of Jewish refugees to take the Trans-Siberian Express – or at least turned a blind eye to their passage. The lingering question is why. The pivotal Soviet official was Vladimir Dekanozov, the people's commissar for Lithuania and the former NKVD head of foreign intelligence. In talks with the Russian army and the party leadership, he is said to have described the Jewish refugees as 'future agents of the USSR'. The Lithuanian historian Linas Venclauskas learned of this statement, but was unable to determine exactly where and when it was made. Almost all information about Dekanozov is in files that cannot be viewed or have been destroyed. Like his boss, the Soviet internal affairs minister Lavrentiy Beria, he fell out of favour during the struggle over Stalin's succession.

'Future agents of the USSR' ... the words keep running through my head. Was Dekanozov referring to the Jewish Autonomous Republic established at Stalin's insistence in 1928? In the late 1920s, the party leader was mulling over a plan to send all Soviet Jews to the barren region around Birobidzhan. Most of them lived in Belarus and Ukraine, but Birobidzhan was on the Trans-Siberian Railway, eight thousand kilometres east of Moscow and nine hundred kilometres north of Vladivostok, so it would have been easy to transport them there.

In the Jewish Autonomous Republic, Yiddish would be the everyday language, and a proletarian Jewish culture would blossom.

Instead of religion, the main form of cultural expression would be literature and art; without question, the Soviet Republic would remain atheistic. It was envisaged as a kind of Israel within the Soviet Union, but without religious implications or myths like the Promised Land. Yiddish would be permitted there, as long as the Cyrillic alphabet was used rather than Hebrew script (to make life easier for the censors).

Voluntary relocation began in 1928, when three hundred Jewish families decided to take the risk of moving to the region. By 1938, the number of settlers was still only five thousand, a negligible fraction of the three million Soviet Jews. By steering Polish Jews towards Birobidzhan, the Soviets could breathe new life into their Jewish republic.

A few dozen refugees with Curaçao visas, who waited too long to leave Lithuania, ended up in Siberian camps in late 1942, where they survived the war – but not in the Jewish Autonomous Republic. Most of the refugees saw Birobidzhan only in passing, through the windows of the Trans-Siberian Express.

In the personal archive of Jan Zwartendijk junior, which he handed over to his brother, Rob, shortly before he died, I found a report of a conversation he had in 1996 with Victor Israelyan, a former senior official at the Soviet foreign ministry, who had spent five decades in the Kremlin's corridors of power and concluded his diplomatic career as the USSR's ambassador to the United Nations. After the fall of the Wall and the collapse of the Soviet Union, he had remained in Pennsylvania to write his memoirs in peace. Victor Israelyan knew every member of the Russian nomenklatura, and had witnessed Dekanozov's rise and fall.

Vladimir Dekanozov became one of Moscow's most feared individuals in 1938, when Lavrentiy Beria made him the NKVD security service's head of foreign intelligence. The new department head had no international experience whatsoever and had never set foot outside the Soviet Union, but that didn't seem to matter to Beria. Over the next two years, Dekanozov proved that he was equal to the job.

On 14 June 1940, Stalin appointed him people's commissar for Lithuania. The day the Red Army tanks rolled into the country, Dekanozov flew to Kaunas on a bomber. As soon as he arrived, on the evening of 15 June, he took measures to dispel any doubt about who would be in charge from then on in Lithuania. The next day, Edith and the young Jan Zwartendijk saw the outcome: the portraits of Lenin and Stalin in every display window.

Still, Dekanozov was on his guard. He lied to Lithuanian farmers, telling them he would not collectivise agriculture. He even waited a while before nationalising foreign companies or abolishing free trade and the middle class. He ordered the arrest of the nationalists he considered most dangerous, and had a number of them hanged as a warning to everyone else. About two thousand Lithuanians were detained in this action – a small number compared to the twenty thousand intellectuals deported to Siberia a year later. Aside from a few arrests, he left the Jewish Lithuanians alone. His main responsibility was to keep the population quiet while he forced the country into the Soviet Union.

Dekanozov left Lithuania in early August. In just six weeks, he had more or less completed the process of Sovietisation. He had installed a government that consisted wholly of Lithuanian communists (who were few and far between), organised elections in which only communists could run for office, and then asked the newly elected parliament to chart a course for the country's future. Their unanimous vote was for integration into the USSR. He told farmers and shopkeepers what they wanted to hear, knowing his successor would make short work of them. He did nothing to stop the exodus of Polish Jews, and permitted them to travel straight across the USSR to Vladivostok. He kept a close eye on consul Zwartendijk and consul Sugihara, but did not intervene; the Dutch and Japanese consulates were the last to remain open. They were not closed until after the commissar's departure in August. Dekanozov's strategic priority was to keep the peace, or in any case to discourage public protest. A rebellion would give Germany a pretext for intervening.

He did nothing without the consent of the foreign minister, Vyacheslav Molotov. When in doubt, he consulted with Beria, his former boss at the NKVD and the second-most-powerful man in the Soviet hierarchy. Molotov and Beria, in turn, did nothing without Stalin's consent. All four of them knew about the refugees, and none of them saw any reason to staunch the flow or redirect it to the gulag.

When Victor Israelyan spoke to Jan Zwartendijk junior, he said Stalin believed, in 1939, that the Soviet Union did not stand a chance in a clash with Nazi Germany. The prospect of German aggression quite simply frightened him. By signing a treaty with Nazi Germany, he could buy time to prepare the Soviet Union for war. Israelyan described the pact between Hitler and Stalin as 'two scorpions in a bottle'. It allowed the Baltic countries to remain within the Soviet sphere of influence, but prohibited their annexation into the USSR. Stalin wanted to avoid provoking Hitler in the Baltic region, no matter what the cost. By this time, the Führer was already falling into a pattern of finding pretexts for military operations; that was what he had done in the Sudetenland, the Memel Territory, and Poland, and Lithuania faced the same threat.

Stalin wanted to use the Baltic countries to shield the vulnerable city of Leningrad. Finland served the same purpose. But for the time being, he controlled all those countries without occupying them – because he feared Hitler's wrath. Not until June 1940, as Germany stormed into France and prepared to invade Britain, did he see an opportunity to occupy the Baltic states. Stalin predicted that Hitler would have his hands full on the western front – and he was right. But he also knew that Hitler would strike back once he had western Europe under control.

Stalin's ploy won him almost two years – until 22 June 1941, when the Germans launched Operation Barbarossa. Meanwhile, Stalin tried to bring the Red Army up to full strength and arm it with the heaviest weapons available. To keep Hitler guessing, Stalin purged his ministries of senior Jewish officials (he called this 'sweeping the synagogues clean'), and invited Dekanozov to stand beside him at the

Red Square parade on 1 May 1941. This act had a powerful symbolic meaning, because soon after Dekanozov had left Lithuania, Stalin had appointed him ambassador to Berlin.

Stalin, Beria, and Dekanozov were part of the Communist Party's Georgian group. They knew each other so well that they were even scared of each other's shadows. Stalin and Beria rivalled each other in cruelty, and no woman was safe around Beria. Even Stalin, without a doubt the most powerful man in the Soviet Union, urged his daughter, Svetlana, to stay as far from Beria as possible. The toll of girls and women abused by the head of the state security service reached the hundreds.

Beria was nineteen years younger than Stalin. In 1921, he joined the Georgian secret police, and within two years he had remade the organisation to suit his purposes. He worked all night, and slept for a few hours at most in the morning. He spent most of his time plotting coups and carrying out political purges. He conducted many interrogations himself, and bragged that he could make anyone confess to being the king of England in less than an hour. In the 1930s, he rose to become party secretary in Georgia. In 1938, Stalin brought him to Moscow.

As a people's commissar and the head of the NKVD, Beria ordered the execution of the theatre and film director Vsevolod Meyerhold, the writer Isaac Babel, and the star reporter Mikhail Koltsov, who had covered the Spanish Civil War in lyrical reports in *Pravda*. All three were of Jewish descent, and all three were accused of Trotskyist sympathies. Beria was also primarily responsible for the Katyń massacre in the spring of 1940, in which 25,700 Polish intellectuals, clergymen, and officers were murdered. Stalin told Von Ribbentrop that Beria was 'our Himmler', the boss of the Russian Gestapo – a striking comparison.

From 1938 to 1940, Beria's right-hand man was Vladimir Dekanozov, who had come with him from Georgia. They spoke Georgian to each other, as did Beria and Stalin, to the irritation of the

Joseph Stalin's daughter, Svetlana, on Lavrentiy Beria's lap. In the background,
Stalin is reading the newspaper.

people around them. Even Dekanozov's appointments as Lithuanian
people's commissar and, a few months later, as Soviet ambassador
to Berlin, were partly Beria's doing. The Georgian was determined
to have an underling in those positions, so that he could form an
independent opinion from Stalin's on developments to the west of
Russia.

Stalin, for his part, trusted Dekanozov as much as he dared to trust
anyone, valued his intelligence, and was impressed by how quickly
he had purged the diplomatic corps of 'kulaks'. But he also called
him 'the Slow Kartvelian', after his birth region, and taunted him for
his ugliness. When Stalin spotted Dekanozov entering the room, he
would grin and say, 'What a handsome man! Look, I've never seen
such a handsome fellow!'

Dekanozov was a dwarf, less than 150 centimetres in height. In
Berlin, no one thought much of him. Hitler regarded Dekanozov
as the model of the Caucasian *Untermensch*, and humiliated him by

always assigning two exceptionally tall SS officers as his escorts at official meetings. At the second meeting between Molotov and Von Ribbentrop, on 10 November 1940, and just before the meeting between Molotov and Hitler, Dekanozov was shown to a tall gilt Bismarck chair in which his feet did not reach the ground.

Despite Dekanozov's bitter hatred of the Nazis, he dismissed the German threat, in his telegrams to Moscow, as mere bluster. Even when a German typographer who secretly belonged to the German Communist Party had one of the nine printed copies of the battle plans for Operation Barbarossa delivered to the Soviet embassy, Dekanozov did not sound the alarm. He informed Molotov, who passed on the news to Stalin, but Stalin cautioned him not to get bogged down in panicky messages and Western propaganda. In the knowledge that his army was still not at full strength – for the simple reason that he had purged one division after the next, and had had thousands of officers murdered on suspicion of high treason – Stalin buried his head in the sand. But when the German attack came, and three-and-a-half million soldiers, three thousand tanks, and twenty-eight hundred aircraft invaded the Soviet Union, he did not blame the messenger. Dekanozov was recalled to Moscow, but when he arrived, he was granted a position as Molotov's number two, and was not demoted or liquidated.

In 1943, Stalin called on his services for another diplomatic mission. In Sweden, Dekanozov held secret negotiations with the Germans on a separate peace treaty – an idea Stalin had never entirely put out of his mind, which he saw as a means of putting pressure on the Allies. But the talks were unsuccessful, and Dekanozov advised Stalin instead to seek victory on the battlefield.

Stalin pictured the division of Europe, in his own words, as 'a poker game' with three players, in which each player hoped to persuade the other two to destroy each other so that the third could run off with the spoils. That was an accurate description of the situation from 1939 to 1941. The three players were the German and Austrian Nazis; the British and French capitalists; and the Bolsheviks. For Stalin, part of this

Soviet ambassador Vladimir Dekanozov arrives in Berlin,
November 1940.

Hitler receives the Soviet ambassador Dekanozov in Berlin, 19 December 1940.
Dekanozov is the second man from the left.

poker game was winning over Hitler. He believed he could do business with the 'Austrian corporal'. Until Operation Barbarossa, he saw Great Britain, and not Nazi Germany, as his most dangerous enemy.

After the war, Dekanozov became embroiled in a sex scandal. Like Beria, he exploited his power and influence to indulge in violent sex, and preferred underage girls. That was Stalin's opportunity to get rid of him, but instead he merely demoted Dekanozov to vice-president of the radio propaganda ministry.

Less than a week after Stalin's death, Beria used Dekanozov in his struggle to succeed the Soviet leader. In March 1953, he appointed Dekanozov as internal affairs minister in Georgia, with the intention of bringing him to Moscow as soon as he was calling the shots in the Kremlin. By that stage, Beria was the Soviet defence minister and first deputy premier. He believed that power was within his grasp, but he had made too many enemies in the party. On 26 June 1953, after a tumultuous meeting of the Soviet Presidium, Beria was arrested; on 23 December of that year, he was condemned to death. That same day, he was executed, along with Dekanozov and six other cronies. Each received a bullet in the head.

In the 1950s, Dekanozov's name was clipped out of the foreign ministry's files and erased. Photographs of him were destroyed, and he vanished, aside from a few brief mentions in Russian history books.

By the start of the Second World War, the Soviet Union was desperate for foreign currency. Beria, prompted by Stalin, established the Jewish Anti-Fascist Committee in April 1942. It consisted of seventy prominent Jews from Russian political, economic, scholarly, cultural, and military circles. The committee was chaired by Solomon Mikhoels, a famous actor and the director of the Yiddish State Theatre in Moscow. Its task was to compile a black book of crimes against Jews committed by Nazis within the Soviet sphere of influence – in Lithuania, Latvia, Belarus, Poland, Ukraine, and large German-occupied areas of the Soviet Union. But the committee's main objective was to raise money from around the world to support the Soviet war effort in the struggle against fascism.

In 1943, Stalin sent Mikhoels and the vice-chairman, the poet Itzik Fefer, on a tour of the United States, Canada, Mexico, and Great Britain. In seven months, they raised US$45 million. Most of the money would be spent on medicine, ambulances, and mobile operating rooms for the Red Army; a smaller portion would be used to buy weapons. In the United States, Mikhoels and Fefer were welcomed by Albert Einstein, Charlie Chaplin, Marc Chagall, and Lion Feuchtwanger. They collected not only money, but also penicillin and morphine.

But the Jewish Anti-Fascist Committee came to a bad end. It continued its work after the war but, from 1948 onwards, was the target of a smear campaign ordered by Stalin and Beria. Solomon Mikhoels died in Minsk, in a murder staged as a car accident. After winning the war against Nazi Germany, the Soviet leaders no longer needed the Jewish intellectuals. A series of trials followed; a military tribunal charged committee members with treason and subversive activities. During the night of 12 to 13 August 1952, which would become known as the Night of the Murdered Poets, thirteen members of the committee were murdered, including the poets Leib Kvitko, Peretz Markish, and David Hofstein. Only a few members – such as Moscow's chief rabbi and the writers Ilya Ehrenburg and Vasily Grossman, who had edited the black book – were allowed to live.

Stalin had always distrusted Jews because they had no homeland. In his eyes, that made them 'mysterious, elusive, and otherworldly'. But most of the women around him and his most devoted officials were Jewish.

In the early 1940s, he decided that his regime should stand up against anti-Semitism. He made notes for a speech in which he described anti-Jewish hatred as 'cannibalism' and 'a crime'. He would never stoop to such a thing, he wrote with pride. And he boasted about Birobidzhan, the Jewish homeland he had established near the Chinese border: 'The tsars wouldn't give the Jews any land, but we have.'

The Communist Party had always had many Jewish, Georgian, Latvian, and Polish members, because those minorities had been persecuted in the tsarist period. In 1937, 5.7 per cent of party members were Jewish, and they formed a majority in the government. Lenin, who had a Jewish grandfather, was worried in the early days after the October Revolution that some groups would become too influential, so he made it an informal rule that if a people's commissar was Jewish, his deputy should be Russian. Stalin maintained this policy, not becoming wholeheartedly anti-Semitic until after the foundation of the state of Israel in 1948.

In the summer of 1940, Dekanozov must have come up with a plan for acquiring foreign currency quickly and cheaply. Consul Zwartendijk and consul Sugihara wrote 2,139 visas. A visa was usually issued to the head of the household, and covered at least three people. And it didn't cost much. I puzzled over the numeral '2' that followed every name on Sugihara's list, until I read in a survivor testimony that one visa had cost two *litai*, then equal in value to $2. The exit visas were not much more profitable; the NKVD charged eight *litai* for each. But the Soviet Union could earn a great deal from the trip on the Trans-Siberian Express: as we have seen, up to $400 for a single journey to Vladivostok.

'In those days $400 was a fortune,' wrote one of the refugees, Chaim Shapiro, in his memoirs. 'We were desperate. How to succeed? The balance of our requirements was supplied by the Joint Distribution Committee'.

If an average of three refugees travelled on each visa, the Soviet Union made $2.6 million. In her memoir, *Visa for Life*, Sugihara's widow arrives at a much larger number of refugees: ten thousand. According to her, the refugees, after reaching Japan, often sent their visas back to Lithuania so that their relatives could travel on the same documents. This certainly happened in many cases, especially if the visa-holder had a common name such as Finkelstein, Friedman, or Goldberg. Seventeen visas were issued with the surname Kaplan.

Near the end of his life, Jan Zwartendijk junior complained about this 'flagrant exaggeration'. 'Sending ridiculous figures out into the world makes the whole story seem unreliable and doesn't do justice to Pa's legacy,' he wrote to his brother, Rob. 'He wrote 2,139 visas. That's plenty, isn't it?'

The refugees were accommodated in Kobe and Yokohama. The Japanese journalist Akira Kitade traced 3,080 of them, using information from the archives of various Japanese shipping companies.

But if Mrs Sugihara's figure is correct, and around ten thousand men, women, and children took the Trans-Siberian Express, the Soviet Union must have earned some $4 million – money they could use at once in the war against fascism.

In 2002, the director of the Russian Research and Educational Holocaust Center in Moscow, the historian Ilya Altman, decided to go through all the archives one more time with a fine-toothed comb, in search of documents about the Jewish refugees. In the autumn of 2017, he published a brief report. The NKVD and police archives allowed Professor Altman to settle two questions once and for all.

In a letter dated 21 April 1940, Vladimir Dekanozov informed Molotov, the foreign minister, that the USSR 'can definitely obtain 1.5 million US dollars from Jewish refugees and international Jewish organisations' in exchange for safe passage. Dekanozov's first idea involved a train journey to Odessa, a boat trip to Turkey, and an overland route to Palestine. A few months later, he had a new plan: the journey on the Trans-Siberian Express to Vladivostok.

Altman found an even more important document in the archives of the leading organs of the Communist Party. On 29 July 1940, as consuls Zwartendijk and Sugihara were furiously writing visas, the Politburo gave 'Jewish refugees from Poland now staying in Lithuania the right of transit via the USSR'. This decision was signed by Stalin himself; copies were sent to Molotov and Beria.

In other words, Stalin gave his personal consent to the orchestrated journey, and informed Molotov and Beria of this in no uncertain terms. This decision made it possible for Dekanozov to collect the foreign currency he was after.

Professor Altman also went through the Intourist archives. In the annual report for 1940, he found the names of 1,472 Jewish refugees who took the Trans-Siberian Express. In the months of January and February 1941, another 1,500 followed. That makes 2,972 in total. Children under the age of two could travel free of charge; there were eighty-five of them in 1941. So a total of 3,057 refugees reached Vladivostok in that time.

But most of the refugees took the train to Vladivostok and the boat to Japan in March and April 1941. The Intourist archives contain no information about those two months, so the actual figure may be considerably higher than the archives suggest.

18

Pan Tadeusz

Marcel Wejland's father was one of the last refugees to obtain a visa. Or so he thought when he saw the doors of the Dutch consulate shut behind him. 'We've been incredibly lucky,' he said back at home in Vilnius, waving his passport.

Thirteen-year-old Marcel understood how important that stamp was to his parents, his sisters, and himself, but he resented every step he took outside Poland. He didn't see why everything had to change. If Poland had only stayed the way it was, he could have spent the next summer again in a wooden hut at the foot of Wiśniowa Góra, 'Cherry Mountain'. After the holidays, he could have returned to Łódź, where he'd grown up and where he went to school. In the autumn and winter, there was no cosier place than his family's apartment, with cornices and mouldings on the ceiling, oak parquet floors, a bay window in front, outward-opening doors, and a balcony with small, graceful columns. That such details stuck in his mind is no coincidence; Marcel would become an architect and design luxurious urban homes, but on the other side of the globe, in and around Sydney.

He loved Łódź, even though the brown coal used for heating did blanket the city in a yellow-brown haze all winter. He looked forward to school every day, was already in his second year of classical grammar school, and had friends named Janusz and Janek. They were Catholic, but that didn't matter to him, just as it didn't matter that

Marcel Wejland and his mother Estera, Łódź, 1936.

he was Jewish. In that respect, he was no exception; one out of three students at his secondary school in Łódź was Jewish, and the biggest difference from the others was that they gained the highest marks for Polish.

Marcel read Polish historical novels and Polish poetry. He had memorised parts of *Pan Tadeusz,* and competed with his friends to recite the most stanzas from that long epic poem by Adam Mickiewicz, the Polish Pushkin. More than anything else, Marcel felt Polish, and the moment he finally felt satisfied with what he'd achieved in life was when, after retiring as an architect, he presented the first complete English translation of *Pan Tadeusz* in Warsaw in 2004.

Of course, on the eve of the Second World War, he was not blind to his country's dark side. His sister, Maria, seven years older, had had to study in Antwerp because the Polish government had capped the number of Jewish students, calling it 'disproportionate'. Anti-Semitism, which had always been present in varying intensity, gained an official status in the late 1930s, seeping into government measures and regulations. The situation made his family indignant. Marcel's father had a good job as an importer at a Danish company, Aarhus

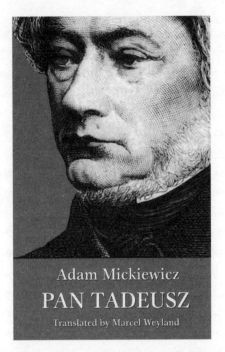

Pan Tadeusz, translated by Marcel Wejland.

Oliefabrik, and strong working relationships with Polish businessmen, accountants, and bookkeepers.

He would have spent the rest of his life in Poland, if German Stuka aircraft had not dropped a string of bombs over the city on 3 September 1939. What a shock it was when his eldest daughter, Halina, who worked for the daily newspaper *Republika*, stormed into the house and shouted, 'We have to leave now!' She knew so much about the swiftly advancing Wehrmacht and the first SS actions that she was sure any delay in their departure would leave them exposed to certain doom. That very afternoon, Mr and Mrs Wejland, Halina, Maria (home from Antwerp on holiday), Marcel, and Mrs Wejland's brother, Bolek, headed towards Warsaw in their car, a Polish Ford Eifel.

Once they had passed the capital and were on their way to Białystok, Mr Wejland picked up a hitchhiker, a corporal in the Polish army. That didn't make any sense to Marcel; there were six of them in the Ford Eifel, which was not a big car. To make things worse, the heat that day was stifling. But he kept his mouth shut, and so did his sisters. Mr Wejland was not a great talker, and it was always a mistake to ask him the reasons for his actions. Fifty kilometres on, he stopped at a petrol station. The tank was practically empty. He said nothing, simply nodding at the corporal – who took the hint, stepped out of the car, and ordered the attendant, 'Fill 'er up.' Right after the German attack, petrol had been rationed. It could only be supplied to Polish army vehicles and Polish soldiers. They were given fifteen litres, just enough to reach the border. Marcel never figured out if his father had known about the petrol rationing or just had a feeling it might be useful to have a soldier in the car.

In Białystok, they left the car behind and took the train to Vilnius. The crowded train spent more time standing still than moving; it took them a day and a night, but the border crossing went smoothly. Even a day later, it would have been much more difficult, and within a week, the area had turned into a kind of no-man's-land controlled by Poles one moment and Russians the next.

In Vilnius, Mr Wejland rented a house outside the ghetto and sent his son to a Polish classical grammar school, where Marcel learned still more stanzas of *Pan Tadeusz* by heart. He had no complaints, until the school was closed and he had to attend a Lithuanian grammar school. Lithuanian, which is more archaic than Ancient Greek, was hard for him to master. He always hesitated over the seven different cases, and that gave him a childish stutter.

Marcel would remember that winter as the coldest in his life; the temperature dropped to minus 40 Celsius. On his way to school one morning, he saw two starving wolves on the frozen river, just a few hundred metres from the centre of Vilnius. Their howls were heart-rending and went on for a while even after a police officer shot them from a bridge.

As cold as that winter was, it was just as hot in the spring of 1940, yet life in Vilnius was anything but harsh. Like most of the refugees, Marcel's father passed his time in coffee houses, restaurants, and cabarets where satirical songs were performed in Yiddish. He managed to exchange his wife's jewellery for foreign currency: American dollars and British pounds. He thought British currency might be useful when he and his children went ashore in Curaçao. You see, that July everyone in the cafés and restaurants of Vilnius was suddenly talking about an island in a warm, distant sea, with a name none of them would have recognised a month earlier.

Michal Wejland waited until 2 August before going to Kaunas for a visa. He took a leisurely stroll down Laisvės Alėja, enjoyed the sunshine, and looked into a few shop windows. Even the hat shop was displaying a portrait of Stalin, a man who surely wore nothing but caps and *ushankas*. It was a strange experience for him to be walking through a city clearly run by communists, but where the shops still told a very different story with their decorative arts and *Jugendstil*. At a table outside the Metropolis Hotel, he drank coffee and, feeling peckish, ordered a piece of apple pie with whipped cream. The scoop of whipped cream was small; the waiter said dairy produce was scarce. After the coffee, he smoked a cigarette. Wonder of wonders, he had found a pack of Lucky Strikes at the station – in Vilnius, he'd had to switch to heavy Russian cigarettes. He took a slow, deep drag, free of care, until he noticed the crowd at the entrance to the Dutch consulate. The street was swarming with people.

Beside the door were two men so tall they had to be Dutch. The dark-haired man was especially gigantic. Every time he opened the door to let in three or four men, he had to use his whole weight to stop the crowd from pushing inside. The other man was clearly suffering in the heat. He kept threatening to get the police, or 'those Cossacks', involved. Both men were on the verge of exhaustion.

Wejland was a polite man, but if he'd behaved as he always had towards his customers in Łódź, he would still have been out in the street two days later. He soon caught wind of a rumour that the Dutch consulate would be closed that very day. Elbowing his way straight through the crowds was not an option; his only chance was to sneak his way around to the door and take advantage of a moment of panic. That moment happened to come soon afterwards, when the taller man at the door staggered and half collapsed. Wejland sped to his aid, waving a bottle of spring water that he'd bought at the Metropolis with his coffee and pie and hadn't finished. The Dutchman put the bottle to his lips, rose to his feet, and clapped his new friend on the shoulder. They wobbled their way into the consulate together, and the other Dutchman locked the door behind them.

Still, it took Wejland another three hours to make it up the stairs, plenty of time to take in the details of the interior. The consulate had obviously been a radio shop, but almost all of its merchandise was gone – probably in storage, awaiting less turbulent times. The display window had been cleared out, but unlike in the other shops on Laisvės Alėja, there was no picture of Lenin or Stalin on display.

When he finally reached the consul, his first thought was, *Just like my boss at Aarhus Oliefabrik … just like a Dane*. Stiff, dark hair, a severe part on the left, and those blue, almost transparent eyes. Seated behind the desk, he'd removed his jacket, but still wore his necktie. 'Wejland,' said the consul, 'that's nearly Dutch.' Did he speak English or German? Wejland wanted to thank the consul, but before he could say anything, the man behind him had started poking him in the ribs.

The walk to the Japanese consulate took around forty-five minutes. Others may have done it faster, but he panted with effort as he trudged up the Green Hill.

'Hurry up,' other Poles said to him, 'the Japanese consulate is about to be closed today, just like the Dutch one.'

This wasn't true; the Japanese consulate didn't close until three weeks later. But there were so many rumours.

A white flag with a red sun showed him where to go. Russian soldiers were standing in front of the fence. Someone said the consul had already left. He thought of the time he'd given Marcel a tricycle. The delighted boy had spent day after day on that iron contraption, pedalling down the pavements of Łódź and under the tall pines of the resort where they spent their summers. That boy with his girlish fringe had suddenly become a young man of thirteen who would declaim one verse after another of Adam Mickiewicz as if standing on stage ... He thought of Halina, his eldest daughter, the only child of his first marriage and a woman of twenty-three now, showing him her first published newspaper articles with pride ... He thought of Maria, who loved student life in Antwerp, but was happiest when she was with her family, wherever her family was ... His mind filled with a single thought: he had to secure his children's future.

How he got past the Russian soldiers and entered the house was a mystery to him later. He did remember the cramped entrance hall, in which ten or twenty applicants stood shoulder to shoulder, and one man's elbow gave him a bloody nose. Then the office. He didn't reach it until late afternoon, advancing step by step. It was quiet there, so quiet that for a moment he thought he had entered a sanctuary. A man in a dark suit, his arms spread wide on his desk, leaned forward and made calm brushstrokes in the travel documents. He told himself that this somewhat fragile-looking man was his guardian angel. No, a guardian angel to his children. Or would it be more appropriate to compare him to the Buddha?

'British?' the man said.

No, he had fled Łódź in such haste that he had forgotten his passport. The British consulate in Kaunas, acting on behalf of the Polish government in exile, had given him a substitute document a few months earlier.

The consul didn't seem to hear his explanation. As if in a trance, he brushed the characters into the document. He bowed deeply. And when he handed over the passport, he smiled.

'I wish you good luck.'

When Wejland left the consulate, he asked someone standing in front of the fence what the consul's name was.

'Sempo Sugihara.'

'Sempo?'

'It's really Chiune, but no Westerner can pronounce that. He goes by Sempo.'

But Michal Wejland decided to burn 'Chiune Sugihara' into his memory.

With his two visas in his pocket, Wejland imagined it would be safe for his family to stay in Vilnius a while longer. Halina said nothing to change his mind; like her father, she saw no immediate threat. After the first wave of arrests, the NKVD was keeping a low profile. The Red Army was transforming Lithuania into a communist society, and seemed willing to protect Jews from local anti-Semitic groups.

Marcel stayed at the Lithuanian grammar school for the whole autumn. He was having a very hard time there. In chemistry and maths, he was falling behind simply because he couldn't always follow the explanations in Lithuanian. Halina began hearing more and more talk of troop movements near the border. A German invasion of the Soviet Union seemed more likely every week. The treaty between Stalin and Hitler was on its last legs.

At the start of the new year, the Wejland family planned their unavoidable journey. By the third week of February 1941 they were in Moscow, boarding the Trans-Siberian Express. Sitting by the window, Marcel would decipher the names of the stations: Sverdlovsk (the former Yekaterinburg, where the tsar and his family had been murdered), Omsk, Chita, Tomsk, Novosibirsk, Vladivostok ... The train trip took two weeks.

On 10 March, the family boarded a ship in Vladivostok that would take them to Tsuruga. On the gangway, a Russian border guard checked their papers. They each had their own passport, except for Marcel, who was listed in his parents' documents. But only Mr Wejland had Zwartendijk's Curaçao visa and Sugihara's Japanese transit visa in his passport, and all five of them travelled on those.

The guard stamped the exit visa in Mr Bolek's passport. Then he stamped Halina's passport. Maria's. And Mr Wejland's.

When he reached Mrs Wejland, he paused. Mr Wejland turned

pale. Marcel was terrified. The guard stared at his mother with a sullen look in his eyes. He checked her passport again, extended his hand, and said, '*S dnem rozhdeniya.*'

Happy birthday.

19

Chanson russe

For the Zwartendijk children, the summer of 1940 was turning out to be as boring as a damp autumn. Edith and Jan weren't allowed to go out anymore, or play in the nearby city park; they had to spent most of their summer holidays indoors. Jan picked up his violin more and more often. What else did he have to do?

'Something cheerful,' his mother would tell him.

He would pace the room as if wondering what to play. His steps echoed in the empty space.

All the furniture had been sent to Uncle Piet in Eindhoven – all the chairs, all the beds. Even the attic rooms were empty. For the past six nights, he and Edith had been sleeping on bales of wood shavings, and so had their Pa and Ma. Robbie was the lucky one, lying in his own cradle – which was portable.

They had spread double-folded sheets over the shavings, but the thickest ones pricked straight through them and into their backs and behinds. Ma had hay fever and lay awake half the night, sneezing.

Grandma's grand piano had been shipped off in a box nailed tightly shut. The crockery, along with the forks and knives, was packed in newspaper. They were camping in their own home, using plates and tableware that had belonged to the professor and his wife, who had been arrested and taken away. After dinner, they would do the washing-up as fast as they could and put the plates back in the sideboard, worried that one of the professor's relatives might turn up unannounced. It had already happened once, although the woman who visited, the professor's sister, had said only that she still hoped every day that her brother would return and that his arrest was just a misunderstanding. Ma had advised her to take away the contents of the house so that the Russians wouldn't steal them, but she hadn't wanted to.

Six weeks later, sure enough, a Russian officer moved into the upper floor and laid claim to everything he found there.

But Edith and Rob didn't hear about that until seventy-six years later, when they went with me to visit their old house. We were invited in by the new owner, whose father had moved into the ground floor in 1945 and discovered the chaos left by the Russian officer.

Those summer days were endless. 'On fine days, we were allowed to go out into the garden,' Edith recalls. 'We would pick and eat the most delicious sweet tomatoes. In the house, we would spend a lot of time playing with Robbie, who by then could crawl across the floor. The rest of the time, we just had to wait.'

The coats and winter clothes were boxed and shipped, and so were the radio, the gramophone, and the books – including the schoolbooks, even though they'd received a notice that the Deutsche Schule would start up again as usual on 2 September. That was in twenty-seven days' time.

'Do we have to go back to school then?' Jan asked.

'Yes, if we don't yet have an exit visa,' his father told him.

They had to leave, but weren't allowed to go. It was strange and scary, both at once. What were the Russians up to? What had their father meant when he said he felt like a hostage?

Pa's business had been nationalised and the consulate closed, by order of the military authorities, but they still hadn't been issued an exit visa. No one understood why. The Japanese consul was in the same predicament. Sugihara hadn't received an exit visa either – not for himself, his wife, his children, or his sister-in-law – even though

Young Jan practising violin in the roof gutter.

he'd already been assigned to a new post. Sugihara had been appointed consul in Königsberg, less than two hours from Kaunas. Van Prattenburg and De Haan couldn't leave either.

'So?' his mother asked.

Jan looked out the window and started to play. It was a tune he'd learned from his teacher. Like Edith's piano teacher, his violin teacher was Russian, too. But she couldn't be all that Russian, he thought, because she had a German name and the same accent in German as Mr Markus at the pastry shop, who spoke Yiddish. He hadn't been taking lessons from her for very long, and he never dared to look her in the face – even though she was very nice to him.

He played a false note, and started over.

'Sounds Russian,' his mother said over the music.

'Don't ask me.'

'It brings tears to my eyes. Play something fun.'

But he was addicted to the tune, even though he couldn't play more than the opening measures, and wouldn't stop until he heard his father's car pull up outside.

It was convenient for Sugihara that he didn't have to leave Kaunas just yet. By the time Zwartendijk issued his last visa, the Japanese consul had built up quite a backlog. Zwartendijk had given out 2,139 visas in total. On the afternoon of 2 August, Sugihara signed transit visa no. 819. At least, that's what Zwartendijk thought he heard on the phone – he may have misheard. On the morning of 2 August, according to his own records, Sugihara issued visa no. 717. In any case, he had a lot of catching up to do.

He would keep at it throughout the month of August, in a race against the clock. His list of visas issued was no longer kept by his Lithuanian secretary, but by his wife, Yukiko. At some point she must have stopped – on 28 August, or maybe even earlier.

On that day, Wednesday 28 August 1940, Sugihara could no longer coax any more time out of the Soviet authorities, and had to close the consulate for good. By this time, his personal effects had already been sent on to Königsberg. He and his wife and children moved into the Metropolis Hotel, less than one hundred metres from the Philips office. He could even have met Zwartendijk in person, since he had to stay in Kaunas until the end of August. But Sugihara was too busy; even in the Metropolis, he kept writing visas, up to twenty hours a day.

In the early evening of Saturday 3 August, Zwartendijk unscrewed the sign from the wall that read 'Consulate of the Kingdom of the Netherlands'. As Russian soldiers looked on, he locked the door, and told Van Prattenburg and De Haan not to return to the office until Tuesday 6 August, some time in the afternoon. He did not explain why.

On Monday morning, he drove his Buick Roadmaster past Lietuvos Philips at a snail's pace. Two Russian soldiers were stationed in front of the door; no one else was waiting there. The news that the Dutch consulate was permanently closed must have spread like wildfire among the refugees. On Tuesday morning, he took the same slow drive down Laisvės Alėja. The soldiers were gone.

Jan junior would always remember the strangeness of the next morning. He later asked himself why his father had brought him along and not Edith. Was he worried she might spill the secret?

In the burly Buick Roadmaster, Pa drove him to Laisvės Alėja. Mother wasn't with them. Pa didn't park right in front of the office, but down the street, near the Metropolis. They took an unusual route to the showroom: not along Laisvės Alėja, but through a narrow street that led to a little square at the rear of the building. Pa must have looked around six times before entering the storeroom. Once they were in, he lit the pot-bellied stove. It seemed he'd made thorough preparations: the wood was there waiting for him.

Van Prattenburg was the first to show up, bearing two bags with the most important Philips business documents. Plus a third bag: the petty cash.

'It's up to you,' Zwartendijk said. 'Burn it all here, or smuggle it into the Netherlands.'

'The latter,' Van Prattenburg said without hesitation, as if he'd thought it over at length.

Then De Haan came in with all the consular stamps and paraphernalia. Zwartendijk stoked the fire again, and De Haan slid the documents into the stove, one by one, without saying a word. The stamps and ink pads also disappeared into the fire. This had all clearly been planned.

The last thing De Haan pulled out of his bag was the list. But he hesitated. 'Are you sure?' he asked.

'Not a doubt in my mind. Whoever is on a list can be tracked down – a day from now, or a month, or a year. Forever …'

'OK, here.'

De Haan handed him the sheaf of paper, as if he couldn't bring himself to put it in the stove.

It was Zwartendijk who consigned the list of 2,139 Jewish visa recipients to the flames. He made certain that every last shred of paper was reduced to ash.

'What have you two been up to?' Edith asked when her father and brother returned hours later.

'Nothing,' Jan junior mumbled.

On the drive home, he'd promised he wouldn't tell. His father had been very insistent: 'Not one word about this until the war is over. That's your mission. Are you up to it?' But Edith suspected something was afoot.

That evening, her father called De Decker. Without giving any details, he simply said, 'I got rid of everything.'

20

Please forgive me. I cannot write any

more.

Officially, the Japanese consulate was closed. But Chiune Sugihara was still issuing visas – even more than in July, he told the Japanese TV reporter Michinosuke Kayaba in a 1977 interview:

> The peak came when I had just closed the consulate and was about to get out of the country on the international train to Berlin before the September 1st deadline. It lasted about two weeks. Workers came to my place about a week before my departure to pack our things. I was still working while they packed. As the packing progressed, I had to have the boxes removed from the house as it got so cluttered. About three days before departure, we moved to the Metropolis. I was working throughout the day as consul but found refugees coming to see me regardless of what I was doing. They came to see me at such times. They even came to see me on the morning of the 1st at the Kaunas station platform where we were departing from. I didn't know what to do, for I just couldn't say no to them ... I don't remember refusing anyone, so I probably issued a visa to everyone.

On Thursday 5 September, Sugihara went to the station in Kaunas with his wife, sister-in-law, and three children. He was surrounded by a crowd of people. Men grabbed him and begged, 'Visa, visa.'

Sugihara no longer had time to write six or seven columns of characters, but in his briefcase he had a stack of blank sheets of paper bearing the stamp of the Japanese consulate. He handed out these sheets to everyone who asked for one, and signed them on the spot. He assumed the words of the visa could be copied onto the sheets later by an experienced forger.

In the concourse, so many refugees gathered around him that he could not proceed any further. He kneeled, placed his left knee on the floor, rested the sheets of paper on his right knee, and signed one after another. Rail workers had to cordon him off so that the crowd wouldn't tumble over him.

His time was short; the international train to Königsberg–Danzig–Berlin was on the point of departure.

Sugihara stood and said, 'Please forgive me. I cannot write anymore. I wish you the best.' He made a deep bow.

Silence fell. No one had expected so much courtesy from a man who had nearly been trampled by a desperate mob.

Then one young man put an end to the confusion by shouting, 'Sugihara, we'll never forget you. I'll surely see you again.'

The consul pressed his hand to his mouth, almost shocked by these words, and went onto the platform. Railway staff had to clear a path for him.

His wife, who described their departure in her memoirs, was already seated in their compartment with her sister and children. Mrs Sugihara wore a dark suit and a black hat with a veil, as if on the way to a funeral. She was conscious at all times of the gravity of the situation.

Sugihara boarded the train, removed his jacket, handed it to his wife, and opened one of the windows along the aisle. He was very hot; his forehead shone with sweat.

From the platform, a boy handed him a blank sheet of paper. He made a scribble; the whistle blew.

Another boy thrust a sheet of paper into his hands; the train lurched into motion. Another quick scribble, and he tossed the sheet of paper out the window.

Sugihara's wife and children leaving Kaunas. The consul leaned
out of the next window and continued to hand out visas.

A third boy tried to reach him, but the train was going too fast.
'Please, please,' the boy cried, but there was nothing more the consul
could do for him.

Sugihara pulled a handkerchief out of his pocket and wiped the
sweat from his forehead. It appalled him that he had to go when so
many people still needed him. In tears, he left Lithuania.

Sugihara remained in Königsberg for seven months. Under the regime
of Erich Koch, the Nazi *Gauleiter* of East Prussia, the city was sinister,

its prisons filled with opponents of Nazism. The synagogue had been destroyed on Kristallnacht, and most Jews had fled the city. Sugihara never felt at home there for one moment, and breathed a sigh of relief when he was transferred to Czechoslovakia.

From March 1941 to the end of 1942, he was consul general in Nazi-occupied Prague. The situation there proved to be much worse even than in East Prussia. *Reichsprotektor* Reinhard Heydrich presided over a reign of terror; no one in the city was safe, not even a consul.

Soon after arriving, Sugihara sent his list of refugees to the foreign ministry in Tokyo – by diplomatic bag, to be sure, but even so it was a risky and amateurish move; the list could have fallen into Nazi hands. Heydrich was not only 'the butcher of Prague' who had practically wiped out the Czech Resistance, but also the brains behind the physical substance used for the mass murder of the Jews: the poisonous gas Zyklon B. He chaired the Wannsee Conference, held on 20 January 1942, where he presented the *Endlösung der Judenfrage*, the 'final solution to the Jewish question'. For Heydrich, who was assassinated with a bomb in Prague in June 1942, the removal of the Jews from public life and their mass deportation was not enough; his goal was systematic genocide. If Heydrich had seen the list, he would no doubt have demanded that Germany's ally Japan return all the Jewish refugees to Europe.

What horrors might have followed, we can only speculate about. In fact, the list arrived in Tokyo unseen, and was whisked away into a safe, where it would remain until several decades after the war. Only after it resurfaced was it possible to see how many people had been saved by consuls Jan Zwartendijk and Chiune Sugihara, according to the original list. In a telegram sent by Sugihara to the Japanese foreign minister on 5 February 1941, he estimated that 1,500 of the 2,139 applicants were Polish Jews. The true figure was much higher, and he knew that. Sugihara – like Zwartendijk, later – had begun to play down the scale of the rescue operation, in order to draw less attention to it.

The same foreign ministry archive in Tokyo also contains a document showing that the total number of transit visas issued in

Kaunas in 1939 and 1940 was 5,580, and that the large majority went to Jews.

Sugihara must have issued many visas that are not listed anywhere. In his TV interview with Kayaba in 1977, he said 'there were about 4,500 people'.

21

Every man for himself

As I reconstructed these events, it remained unclear to me why Zwartendijk had agreed to close the Dutch consulate on 3 August 1940. If he had strung along the Russian military authorities until 28 August, like his Japanese counterpart, he might have been able to keep the consulate open and issue many more Curaçao visas.

Sugihara had persevered all the way to the platform in Kaunas, and even on the train as it departed for Königsberg. He had taken huge risks. So had Zwartendijk – until August came. Maybe he thought he'd reached the limit and that persisting would look too much like defying or provoking the authorities. He not only feared that the Russians might intervene at any moment, but also that the visas he and Sugihara had already issued might then be declared invalid. Better to help fewer people, he may have decided, than to put all the refugees with visas in danger.

I can't say for certain. What I do know, from Edith and Rob and from Jan junior's letters, is that Zwartendijk felt responsible for the visa recipients. When fifteen years after the war he still hadn't received news of any of them escaping death, he was consumed with worry. The true scale of the Shoah had become public knowledge by then, and he began to fear that most of 'his' refugees were among the six million victims.

He had known from the start that the rescue operation would

be dicey. Some of the earliest refugees with Curaçao visas had been arrested by Russian soldiers on returning from Kaunas to Vilnius. Their visas had offered them no protection. He'd heard about their miserable fate the last time he saw Nathan Gutwirth. Even those who managed to leave the country could always be removed from the train between Kaunas and Moscow, or between Moscow and Vladivostok. And how would the Japanese authorities respond? Would they allow the refugees to travel on, or send them back to Europe – to Poland, where they came from, or maybe straight to Germany? Zwartendijk had no idea in 1940, and he was none the wiser in 1962.

It was not until 1963 that he received the first message from a survivor – a man who had reached Los Angeles and wanted to send his belated thanks. Zwartendijk wrote a crotchety reply. Only one survivor – had the whole operation achieved no more than that?

It's possible that his superior, De Decker, advised him to accede to the Russian demand for the immediate closure of the consulate. In August 1940, various parties outside Lithuania learned of the exodus that had been enabled by the Dutch and Japanese consuls; the great powers were sure to respond. The American ambassador in Moscow, Laurence A. Steinhardt, sent an alarming telegram to the State Department in August, which showed how apprehensive he was that the refugees might eventually reach the United States:

> I assume the Department is aware of the fact that Japanese transit visas were issued to these individuals on the basis of assurances made to the Japanese Legation in Kaunas by the Dutch consul at the instance of the Joint Distribution Committee in Kaunas that entrance visas to the Dutch possessions in the Americas were not required and that approximately 2,000 Japanese transit visas of this type were recently issued in Kaunas, specifying on the face of the visa that the applicants were en route to the Dutch possessions in the Americas.
>
> Each of the applicants thus far examined by the Embassy in Moscow regarded his Japanese transit visa marked as en route to the

Dutch possessions in the Americas as merely a means of obtaining a Soviet exit visa and transit across Japan with the intention of entering the United States and remaining there for at least the duration of the war.

The Americans had by no means forgotten the ill-fated voyage of the *St. Louis*, and ambassador Steinhardt warned the state department that another such tragedy could be in the making. But he did not send this telegram until 6 October, and we may assume that, in the first week of August, the foreign embassies had not yet been alerted to the situation.

This is why the question arises of whether Zwartendijk could have continued until at least 17 August, the date when De Decker had to close the Dutch legation in Riga by order of the Russians. This may, in fact, be the strangest thing of all: Zwartendijk shut down the consulate fourteen days before De Decker closed the legation in Riga.

As it turned out, the problem was that the Dutch consulate was headquartered in the Philips office. Like all companies with more than twenty employees, Lietuvos Philips had been nationalised on 1 August. On 2 August, the communist overseer showed up and demanded that the Dutch managers clear out the office so that he could get to work on Monday 5 August. This made it impossible to continue using the location as a consulate.

'While at first we'd had people in the company who had expressed their political colour by wearing brown shirts,' Robert van Prattenburg later said, 'by this stage the colour was red, and one of them became a people's commissar.'

He wasted no time in demanding that Zwartendijk, Van Prattenburg, and De Haan pack their things and leave at once. And he asked the Russian military authorities to order the closure of the consulate.

On 1 August, Zwartendijk sent his last message from Lithuania to Eindhoven. It reached his immediate supervisor at Philips headquarters on 8 August:

One of these days the whole family may turn up on your doorstep, with or without our moving boxes. You must have figured out by now that the horizon here is still far from cloudless, but don't expect me personally just yet!

He hadn't yet applied to the Soviet authorities for an exit visa for himself and his wife and children, and he had heard there was a waiting period. Nor had he yet accepted the nationalisation of his office.

According to Van Prattenburg, they had no choice but to leave: 'The last light bulbs were removed from the stockrooms. We knew there would be no new supplies of radio parts. Lietuvos Philips was history.'

Every day, Edith heard her father grumbling: 'It was a dismal, mixed-up situation for him. You could cut the atmosphere in the office with a knife.'

One of the commissar's first measures was to rehire all former employees, including those suspended in May because of the low turnover. The remaining employees received permanent positions; their worries about the future were over. Maschewski – who was in fact responsible for day-to-day management, since the people's commissar had no idea what he was doing – accepted the nationalisation of Lietuvos Philips as an irreversible fact. He was careful to avoid controversy. Zwartendijk continued to go to the office and showroom on Laisvės Alėja every day of the week for the whole month of August. He usually left before noon, so that – like Van Prattenburg and De Haan – he could join the queue for an exit visa. They found themselves in the same boat as the Polish Jews they had helped to obtain visas, and could see the humour in it.

While Zwartendijk kept the people's commissar preoccupied, Van Prattenburg managed to pack up all the important business documents so that they could be taken back to Eindhoven. He was also able to empty the safe before the people's commissar found out its code.

The radio-assembly plant was slow to resume production. The stockroom was relocated to the Aartsengel Michaelbasiliek in Kaunas, the blue-domed church that Zwartendijk had passed every afternoon on his way home. The accounts and records were moved to the Church of St Michael the Archangel in Vilnius. This type of thing drew no protest or complaint from the Lithuanians, because they hoped to avoid worse; if Moscow saw no practical use in a church building, it would be demolished.

On 13 January 1941, Lietuvos Philips would be incorporated into the Russian State Radio Trust Pamprekyba. The brand name would be changed to Banga, and the parts would come from Leningrad.

If the Soviets had asked permission to continue using the brand name Philips, the answer from Frits Philips would have been no. Frits was a religious man, a member of the Moral Re-Armament movement, and a staunch opponent of communism; his world stopped at the Iron Curtain. Any cooperative initiatives took the form of joint ventures, and the products were marketed under other brand names. Yet they sometimes found their way through Asia into the Soviet Union and into the Banga assembly factories in Kaunas, Vilnius, and Riga.

Once production was in full swing, from 1946 onwards, Zwartendijk, Van Prattenburg, and De Haan's little company grew into a colossus. In the 1960s, Banga produced millions of transistor radios for the entire Soviet Union.

For the Dutch expats in Lithuania, the process of leaving was difficult and chaotic.

'The best idea is every man for himself,' Jan Zwartendijk said. From deciding to leave, it was a long road to actually leaving. Van Prattenburg knocked on the doors of one Soviet official after another until he found a lieutenant colonel who called himself a people's commissar. A fierce anti-German, he couldn't imagine why anyone would want to return to the Netherlands, which after all was occupied by the Nazis. After a lot of back and forth, Van Prattenburg hit on the winning argument; he said he planned to join a Resistance cell. 'Ah, a partisan,' the officer said. Van Prattenburg received an exit visa for himself and his wife, who was expecting to give birth to a son on 9 September.

They departed on 27 August, travelling by way of Königsberg, Danzig, and Berlin – from Lithuania and East Prussia through part of Poland, and then all the way across Germany. At every border crossing, the currency and the papers in the suitcases caused trouble. But Mrs Van Prattenburg saved the day. She would almost lie down instead of sitting, with both hands on her belly, and she was hot – so hot that she could hardly breathe. The border guards took pity on her every time.

On 29 August, Koen de Haan was allowed to leave with his wife and son. The Zwartendijks were the only ones not to receive an exit visa. The Soviet authorities gave no reason. Erni had to remind herself ten times a day not to panic and not to show her children any hint of her fear and anxiety.

On 2 September, Edith and Jan began the new school year in Lithuania. It was Jan's first year in secondary school, and Edith's second. In the afternoon, they were all led to a field just outside Kaunas, and each student had to plant a tree. They had done the same thing once before the summer holidays; they didn't really understand why. During that September field trip, Edith sank deep into the mud. It would be her last memory of Kaunas.

On 3 September, Jan Zwartendijk was finally informed that he could pick up his exit visa. On 4 September, he and his whole family boarded the train. They stopped for the night in Berlin, in the hotel where Erni and little Robbie had always stayed on their way to the Netherlands and on the return trip to Lithuania.

The next day, they continued their journey. Edith remembers only one thing about it: 'You would get so dirty. The windows were open the whole way, and you could hear the locomotive puffing. Wisps of smoke blew into the car, and by the end of the day you were black all over. The dust covered your forehead, your cheeks, your hands.'

On the platform in Utrecht, their cousins, Piet and Mien, were waiting for them. Zwartendijk had called from Berlin to ask if the family could stay with them for their first night in the Netherlands.

Dr Piet Nieuwenhuijse, a pathologist, was an eminent man of medicine. He looked them up and down – first the children, then Erni, and finally Jan.

'You look dog-tired. The first thing you need to do is sleep for days. And cut down on the smoking. You'll give yourself a heart condition. Your face is rigid with tension.'

'It can't be as bad as all that,' Zwartendijk said. 'Nothing much out of the ordinary has happened to us.'

'Oh, no?' said Jan junior.

'No,' his father said, bringing the conversation to an abrupt halt.

It was the first time Jan had ever caught his father lying. He got the message right away: they weren't supposed to talk about Kaunas anymore. Nothing had happened – full stop.

Two days later, the Zwartendijks travelled on to Eindhoven. There they stayed with Jan's brother, Piet, who had already applied to Philips for a house for them. They were able to move before the end of the month.

The last thing to arrive in Eindhoven was the grand piano. The instrument had been sent in early August. As if there were no war, it had travelled from Kaunas straight across Poland and Germany to the Netherlands, and arrived in Eindhoven in early October 1940, still packed neatly in its box, along with the lace cloth crocheted by *Grossmaman* that had always been draped over it.

The piano would remain in the sitting room in Eindhoven until 1944, when they had to trade it for food.

22

The Swedish route

De Decker closed the Dutch legation in Riga on 17 August 1940, under the watchful eyes of two Russian officers and four soldiers. He stepped into a government car commandeered by the Red Cross, which took him straight to the airport. The envoy was accompanied by his Dutch assistant, Archibald van der Stal, chancellor first class, and Stal's wife. They had been permitted to send off their personal possessions to their first destination, Stockholm, a few days earlier.

When Leendert de Decker stepped into the aircraft, a Douglas DC-3 in the fleet of the Swedish airline SILA, he could see he wasn't the only diplomat who had been ordered out of the country by the Soviets. A quick scan of the cabin revealed eight others, most accompanied by their wives.

He had thought he might be put on a boat to Sweden; the sea voyage from Riga to Stockholm took twenty hours. The coasts of Courland and the Gulf of Riga were under Russian control, but German submarines had been reported in Baltic waters, so it was safer to fly to Sweden. At the airport, he heard that this was certain to be one of the last passenger flights to Stockholm, but the mail flights to and from the Baltics would continue for the time being. He made a mental note of that last fact.

Leaving was difficult for him. The years in Riga had been the hardest of his life, but even after his wife's death he still loved the Baltic states: the atmosphere, which always reminded him of Christmas, and the scent of pine trees, even in the middle of town.

The evening before, he had called the consul in Kaunas – his last act as envoy. Zwartendijk had sounded tired and tense, although he did his best to stay businesslike. 'I don't know why the Russians want to hold me here,' he had said. 'It's starting to seem a bit odd, to say the least.'

This news had worried De Decker, too. All the diplomats had been told to leave, except for Sugihara and Zwartendijk. Still, he felt certain the Russians wouldn't find any evidence against the Dutch consul. Zwartendijk's hints had made it clear to him that all of the consulate's papers and documents had been destroyed. Of course, this didn't mean all traces of the operation had been erased. After all, every visa issued was proof of what Zwartendijk had done.

In Stockholm, De Decker stepped into the middle of a huge mess. None of the Dutch officials there could handle the situation any longer. The government in exile in London was sending conflicting orders, while the Swedish government tried to avoid any appearance of sympathy for occupied countries. Diplomats and secret agents from Nazi Germany kept a critical eye on the situation. Gestapo agents tapped telephone calls to and from the foreign embassies day and night to find out whether Sweden was as neutral as it claimed.

For the time being, De Decker was between assignments. The Netherlands already had an envoy in Sweden, who had been there since 1934: Baron J.E.H. van Nagell. And besides De Decker, another envoy had fled to Stockholm: Dr G.A. Scheltus, from Norway. There was also a consul general, appointed in 1938.

The fact that Van Nagell had been sidelined on 1 May 1941 – placed *en disponibilité*, in diplomatic jargon – made little difference for De Decker's purposes. Van Nagell had fallen seriously short in keeping the government in exile up to date – though he claimed the problem was that Eelco van Kleffens, the foreign minister, regarded his messages as 'impolite'. The envoy was also said to have been too cautious in his dealings with the Germans. 'He's worse than the Swedes,' said

Stockholm's first Engelandvaarders – Dutch refugees who planned to travel on to England as soon as possible to join the Dutch Resistance. Van Nagell was no Nazi sympathiser; he did go to the trouble of arranging a passage to England – by way of Vladivostok, Kobe, and Batavia (present-day Jakarta) – for his own son. But the eminent Dutch war historian Dr Loe de Jong investigated the baron's Swedish period, and rendered a devastating judgement: 'Not without occasional good impulses, but otherwise a diplomat of minor accomplishment, despite nineteen years of experience in five different missions.'

Van Nagell was replaced by Scheltus, who decided that it would be more sensible to speak to the relevant ministers in person in London, so that at least the Gestapo could not listen in to their conversatioins or intercept their messages. But the aircraft that took him to England was unheated; he contracted a lung infection and, three weeks later, drew his final breath.

Just before his death, Scheltus made a huge blunder. After the American invasion of North Africa, he made it clear that he expected an immediate protest from the Dutch government in exile, because he considered it equivalent to the German invasion of the Netherlands. Four decades later, Loe de Jong could still work himself into a lather about Scheltus: 'This statement evinced no great understanding of what was at stake in the Second World War.'

After Scheltus's sudden death, De Decker filled in for three months as an interim *chargé d'affaires*. Then a replacement was found: a diplomat who was much younger but stemmed from an old aristocratic line. Willem Constantijn, Count of Rechteren-Limpurg, came from Washington. In the dead of night, he was flown from London to Stockholm.

De Decker remained active behind the scenes. So did the former envoy Van Nagell, a situation that led to great confusion about who exactly was responsible for what. Meanwhile, the Engelandvaarders were arriving in Sweden by the dozens, and Van Nagell didn't seem capable of doing much to help them. Their business was handled by the consul general.

A.M. de Jong in his hardware factory, seated in a ball bearing, Malmö.

Less than a week after his arrival, De Decker had figured out that only one Dutch official in Stockholm was keeping a cool head: consul general Adriaan Mattheus de Jong, a businessman who reminded De Decker very much of Zwartendijk. Forty-three years old – more or less the same age as the consul in Kaunas – he hated fuss, and was fast and efficient. De Jong came from Sliedrecht, a centre of the dredging industry along the Merwede River. He had emigrated when he was nineteen and, at the age of twenty-one, married a Swedish woman. He was a hardware wholesaler in Malmö, selling nails, bolts, and screws. He had turned a sleepy little shop into a flourishing business. In 1938, he had been appointed as Dutch consul in his southern Swedish city. In 1940, he opened a second branch of his business in Stockholm, moved to the capital with his wife and two sons, and was promoted to consul general.

De Jong laid the foundation for a robust company that remains in operation, managed by the third generation of De Jongs. As a consul, he was at least as effective, showing more resolution than all the career diplomats put together. But in 1943 he made an excruciating mistake.

My advertisement in the weekly *Australian Jewish News* ('Dutch author looking for testimonies on "The Angel of Curaçao"'), led to a response within two weeks from a barrister in Melbourne, Deborah Wiener. Her father, Ascher Wiener, had used a Curaçao visa.

The name Zwartendijk meant nothing to her, as her father's visa had been issued by the Dutch consulate in Sweden. At my request, she sent a copy. The note in the passport, written in French (!), is identical, word for word, to the formula used by Zwartendijk. The visa bears the clearly legible signature of A.M. de Jong.

The date of issue is surprisingly late: Stockholm, 17 January 1941. Underneath that is a number I cannot explain: 274/211. Was this the 274th visa in note form that De Jong issued?

In 1941, Abram Wiener used his mother's maiden name as a pseudonym. The visa is in the name of Erazm Übersfeld. The address: Gedimino 9, Vilnius.

Gedimino Prospektas, a broad boulevard, was and remains the main shopping street in Vilnius. Department stores stand side by side with ministries, banks, and the parliament building. The historic building at number 9 dates from the nineteenth century. It could never have been the home address of Ascher Wiener, alias Erazm Übersfeld.

On my next visit to Vilnius, I walk over there. The post office is at number 7. It was already there in 1941, I am told, and the poste

CONSULAAT-GENERAAL
DER
NEDERLANDEN
VOOR
ZWEDEN

STOCKHOLM
Postbox 727
HOLLÄNDAREGATAN 3
Telefon 23 5115
Tel. adress Dejong

Le soussigné, Consul-Général des Pays-Bas à Stockholm,
déclare par la présente que pour l'admission au Surinam, au
Curaçao et les autres îles néerlandaises dans les Antilles,
un visa n'est pas requis.

Le Consul-Général

Stockholm le 17 janvier 1941.
№ 274/211.

Erazm ÜBERSFELD
Gedimino 9,
Vilnius.

Abram Wiener's Curaçao visa, signed by A.M. de Jong.

restante could be picked up at number 9. Refugees who stayed in the
Vilnius ghetto used this address.

Without a transit visa, Ascher Wiener could not travel to Japan.
Consul Sugihara could no longer issue him one, since he had left for
Königsberg and, by 17 January 1941, was already on the way to his
following post, Prague. Wiener must have got hold of one some other

way. I can't ask him how; he is no longer alive. His daughter can't tell me either. Apart from the visa issued by A.M. de Jong, no other travel documents have been preserved.

In *Go, My Son: a young Jewish refugee's story of survival*, published in 1989, Chaim Shapiro described the different escape routes taken by the refugees. He presented an even more detailed overview in the 3 February 1998 issue of *Jewish World Review*. Shapiro, who became a rabbi in Baltimore in the 1960s, has no doubt that the main issuer of Curaçao visas was Zwartendijk. As he tells it, the idea for these visas arose from the friendship between Zwartendijk and Nathan Gutwirth. They knew each other before the war, and exchanged the sports sections of Dutch newspapers.

Shapiro does not mention Peppy Lewin. According to him, it all started with Zwartendijk and Gutwirth. Zwartendijk got De Decker involved, and Gutwirth told Warhaftig, the lawyer from Warsaw who tried to persuade as many Jewish refugees as possible to leave for Japan on Curaçao visas. But after the Dutch and Japanese consulates in Kaunas were closed, the refugees had to find alternative routes. The first was the USSR–Palestine route, which led either through Turkey and Syria or through Iran. An underground printery in Vilnius supplied forged British entry visas for Palestine, barely distinguishable from the real thing. This operation was organised by Jabotinsky's Zionist Revisionists, a group that later became part of Israel's Herut party, which in turn was absorbed into Likud. The Revisionists distributed the British documents to their members and to *halutzim*, 'pioneers' who migrated to lay the groundwork for the state of Israel.

After a protest from the British government to the Soviet Union that a remarkable number of refugees were entering Palestine through Syria with forged British papers, the underground printshop in Vilnius was shut down, and the printer banished to Siberia. He was released ten years later, and spent the rest of his life in Jerusalem.

After that option was eliminated, the main route was through Sweden. Very soon after De Decker arrived in Stockholm, in

September 1940, he was contacted by the German rabbinical student and refugee Shlomo Wolbe. Wolbe had heard about De Decker from Gutwirth and Warhaftig, who were still in Lithuania.

De Decker provided Wolbe with the wording of the Curaçao visa, and sent him to Adriaan Mattheus de Jong. Without a moment's hesitation, De Jong went to work – without informing the Dutch envoy. Wolbe delivered the applications, and sent the visas typed and signed by De Jong back to the main post office in Vilnius, from which they were distributed among the applicants.

The problem was the transit visa. On De Decker's recommendation, Wolbe sent the applicants to the Japanese embassy in Moscow. But they were rejected and returned. The Japanese consul in Moscow had submitted the Curaçao visas to the Dutch consul in Moscow for examination. He called them false documents, because the wording suggested that you could easily enter Curaçao or Suriname, which was not the case.

Shlomo Wolbe then went looking for another Japanese consul, one in a city without a Dutch consul to spoil things. After some searching, he found a consul in Chita, eight hundred kilometres east of Irkutsk, on the Trans-Siberian Railway. Furthermore, the Japanese consul in Chita proved to be a man of action; he sent the signed visas back by return of post.

Chaim Shapiro's story is not entirely accurate. In 1941, the Netherlands had not yet established diplomatic relations with the Soviet Union. After the Bolshevik revolution, every country in Europe had taken that step – Germany first, in 1922, and then all the others – with the sole exception of the Netherlands. Serious attempts kept running up against ethical objections from a majority in the nation's lower house of parliament. For the confessional and liberal parties, the 'original sin' of the Soviet Union, 'born in blood', and the ongoing religious persecution there ruled out any possibility of normalising relations. And this is not to mention another formidable opponent: Her Majesty the Queen.

On 22 June 1941, the Soviet Union became involved in the war.

The day Russia was attacked by Nazi Germany, the USSR joined the Allies. The response from the Dutch government in exile was frosty: 'Russia should be praised for its struggle, but not recognised.'

Queen Wilhelmina was a staunch opponent of recognition. Her grandmother had been a Romanov, and Her Majesty refused to see a representative of the people who had slaughtered her relatives. As recently as 1899, the last tsar, Nicholas II, had opened a letter to Wilhelmina with '*Madame ma Soeur*' and closed with '*le bon frère, Nicolas*'. And although she'd had little respect for her late 'brother', she was put off by the presumptuousness of her foreign minister, Van Kleffens. Paul I may have been her great-grandfather, Van Kleffens said, but he could hardly imagine that the queen's distant kinship 'to that Romanov ruffian would be any reason for Her Majesty to deem herself closely connected to that House'. That did it; Queen Wilhelmina deplored, in the strongest possible terms, the description of her ancestor as a 'ruffian', and refused to cooperate. In the end, the American and British governments had to intervene, and prime minister Gerbrandy even had to offer a half-baked apology ('It is not, in fact, general knowledge that Paul I was a ruffian') before Wilhelmina finally gave in, on 3 June 1942. 'Oh, let's get on with it then,' she is supposed to have said, and on the official document she wrote, 'Approved. W.'. But the first Dutch ambassador would not arrive in Moscow until September 1943.

Nonetheless, the Netherlands and the Soviet Union were trading partners in the 1930s. There must have been the occasional businessman who acted as the voice of the Dutch business sector, shouldering responsibilities that would normally have belonged to a consul. But in 1940–1941, the Netherlands did not have consuls in Russia – whether in Moscow or anywhere else.

Consul De Jong went on issuing Curaçao visas from Stockholm for another year, until Germany occupied the Baltic states in 1941. He would type the same words that Zwartendijk had written in the passports, and send the document – signed, dated, and bearing the stamp of the consulate general of the Netherlands in Stockholm – to the applicant in Lithuania. He issued nearly five hundred visas of this kind (I found one numbered 368, and another numbered 472) to Jewish refugees from Poland or Lithuania, and around one thousand men, women, and children used them to travel to Japan.

Those who left in the early months of 1941, such as Ascher Wiener, could travel on to Japan a few weeks later, and from there to Shanghai. Wiener ended up in New Zealand. Those who travelled from Lithuania to Vladivostok in May and June 1941 had vastly greater difficulty.

Among them was Chaim Shapiro, who was stuck in the Siberian gulag with thirty other Jewish refugees for the duration of the conflict. But, as he wrote after the war, 'Siberia was better than Auschwitz, and 80 to 90 per cent of the prisoners survived the war.'

Adriaan Mattheus de Jong became a second Jan Zwartendijk, also operating under the supervision of Leendert de Decker. But De Jong was less cautious. From his appointment as consul general in Stockholm in 1940 to September 1943, De Jong was responsible for 'emigrants' (*uitgewekenen*), seafarers who came to Sweden to join the fight for the liberation of the Netherlands, and Engelandvaarders, who came from Delfzijl in the Netherlands on coastal trading or fishing vessels, and hoped to travel on to England to join the Allied forces. The term 'emigrants' also covered seafarers and students who had no interest in fighting for any cause and had come to Sweden to sit out the war in peace and safety.

After the war broke out, Dutch coasters kept up a regular service to Swedish ports, departing from Delfzijl except in the coldest winter months. In his magnum opus on the Netherlands in the Second World War, Loe de Jong (no relation to the consul) wrote, 'The idea of using the coasters to establish a "route" to occupied territory didn't occur to anyone in London; the initiative lay entirely with the Dutch consul general in Stockholm, A.M. de Jong.'

He contacted the Resistance group 't Zwaantje, led by Dr Allard Oosterhuis, a physician in Delfzijl and a shipowner. In Groningen, this

The Dutch consul general in Stockholm, Adriaan Mattheus de Jong.

combination was less unusual than it may seem; when a gentleman farmer's eldest son took over the family farm and estate, a younger brother often received a ship as his inheritance. Dr Oosterhuis operated two coasters, one of which he used to send Jacques de Vries to Sweden. The men had become acquainted during the short-lived mobilisation of the Dutch forces in 1939, when they played billiards together in the Hotel De Witte Zwaan ('The White Swan') in Leiden. In memory of that time, they gave the Resistance group they set up in 1941 the code name 't Zwaantje ('The Little Swan'). De Vries had a Jewish father – another reason to send him away from the occupied Netherlands to neutral Sweden, hidden in the coaster's forepeak and carrying a forged seaman's book.

In Stockholm, De Vries made contact with the British and was given a job at the British embassy, where he could quickly and easily pass on all messages and requests from 't Zwaantje to London.

That's the way to go about it, thought Adriaan Mattheus de Jong, who kept himself informed about the whole operation. The consul already had close ties to the British secret service, and had hired a Dutch merchant ship captain, E.H. Schuur, to maintain contact with all Dutch coasters that visited Swedish ports. He passed on the information collected by Schuur to British foreign intelligence, the Secret Intelligence Service (SIS or MI6).

De Jong was unmistakably excited by the whole thing, and enjoyed dipping his toes into espionage. He even more or less looked the part of a secret agent, with his thin, stylish David Niven moustache and a charming smile that never betrayed his true intentions. But his most conspicuous trait was acting fast. Less than a month after De Vries's arrival, almost all messages and requests from the Resistance were going through the Swedish route. And on the return voyages, radio transmitters and other espionage devices were sent to the Netherlands.

For the first six months of 1943, 't Zwaantje could send five people to Sweden on each voyage, usually on board the *Corona*, one of the coasters belonging to Dr Oosterhuis, commanded by Captain Harry Roossien. Young Resistance fighters were sent by way of Stockholm to England for military training, so that they could be dropped back into the Netherlands well trained and with the most up-to-date transmission equipment. Couriers, too, arrived in Sweden with priceless information about the situation in occupied territory. On its way back to the Netherlands, the *Corona* carried money for the Resistance and sometimes a returning courier. It was a well-oiled organisation, which ran much more smoothly than the reception and support offered to Engelandvaarders. Those young men who had succeeded in escaping from the Netherlands had to chop wood in Swedish work camps for ten, twelve, or fourteen months before they were finally sent on to England to join the Allied forces.

The Swedish route ran into trouble when Captain F.J.M. Aben came to Stockholm. He said he was tired of looking on passively and wanted to do the same thing with his ship, the *Excelsior*, that Roossien was doing – to become an active participant, transporting people. There was nothing he wouldn't do. Of course, he added, he did expect payment. And when the people he took on board were especially valuable to the Resistance, he wanted some kind of danger money.

At first, consul De Jong played for time while collecting intelligence on Aben and asking the British secret service for advice. They were not entirely opposed to making use of the Groningen captain, but did recommend that Aben be kept in the dark about the ins and outs of the Swedish route. More alarming news came from Dr Oosterhuis in Delfzijl, who informed the consul by courier that Jos Aben had, for a time, belonged to the NSB, the Dutch Nazi party.

When Aben remained insistent, De Jong took a big risk. He decided to work with Aben, put him in touch with Dr Oosterhuis, and make him responsible for bringing one of the leaders of the Dutch intelligence service, W.L.Ch. Lindenburg, to Stockholm for a fee of 2,000 guilders.

In fact, Aben was a *Vertrauensmann*, a paid informant of the Nazi intelligence agency, the Sicherheitsdienst (SD). He supplied the SD with information about the people he took to Sweden, receiving bonuses from the agency that were many times his usual salary. To camouflage his traitorous role, he transported members of the underground at regular intervals. Many people therefore thought he supported the Resistance. But the opposite was true; he was delivering them straight into the hands of the occupiers. On 23 July 1943, Dr Oosterhuis was arrested in Delfzijl by the SD. The other members of 't Zwaantje also ended up imprisoned in Scheveningen. In the spring of 1944, all these prisoners were condemned to death. However, for reasons that remain unclear, not one of the sentences was carried out. The members of the Resistance group were sent to a German camp, from which they were liberated by Americans at the end of the war.

These arrests led to the permanent closure of the Swedish route. By then, there had been thirty-eight shipments from Delfzijl to England by way of Stockholm. This makes it all the more surprising that – in August 1943, more than a week after the arrest of Oosterhuis and his group – Captain Aben still had the nerve to take Anton van der Waals to Stockholm.

Van der Waals, who had left a trail of destruction in the Dutch underground and informed on at least eighty-three Resistance members, insisted that Aben transport him and him alone, without any other passengers on board. Otherwise he might be recognised, especially by someone in the Resistance. Things had become too hot for him in the Netherlands. 'With growing speed and precision, his description was compiled and distributed,' writes his biographer Auke Kok. 'Even the smallest details – a pimple here, a golden tooth there, his slightly misshapen nose – were well known to those who considered him their archenemy. It was fair for him to assume that dozens of Resistance members were walking around with plans to eliminate him, armed with revolvers, copies of his photograph, and enough hate to strike without hesitation.'

In Stockholm, Captain Aben introduced the traitor to consul General De Jong and to W.A. Gevers Deynoot and W.L.Chr. Lindenburg, the leaders of the Dutch intelligence service. Van der Waals, under the pseudonym of Baron Henk van Lynden, explained that he was trying to contact London because he planned to blow up a number of ammunition depots and the lock near Maasbracht. He was out of luck; Gevers Deynoot had noble blood, and decided to check the lists of aristocratic families to find out exactly who this so-called baron was. Van der Waals then admitted, without batting an eyelid, that he had falsely assumed the title 'baron' and refused to say who he really was.

He stayed in Stockholm for a few more days, in a residence for staff of the Dutch diplomatic mission, but soon asked Aben if he could be taken back to Delfzijl. He sensed that the secret service men were suspicious, and decided his mission had failed. Back in the Netherlands, he went on using his special talent for betrayal.

Captain F.J.M. Aben was sentenced to twenty years' imprisonment in 1950 for betraying Engelandvaarders and passing on intelligence to the Germans. Anton van der Waals was sentenced to death, and Queen Juliana rejected his application for a royal pardon. On 26 January 1950, that most notorious of Dutch traitors was shot dead on Waalsdorpervlakte, a clearing in the dunes near The Hague where hundreds of members of the Dutch Resistance had been killed by the Germans.

A year after the war, Adriaan Mattheus de Jong was nominated for a medal for his many accomplishments in the Second World War. This led to the ministries in The Hague receiving complaints about De Jong's actions in wartime. The government asked the Van Rappard Commission to investigate De Jong's involvement with the reception of Engelandvaarders, the Dutch intelligence service, and the purchasing centre charged with providing for Dutch refugees in Sweden.

The commission released its report with remarkable speed, in September 1946. The conclusion was that De Jong had 'certainly not been lacking in dedication', and that almost all the witnesses interviewed in Stockholm had praised his great appetite for work, but that he had made 'serious errors of policy' in his work with the emigrants and as a representative of the Dutch intelligence service. His approach as the head of the purchasing centre had been more successful, but that did not change the fact that his actions as a consul had been rash. He had not kept adequate records; he had lost the receipts, so to speak, and could no longer account for all his spending. He did not appear to have embezzled money – on the contrary, he had sometimes paid out of his own pocket – but he couldn't account for all the payments to Engelandvaarders staying in the work camps.

The foreign minister – still Van Kleffens – accepted the conclusion that the consul had acted too fast and too rashly, and added that he had shown too much personal initiative.

Adriaan Mattheus de Jong was furious. Throughout the war, he had run himself ragged trying to help hundreds, if not thousands, of people, and this was the thanks he got. He requested an immediate discharge from the service, which was granted on 1 January 1947.

That same day, the Dutch consulate general in Stockholm was closed, and the consular work was transferred to the embassy.

But the Dutch authorities were not yet finished with De Jong. He was summoned to The Hague to appear before a committee of inquiry into wartime government policy on 3 and 4 March 1949. During the long hearing he faced numerous accusations, to which his answer was, 'Necessity knows no law.'

He explained that he had sent the very first Engelandvaarders on a route leading through Moscow, Vladivostok, Japan, and the Dutch East Indies. Flying directly to England would have been too risky and too expensive (mainly the latter). The first group, thirty to forty young men, had gone by way of Japan to Batavia, from where they had travelled by sea to London. De Jong did not mention that the route had been recommended to him by the former ambassador to the Baltic states, L.P.J. de Decker. Nor did he say a word about the visas he had posted to Polish and Lithuanian Jews. He kept De Decker completely out of the spotlight. But he did note that the route through Moscow and Vladivostok had become unusable after the Japanese attack on Pearl Harbor.

His account of his own actions was very lucid. One day, he told the committee, he had been summoned by the Dutch envoy in Stockholm, Dr G.A. Scheltus. The envoy had asked about certain things the consul had done in great haste: 'Mr De Jong, can you square those acts with your conscience and justify them to God?' De Jong had replied, 'I'm awfully sorry, Your Excellency. My country is at war, and I feel I owe this to my homeland. Then my conscience doesn't come into it, so I can't be in conflict with it. We've too often had no choice but to do things that don't exactly sit well with your conscience.'

At the end of the hearing, he made one last remark: 'If you don't do anything, you won't make any mistakes.'

23

An overlooked date

Studying all the documents about Adriaan Mattheus de Jong, I picture a consul general caught between what was possible and what was allowed. Of course De Jong made mistakes, but his goal was always to get the most out of the escape routes.

'We've too often had no choice but to do things that didn't exactly sit well with your conscience.'

This statement by De Jong to the committee of inquiry keeps coming back to me.

One morning, I reach for a folder I first saw in Vilnius fourteen months earlier and see, to my astonishment, that this secret file from the Lithuanian state archives contains a crucial date I have completely overlooked.

There had always been something strange about the documents from Vilnius; at first they were promised and even shown to me, but I couldn't obtain any copies. I was offered the opportunity to see them by the Lithuanian vice-minister of foreign affairs, Mantvydas Bekešius – a nice guy, only thirty-five years old, enthusiastic, open-hearted, and a member of the centrist labour party, Darbo, which has some populist tendencies but is staunchly pro-European. I spent an entire morning talking to him in Vilnius. In perfect, melodious English, Bekešius said it was time to stop suppressing the truth about what happened in Lithuania during the war. He promised me full disclosure

of the Lithuanian side of the Curaçao visa affair, although he added
that 'the Lithuanian side' is a concept open to interpretation. When
Jan Zwartendijk arrived in Kaunas in 1938 to run the Philips office
and applied for a residence permit, he went to the government of the
independent Republic of Lithuania. When he was appointed consul,
the national security service conducted a routine security vetting,
even though by then Lithuania was already in the Soviet sphere of
influence. When he issued visas to Jewish refugees, the NKVD was
keeping an eye on him. When he left Lithuania, he needed an exit visa
from the occupying power: the Soviet Union.

To make certain that I really would receive all the information,
minister Bekešius proposed not to request the file himself but to ask
Emanuelis Zingeris, a Jewish member of parliament, to request the
documents and send me copies.

I had met Zingeris the day before, in the company of Edith and
Rob Zwartendijk: an emotional man, born before the war. His mother
had been one of the very few Lithuanian Jews to survive the conflict.
She came from Kaunas, was eighteen years old when the war broke
out, was interned in the Ninth Fort, and, a year later, was transferred
to Stutthof, the first Nazi concentration camp outside Germany. She
always had a smile on her face, and was punished for it in Stutthof
by the SS guards, who felt any Jewish woman in the camp should be
filled with despair. After all, they don't smile on death row, do they?
Her indestructible optimism got her through her ordeal in the camp,
but when she returned to Kaunas she was arrested by the NKVD. The
Soviet agents argued that, since no Jews had come out of the camps
alive, she must be a German spy. Zingeris told the whole story to
me, Rob, and Edith, whose hands he held the whole time because his
mother had undoubtedly gone to school with her in Kaunas. This was
the man who took responsibility for having all the documents sent to
me, and I had the fullest confidence he would do so.

Four days later, Faina Kukliansky showed me the copy of the file
during intermission at a concert in the former Jewish grammar school
in Vilnius. Emanuelis Zingeris, overcome with emotion, had come

down with a serious case of flu, but he had wanted to make sure the file would reach me anyway, so he entrusted it to Faina, the leader of the Jewish community in Lithuania. Since the intermission was fairly long, Faina had more than enough time to translate the main passages from the files for me. But she hadn't had time to make copies of all the documents. She promised to do so the next day, so that I would have the complete file before leaving Lithuania.

But the copies never arrived – not even when I sent reminders from Amsterdam – two, three, four times. I asked the Dutch ambassador to Lithuania, Bert van der Lingen, for help. When he contacted Faina, she finally confessed in embarrassment that the file had gone missing. She had left it lying around somewhere that evening after the concert, and then it was gone. Or ... well, she didn't want to accuse anyone ... but maybe someone had deliberately walked off with it when her back was turned.

It took another twelve months before ambassador Van der Lingen was able to send me a new copy of the file. He'd had to go through the entire hierarchy again, and, to make matters worse, deputy minister Bekešius's party had lost the elections. Darbo had plummeted from twenty-seven seats to two in the wake of a corruption scandal, and Mantvydas Bekešius had not returned to government.

I started to wonder if there was more to those papers than met the eye. But once I finally got a hold of the file, I couldn't figure out at first what could be so significant. There were various reports showing that the NKVD distrusted Erni Zwartendijk more than Jan. Other than that, it seemed to me there was nothing of special interest, except perhaps for the black bowtie and snow-white dress shirt worn by consul Zwartendijk in his identification photos. That must have struck the Soviet agents as rather decadent.

The NKVD dossier includes samples of a Curaçao visa issued by consul Zwartendijk, and a handwritten visa from consul Sugihara.

The words of the Dutch visa are stamped in green ink; only the number, date, and signature are written by hand. The opening words of the Japanese visa are also stamped, in bluish-purple ink.

Sugihara had apparently followed Zwartendijk's lead, and had a stamp made, partly in English and partly in French:

TRANSIT VISA.
Seen for the Journey
through Japan (to Suranam,
Curacao and other Netherlands' colonies.)
Consul du Japon à Kaunas.

These words were followed by the usual seven columns of Japanese characters.

The two visas were issued on the same day to the same person: Jankiel-Mendel Grzebiułka, a widower. The photograph in his travel document shows him with his son, who apparently travelled with him. The date of issue is handwritten on the Dutch visa and stamped on the Japanese one: '23 VIII 1940'.

I have leafed through the file dozens of times; dozens of times I've looked at the visa and grinned to see the misspelled word 'Suranam'. But now, for the first time, I notice the date: 23 August 1940.

But by this time the Dutch consulate had been closed for three weeks, hadn't it? And surely Sugihara would have been busy packing his bags that Friday 23 August, even if he did manage to keep the Japanese consulate open until the 28th?

In the late afternoon of 6 August, Zwartendijk had taken his son to the courtyard behind the Philips office. He had invited his employees, De Haan and Van Prattenburg, to join him as he burned all the consulate's papers and paraphernalia: the archives, the list of visas issued to Jews, and the stamps. After 6 August, so the story went, no hint of the rescue operation remained; all the physical evidence had been destroyed.

But what do I see on the visa that Jan Zwartendijk had issued on 23 August 1940? Three stamps! First, the green one with the note in French. Second, the round green stamp with the coat of arms of the Netherlands encircled by the words CONSULATE OF THE NETHERLANDS *

KAUNAS. Third, the stamp beneath J. Zwartendijk's signature: 'Consul des Pays-Bas a.i.'.

He had apparently kept a separate set, duplicates of the actual stamps, with which he went on issuing visas throughout the month of August.

The Dutch visa has a handwritten number: 180. By the time Zwartendijk closed the consulate on 3 August, he had written 2,139 visas. But this visa, dated 23 August, is numbered 180. The recipient, Jankiel-Mendel Grzebiułka, is not to be found on Sugihara's list. I think '180' refers to the number of visas issued by Zwartendijk after the Dutch consulate closed. The recipients of those 180 visas are not on any list, including Sugihara's. So to the list of 2,139 visas, we must add at least 180 more.

Where Zwartendijk issued these visas I do not know. Maybe in the lounge of the Metropolis Hotel, a well-known meeting place for diplomats. (Sugihara became a guest there on 28 August.) Or maybe back at the Philips office after all. Or at Markus, the Jewish pastry shop across the street, where they had such delicious ice cream, and where, in front of the left side of the counter, there were two tables and four chairs …

So Zwartendijk's motive in closing the consulate early was obviously not to play it safe. On the contrary, he took great risks and went on issuing visas, in utter secrecy, until just before his departure. It's no coincidence that the visas in the NKVD file were issued on 23 August. If the Russian secret service ever needed any dirt on Zwartendijk, they had proof that the consul had gone beyond his mandate, continuing to issue visas almost three weeks after the Dutch consulate was closed by order of the Soviets. That would have been plenty of justification for arresting him.

And suddenly I realise something else. Edith told me that in the second week of August she and her brother, Jan, had stayed with a farmer and his wife about one hundred kilometres from Kaunas. Jan, too, made a written note of a two-week stay in the countryside, because his father

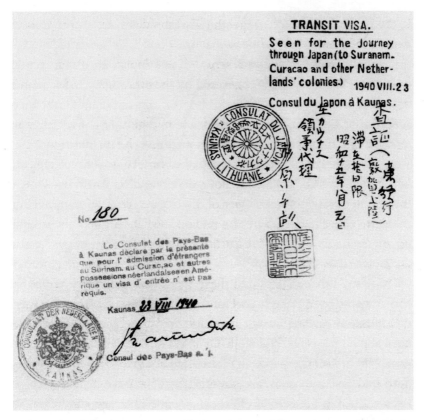

Visas issued on 23 August 1940 by consul Zwartendijk and consul Sugihara,
from the secret Lithuanian file.

felt the city was becoming too dangerous for the children. He didn't
give dates, and I had suspected that Edith was wrong. I had believed
the two-week trip to the country must have taken place in June, right
after the Russian occupation of Lithuania, and not in August, when
they were poised to leave for the Netherlands.

But Edith was right: immediately after their father had burned the
list of names and destroyed the stamps, he had taken Edith and Jan to
a place outside the city. He must have known by then that he would
go on issuing visas and that it would get riskier by the day, since the
consulate had been closed on Soviet orders.

In the Buick Roadmaster, Zwartendijk drove Edith and Jan to a farm along the Memel. The name and address had been given to him by the Stoffels. He felt it would be irresponsible to take Erni and Robbie there, too. Robbie was still bothered by the strawberry mark on his nose, and Erni wanted to stay as close to him as possible. But Erni agreed that Edith and Jan should be sent into hiding, and Jan was terrified that the Russians would do something to his children.

It was a one-and-a-half-hour drive to the farm. They were not stopped once. That wasn't because of their diplomatic plates or the Dutch banner on the right fender. Outside the city, no tanks were visible, no columns, no military transports – and no Russian checkpoints, at least not on the narrow road along the south bank of the Memel.

Zwartendijk dropped off Edith and Jan, slipped the farmer and his wife a hefty sum, and left for home right away, wondering whether he had done the right thing in leaving the children without their parents.

Edith and Jan had travelled one hundred years back in time. The farm had no electricity and no running water. They had to bathe in the river. There wasn't an icebox either; milk and butter were kept in a cellar deep underground, underneath a shady spot in the vegetable garden. Everything they ate came from the garden, the chicken coop, and the rabbit hutch. The farmer and his wife never went into town or even to a nearby village. Their closest neighbour was three kilometres away.

The farmer's wife made clothes herself. In the back of the farmyard, they had wood piled up for the winter, and even in the summer they used a wood-fired oven. They baked their own bread. The curtains of the farmhouse were shut all day. The farmer's wife kept her house and herself spotlessly clean. She was scared of flies and mosquitos, and had an eye out for them whenever she sat at the table. Without warning, she would spring from her chair, and another mosquito would bite the dust. She caught flies by crushing them between her hands, and never missed. Before sitting back down, she would wash her hands at the pump.

Edith and Jan had little way of knowing whether children had ever crawled across the tiled floor of the farmhouse. There were no photographs anywhere in the kitchen or the two bedrooms, but that didn't mean much; apart from a crucifix on the mantel, the walls were bare. They didn't dare to ask questions.

Meals went by in almost total silence. Afterwards, the couple would return to work. They had a cow in the field between the yard and the river, which they pampered like a lamb. They spoke only Lithuanian, with such a strong accent that Edith, who had picked up quite a few words, could make out nothing but *taip* and *ne*, yes and no.

The children stayed on the farm for two weeks. One Saturday, they drew back the curtains and saw that across the river a Russian army camp had been hastily pitched the night before. Hundreds of soldiers and dozens of tanks, trucks, and motorcycles with sidecars.

That happened to be the day their father and mother came by to check on them. When her mother noticed the Russians, the shock gave her hiccoughs.

Their father slipped the farmer's wife a bonus and took off for home, barely giving Edith and Jan time to gather up their things.

Unbeknownst to his children, and probably to Van Prattenburg and De Haan, Jan Zwartendijk had gone on issuing visas for twenty more days. Only Sugihara must have known, since he saw the dates written in pen by the Dutch consul.

Once the children were back in Kaunas, Zwartendijk stopped. Why? At Erni's urgent request? Or did he keep even her in the dark?

By then it was 29 August. Four days later, Edith and Jan went back to school; two days after that, the five of them were on the train, bound for Berlin.

Zwartendijk left Kaunas in silence. No one came to the platform to wave or shout as the train departed. But, like consul Sugihara, he had gone on as long as he could.

Twenty-three years after the war, Sugihara said, 'If I had obeyed my government, I would have been disobedient to God.' Zwartendijk was much too down-to-earth for such pronouncements. All he said – just before his death, to his youngest son – was that he had left Kaunas with a clean conscience.

24

Towards the ends of the east

The sea voyage from Vladivostok to Tsuruga took three to four days, depending on the weather. The large majority of refugees travelled on the *Amakusa Maru*, a small, old passenger ship weighing 2,345 metric tons, built in 1902. Along with its smaller sister vessel, *Harbin Maru*, it maintained the connection between Vladivostok and Tsuruga.

The *Amakusa Maru* made twenty crossings in total with Jewish refugees on board. In the autumn of 1940 and the spring of 1941, almost all its passengers were Jews. No other travellers took it into their heads to go to Japan by rail and ship in those days, aside from a few Engelandvaarders sent that way by consul De Jong.

On the way to Japan, the ship would be filled beyond capacity, sometimes carrying 350 passengers. On the way back, it was almost empty apart from the crew.

The *Harbin Maru* made the voyage four times, also with Jewish refugees as its only passengers.

It was a turbulent crossing, with huge swells on the Sea of Japan. According to eyewitnesses, the waves were an unchanging black. Almost every time, the ships had to battle their way through swells that were metres high. As if that weren't bad enough, the *Amakusa Maru* also tended to roll from side to side. Few passengers could help becoming seasick; the most popular part of the ship was the toilets.

The *Amakusa Maru* in Tsuruga Bay.

Almost all the refugees travelled third class, sleeping on mats on deck. Only a few could afford a place in one of the cabins, which were also packed. From late December to early February, the departures were irregular; when the Vladivostok harbour froze over, the voyage had to be delayed. Most of the refugees reached Japan either just before or just after the winter of 1940–1941.

Jan Krukowski recalls that all the Jewish passengers came on deck when the *Amakusa Maru* left Russian territorial waters. It was one of the last days in February, light snow was falling, an icy wind was whistling in the masts, and suddenly someone started to sing 'Hatikvah'. His voice was joined by a hundred others. Jan Krukowski looked on in surprise:

> My father, who was standing next to me, laid his hand on my shoulder and said, 'Everything will be fine now. From now on, the Japanese emperor will protect us.' All around us was an explosion of joy. I hadn't even known that Japan had an emperor, but I thought he must be a fantastic man. The people around me sang as if their lives depended on it.

That must have been the first moment that the refugees felt some measure of freedom. The Soviet border guards had let them go; they had left dark Europe, which had sought to destroy them, far behind. Now no one would stop them from singing the Hebrew song that seven years later would become the Israeli national anthem:

And onwards, towards the ends of the east,
an eye still gazes towards Zion.

Our hope is not yet lost,
The hope two thousand years old,
To be a free nation in our land,
The land of Zion and Jerusalem.

When Jan Krukowski went ashore in Tsuruga, it was dark and cold. His sister had a fever, and his parents rushed out to find a place to sleep. They checked into the first hotel they found, the Kumagai, where, on a *tatami* (rice straw) mat in the centre of a large room, charcoal was glowing in a *hibachi* brazier. They warmed themselves and drank hot tea, but thought their surroundings were a little strange. There were many heavily made-up women in kimonos who looked different from the waitresses. They heard music in the distance, and laughter. Men came in as if they were regulars, and left an hour later.

Jan, though only eleven years old and not exactly wise beyond his years, began to suspect that they may have been in the kind of hotel that they called a brothel. A few weeks later, he learned the Japanese word: yūkaku. But in Kobe, where they went by train, he also learned that there was a huge difference in status between the prostitutes who worked in a yūkaku and geishas – high-class courtesans – and he thought they had probably stumbled into a geisha house. In any case, they had felt safe there, despite the clients coming and going. In Tsuruga, I learn that the Kumagai Hotel was then at the edge of the red-light district.

When Leo Melamed set foot in Japan, he felt certain the nightmare had come to an end:

> The town of Tsuruga I saw after landing looked like a miniature garden. Most of the houses were built of wood and the doors in the houses looked like they were made of paper. It seemed that people were shovelling the snow with straw hats. My impression about them was that they were very happy and kind. The language sounded as if I were on another planet and I felt that I had really come to a foreign country.

The refugees with prearranged places to stay in Kobe could travel onwards right away. As schoolchildren stared at them, they went down the avenues of Tsuruga in a long line headed for the station. From the docks, it was about a forty-minute walk. Around the halfway point, they passed through the Kehi-jingū, a Shinto shrine. They hesitated a moment before proceeding through the red *torii*, the impressive entrance gate made up of two vertical pillars supporting two horizontal lintels curving upward at both ends. They looked around the sprawling temple grounds, used the bamboo ladle to scoop the temple water from the well, and continued towards the station.

From a doorway opposite the bathhouse, a boy from Tsuruga was watching:

> When I was in 5th grade (10 years old), I think it was in September or October, I saw Jewish people walking in front of the drugstore that used to be in front of the bathhouse. There were young and old, men and women, they were walking from Kehi Shrine to Tsuruga station in line. Their clothes looked normal; they were not rags. But they were not carrying any bags. There was an old lady with white hair; and she was wearing a red dress. Japanese didn't wear bold, solid colours like that, so it surprised me. Another woman had either a fox or raccoon wrapped around her neck, and when I saw its legs it was a little sickening to me. I went home and asked my Grandpa who these people were. He said, 'They are called Jewish and they do not have their own country.' They

walked on, without talking. I do not remember seeing any policeman around them. That was the only time I ever saw them. When I heard what Grandpa had to say, I felt sorry for these people.

The daily newspapers sketched doomsday scenarios. The local newspaper *Fukui* commented, 'There are still some 300,000 refugees wandering around in Europe. Since their only remaining escape route is by rail to Vladivostok and by ship to Tsuruga, the number of refugees coming here is bound to reach excessive proportions.'

In the Japanese state archives, Akira Kitade found telegrams from the national security service to Tsuruga's port authorities, police, and local administration: 'Jews fleeing from the new reality in Europe / are streaming into our country / 300–400 per voyage to Tsuruga.' The service went on to say, 'Total number of refugees / coming this way via Siberia / estimated at 300,000.'

After these alarming messages, you might have expected the Japanese government to hermetically seal the border, but they did not. The local authorities in Tsuruga merely issued an urgent request to the station masters, platform masters, and ticket sellers to give the refugees clear instructions ('keep to the left while in the queue') and effective assistance.

After a complaint from the staff that the refugees were asking so many questions they fogged up the ticket windows, the local authorities issued a directive to clean the windows once an hour.

I visit the Port of Humanity Tsuruga Museum, where I hear that the name should actually be spelled 'Port of Humanity *Tsuruga Muzeum*', the Polish way. It is housed in the former customs office, a European-style building with a red roof that looks completely authentic but is a stone-for-stone reconstruction. The original building was razed in the American bombing of 1945.

I had pictured Tsuruga as a sleepy port town far from Tokyo, dreaming away on a bay behind mountain ranges, difficult to reach. I discovered the opposite was true. In two hours, the Shinkansen took

me from Tokyo to Maibara, where I changed to the Osaka–Kyoto–
Tsuruga Special Rapid Service, which takes less than an hour to reach
its terminus.

Thanks to this railway connection, Tsuruga blossomed. After the
completion of the Trans-Siberian Railway, Japanese travel agencies
advertised that it was possible to go to Berlin or Paris almost entirely
by land. The train to Tsuruga was dubbed the Eurasia International
Transfer Train. The Japanese also hoped that wealthy Russians would
come from Moscow to visit Tokyo. In June 1911, the *Houzan Maru*
entered the harbour of Tsuruga with the first seventy-seven Russian
tourists on board. But Tsuruga's heyday did not last long. Before
Tokyo and Kyoto could become popular destinations, the First World
War broke out, followed by the Russian Civil War.

In 1920, Japanese naval vessels brought passengers of a very
different sort to Tsuruga: worn-out, malnourished Polish orphans
who had roamed the Siberian taiga for years. Thousands of Polish
labourers had been forced to work on the Trans-Siberian Railway.
After its completion, they had stayed in Siberia with their families, but
when the Russian Revolution broke out in 1917, they were trapped
between the warring sides. Polish settlements were burned to the
ground and their inhabitants murdered; children fled and wandered
the boreal forests alone or in small bands. Anna Bielkiewicz – born
in Siberia, the daughter of a Polish railway engineer – wanted to
help these half-wild orphans. She founded a rescue committee, and
arranged for 770 of them to be sent to Tsuruga.

At the museum, greatly enlarged photos and newspaper articles
tell the story of the Polish orphans; the ground floor is dedicated
entirely to their story. Director Akinori Nishikawa, accompanied by
an interpreter, shows me around. In the autumn of 1921, 370 orphans
left for the United States. That same year, the four hundred other
children, finally restored to health and vigour, were sent on a Japanese
ship to Danzig (present-day Gdansk).

Twenty years later, much larger groups of Poles arrived in
Tsuruga; this time, they were Jews. The entire upper level of the

museum is devoted to their arrival, with photos, documents, and explanatory texts about the escape route that was mapped out by consuls Zwartendijk and Sugihara.

When the museum opened in 2008, the keeper of the Tsuruga city records, Takaharu Furue, sent out an appeal for eyewitness accounts of the events of 1940–1941. He collected thirty testimonies, some in writing, some on audiotape, and some on video. These can be read, heard, and viewed in the museum. I received an English translation of the brief accounts, which were also read aloud to me by the interpreter.

All the testimonials came from men and women who were children when the Polish Jews arrived. The first thing that surprised them was the refugees' clothing. They wore thick, dark winter clothes in September and October, when the climate in Tsuruga is still warm and pleasant. And despite being international migrants, they had little or no baggage; that, too, surprised the children. Japanese onlookers noticed their communal spirit; the Jews had little, but they shared everything:

> As the Jewish people walked from the port to Tsuruga station, they were sharing an apple by taking a bite of an apple and passing it on to the next person. As a child I was told never to eat outside or especially while walking, so this story stuck with me. The Jewish people's clothing was all dark with hats. They were wearing coats because it was winter.
>
> I noticed about twenty foreigners were passing in front of the window, and obviously my eyes went to a child. Everyone had very tired-looking clothes, but I remember this child was walking towards Kehi Shrine, with no shoes, while eating an apple. I suppose they were hungry, and very poor.

In the autumn of 1904, most of the refugees were able to travel on to Kobe without delay. But the shelters filled up, and in the spring of 1941, the Polish Jews had to wait in Tsuruga for days, sometimes weeks. They were put up in pensions or *ryokans* (traditional Japanese inns), in private homes, or in the city's only hotel. The locals began to notice that the refugees' clothes gave off a musty odour and that both the men and the women were starting to smell offensive. So the mayor decided to open the bathhouse to the Jews, free of charge. While they were using it, it was closed to the locals. According to eyewitnesses, the water in the baths turned black. This was said to show how long and hard their journey must have been.

In one display case, a silver lady's watch glittered. Akinori Nishikawa mentioned, more or less offhandedly, that the Jews offered their watches, jewellery, and precious stones for sale to the local jeweller. When they were asked why they were selling such beautiful and personally meaningful possessions, they would open their mouth and point inside; they needed money for food.

'Then they can't have been paid much for them,' I venture. Akinori Nishikawa, a good-looking man in his forties in a spotless blue suit, gives me a puzzled look. The idea that some people profit from others' misery doesn't seem to have occurred to him.

Leaning in closer to the display case, I notice that the watch is damaged on one side.

In June 1945, Nishikawa tells me, American B-29s dropped a carpet of firebombs onto the city. All the wooden houses in Tsuruga went up in flames; 80 per cent of the city was destroyed. The heat melted one side of the watch.

The bombing also affected my story in a different way. Japanese customs officials and border police kept close track of who landed in Tsuruga. The ships' registers and passengers lists of the *Amakusa Maru* and *Harbin Maru* were among the records kept in the Custom House. Not one Jewish refugee entered Japan through any port but Tsuruga. Those records could have been used to determine exactly how many Jews had been able to flee Europe thanks to a Curaçao visa. But only the papers from October 1940 were preserved. The other records went up in flames in 1945.

In May 1941, mounting international tensions led the Japanese shipping company Kita Nippon Kisen to cancel the line running between

The Japan Tourist Bureau representative, Tatsuo Osako, with a Jewish
refugee aboard the *Amakusa Maru*.

Vladivostok and Tsuruga. The *Amakusa Maru* and the *Harbin Maru*
were confiscated by the Japanese navy and used for troop transports
to occupied Taiwan. From one day to the next, Tsuruga changed back
into a fishing port and a provincial town.

And so it remains to this day. Apart from the trawlers, the only
ships in the harbour are Japanese coast guard frigates. They still bring
the occasional refugee into town, perhaps a North Korean fisherman
who has crossed the Sea of Japan in a rickety little boat bashed by the
waves. But such boat people receive little attention.

On every crossing, the *Amakusa Maru* carried a representative of the
Japan Tourist Bureau, a government organisation. This staff member
wore the uniform of a merchant marine officer. Tatsuo Osako was
twenty-two years old in 1940, when he made his first voyage on the
Amakusa Maru. A handsome young man with a full head of hair, he

enjoyed talking to the passengers and kept a scrapbook in which the passengers wrote friendly messages above, below, or beside their photos. The scrapbook has been preserved; facsimiles of some pages are on display in the *muzeum* in Tsuruga.

On the first page, Vera Harraug, a Jew from Norway, compliments Tatsuo Osako. Henii Hilre, a Jew from Bulgaria, writes an equally warm message. Marie (surname unknown), writing in French, likewise extends a *grand merci*. Toni Altschul ('*Zum Andenken* ['As a souvenir'], 22/3/1941') was a German Jew. Not one of these names is included on the list that Sugihara sent from Prague to the Japanese foreign ministry in Tokyo in 1942. I am now really starting to believe that the number of refugees must have been much greater – and that many of them did not come from Poland.

25

No way forward, no way back

Benjamin Fishoff was unlucky when he arrived in Japan. He was on the *Amakusa Maru* with 350 other Jewish refugees when it entered Tsuruga's harbour on 13 March 1941. Japanese border guards boarded and checked their passports. According to Fishoff, he was one of seventy-two passengers taken aside. All seventy-two had transit visas for Japan but no Curaçao visas.

By the time he had reached the Dutch consulate in Kaunas, he had found it already closed. It was towards the end of August. He was too late to obtain a visa from Zwartendijk, but Sugihara was still at his desk.

The Japanese consul spelled Benjamin's surname 'Fiszof', wrote 'chil' after that, and noted the first name. Benjamin was nearly eighteen, hardly a 'chil[d]'. He had been separated from his parents and brothers while fleeing Poland. Consul Sugihara was not allowed to issue visas to minors, but in this case had made an exception.

Even without a Curaçao visa, Benjamin Fishoff had decided to take the risk. *First Japan*, he told himself, *and then we'll see*. The other refugees taken aside must have thought the same thing. But now, the Japanese authorities insisted that all seventy-two illegal immigrants had to return on the next ship to Vladivostok. That happened to be the very same ship; on 16 March, the *Amakusa Maru* returned to the Soviet Union.

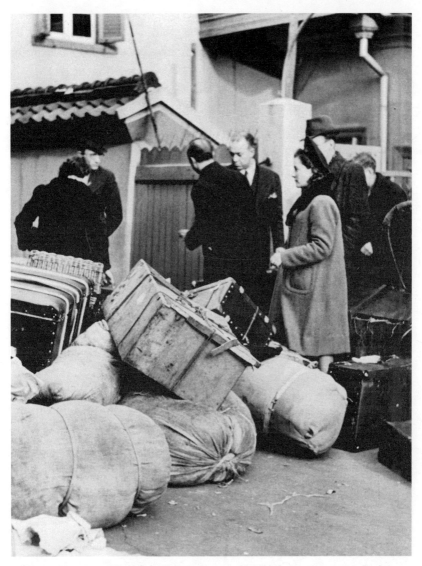

Arrival in Kobe, a photograph by Tetsu Kono for the exhibition *Wandering Jew*.

In Vladivostok, border guards and NKVD agents came on board and accused the Jews of spying for the Japanese. The seventy-two of them had to stay on board. They feared they would be sent to do forced labour in the Siberian gulag.

By this time, the passengers allowed into Tsuruga had spoken to the representative of Jewcom in Kobe, who had wasted no time in contacting the Dutch consul in Kobe, Nicolaas de Voogd.

Unlike Zwartendijk, De Jong, and Sugihara, Nicolaas de Voogd would go on to have an illustrious diplomatic career. Towards the end of the war, Lord Mountbatten attached him to his staff in Ceylon as an adviser on East Asian affairs. In April 1950, six months after Mao Zedong's communist takeover, De Voogd became the first Dutch *chargé d'affaires* in China. His first posting as ambassador was to Bangkok, his last to Tokyo. From 1960 onwards, he had the task of trying to mend the damage done to the Dutch–Japanese relationship by the Second World War.

At the foreign ministry in The Hague, De Voogd is still remembered as a skilled diplomat who could break through walls of pent-up emotion by understanding the context of every individual he spoke to. He was able to do that thanks to his thorough understanding of the languages, cultures, religions, customs, and traditions of the countries where he worked.

Nicolaas de Voogd had begun his career as a ship's radio officer. He had expected a future on the high seas, aboard a rusty freighter. At the age of sixteen, he had been a fanatical radio operator; after his final secondary school exams (focusing on science and maths), he took a two-year course to become a radio officer. Under pressure from his father, who saw a physician in him rather than a sailor, he then went on to study medicine. Whether it was his imagination at work or a microbe, he fell ill, and was advised not to work so hard anymore and to get plenty of fresh air. This gave him the chance to pursue his own dream, and he became a radio officer for the shipping company of Rotterdamsche Lloyd.

He would have spent the rest of his life plying back and forth between Rotterdam and the Far East, if one of the passengers hadn't noticed the ease with which he picked up languages. Japanese characters came as naturally to him as Morse code. Nico de Voogd was persuaded to try of studying Oriental languages at the University of Leiden for a year. Five years later, he received his diploma in Japanese, with a minor in Mandarin. He joined the Interpretation Service, a department of the foreign ministry established early in the century as a source of specialised interpreters for the diplomatic and consular missions in China and Japan. Even so, he decided that wherever he served he would set up a 'radio room' with four or five short-wave receivers.

From 1927 to 1930, he worked as an interpreter in Her Majesty's legation to Tokyo. After six months' leave in the Netherlands, he returned to Japan in 1931 for readerships at the Universities of Kyoto and Osaka. He spent four happy years in that academic setting and perfected his Japanese. Then he returned to the Interpretation Service, becoming a second-class interpreter with the personal title of consul at the consulate general in Kobe. He was assigned a house, large by Japanese standards, and his radio room proved its value when the international situation rapidly deteriorated and, after the German invasion, communication with the Netherlands became nearly impossible. The messages he picked up from Dutch and British vessels gave him an impression of what was going on in Europe.

In 1940, the Interpretation Service had eleven members. It was a small, elite group that included Robert van Gulik, the sinologist, Orientalist, diplomat, musician (he played the *guqin*, the Chinese zither), expert on ancient China, illustrator, and author of the Judge Dee crime novels, which he wrote first in English and later in Dutch. Van Gulik interpreted for the embassy in Tokyo. He, too, had a great diplomatic career ahead of him; in 1965, he would succeed Nicolaas de Voogd as ambassador in Japan.

Those two brilliant young men began their service in the Far East before the Second World War broke out. Their superiors in Japan were Jean Charles Pabst, an authoritarian officer with a heart condition who would die six weeks after the Japanese invasion of Pearl Harbor, and Jan Pennink, a former trade commissioner interested only in lucrative business deals.

Major General Pabst; ret., the Dutch envoy, had been in Tokyo since 1923. He had been appointed to the post because he had served as military attaché there from 1910 to 1916. A bachelor, he led a secluded life in his official residence, a magnificent country house in the English style, and was exposed to the Japanese as rarely as a rear admiral is to deep-sea fish. In his diplomatic work, he was tentative and insecure – until he made an abrupt decision to rattle the sabre, usually at just the wrong moment. He never asked Van Gulik for advice, because he despised 'scholars or pseudo-scholars who turn up their nose at the real work'. When the Second World War broke out, he was sixty-seven years old, had eye and heart trouble, and was eagerly anticipating retirement. But when he requested it, it was denied, because minister Van Kleffens could not find a suitable replacement in the short term.

The envoy did not get along with the consul general in Kobe either. But that wasn't entirely his fault. Consul Pennink was a highly strung man, unequal to the strain of living in a country with an unfamiliar language and culture. In fact, Pennink loathed everything Japanese and could not look a Japanese person in the eye without feeling disgust. That may have been understandable under the political circumstances of the time, but it was not a convenient trait for a man in his position. Pennink shunned Pabst and began to manage his affairs on his own.

The port of Kobe was Japan's centre of foreign trade; all the country's exports to the Dutch East Indies went through the city. Japanese bicycles, sewing machines, and cheap cameras were sent to Batavia and Surabaya by the thousands. Pennink negotiated directly with the colonial officials in the Dutch East Indies, and secured import and export permits. Batavia was his business. He left all other consular matters to Nicolaas de Voogd, jeering that the son of a pastor from Zeeland must know how to deal with souls in need.

But Nicolaas de Voogd felt no urge to distance himself from his roots. Everywhere he was sent, he brought his portable church organ with him, like the pastor's son he was. No matter what part of Asia he found himself in, he could not go a day without Bach.

Consul De Voogd's family in Kobe.

When the seventy-two Polish Jews were sent back because they had no Curaçao visas, Nathan Gutwirth asked De Voogd for help. Nathan had left Lithuania on 8 December 1940 and crossed over to Tsuruga on the last boat before winter fell. Before the year was out, he approached De Voogd in Kobe. Nathan had Dutch nationality, and explained to De Voogd all the ins and outs of the Curaçao visa.

He and his wife, Nechama Gutwirth, had found temporary lodging in Kobe. Just before leaving Lithuania, she had been issued her own Dutch passport by De Jong in Stockholm – by post.

In March, they were informed that seventy-four refugees had been sent back. Not seventy-two, as Fishoff later recalled, but seventy-four. Nathan made a beeline for the Dutch consulate with his friend Lev Sternheim, Peppy's brother:

> The consul, Mr de Voogd, received us very cordially, but after listening to our story and hearing our request for a false Curaçao declaration, he replied that he could do nothing without the consent of the Netherlands ambassador in Tokyo. Realising that this would result in a refusal, I was fortunate enough to have with me a letter from Mr de Decker,

the ambassador in Riga, in which he opted for the Curaçao declaration (as we called it). After reading the letter and thinking, Mr de Voogd replied, 'This is sufficient for me.' Needless to say we were relieved, and thanked G-d that the way had been opened to rescue these people. In that moment Mr de Voogd showed great humanity. After all, he took the risk of a reprimand from his ambassador.

They had to hurry. The Japanese captain of the *Amakusa Maru* had promised not to make the seventy-four passengers disembark in Vladivostok, but he did demand speedy confirmation of their status by radio. Nathan Gutwirth and Lev Sternheim visited the Dutch consulate late on a Friday afternoon, not long before closing time. The consulate would do no business for the next three days, because of the first day of spring, a Japanese national holiday.

But De Voogd gave Nathan and Lev hundreds of sheets of stationery with the official letterhead: 'CONSULATE OF THE NETHERLANDS'. He told them to type the declaration on the blank sheets and, as soon as they were done, to come to De Voogd's house for his signature and the consular stamp. A hundred sheets, so that if they made an occasional error, they wouldn't have to return for more paper. But he did ask them to give back the leftover blank sheets, so that they wouldn't end up in the wrong hands.

Nathan and Lev hurried off to the office of the Jewish community, where three men stayed up all night to type the declaration on the sheets. The Curaçao visas, signed by Nicolaas de Voogd, went into the satchel of a representative of the Committee to Aid the Victims of War who was headed for Tsuruga. The rail journey from Kobe to Tsuruga took three hours. At the shipping company office, the captain was able to reach the *Amakusa Maru* by radio. When the ship arrived in Vladivostok the next day, the captain informed the Russian authorities that he could take the seventy-four refugees back to Tsuruga, because they had been issued the visas required for admission to Japan.

In the archive of the consulate general in Kobe, kept in the National Archives in The Hague, I found the list of the seventy-four Polish Jews issued with Curaçao visas. This list was made on 18 March 1941, and is consistent with all the information provided by Nathan Gutwirth. The only surprising thing is the signature: 'Tokyo, The Netherlands Minister, J.C. Pabst.'

Upon reflection, consul De Voogd had apparently felt it wiser to ask for his superior's approval after all – and Pabst had not refused.

The archive of the legation in Tokyo, also kept in the National Archives in The Hague, includes a furious letter from the Dutch envoy. In it, Pabst accuses De Voogd of having vastly overstepped the limits of his authority. He complains that the consul should never have become involved in an affair that could have had serious consequences for the already tense relations between the Netherlands and Japan. But when push came to shove, it was the envoy who signed his name under the list of visas issued. And not the consul!

Pabst was a true military man. A lieutenant who blundered would face his wrath, but he, the general, would take final responsibility.

Pabst let De Voogd know that he could expect consequences. Nathan Gutwirth was right to praise the consul, later, for 'the enormous risks' he had run. But, in the end, Pabst took no disciplinary measures.

There was another fact that Nathan Gutwirth left out of his account of these events, again to avoid creating difficulties for De Voogd. The man at the shipping company office who contacted the *Amakusa Maru* by radio was not the representative of the Committee to Aid the Victims of War, but the consul himself. De Voogd communicated with the Japanese ship's radio officer in Morse code.

Nathan Gutwirth would remain in touch with De Voogd until the latter's death in 1977. In all their face-to-face meetings and correspondence, as well as in his memoirs, he always addressed him as 'Mr' De Voogd. He showed equal respect for 'Mrs' De Voogd.

Mr and Mrs De Voogd had a striking similarity in their backgrounds.

GEZANTSCHAP
DER
NEDERLANDEN.

The Netherlands Legation hereby certifies that the
undermentioned persons all of Polish nationality do not
need a Netherlands visa in order to proceed to the
Netherlands West-Indies (Curaçao, Surinam, etc.)

1. Beiler Abraham Mojzesz
2. Goldberg Chaim
3. Gastner Hirsz
4. Tanienter Szaja
5. Seroka Szymon
6. Ruchlejmer Izak
7. Szwarcman Szlama Uszer
8. Lewin Szepsel
9. Lew Mejer Dawid
10. Altszuler Antonina
11. Krakowski Wolf Abram
12. Mendelson Manus
13. Arabczyk Beniamin
14. Guberman Efraim
15. Guberman Sara
16. Ulrych Baruch
17. Wajngarten Jakub Berek
18. Goldberg Boruch Icko
19. Wajntraub Josek
20. Fiszow Chil
21. Bryzman Szymon
22. Znamirowski Symcha
23. Znamirowska Leonia
24. Znamirowski Izrael
25. Mandelbaum Berko Jakub
26. Garden Izrael Mojasz
27. Podchlebnik Szlama
28. Goldszmidt Henoch
29. Kozlowski Beniamin
30. Sezenen Jecheskiel
31. Celbron Boruch Mojsze
32. Mlotek Abram
33. Rubinstein Daniel
34. Sztiglic Izrael
35. Szepsenbaum Rytla
36. Zaulner Aron
37. Bursztynarz - Abramczyk Michel

38. Bursztynarz - Abramczyk Jankiel
39. Goldberg Szmuilo Morduch
40. Korentajer Szymon
41.   "   Emma
42.   "   Felicja
43. Fuks Abram
44.   " Szajna Hendla
45. Kalisz Szymon
46.   "   Icchok
47. Epsztein Abram
48. Bimbad Szloma
49. Podchlebnik Efraim
50. Finkelsztajn Benjamin
51. Sztycer Nachman Boruch
52. Jakubowicz Moszek Lajzer
53. Langer Mozes Izak
54. Szejnbaum Lejb
55. Sznajder Nachman
56. Susel Sosia Mariam
57 Prokosz Szmul
58.   "   Perla
59. Kandel Abram Josef
60. Lewi Josef Chaim
61. Apsztajn Salomon
62. Apsztajn Sara
63. Berezowski Zelezniak Oskar
64. Berezowski Zelezniak Maria
65. Zalc Jakub
66. Schmert Maks
67. Pinkus Henryk
68. Fajgenblum Cyrla
69. Warhaftig Ignacy
70. Kozlowski Rubin Josef
71. Margolis Izrael
72. Gerichter Szaja
73. Szechter Dawid Samuel
74. Szymkin Jozef.

Tokyo, March 18th, 1941.

The Netherlands Minister,

J. C. Pabst.

The list of seventy-four names, signed by J.C. Pabst, the
Dutch envoy in Tokyo.

Nicolaas de Voogd was a pastor's son from the island of Noord-Beveland. In 1930, he married Amarintia de Vries, the daughter of a pastor from the neighbouring island of Zuid-Beveland.

Nicolaas and Amarintia de Voogd had two sons, both born in Kobe, Jan in 1932 and Bert in 1934. Both emigrated to Australia, and were not hard to find. Jan lives in Sydney; Bert, in Bairnsdale in the state of Victoria.

Jan de Voogd remembers that in 1941 his father took the night train from Kobe 'on business'. It had to do with the transit visas. He helped 'at least two hundred' Jews obtain travel documents and, according to Jan, 'usually without the knowledge' of the ambassador'. When I ask him why his father did it, he sends me a copy of a letter he sent to his brother, Bert, in January 1975.

> Dear Bert,
>
> You asked me recently why our father helped so many people without making it public, and why he was willing to defy rules and laws for that purpose. Our father conducted himself according to a system of values. He had three rules he lived by:
>
> 1. 'Try to see it from someone else's point of view.'
> 2. 'Have more respect for the spirit of the law than for the letter.'
> 3. 'Always be generous in your dealings with people.'
>
> Yours sincerely, your brother Jan

Mrs De Voogd made her own personal commitment to the refugees whose journey brought them to Kobe. In particular, her heart went out to the Nussbaum family: Chaim and his wife, Rachel, who was expecting a baby soon, their two children, and his brother, Samuel. They had arrived in Kobe exhausted. Chaim Nussbaum told Mrs De Voogd something she barely thought about at the time, but that would later come back to her vividly: he was born near Auschwitz in 1909.

Chaim left Poland at a young age and went to Scheveningen, where he became friends with Nathan Gutwirth. They were constantly talking football, and kept up the conversation even in wartime. Chaim studied Hebrew in Leiden, and in 1939 he left with his wife, children, and brother for Lithuania, where he became the head of the Hebrew department at the Yavneh School.

On Nathan Gutwirth's recommendation, he went to Zwartendijk and Sugihara for three visas on 18 August 1940. Like Gutwirth, they left in good time, taking the Trans-Siberian Express in late November 1940. But they had a more difficult journey than Gutwirth, who left three weeks later, and faced long stops in Siberia, a raging storm during the sea crossing, and poor accommodation in Tsuruga.

Soon after arriving in Kobe, Rachel gave birth. The baby died the same day. Chaim went to the consulate with the news, partly because he didn't know how to report the death officially at Kobe's city hall. Mrs De Voogd sent a capable doctor to Rachel right away, so that at least she would survive the birth. The doctor recommended professional nursing, and Mrs De Voogd obtained the services of a qualified Japanese nurse who had worked in Singapore for years and spoke fluent English. The nurse visited Rachel twice a day, brought her fruit, and made sure that Chaim and Samuel also ate well. Another striking fact: the Japanese doctor and the Japanese nurse declined payment for their help.

Once Rachel had recovered, consul De Voogd set about trying to repatriate Chaim and all other Jewish refugees with a Dutch passport to the Dutch East Indies (present-day Indonesia, then a Dutch colony). That was not so easy, because the governor in the capital city of Batavia (now Jakarta) was unwilling to admit the refugees unless they had already found work in the colony. So jobs had to be found for them before they left Japan.

That wasn't too difficult in Chaim's case; he could work in Batavia as a rabbi. But finding a job for his brother, Samuel, was a good deal harder. Consul De Voogd was ultimately able to arrange a position for Samuel teaching maths at Batavia's modern grammar school.

Nathan Gutwirth had a cousin in Batavia who ran a jewellery company. It took a few weeks to get in touch with him, but then he made an immediate offer to employ Nathan in the family business.

The Elberg family, who had moved to Lithuania from the Dutch province of North Brabant (but whose names are not included on any list), also had trouble finding work. Consul De Voogd had to send quite a few telegrams before he figured out a way to send them to Bandung, another major city in the colony.

It was even harder to make arrangements for Levie Sternheim, who had arrived in Kobe with his mother, Rachel; his sister, Peppy; his brother-in-law, Isaac Lewin; and their young son, Nathan. It was not too hard for De Voogd to obtain entry visas for the United States for Isaac, Peppy, and Nathan, because one of Isaac's brothers had lived in the United States for many years, and was willing to act as financial sponsor and pay an exorbitant price for their residence permits. Isaac went on ahead with his son, Nathan, while Peppy remained in Kobe, because no arrangements had yet been made for her mother and brother to go to the Dutch East Indies. She refused to leave without knowing where Rachel and Levie would end up.

Peppy boarded the boat for San Francisco only after Levie had joined the Royal Netherlands East Indies Army (KNIL). This was the sole opportunity that consul De Voogd had found for him. Levie left for Surabaya, the colony's second city, with his mother, Rachel.

All the refugees who reached the Dutch East Indies – all Jews with Dutch nationality – were arrested by Japanese soldiers in February 1942. Like all the other Dutch nationals in the colony – men, women, and children – they had three-and-a-half years of confinement ahead of them, behind barbed wire in Japanese internment camps. The Japanese, who had treated them with such human kindness in Tsuruga and Kobe, became their oppressors in the Indies.

Chaim Nussbaum was interned in a camp in Java at first, was later moved to another near Singapore, and then became a forced labourer on the Burma Railway, also known as the Death Railway. His wife and brother remained in Java, Rachel in a women's camp, and Samuel in a camp near Batavia.

Long after the war, Nathan Gutwirth decided to make a written record of everything that had happened to him and his wife, Nechama, with the exception of the years in the Japanese internment camp. He was in a men's camp, and Nechama was in a women's camp hundreds of kilometres away. Nathan said, 'I lost my sense of modesty, I had to. And something else, too: three and a half years of my life.'

It's understandable that after the war Nicolaas de Voogd hardly said a word about his efforts. Amarintia, too, remained silent about her experiences in the camp. The Indies route had proved to be the wrong one, and cost some refugees their lives.

Levie Sternheim joined the KNIL, became a Japanese prisoner of war in 1942, and died on 20 May 1943 in a prisoner-of-war camp on the island of Flores. After the war, his remains were reburied in Kembang Kuning Field of Honour, a Dutch war cemetery in Surabaya.

His mother, Rachel Sternheim, spent the full three-and-a-half years in a women's camp in Java. On 1 June 1946, wasted by dysentery, she returned from Batavia to Amsterdam. It took her more than two years to regain her strength, and at the age of sixty-two she moved to the United States to be with her daughter, son-in-law, and grandson.

Chaim Nussbaum returned from Burma a wreck. It took him years to recover from the hardships he had suffered. Chaim made Canada his new homeland, and spent the rest of his life there, working as a rabbi. He died in 1994, not long after publishing his war diary *Chaplain on the River Kwai* – three hundred pages of adversity.

De Voogd had gone to Japan in 1927. He remained there, with a six-month interruption for leave, until 1942, witnessing Japan's transformation into a warlike imperialist nation. He spoke the language as few foreigners did, read the newspapers, and listened to the radio.

All diplomats stationed in Japan observed the struggle – sometimes open, but more often half-concealed – between the civil servants striving for good international relations and the ever more warlike military. Japan claimed the right to become a colonial power; that was no secret after the annexation of Taiwan, Korea, Manchuria, and Shanghai. Why, Japan reasoned, were only the Netherlands, Great Britain, and France allowed to conquer and exploit large parts of Asia? Japan wanted a piece of the action. But within Japan's borders, the mood never turned hostile or xenophobic.

Between 1900 and 1940, Japan had made a huge industrial leap. But the country had to import 90 per cent of its raw materials. It came as no surprise to De Voogd that Japan had its eye on the Dutch East Indies, with its vast oil reserves. But he could hardly have suspected that Japan would unleash a war of civilisations aimed at subjugating and debasing all its conquered peoples, from the Dutch to the Chinese, and from the British to the Koreans.

The Japanese annexation of Asia was barbaric. Both the military and the politicians were flushed with victory, perhaps because the attacks on Malacca, the Philippines, and the US naval base Pearl Harbor on 7 and 8 December 1941 were such a resounding success. Like Hitler's Germany, Japan felt unbeatable. But the country had rushed into conflict on too many fronts at once, and it encountered opposition from too many sides. The war turned into a desperate offensive marked by frustration and brutality.

De Voogd could offer refugees only one alternative to the Dutch East Indies. South Africa was willing to admit around fifty Jewish refugees. But Lev Sternheim, Chaim Nussbaum, and Nathan Gutwirth saw greater short-term opportunities in the Dutch colony, and politely turned down the offer.

On 14 February 1941, De Voogd put his wife and two sons on board the SS *Tjisalak*, a ship of the Java–China–Japan Line, and sent them to the Dutch East Indies – the best possible evidence that he saw no acute threat in the colony. Or did he? A month later, on 22 March 1941, Amarintia de Voogd and her two sons boarded the MS *Poelau Roebiah*, which took them by way of the Panama Canal to Canada. This was at the urging of Nicolaas de Voogd, who had stayed behind in Kobe.

In September 1941, the consul was placed under house arrest by the Japanese authorities. He realised then that Japan was much more aggressive than foreign diplomats had expected and that the Dutch East Indies had been the wrong choice of destination. But by then all the refugees with Dutch nationality had left; it was too late.

Nathan Gutwirth bore no grudge against De Voogd. After the diplomat's death in April 1977, he placed a death notice in the *Nieuw Israëlietisch Weekblad*, a leading Dutch Jewish periodical, on behalf of his whole family:

> In his capacity as Dutch consul in Kobe in the years 1940 and 1941, he saved many Jews. In him, the Jewish people have lost a genuine friend.

Nathan Gutwirth expressed himself in even clearer terms in a letter he sent on 22 August 1992 to the journalist, legal professional, author, and poet Hugo Pos, who was writing an article about Jews for the weekly Dutch magazine *Vrij Nederland*. This letter eventually came into the hands of consul De Voogd's sons in Australia. Gutwirth wrote:

> Judging by my experience, consul Sugihara's role has been somewhat exaggerated. Japan itself deserves a great deal of credit for admitting and accommodating the refugees and not creating difficulties after the term [of the transit visa, twelve days] expired. What still troubles me is that the role of the Dutch authorities is not acknowledged as it should be. It was they who made the operation possible, in the full knowledge that it was a fiction. I will not diminish Mr Sugihara's role, but he took fewer risks than some others, such as the Dutch consul in Kobe, Mr N.A.J. de Voogd, who – without consulting with the Dutch ambassador in Tokyo – made statements that would land him in trouble with both the ambassador and the Japanese authorities. Too little credit is given to ambassador De Decker in Riga and Mr J. Zwartendijk in Kaunas. Without their contributions, nothing would have happened. From time to time, I'm sent books about this period. Most of them focus entirely on personal experiences and do not provide an objective view. In a

sense, that's understandable, because the whole thing was organised by a few people, whose names were kept out of the spotlight as much as possible, since they could have found themselves in trouble with the Russian authorities. To this day, most refugees do not know the names of the people who made all this possible.

Gutwirth had apparently never heard that De Voogd *had*, in fact, consulted with the ambassador.

Nicolaas de Voogd also saw to it that the fifty entry visas pledged by South Africa were issued to Polish Jews. In May 1941, Israel en Syma Oberman, Julian Glass, Jehuda Leib Blum, and Chaim Belfu departed from Kobe for South Africa aboard the *Africa Maru*. The others left that same month, also from Kobe, on board the *Manila Maru*. All of them reached South Africa, and escaped the violence of the war for good.

26

The house with the green shutters in Kobe

It was raining cherry blossoms when Marcel Wejland arrived in Kobe. He loved the city right away, just like he had fallen under the country's spell during the railway journey from Tsuruga on the Sea of Japan to Kobe on the Pacific.

Half a century later, Marcel would describe his stay in Japan as 'a peaceful interlude in our wanderings'. The passage from Vladivostok to Tsuruga had not just brought him from one country to another, but 'turned out to be the transition from one season to another and from one world to a much better one. From a harsh winter to an enchanting spring of sudden cherry blossoms and sweet, doll-like girls in flowery kimonos. It was a passage out of darkness and, finally, into daylight …'

Kobe, with fewer than a million inhabitants, was a city on a human scale against a backdrop of densely forested mountains, a green wall of maple and bamboo. Below, the ships bided their time in the harbour; beyond them was the glitter of the ocean. It was a wonderful city for children, with little alleyways between houses and stairways up the steep slopes – like a Montmartre by the sea.

As soon as Marcel arrived, he enrolled at an American high school run by Methodist missionaries. After the long break in his education, he was raring to go. It was almost like having private tutors; there were only a couple of students in his class. Of course, Marcel still recited from *Pan Tadeusz*, but his biggest challenge was no longer memorising

Jewish refugees in Kobe, Japan, photographed by Tetsu Kono
for the exhibition *Wandering Jew*.

Adam Mickiewicz's poem; rather, it was learning English as fast as he could. Again, Marcel distinguished himself; he was practically fluent by the time he and his parents and sisters stepped onto the ship to Shanghai.

After school, he roamed the streets of Kobe, sketching European-style Gothic Revival houses and Japanese wooden houses, classified by the number of sleeping mats that fitted into a room; there were four-mat and six-mat dwellings. At a casual restaurant he had *yakisoba* (a stir-fried noodle dish), which was so delicious that he never tasted anything like it again. He would observe the Japanese people around him, and they would give him nothing but friendly and curious looks in return.

Jan Krukowski and his parents moved into a hotel room that the three of them had to share with another Polish-Jewish family. Despite the cramped, stifling quarters, they all adjusted to the situation. They knew that in just a few weeks they'd be travelling on, though they had no idea where to. The same thoughts went through the minds of all the refugees: *Just a few more weeks, and we'll be on our way to our new homeland.* Almost everyone hoped it would be the United States. No one expected that some of them would remain in Kobe a whole year, and most of them for more than six months.

The long wait may have bothered some of the adults, but not Marcel Wejland, and not Leo Melamed, who felt like he was on a long vacation:

> In Japan, we weren't refugees anymore but tourists. My parents didn't work. They sometimes found something to do, but they weren't preoccupied with earning a living. We travelled to different places, took the train to Kyoto; I remember the pagodas … In the summer, we went to a holiday resort and went for walks, explored the mountains, visited Buddhist temples, and took snapshots … things like that. Later, of course, we talked about the trials and tribulations of the long exodus. But those months in Japan are also part of the story, and they were delightful. Whoever says otherwise is lying.

Most of the refugees, about 90 per cent, stayed in Kobe. Why not Tokyo, home to all the embassies? Or the much larger port of Yokohama, the place of departure for the ships to Vancouver and San Francisco?

In the Kobe Synagogue, I have a pamphlet pressed into my hand: *The Jews of Kobe* by Tamar Engel, a brief history of the Jews in the city. In 1858, Kobe became one of the first ports open to foreigners. Right away, it was flooded with merchants and diplomats; six countries, including the Netherlands, opened consulates there. The foreigners had beautiful houses built, mostly in wood and stone in the Victorian neo-Gothic style. But there were also German-style timbered houses, and houses with dark-green shutters. The Japanese called them *ijinkan*, 'foreign houses', and they were all in the district of Kitano, high in the city near the mountains. Alongside the Dutch, Danish, French, British, and American merchants, a striking number of

German businesspeople settled in Kobe. The group included German Jews, who were joined by Sephardic Jews from Iraq and Iran, and Ashkenazim from Russia.

The Jews were welcome guests in Japan after a Jewish banker from New York City, Jacob Schiff, lent the Japanese state $200 million, about half of what was needed to finance the 1904–05 Russo-Japanese War. Not one European bank had been willing to lend Japan money to purchase naval vessels. After the Japanese victory, Jacob Schiff was given a hero's welcome in Tokyo, and became the first foreigner to be awarded the Order of the Rising Sun by the Japanese emperor.

Jewish businesspeople settled in Yokohama. In 1923, when the Kanto earthquake destroyed large parts of Tokyo and obliterated Yokohama almost completely, killing 140,000 people, most of them moved to Kobe. In 1940, around one thousand Jews were living in Kobe; they saw each other in synagogue every Saturday, and their interests were represented by a well-oiled organisation, the Jewish Community (Jewcom).

After the first, sketchy reports that large numbers of Jewish refugees had arrived in Tsuruga, Jewcom decided to take action. The organisation hired two aid workers, paid for the refugees' trips from Tsuruga to Kobe, rented a number of large European-style houses and a few hotels and guesthouses to accommodate them, provided clothes, food, and medical assistance, and offered financial support or low-interest loans to refugees who had obtained visas for Australia, New Zealand, the United States, or Canada. Helping them on their way was the most difficult step, but Jewcom did what it could – with extreme efficiency.

I had not expected to find any remains of Kobe's old houses or traditional atmosphere. In 1945, three bombing raids destroyed more than half the city. During the heaviest bombing, on 16 and 17 March, 331 American B-29s dropped napalm incendiary bombs that burned down almost all the wooden houses. The death toll was 8,841. The city was quickly rebuilt and regained something of its former lustre, but forty years later it was hit by another disaster. In the earthquake of 17 January 1995, some two hundred thousand buildings collapsed, and 6,434 of the city's inhabitants died.

But as if it were the most normal thing in the world, the roads, bridges, and railways were repaired, the shopping centres, hotels, and offices rebuilt, and the European-style houses restored to their former condition or recreated, board by board, stone by stone. The duplicates are perfect, right down to details like chipped paint. The only house not yet fully restored is the four-storey urban villa from 1924 designed by the American architect Frank Lloyd Wright. But work is well underway there. To show that all these houses were heavily damaged or utterly destroyed, the clocks on some house fronts are set permanently to 5.46 a.m., the time when the four-minute earthquake began in 1995.

The former home of the US consul general has become a museum. The Parastin House, built for a Russian businessman, is now a tearoom; the Wien-Austrian House is a wedding centre; and La Maison de Graciani is a restaurant, as is the former home of British businessman Ferdinand Bishop. The house with the green shutters is now a Starbucks. Among the *ijinkan* are new houses and shops with jazz clubs in the basements. Kobe is as open and international as it was in 1940–1941 The school attended by Marcel Wejland is now called St. Michael's International School; it's in the same street as the mosque and, further down, the synagogue.

While the younger refugees were enjoying themselves in Kobe, their elders were growing tired of the crowded houses.

In the archives of the Japanese foreign ministry, Akira Kitade found a report about the Jewish refugees in Kobe, sent by the district manager of the Nippon Yusen Kaisha (NYK) shipping company to senior management on 31 March 1941. The refugees were future NYK passengers, but what sort of people were they?

With respect to life conditions, for approximately 1,000 Jews with no money to spend, the Kobe Jewish Community has supplied 1 yen and 20 sen per day as pocket money with help from the US Jewish community. One loaf of bread a day has been provided by Hyōgo's foreign affairs department. That is to prevent them from walking around in the city looking for bread. The thousand or so destitute Jews are mainly scattered around Nada, Aoya, Kitano, and Yamamoto Avenue, enduring a miserable lifestyle by sharing twenty-one western-style houses, sometimes with twelve people living in one room. The sight of these people wandering around in the city has become an odd scene in Kobe city. It is a growing problem for local officials and it is causing rumours in the street. The city government is struggling to arrange their early departure. The remaining 700 Jewish people came here with almost no money. Using funds they received from relatives and friends in the US, they share apartments and hotel rooms. These people do not require the direct bailout of the Kobe Jewish Community, but they take all their meals in their hotel rooms. They buy nothing, not even a cup of tea. In one case, a number of friends visited one guest and shared a bath, damaging the carpet. One first-class hotel used to take care of as many as twenty such people but that number has been reduced to four.

Not everyone took such a dark view. Osaka, less than an hour away from Kobe, was home to a group of six experimental photographers, the Tanpei Shashin Kurabu (Tanpei Photography Club). At the suggestion of their most talented member, Nakaji Yasui, the group decided in May 1941 to organise a thematic exhibition in Osaka entitled *Wandering Jew*.

The fourteen photos portray the lives of the refugees without leaving out any of their loneliness, longing, disillusionment, and nostalgia. They are, without exception, works of profound humanity, in which the Wandering Jew becomes a timeless symbol of the displaced person. The photos are now on display in the Hyōgo Prefectural Museum of Art in Kobe.

Hiroko Yamagata was six years old and in the first year of elementary school when hundreds of foreigners dressed in black were strolling

'Mother', a photograph by Nakaji Yasui.

through the streets of Kobe. She lived near Hankyu Rokkō Station, in an area where for decades many Westerners had owned houses. Hiroko Yamagata would later become a well-known poet. What she remembered about the Jews, she told Akira Kitade, was a little boy whose grandmother had given him a paper parasol he never used:

> One day I saw the boy with his father. He had slipped his left hand under his father's right arm. Now and then, he pressed his face against his father's jacket. I felt an upwelling of jealousy. I could never do anything as intimate as that with my father. I envied the boy, envied his spontaneous way of expressing his feelings.

Hiroko's German friends warned her off the newcomers: 'They may speak German, but they're Jews.'

Jewcom asked a Japanese professor of religion, Setsuzo Kotsuji, to raise the issue of the Jewish refugees with the Japanese government. He received assurances from the interior minister, Yosuke Matsuoka, that the refugees could stay in Kobe for the time being, even though their visas had expired many weeks or months earlier. The Kobe police were told not to carry out identity checks and to leave the refugees in peace.

In Marcel Wejland's memoirs, he tells a funny story. Apparently, at one stage, the interior minister in Tokyo asked the headmaster of the Mir Yeshiva to come and see him. With the aid of an interpreter, and in the presence of all his senior officials, the minister asked the rabbi, 'Please, would you tell me why the Germans hate you so?' Without even blinking, the rabbi said, 'Because we are Asians!'

At that, all the heads around the table nodded.

27

Zorach Warhaftig

No one was very fond of Zorach Warhaftig. No doubt that was because of his strong will and independent mind. In Lithuania, he had pointed to the way out for the refugee community. And in Japan, he remained a tireless organiser, blazing his own trails. He seemed almost like a party boss, and later, in fact, became a major figure in Israel's United Religious Front. Warhaftig was a born leader, incapable of just looking on passively. But he could also be pushy.

Zorach was the name as Sugihara wrote it on his list of visas. It can also be spelled Zorah or Zerach or Zerah. Zorach was the lawyer from Warsaw who had sent Nathan Gutwirth to the Dutch consul with the urgent request to issue Curaçao visas to all the students in Talmudic academies. Once Zwartendijk agreed, Warhaftig travelled all over Lithuania to persuade students to apply for visas and leave as soon as they could. Warhaftig felt almost as if he was herding a flock of stupid, stubborn sheep.

Ultimately, the sceptics were convinced by a multiple homicide. In October 1940, the Soviet authorities decided to close every church in the country, along with the monasteries and all the other religious schools and institutions. When they came to close the synagogue in Telšiai, four yeshiva students grabbed the Torah scrolls and made a run for it. They were shot dead. In the days that followed, hundreds of Jews applied for Curaçao visas and began their exodus. Scores of

Zorach Warhaftig's travel documents, signed by
Jan Zwartendijk and Chiune Sugihara.

them travelled by rail to Moscow and took the Trans-Siberian Express
to Vladivostok.

Zorach Warhaftig and his wife and daughter, partly to set an
example for the other refugees, boarded the Trans-Siberian Express
in September 1940. Their journey went smoothly, and they arrived
in Japan in the first week of October. In Kobe, Warhaftig went to see
the Dutch consul, De Voogd, and to offer his services; in Tokyo, he
conferred with the Polish ambassador; and in Yokohama, he contacted
a variety of refugee organisations.

Warhaftig calculated that at least 4,700 Jewish refugees would be
coming to Japan, including at least 2,200 from Lithuania. He feared
that this large influx would become a problem if Japan took an active
role in the war, because its ally Nazi Germany would demand that all
Jews be sent back to Europe. It would be better, he concluded, to send
them on as soon as possible to safe destinations.

Warhaftig did not stay in Kobe – it was too far from Tokyo, where
the big decisions were being made. Too small-scale, too provincial.

Most ships leaving Kobe's harbour were bound for Asia. He chose to be based in Yokohama, an open city looking outward to the sea, and the point of departure for all ships crossing the Pacific. Besides, Yokohama was close to Tokyo, just twenty-five minutes by train. In Tokyo, Warhaftig hoped to make swift arrangements with the ambassadors of Canada, the United States, Australia, and New Zealand – countries he was certain would agree, sooner or later, to take in Polish refugees. To achieve that goal, he sought the support of the Polish embassy in Tokyo. To ensure the departure of large groups of Jews to Palestine, he also needed the assistance of the British embassy. After all, the British controlled Mandatory Palestine.

In Yokohama, Warhaftig gathered around him as many rabbis and yeshiva students as possible. He believed reciprocal social control would keep the young men in check – a miscalculation. Once the students reached Japan, they tired of all the strict requirements and proscriptions. Knowing that soon they would once again be subject to those rules and laws, they seized the opportunity Kobe offered for a quick taste of freedom. They were captured by the Tanpei Photography Club sitting outside in the warm sunshine playing chess.

Warhaftig avoided the Dutch embassy. He had a rather low opinion of the Dutch – including Zwartendijk, even though they'd never met. The Curaçao visa in his passport, issued on 24 July 1940, had been arranged for him by Nathan Gutwirth. Warhaftig spoke to the Polish and British ambassadors, urging them to allow the refugees to depart for Palestine at once. In Yokohama, he contacted the Japanese shipping company NYK. For them, the passage to Palestine was a lucrative proposition, because of the length of the journey and the risks. NYK made a proposal. The first group of five hundred refugees could depart on one of their ships before the new year. The company demanded a security deposit of [US]$20 per person, $10,000 in total.

Warhaftig got in touch with the World Jewish Congress in New York, and asked them to advance that sum. The WJC, an international federation of Jewish organisations established in 1936, was willing,

Zorach Warhaftig.

but slow-moving. Warhaftig told them that after the refugees arrived they would repay the deposit and the costs of the voyage, but this commitment was too vague for the WJC's taste. Long-drawn-out negotiations followed, with telegrams whizzing back and forth. Warhaftig kept the Japanese shipping company on the line for weeks, but when the deadline for the deposit passed, NYK cancelled the trip. Warhaftig had dozens of telegrams to show them, sent to organisations all over the world to raise funds. But that made no difference; the shipping company manager did not doubt his good faith, but insisted on seeing money on the table. Warhaftig described the shipping company's attitude in his memoirs:

Then I saw a side of the Japanese that was unfamiliar to me. It was as if I had insulted them deeply. The representatives of the shipping company were in a state of fury I could not reconcile with the simple annullation of an agreement. I thought the break would be permanent, but no.

Many Jewish refugees had already reserved a ticket for the voyage to Palestine. That brought it home to the NYK that thousands more Jewish refugees would be coming to Japan, and that they, too, would eventually have to leave Japan by ship. The migrants were a gold mine.

The shipping company made a new proposal – a voyage to the United States. This plan succeeded, thanks in part to assistance from the Polish embassy in Tokyo. On board were 120 Russian Jews and 88 refugees who had received visas in Kaunas.

Another ship went to Vancouver. The passengers included Zorach Warhaftig and his family. The *Hikawa Maru*, a comfortable passenger ship with a grand Art Deco interior, left the port of Yokohama on 5 June 1941 and arrived in Canada on 17 June. From Vancouver, it went on to Seattle.

Warhaftig recalled the voyage: 'The prevailing mood on board was that of a wonderful summer holiday. We were surrounded by luxury and almost forgot that a terrible war was ravaging the world.'

But once they reached Canada, he felt guilty. Every day, he asked himself why he couldn't have helped more refugees, why he hadn't done more.

Zorach Warhaftig and his family emigrated to Palestine in 1947. In 1949, he was elected to the Knesset. He was minister of religious affairs from 1961 to late 1974, as the fledgling state of Israel was going through its most trying and tempestuous years. He left the Knesset in 1981, and died in 2002 at the age of ninety-six.

Abraham Liwer also crossed the Pacific on the *Hikawa Maru*. He came from the town of Będzin in Silesia. After the German invasion, he had fled with his wife, Chava, and daughter, Johevet, for Lwów, present-day Lviv, which was then in eastern Poland and is now in western Ukraine. The stream of refugees swelled the Jewish population of Lwów from 125,000 to 160,000 in a matter of weeks. In September 1939, the city was occupied by the Red Army. The Molotov–Ribbentrop Pact provided that the Soviet sphere of influence would extend even beyond the Baltics, into south-eastern Poland, and the Russians wasted no time in snatching this piece of Ukraine. In Lwów, unlike in the Baltics, they cracked down right away.

After the NKVD received an anonymous tip, they interrogated Abraham Liwer. Was it true that he had been the director of a bicycle factory in Będzin? He could hardly deny that. Had he done well for himself? Again, he could hardly say otherwise. Was he a capitalist? No, he replied, he was an Orthodox Jew who believed in the justice of the Most High. Liwer was permitted to go, but he decided it would wisest to flee to Vilnius, seven hundred kilometres to the north. On the last night of the year, he crossed the Memel with the help of a human trafficker. It was just the right moment; the guards were in the middle of a drunken New Year's Eve celebration. The temperature was so far below freezing that he lost a toe to frostbite.

Liwer hoped his wife and daughter would soon follow, but, back in Lwów, they had to fill in a form with a series of questions, and gave a wrong answer. The question was whether they wished to return to their place of residence in the German zone or remain in the Soviet Union. Those, like them, who ticked the first box were immediately flagged as spies and accomplices of the Nazis, and less than two days later they were on a freight wagon headed for a camp in Siberia. Liwer heard about their deportation when he received a request to send food to a certain address in the Soviet Union.

In Vilnius, Liwer heard about the visas being issued by the Dutch and Japanese consuls. He went to Kaunas, and applied for a visa not only for himself but also for his wife and daughter. According to the Sugihara list, he received the transit visa on 3 August 1940. This is one of the few cases in which Sugihara noted the applicants' ages: Abram was fifty-one years old; his wife, Chava, forty-eight. He added, 'with

Abraham Liwer and his wife, Chava, and daughter, Johevet.

a child (18)'. A surprising addition, since the wife and child were not present in the consul's office but sharing a three-by-four-metre hut with six other prisoners in a camp in Siberia.

In the forced-labour camp, Johevet had been assigned the plum job of making coffins. The great advantage was that she could do it indoors, without going out into the Siberian cold. Her mother soon came to assist her; it was pleasant work.

Abraham Liwer began his journey to Japan in September, and stopped in Vladivostok. Foreign visitors waiting for the next ship to Japan were not allowed to stay in the city, home to Soviet naval headquarters, for more than four days. Abram Liwer reported to the NKVD office after a week, and informed them he would not leave the Soviet Union unless he could take along his wife and daughter.

Liwer was a tall man with a blond quiff and blue eyes. He happened to be talking to the right NKVD people's commissar: a husky woman in a leather jacket who couldn't keep her eyes off him. She asked Liwer many more questions than necessary in order to keep him in her office. She also promised to do everything she could to track down Abraham's wife and daughter. The most important thing, she said, was to find out which camp Chava and Johevet were in. She contacted NKVD headquarters in Moscow, and found out they were in a camp near the copper mines of Krasnouralsk. That was good news, in a sense: Krasnouralsk was 120 kilometres from Yekaterinburg, and that was on the Trans-Siberian Railway. Chava and Johevet were released the very next day, and the day after that they boarded the train to Vladivostok.

When the Liwers reached Japan, they had to tell their story to journalists at least ten times. The newspapers printed long articles about 'the one man to succeed in liberating his wife and daughter from the Siberian gulag'.

Abraham, Chava, and Johevet stayed in Tokyo. They became so well known that Johevet was offered a job at the Polish embassy. For eight months, she served as secretary to the ambassador – until His Excellency found a place for her and her parents aboard the *Hikawa Maru*.

28

Zofia and Count Romer

Tadeusz Ludwik Romer is said to have been the first to use the nickname under which Zwartendijk became known among survivors. Romer, the Polish ambassador to Japan, asked every Polish Jewish refugee who came to him, 'Where did you get your visa?' The answer was always, 'From the Dutch consul in Kaunas.' To which the count would reply, with a charming smile, 'Ah, the Angel of Curaçao.'

The Polish ambassador was married to the high-spirited Zofia Romer née Wańkowicz. The couple had three daughters: Teresa, Gabriela, and Elżbieta. Like Zwartendijk, Romer cannot be found in his country's history books. That's stranger in the case of the Polish count than in that of the Dutch businessman, because his wife was a living legend.

Zofia was the niece of Melchior Wańkowicz, one of Poland's best-known authors, who had begun his career as a reporter on the eastern front in the Polish-Soviet War. He used Zofia's war diaries as raw material for his epic *Szpital w Cichiniczach* (*The Cichinicze Hospital*), which was published in 1926 and drew immediate attention from masses of Polish readers thanks to its intense, romantic storyline. Three nurses are caring for the wounded in a ramshackle country house in 1919–1921, during the ruthless struggle between the Polish and the Bolsheviks. When desperadoes from the Red Army attack the field hospital and kill the doctors, the nurses take charge. Zofia is one

Zofia Romerowa Wańkowicz in 1920.

of them, and her smouldering, piercing gaze and fierce demeanour make her the most formidable of them all.

In 1999, the book was filmed by Jerzy Wójcik under the title of *Wrota Europy* (*The Gateway of Europe*). This true-to-life feature film made a deep impression on Polish viewers, but because its historical backdrop is so unfamiliar, it was not released in any other European country. Outside Poland, the war of 1919–1921 against the Bolsheviks has been forgotten.

During the turbulent years on the front, Zofia fell in love with the ultra-aristocratic young officer Prince Konstanty Drucki-Lubecki. 'Fell in love' may be an overstatement, actually. She was trapped in the fortified city of Babruysk with the captain and an entire Polish regiment. German troops were approaching on one side, the Bolsheviks advancing on the other; the Polish troops were trapped in between. In a matter of weeks, they would have no choice but to surrender. It was then that – in the words of Zofia's daughter – 'my very pretty mother agreed to marry one of the young officers in the fortress' on the condition that he should take her straight through the battlefield and the chaos of Russia after the revolution to the port of Murmansk. That was her only way of reaching the newly formed Polish army in France.

Something resembling a marriage ceremony was hastily organised. Konstanty tried to persuade Zofia to give up her desperate plan, but she would not be swayed. He hesitated and tried to back out, which infuriated her. Soon after saying 'I do,' she began to accuse Konstanty of seeking to renege on his promise to take her to France. Before the wedding could even be well and truly celebrated, Zofia took off.

She would see Konstanty one last time in 1930, at the Polish embassy in Rome; he was in the Polish military delegation, and she was standing beside the young diplomat with whom she would spend the rest of her life.

Zofia had no need to divorce Konstanty – and in the very Catholic country of Poland in 1921, that would have been impossible. Instead, her first marriage was simply annulled by the Catholic Church, because the bride and groom had never consummated it, and it had not taken place legally – Konstanty and Zofia had been unable to find an official to marry them anywhere near the fortress. Not until 1924 did the Wańkowicz and Drucki-Lubecki families reach a settlement about what Zofia's daughter called 'this youthful wartime folly of my mother's'.

Soon after that, Zofia met Tadeusz Ludwik Romer, who came from a wealthy landowning background, but had lost his parents at an early age and had led a wandering life ever since. The laconic, reserved, almost mysterious count greatly intrigued her, and she would remain in conversation with him for the rest of her days, in an unusual way: by writing him long letters. The count responded with equally long letters setting out his ideas, his concerns about political developments, the terrible fate that menaced the independent Polish nation, and his passionate belief in family, which he saw as the reflection of divine love.

Zofia wrote about her life at the count's side in her diary: 'Everyone who spends time with us is surprised by our respect for one another. It stems not from foolish admiration but from the sum total of everything we have been through together over the years. I dare

Count Tadeusz Ludwik Romer, October 1928.

not say what he thinks of me in his most secret thoughts, but time after time, I am surprised by his wisdom, which he always conveys modestly, with the kindness of a smile.'

After Tadeusz was appointed ambassador to Japan, Zofia continued to write about everything that happened to her or troubled her conscience. One of her last diaries is entitled 'Kneeling before the Emperor', meaning Hirohito. It was not published until 2002, by a small Polish publishing house in Canada.

Tadeusz and Zofia died decades ago, but the Polish foreign ministry was able to help me track down their eldest daughter. Her younger sisters have passed away.

Teresa was fifteen years old when the first refugees came to the Polish embassy in Tokyo. She is now ninety-one, but still recalls her time in Japan as if it was yesterday. Her memory is as photographic as Edith Zwartendijk's, and even though I couldn't take her with me to Tokyo ('I'm no longer physically capable of that'), she was eager to tell me the whole story, in writing, from her home city of Montreal. Like her mother, she loves to write, and does it with such verve that I feel I can hear her voice when I read her letters. When I reach Tokyo, I have no trouble whatsoever finding the places she described.

The Polish embassy was in a street called Mita Tsunamachi. The only thing Teresa Romer is unsure about is the house number. She thought it was 9. In any case, it was a large, European-style building surrounded by a secluded Japanese garden with magnificent trees, stone lanterns, steep paths to secret caves, and even a charming Japanese teahouse, strictly off limits to children. A country estate in the city. It belonged to Marquis Hachisuka Mochiaki, a cousin of Emperor Hirohito, who had fled the Japanese court and devoted all his time to studying birds in the African rainforests. On all sides of the park-like garden was the bustling city, with a mixture of broad motorways, tall office buildings such as the main post office just behind the garden, and narrow, winding streets lined with wooden houses and Japanese shops: a porcelain dealer, a florist, and even a goldfish shop with so many ponds that it took some time to pick out a fish there.

Those wooden houses and shops have vanished. The houses went up in flames in the 1945 bombing, and the shops have been replaced by luxury apartments. The embassy became the prestigious Tsunamachi Mitsui Club, but the garden remained intact and is as enchanting as ever, a place to unwind for a while in a city that seems to go on forever. It is also still a private garden, and I am soon chased out by two women in uniform.

The chancery and the ambassador's residence were in the same building, but had separate entrances – the building still has two entrances today. Teresa heard stories about the refugees, but never saw any of them walk up the avenue to the embassy, which lay hidden behind tall trees, and push open the wrought-iron door. In fact, not many refugees came to Tokyo; the trip was too expensive, and only the wealthy thought they might be helped sooner if they went to the embassy in person. Most refugees lived in Kobe. The embassy staff, six men and one woman, travelled back and forth to Kobe to help with the visa applications, 'and my father sometimes went with them if there were real difficulties, but most of his work was in Tokyo, where he had to convince fellow ambassadors from friendly nations to raise their refugee quotas'.

Romer would arrive late to dinner in his residence, and afterwards he would often return to the chancery to continue working. Even though the building was overgrown with ivy, the children could see the light in his office until long after midnight.

The servants and embassy employees lived in small outbuildings hidden from sight by trees. What most struck the refugees who visited – and Teresa confirmed this – was that the house and garden exuded the peace and quiet of perfect order. That stood in stark contrast to the utter chaos that prevailed everywhere else in the world.

When the first Polish Jews came to meet with him, Romer understood that they had a serious problem. Their visas were for a Caribbean island they could not possibly reach, and the transit visas consul Sugihara had issued in Kaunas were valid for only *twelve days*. None of them could leave the country so quickly. At first, the Japanese authorities required the refugees to apply for temporary political asylum, which involved a pile of paperwork. But after a few months, they concluded that it had been a lot of fuss about nothing and that it made more sense for the Polish Jews to move on as soon as possible to a country that was willing to take them in. This was easier said than done; almost all countries not at war had declared that they could not handle any more refugees. Negotiation was required with representatives of friendly powers, and nothing would be achieved without patience. Romer anticipated a months-long process. Meanwhile, the refugees had to be housed, fed, clothed, and maintained.

It would have been unsurprising if ambassador Romer had washed his hands of the whole business. He had arrived in Japan on 1 October 1937 as the envoy of the Second Polish Republic. On 1 September

1939, that republic had been crushed by Nazi Germany. Since then, he had served the Polish government in exile, based in Angers at first and then, from 17 June 1940, in London. He had little political support, or influence over other powers, or room to manoeuvre, and had a meagre budget. And the most awkward fact of all was that circumstances had made him the rescuer of a group of people who even in pre-war Poland had suffered under 'the enemy's hand' and 'the hand of the mighty', in the words of the Old Testament book of Job.

As soon as the first refugees turned up at his doorstep, Romer sent out a message to his British, Australian, and Canadian counterparts:

> It is not appropriate to investigate whether any particular Polish refugee is a Jew or a Christian, but only whether he is or is not reliable and dedicated to the service of his country and hence of the common Allied cause.

He maintained this position in October 1940 when establishing the Polish Committee to Aid the Victims of War. Not the *Jewish* victims, mind you – no, *all* victims of war. He kept the whole Jew business out of his communiqués, messages, and requests, to emphasise that he was working on behalf of *Polish* citizens who had every right to the support of the Polish state.

This obviously made a strong impression, judging by the account of Oskar Schenker, who in October 1940 became one of the first refugees to reach Japan:

> I must admit that I could not contain the emotion that accompanied me when, after a year of wandering and uncertainty about the next day, I was finally able to step on the threshold of the Polish embassy. The white eagle at the gates to the building, the Polish language, spoken loud and openly, the uniform of our defence attaché, all this made such an impression on me, that for a moment during the first audience with His Excellency Tadeusz Romer, the ambassador of Poland, I could not utter a single word. The atmosphere of this and all subsequent

meetings had left a mark on my entire stay in Japan, and, I must say, a very positive one. And so from the very start I decided to serve and use my experience in working in civil service in Poland for the benefit of the Polish Committee to Aid War Victims in Tokyo. This was a time of hard work for the entire embassy staff. Ambassador Romer set the example himself, as he personally oversaw even minute details of planned refugee transit and settlement.

As the president of his Polish Committee to Aid the Victims of War, the ambassador appointed his wife. Zofia ran the organisation like a first-aid post on the front line. Her motives are not hard to fathom. The nurse in *The Cichinicze Hospital* is not inspired by Christian charity or anything of that sort; she goes to the field hospital to search for her missing brother. What matters most to her is helping her family. When, in the end, she finds only the place where her brother lies buried, it changes her for life.

But I suspect Romer had a different reason. He was a staunch supporter of the Second Polish Republic, which, especially in its early years, had made it a point of honour to protect minorities, especially Jews. This had become more difficult in the 1930s, with violent eruptions of anti-Semitism in many parts of the country. But at the national level, ministers and senior officials remained true to the values of religious liberty, equality, and fraternity, even as the tide turned among the general population.

Another motive may have been that he saw himself as a lost soul from a world of customs and traditions that had gone down in blood and tears. He had seen the light of day in the winter of 1894, on the Antanašė estate near the village of Obeliai in the north-east of Lithuania, eight kilometres from the Latvian border. The area was then part of the Russian empire, as was Poland, but before becoming Russian, it had formed the easternmost tip of the Duchy of Courland.

Count Tadeusz Ludwik Romer was descended from an old Baltic German family, and the Baltic German counts and barons had for centuries seen themselves as displaced persons, roaming from one

The three Romer daughters. In the middle is the eldest, Teresa.

sphere of influence and centre of power to another, from Saint Petersburg to Warsaw, from Stockholm to Königsberg. A Polish friend of his father's, Konstanty Przewłocki, had taken an interest in him and offered him a place in his home in Lublin. Otherwise, he might have ended up in tsarist Russia or in the Austro-Hungarian empire. From childhood, this made him sceptical about such notions as bloodlines and nationalities. At rock bottom, he believed, every human being is a foreigner. Only the whim of fate determines where you will end up and under what circumstances.

The woods of Antanašė ran along a lake that shone silver in the spring and autumn. The year Tadeusz was born, Obeliai had a Jewish population of 662 out of a total of less than 2,000. The synagogue was a simple wooden structure, but it had been there for more than a century. Its Yiddish name was Obeliai Abel. The most common names there were Horovitz, Kaplan, Friedman, Zak, Gordon, Klavir, and Bernstein (or Bernsztejn, the Polish spelling).

29

Odd is death; even is life

Masja and Zelda Bernstein made their escape just before the walls were erected around the Warsaw ghetto. They hoped that in Vilnius they would be reunited with Mordechai, Zelda's husband and Masja's father. A journalist and political activist, he had been investigating a story there when the German armies invaded Poland.

For the journey to Vilnius, Zelda brought salt, matches, a needle, and thread. She had grown up in a rural town, and knew what country people needed. One box of matches could be exchanged for two days' food.

Zelda arranged places for her daughter and herself in a farmer's horse-drawn wagon. They left Warsaw, twelve people in all – women, children, and one elderly man. The farmer had talked the women into giving him their jewellery, telling them it would be safe in his inside pocket if the Germans stopped the wagon and patted down the passengers. But once they were on their way, instead of heading east as fast as possible, the farmer took them straight to a German military guard post and said to the soldiers, 'Here's a load of Jews for you.' Then he took off with their valuables.

The Germans ordered the women, children, and the old man to stand up against a wall. They numbered them from 1 to 12, and had them write down their numbers on cards and attach them to their clothes with safety pins. Then the prisoners stood out in the cold all

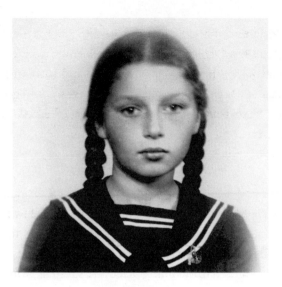

Masja Bernstein.

night, motionless, against the wall. At daybreak, the *Oberscharführer* (squad leader) ordered all the prisoners with even numbers to step aside. Then SS riflemen shot and killed the people with odd numbers. Masja and her mother were numbers 4 and 6.

The six people against the wall included two girls about Masja's age, who had two braids just like hers. The only conspicuous difference between them was that they had odd numbers pinned to their collars. All her life, Masja would ask herself how she could justify still being alive.

Travelling on foot, they reached a village. Hundreds of refugees were clustered there; they kept trying to cross the border, but whenever they came too close to Lithuania, the Russians would shout, 'Go back or we'll shoot you down.' There was nothing for it but to head back. There was no place for the refugees to stay, and the weakest died of hunger, thirst, and cold.

One day, while the Russians were loading the dead onto carts and hauling them away, Zelda and her daughter decided to leave the group behind and head south along the border on their own. An old peasant woman caught sight of them as she was taking her haycart to her hut on the German-occupied side of the border. She hid Zelda and Masja under the hay, smuggled them past the German guards, and offered them shelter in her humble dwelling. The old woman had to nurse both Zelda and Masja back to health before they could go any further. Alternating bean soup with potato soup, she helped them recover their strength. If the Germans had found out she was hiding Jews, they would have not only killed her, but also wiped out her whole village.

Zelda still had some money in her handbag, but the peasant woman refused it, saying it was her Christian duty to help. A few months later, Masja read in her mother's diary that the woman had told Zelda just before they left, 'I want you to know why I'm doing this. When I was a girl, someone offered me a hiding place and saved my life. I believe it is my duty to return the favour in gratitude for that goodness of heart.'

They continued searching for a ponit of escape along the border until they were stopped by a young Russian soldier. He aimed his rifle at them and said, 'Go back or I'll shoot.'

When they had left Warsaw, Zelda had told her daughter that if Russians gave them any trouble, she should start crying. She had known many Russians in her youth, and explained to her daughter, 'Russians have a frosty exterior but a warm heart.'

So Masja burst into tears, and her mother said, 'Masjenka, sweetheart, please don't cry.'

The Russian soldier lowered his rifle and asked in surprise, 'Since when do Poles give their children Russian names?' Zelda showed the soldier her birth certificate, which was in Russian. In her year of birth, Poland had still been part of the Russian Empire. She told the soldier that she had named her daughter after a character from a Chekhov story. That meant nothing to him, because he had never read a book – he was illiterate. 'But,' he said, 'I have a sister named Masja. She's the same age as your Masjenka, and has the same braids. If I shot her, it would be like killing my sister.'

The soldier took the two women to headquarters, gave them bread, and poured them tea from the samovar. The next day, he had a

Zelda, Mordechai, and Masja Bernstein in Vilnius, 1940.

military truck drive them to Białystok. From there, they could travel on to Vilnius.

In the café in Vilnius frequented by journalists, Zelda found her husband, Mordechai. He was overjoyed to see her, but the biggest hug of all was for his daughter.

For six months, the war seemed far away, and the three of them could lead a normal family life. But not long after the Red Army invasion, Mordechai Bernstein was arrested by the NKVD. He had been betrayed by a childhood friend he had seen in Vilnius.

In Jewish circles, Bernstein was known to be an active Bund supporter. He was thrown into a Soviet prison, together with Menachem Begin, who would later become the prime minister of

Israel and write a book about the nocturnal torture sessions in the Vilnius prison, with the ironic title *White Nights*.

Zelda decided to flee with her daughter again. On 17 August, she went to the Japanese consulate in Kaunas for a visa. Sugihara wrote her name the same way consul Zwartendijk had earlier that day: 'Zelda Bernsztejn'.

Afraid the NKVD would arrest her, too, Zelda wanted to leave as soon as they could. But they could not leave until winter. They arrived in February 1941 and ended up in a house in Kobe. There, Zelda told ambassador Romer the story of her escape. He promised Zelda and Masja that he would personally see to it that she had a place on the first ship to Canada.

That ship, the *Heian Maru*, left the Yokohama harbour for Seattle five months later. The girl at the taffrail, who drew the attention of an American photographer, stared stiffly out ahead.

Mordechai Bernstein was transferred from Vilnius to the Gulag Archipelago, and did not see his wife and daughter again for another seventeen years.

Masja was to become one of New York's best-known society columnists, writing for the English edition of the Yiddish daily *The Forward*.

30

Escort to Shanghai

The Polish Committee to Aid the Victims of War, run by Zofia Romer, opened offices in Kobe and Yokohama and sent a permanent representative to Tsuruga to meet refugees as they stepped off the boat. The committee worked in close coordination with Jewcom. The two committees rented twenty-seven dwellings in Kobe, which could accommodate an average of four families each. When a family had to stay there longer, a suitable place was found. The refugees received free medical assistance, clothes, and blankets, and every effort was made to provide education for the children.

All this cost money. For support, Zofia turned to the Committee for Assistance to Jewish Immigrants from Eastern Europe (East Jewcom) and the American Jewish Joint Distribution Committee. There were also the costs of sending the refugees onward to a variety of destinations, from Burma and Vancouver to Mexico and Buenos Aires. The cost of assistance to Polish Jews in Japan totalled US$350,000, scraped together by Zofia and Tadeusz.

Ambassador Romer was in charge of refugee care, procedures for verifying documents, and issuing new Polish passports, since most refugees were still travelling on the permits that had been issued by the Lithuanian authorities. He obtained transit and exit visas from the Japanese authorities. Romer helped 250 Poles, including Zelda and Masja Bernstein, and eighty rabbis and rabbinical students

(Warhaftig's group), gain visas for Canada. And after incessant calling, telegraphing, and pleading, he got his hands on sixty-five visas for Australia, thirty for New Zealand, fifty for Burma (then still a British colony, later occupied by Japan), three hundred for the United States, and one hundred for countries in Central and South America, as well as four hundred certificates for immigration to Palestine. In total, he netted 1,195 visas. All were for adults or heads of families; in those days, children under twenty-one could travel on their parents' visas. Romer offered a future to at least 3,000 refugees.

But all this was not easy. On 23 March 1941, the ambassador sent an alarming message to his government in London:

> It is urgent to enable migration of Jews out of Japan. As there are more than 1,500 of them here, the Japanese government has decided to restrict the conditions for entry. This has put those on their way to Japan, including Poles, whom we care about deeply, in a critical position. I am trying to resolve this crisis with all my might. The Canadian diplomatic mission, which had already started issuing visas from assigned quotas, will probably increase its number to 140 persons.

Germany put the Japanese government under pressure to shut the Polish embassy. Romer was able to avoid this by invoking the long record of information exchange about the situation in the Soviet Union between the Polish and Japanese secret services. This exchange, negotiated at government level, had existed since 1920.

Let me interrupt the narrative here for a moment to give proper attention to an important detail.

I discovered fairly late in my research the role played by the Polish ambassador in Tokyo. In the papers left by Jan Zwartendijk junior when he died, I found a note that he had met with the Polish historian Ewa Pałasz-Rutkowska in Tokyo in 1997 to discuss 'the role of Ambassador Tadeusz Romer'. That was all.

Jan junior may still have been absorbing the impact of his meeting with Chiune Sugihara's widow. Mrs Sugihara, who had made such an impression when he was eleven years old in Kaunas, had annoyed him no end 'by the way she made the whole story about herself and her husband'. In a letter to his brother, Rob, he wrote, 'They are the saints, and our Pa counts for nothing.'

She likewise minimised ambassador Romer's contribution. But whatever Jan discussed with Ewa Pałasz-Rutkowska, he left no written record of it.

On the Internet, I found Ewa's thesis about Romer, published by the University of Warsaw in the late 1990s. What makes it especially interesting is that she includes the full text of telegrams from the ambassador. She had received access to the Polish government's archives, which offer surprising insights.

Romer kept the Polish embassy in Tokyo open a little longer through the sophisticated use of threats. The Polish and Japanese secret services had worked together for twenty years to spy on the Soviet Union. Russia, Poland's age-old enemy, was also Japan's most formidable rival. The two intelligence services had exchanged information from 1920 onwards. Romer suggested that, for the time being, it would be best for them to continue. With Nazi Germany invading the Soviet Union, how would Stalin respond?

All of a sudden, it became clear to me why consul Chiune Sugihara had been sent to Kaunas by the Japanese government: to gather intelligence on the Soviet Union. After all, he spoke fluent Russian. I also realised why he was spying for Poland; not to supplement his earnings, as I had assumed, but with the full knowledge and consent of the Japanese government and for purposes of information exchange. Close cooperation with the Poles was part of his mission.

Romer's Machiavellian approach – cool-headed, calculating, and above all polite – won the Polish embassy months of additional time. But in October 1941, his time ran out. The former chief of the Imperial Japanese Army's general staff office, Hideki Tojo, rose to power, becoming the prime minister, interior minister, foreign minister, and minister of war. In close consultation with army leaders and with the tacit consent of the emperor, he dragged Japan into the Second World War.

The country cut off diplomatic relations with the United States, Great Britain, Canada, and the Dutch and French governments in exile. The immediate trigger was an embargo on exports to Japan instituted by the United States, Britain, and the Dutch government in London, but any other pretext would have worked just as well. The embargo had been a response to Japan moving 140,000 troops into Indochina.

The Polish embassy in Tokyo was the last one closed by order of the Japanese authorities. Those same authorities ordered the transfer of the Polish-Jewish refugees remaining in Japan to the Chinese port of Shanghai, occupied by Japan since 1937.

The Dutch envoy in Tokyo, J.C. Pabst, and the Dutch consul general in Kobe, J.B.D. Pennink, accepted the Japanese ultimatum as an irreversible fact. They closed the legation in Tokyo and the consulate general in Kobe. Consul Van Gulik and consul De Voogd were placed under house arrest.

The Polish ambassador did not comply with the measure right away. He demanded that the Japanese government allow the seven-person staff of the Polish embassy, his wife, and his children to travel with him to Shanghai to make certain that not a hair on the heads of the Polish refugees would be harmed and that they would receive whatever assistance they needed: temporary housing, reception, food, medical care, reorientation, and education.

Before Romer left, he informed the Polish government in London of his decision. He received unconditional authorisation and the title, from 1 November 1941 onwards, of 'ambassador with a special mission'.

As a diplomat's daughter, Teresa Romer was used to moving on every three or four years, leaving behind her home, her familiar surroundings, her school, her friends, and her pets. 'It was normal and just had to be done, so there was no point in being sad or sorry. Better to look forward to something new and exciting.' Moreover, Teresa and her sisters, Gabriela and Elżbieta, left in the knowledge that their Polish governess and tutor, Miss Maria Hubisz, would accompany them. Miss Hubisz would remain with the children until her death in Montreal at the age of 102, and would be buried in the same grave as Zofia and Tadeusz Romer.

But the departure from Tokyo was out of the ordinary. Teresa had become attached to Seishin Joshi Gakuin, Sacred Heart School, and her teachers there, and her nine Western and Japanese classmates had become her friends. In just a few weeks, she was supposed to take her final exams and receive her diploma. She had come to know Japan as a fabulously beautiful and fascinating country. And now she had to go:

> So I remember our departure from the Tokyo train station. No tears as we were saying farewell to a large crowd of friends, including emissaries from the Emperor and Empress. Flowers for my mother. Then a blank. Then click, a group photograph in Nagasaki, where my father wanted us to stop, to say goodbye to a mission of Polish Franciscan monks. In the photo I see, beside my family, the embassy staff and their families – but I wouldn't have known this just from memory. Boarding the boat? Where in Japan? … Docking in Shanghai? Blanks.

The Polish embassy staff made the crossing to Shanghai on the first of the three ships that carried the remaining Polish-Jewish refugees: 946 holders of passports with Curaçao visas, with their families.

The passengers on the second ship included Zofia Romer and her three daughters.

Ambassador Romer took the third ship, which left the port of Nagasaki on 26 October 1941. Also on board were the 320 teachers and students from six yeshivas in Poland and Lithuania, and a group of rabbis with their families, around 80 people. The ambassador felt that these people required special protection.

Shanghai Polish Aid Committee, 1942. Zofia is seated in the
centre of the front row.

In Shanghai, Romer, his wife, Zofia, and their three daughters
moved into a hotel on the Bund. After a few weeks, they moved to
three rooms in the Polish legation villa, in a quiet street in the French
concession.

Tadeusz and Zofia Romer would remain in the city for almost a
year, doing their best every day to help the refugees.

On 25 August 1941, Einsatzkommando 3, led by SS-Standartenführer
Karl Jäger, carried out a roundup in a wide area around Obeliai,
Lithuania, to 'cleanse' the area of Jews. The people they arrested – 112
men, 627 women, and 421 children – were forced to dig a long ditch in
the woods at Antanašė, the former Romer family estate, and stand in
it. It took a twenty-man execution squad no more than a few minutes
to mow down the 1,160 men, women, and children, and less than an
hour to cover the bodies with earth.

Not until twenty years after the war did Count Romer hear about
the massacre on the estate where, as a toddler, he had taken his first

steps. It was the horrifying evidence that, in 1941, he had made the right choice.

'My father,' Teresa wrote to me, 'believed that respect for all is inextricably linked to certain privileges a person may enjoy, such as a good education and a prominent position. He was a caring man, towards his family and others, warm and helpful. His father's death when he was five years old, and his mother's when he was nine, made him wise beyond his years and gave him a strong sense of humanity. Offering a helping hand was the first thing he strove for, making an impression on other people the last.'

According to Teresa, her father's generation had been shaped by Poland's newly acquired independence and by a patriotism born of the centuries-long struggle against Russian, Austrian, and Prussian domination. But their dream of independence resulted in Marshal Piłsudski's absolute rule, while all around the young nation one dictator after another came to power. But Romer, undaunted by the world around him, remained an ardent democrat.

Teresa writes that her parents were 'devastated at the shocking 1939 news of the Nazi and Soviet attacks and atrocities on our homeland – from dreadfully far away. News about these and about the fate of friends and relatives trickled through to our safe, comfortable existence in Tokyo, from which so little help could be offered. A different form of suffering. So when refugees unexpectedly started arriving, it mobilised an all-out effort to help them, in every way possible.'

It's a quality I find in every one of the Just: the will to take real action. Ordinary people with elastic consciences look on passively, or turn away. I would feel the same urge – to bury my head in a book, or lose myself at the piano. In fact, Tadeusz Romer occasionally did the latter; when it all became too much for him, he would pour out his emotion into the keys. And as a Polish patriot, who else could he play but Chopin? Tadeusz had received his first piano lessons from his guardian, Konstanty Przewłocki, who had been his father's friend and classmate at university in Riga. 'Uncle Kot', as Tadeusz called him, had taken the boy into his home and treated him as he did his own five children. Przewłocki had the skill of a professional pianist, and sometimes gave concerts in Kraków. Uncle Kot taught the young count to love music, especially Schubert and Chopin.

Ambassador Tadeusz Romer had a grand piano installed in the Polish embassy in Tokyo. One of his finest moments in Japan, as his daughter tells it, was 'the unforgettable day that Arthur Rubinstein was playing on his grand piano in the embassy's reception room, and gave a concert for diplomatic gatherings and Japanese invités'. Chopin had never sounded so sweet to his ears as there, in Tokyo, just before the Nazis occupied Poland and Arthur Rubinstein's birth city of Łódź.

In the spring of 1942, Japan and the Allies decided to exchange diplomats who were stuck in occupied zones. It took another few months to organise everything. The *Kamakura Maru* took the Western diplomats who had worked in Japan and China to Lourenço Marques (present-day Maputo) in Mozambique; this included Robert van Gulik, Nicolaas de Voogd, and Tadeusz Romer, as well as Zofia Romer and her three daughters.

On top of this, the Polish ambassador had secured places for forty-five Polish Jews on the voyage to Mozambique. In Lourenço Marques, they were exchanged for Japanese diplomats.

No sooner had Romer arrived in Lourenço Marques than he received a telegram from the Polish government in exile asking if he would accept an appointment as ambassador to the Soviet Union. For a Polish diplomat, there was no post more difficult.

He discussed it with his wife. After a whole night of quarrelling, he made his decision. Teresa and her sisters listened in from an adjacent room. Her parents were well aware, she writes, of the crushing hardship the job would entail. She remembers they spent the whole night debating the offer in anguish, weighing all the risks and all the arguments for and against. Yes. No. But. Or a howl of emotion. Her

Tadeusz Romer as foreign minister of the
Polish government in exile, 1944.

mother, who knew better than anyone how dangerous it was in the
USSR, begged her father to refuse, or to accept the post only if she
could go with him. But that was out of the question. More than half
of Russia was then occupied by the Nazis, and the seat of the Soviet
government had been moved to Kuybyshev (now Samara), about one
thousand kilometres east of Moscow. Because of the exceptionally
dangerous situation – the Battle of Stalingrad had begun – the Soviet
Union was not accepting diplomats' families. When her father insisted
it was his duty to serve, her mother realised there was no longer any
point in arguing. Early in the morning, she reluctantly gave in. But
he asked her to stay in the relative safety of South Africa with the
children, instead of leaving for London and braving the bombs, and
she agreed.

Sofia writes, 'So within three days, the whole course of our lives changed. My mother and we were heartbroken – but, well, it was wartime, everyone was obliged to do their duty, however hard. It was the first and only time in my parents' lives that they were separated for more than a few days. My mother, brave as always, found a small apartment in Johannesburg, got her children into schools, and took on several voluntary war jobs as a delegate of the Polish Red Cross. My father, hard-working and altruistic as always, rose to the unusual challenge of his post.'

In 1942 and 1943, Zofia and Tadeusz again wrote each other many letters. Intense, sorrowful, despairing letters. They had no way of knowing whether they would see each other again in good health, or whether Poland would retain its independence. On the horizon, they could already make out the dim contours of their future: a life in exile.

After the discovery of the first mass graves in Katyń on 26 April 1943, the Polish government had no choice but to sever relations with the Soviet Union. Ambassador Romer was summoned back to London immediately. There he would serve for another sixteen months, as the foreign minister of the Polish government in exile.

One of the officers killed in the Katyń massacre of April–May 1940 was Prince Konstanty Drucki-Lubecki, with whom Zofia had had her short-lived wartime romance. It would take many more years before his name would turn up on one of the lists of Katyń victims, the so-called Ukraine List. These were long lists, very long; the total number of Polish officers and intellectuals murdered by the Russian NKVD was around 22,000.

Zofia never found out.

When I write to her eldest daughter to let her know about the prince's name on the list, she replies that I am the first to have told her. But there is no doubt, as Teresa wrote to me, that Katyń was a national tragedy that left its mark on many Polish people and scarred her entire family.

31

The secret of Kaunas

When the Zwartendijks had moved to Kaunas, they had brought only a bare minimum of luggage. The rest of their furniture and possessions had gone into storage in a warehouse in Middensteiger, a street in the centre of Rotterdam. When the city was bombed in May 1940, none of it had survived the flames, not even the silverware. Since they had to buy new furniture, they had the feeling, in the autumn of 1940, that they were starting over with a clean slate.

In Eindhoven, they moved into Goorstraat 2, a semi-detached townhouse owned by Philips. It had the solidity of 1920s architecture; a fresh lick of paint on the doors and the window frames, and it looked newly built. The garden extended far behind the house, and, later in the war, proved large enough for them to dig an air-raid shelter.

They could hear the war creeping closer. Three hundred metres from the house was the railway yard. With growing frequency, Royal Air Force (RAF) bombers were targetting freight trains. The British were trying to shut down the Nazi distribution system and the export of Philips products to Germany. The Zwartendijks often had reason to hide in the shelter they had dug in the garden, which was covered with old doors and sand.

Goorstraat cut across Villapark, a village within the city where everyone knew each other. Edith quickly learned that their next-door neighbours were the Hoekstras, and that the youngest of their five children was a Jewish girl in hiding. No one in Villapark saw any need to make a secret of this.

All the fathers in Villapark worked at Philips; most of the children, including Edith and Jan, went to school at nearby Lorentz Lyceum. This secondary school had been founded with financial support from Anton Philips for the children of non-Catholic senior staff of the electronics company.

Edith had a hard time accepting that Jan was avoiding her. She had the feeling that in Eindhoven she'd become a stranger to him from one day to the next. The days when they had been inseparable felt like part of a distant past in a distant land. He never said to her, 'Remember, in Lithuania ...' Edith would have to wait half a century before her brother spoke those words.

Jan refused to cycle to school with her. She made four new friends in no time; that was some consolation, but losing her intimacy with her brother still hurt. It was cold comfort that he hadn't traded her in for a bunch of new pals. He remained a loner; his best and maybe his only friend was his father. It was hard for him to relate to the lads in his class. They had big mouths, until things got hairy. As soon as they heard the roar of a plane, they would run for cover. But Jan would climb a tree to find out whether it was a British Ventura or a Heinkel. His most amazing experience was when a low-flying German fighter zoomed straight over the garden. He could see both the pilot in the cockpit and the gunner in the nose. Still better, when he said the gunner had given him the thumbs up instead of firing, his father had believed him.

What was much more dangerous was the time when eight British RAF squadrons laid waste to the Philips factory complexes. Jan Sr., Edith, and Jan junior had cycled to the station to pick up Aunt Cootje, who was coming to stay with them for a few days. As they reached the square in front of the station, they saw the Mosquitoes swooping down on the factory in Emmasingel. The bombing went on for four minutes. Edith went looking for a safe place to wait it out in the station,

After the bombing of the Philips factory in 1942.

but her father and brother jumped back on their bicycles to check the damage to the radio factory. Edith could not understand why they wouldn't take shelter. When the siren gave the all-clear signal and she went back outside, her surroundings were unrecognisable. Through the clouds of dust, she ran the whole two kilometres home. When she tried to tell her mother what had happened, all she could say was that he had lost Pa and Jan.

Her father and brother showed up half an hour later, without a scratch. The next day, they realised they'd had a narrow escape from a fiery hell. The incendiary bombs and the fire they started had destroyed not only the Philips factories in Strijp-S and Emmasingel, but also homes, shops, and churches. The hospital sustained heavy damage, and 138 civilians died.

The early months in Eindhoven stood in stark contrast to 1942–1944. The pace of life was sleepy, as if the war were all a big mistake and

Hitler had occupied the Netherlands by accident. They returned to old traditions: every other Sunday, the whole family would go to see Uncle Piet, and the next Sunday, Piet, his wife, Mary, and their three daughters would return the visit. They would do chores together, washing the car or mowing the grass. In the summer, they might cycle out to the heath for a picnic.

Piet was still working at Philips and, as always, had firm opinions about everything. If anyone disagreed with him, he could get so angry he would refuse to speak to them for weeks. His twin brother was easier going; when he disagreed, he kept his mouth shut – or at least he weighed his words more than once before criticising anyone. Piet had a hot temper, like his sister, Didi, who also proclaimed her views vociferously, and would get into spirited arguments with other editors at her newspaper. To Piet, the only good Jerry was a dead Jerry. He could say that ten times a day, and each time he would add, 'Whether inside or outside the company.' No one doubted Piet's fearless commitment to his views. The problem was that Philips had been assigned a German administrator, who worked hand in glove with the Dutch Nazis among the employees. Airing opinions like Piet's on the work floor could land you in very hot water.

Jan, a diplomat by nature, came up with a different approach. He believed in pretending to play along while causing delays and seizing opportunities to sabotage the occupiers' plans. Piet's resistance was more open, until he saw that Jan's tactics were more effective. Then he, too, devoted himself to the art of carefully timed procrastination.

As the war dragged on, both of them spent less time at the office. Jan was bored; Piet advised him to spend his afternoons playing bridge. Jan arranged (and deranged) the company's contacts with Eastern European countries for the foreign sales department; Piet was an assistant director in the commercial department that served the broadcasting industry. Piet's department received major orders during the war, and grew into one of the most important parts of Philips Eindhoven. Most orders came from the occupying regime, and Piet was constantly explaining to the Germans why delivery had to be postponed again. He taught the staff of the production department how to do the opposite of what they'd been hired to do: delay delivery as long as possible and introduce subtle defects into the transmission equipment, so that it would stop working properly within twenty-four hours.

After the ninety-three RAF bombers razed the factory complexes, Piet could finally get serious about playing bridge. Some co-workers were outraged, but he had mixed feelings. The radio factories had been reduced to smoking rubble; years of work had been obliterated, and not even by the occupiers, but by the Allies. But then again, the news had arrived in London 'from numerous sources' that the factories in Eindhoven were hard at work for the Germans.

Frits Philips made no secret of his bewilderment. He told everyone he ran into, inside or outside the company, 'We manufacture so darned little for the Germans that it could never justify a bombing.' But the Dutch government in exile had given its consent to the attack.

Zwartendijk kept quiet about Kaunas, even to Piet and Mary, and certainly to his co-workers and supervisors, including Guépin, the company's number two, who had been swiftly sidelined by the German administrator. For a long time, he also kept secret what had happened in Lithuania from the director, Frits Philips.

He was biding his time until he felt certain of the exact situation at the company. Who was really in charge: the directors in New York, the directors in Eindhoven, or the German administrator? Who was trustworthy, and who was not?

The war had not taken the Philips conglomerate by surprise. Zwartendijk still remembered every step of the evacuation plan made by the directors in 1935, when he was working in Eindhoven. This plan relied on the centuries-old Dutch Waterline, a combination of man-made defences and natural bodies of water, intended to protect Holland from advancing enemies. Some one hundred to two hundred Philips managers were to be moved to an empty factory in Dordrecht, behind the waterline, along with the manufacturing equipment, the

Jan Zwartendijk in his office at Philips in 1942 or 1943.

stocks, the raw materials, the accounts, and the patent records.

Frans Otten, who had succeeded his father-in-law, Anton Philips, as director in 1939, had no illusions about what lay ahead. That had been clear to Zwartendijk even before the war. 'It will happen,' Otten had told Philips directors. 'You can see it coming. If you've read *Mein Kampf*, then you know what he's after.'

He – the name was no longer spoken aloud, because everyone knew at once who the word referred to – sought absolute power over all sectors of society, including industry.

In January 1939, the Philips directors had decided to shift some manufacturing from Eindhoven to Blackburn, in the English county of Lancashire. The next step was to move the company's registered office to a safe area – The Hague at first, and later Curaçao.

Zwartendijk had not heard about this second destination until after his return from Eindhoven. It was a sheer coincidence that, in July and August 1940, he had helped thousands of Jewish refugees to flee Europe by granting them visas for Curaçao, the new location of the Philips head office since May of that year. In both cases, the island offered a way of protecting vital interests. The Philips executives did not sign the decision to relocate the office until 13 May 1940, on the frigate that took them to England; the Dutch justice minister was also on board and looked on.

On the evening of 9 May 1940, Frans Otten had received word from Germany that German troops would invade the Netherlands that very evening. The Philips director heard about the invasion even before the Dutch military leaders. Otten had immediately called a directors' meeting and drummed up Frits Philips, Anton's only son, who held the position of assistant director. Shortly before midnight, the signal was given to evacuate. Machines and stocks were loaded onto lorries; the department heads hurried to the station, where a train had been reserved to take them to Dordrecht. At 4.00 a.m., as the German invasion of the Netherlands began, the lorries began to move. But eighty kilometres along the route, they ran into a trap; German parachutists had blocked the road to the Moerdijk bridge. There was nothing they could do but drive back to Eindhoven.

The special train also had to stop at the Moerdijk bridge and turn back. Only a few smaller lorries and passenger vehicles made it across the Hollands Diep River on the ferry. The next evening, 12 May, the convoy arrived in The Hague. Those passenger cars had held all the Philips directors and their families.

During the long afternoons that Zwartendijk spent twiddling his thumbs, he had heard the whole story ad nauseam, in both first- and second-hand versions. In Eindhoven in 1941, they never tired of talking about how the directors had escaped. The group had spent the night in the Hotel Witte Brug. The next morning, Frans Otten had contacted the Dutch government and learned that two British warships were waiting at the Hook of Holland, one for the Dutch government and royals, and one for the Philips directors, if they wished. Half a day later, the company's top managers arrived in London with their wives and children; six weeks later, they were far from the conflict, safe in New York, where Philips would have its headquarters for the remainder of the war.

Frits Philips was the only director to remain in the Netherlands. As a reserve officer, he had reported to the defence ministry first thing after arriving in The Hague. But before he had the chance to join the Dutch air defence command on 14 May, the Netherlands had given up the fight. He briefly considered crossing to England, but the next day he and his wife returned to Eindhoven.

Had that been the right choice? Halfway through the war, it was still far from clear. His choice had stemmed from a sense of noblesse oblige, a feeling that he had been chosen to take on weighty responsibilities and steer his company through the war. In 1944, he said as much to Jan Zwartendijk, in unmistakable terms: 'I couldn't leave the people and the factory to their fate.'

Hermann Göring, the supreme commander of the Luftwaffe, the leader of German's four-year re-armament plan, and the country's most powerful man when it came to the economy, saw the war industry as no different from ordinary manufacturing. He instructed the Nazi propaganda agency to 'take over and safeguard' the Philips factories. The German administrator assigned to the company began

Frits Philips.

work on 5 July, and monitored every move made by Frits Philips and his right-hand man, legal expert Anthony Guépin. From the summer of 1940 onwards, Philips essentially had three sets of managers: the Germans, the Dutch, and the directors in New York. The first and third wanted nothing to do with each other; meanwhile, Philips and Guépin were stuck in the middle. Frits Philips had the near-impossible task of misleading and deceiving the Germans whenever he could, keeping the employees calm, and being as ineffectual as possible, but without bankrupting the company. Meanwhile, he was in secret communication with the directors in New York, whose priority was to safeguard the company's interests outside the Netherlands. This clandestine contact was made by infrequent delegations to Switzerland.

In the foreign sales department, Jan Zwartendijk could see how tense the relationship was between Frits Philips in Eindhoven and Frans Otten, the company president in New York. He is certain not to have seen Otten's letter to the director of the Swiss Philips organisation, but even so, there must have been whispers in Eindhoven of the high-flown rhetoric that Frans Otten was using against his brother-in-law, Frits:

> He [Frits] and we must always base our decisions and our activities on the principle of upholding the honour and spotless reputation of the nation, the company, and individual employees. Our common goal of ensuring our company's survival in the interest of the shareholders and of providing employment for our managers and workers must never detract from that overriding principle ...

A lofty moral stance. At the same time, Zwartendijk knew, after everything he'd experienced in Kaunas, that it was easy for the big brass in New York to talk. They were safe there – out of reach of the bombs that rained down, more and more often, on the railway yard and the freight trains to and from the factory – and were never asked to deliver parts to subsidiaries in the Balkans or Hungary.

The employees supported Frits Philips, who put the company's usual activities on the back burner, but nevertheless tried to keep it running as well as he could; his greatest hope was that after the war it could make a serious contribution to the economic recovery of the ravaged Netherlands. In time, Frans Otten realised this, and sent a telegram, by way of Switzerland, to make it clear to his brother-in-law that he did not doubt his loyalty in the least.

On 24 March 1941, Zwartendijk received a letter at his home address that had been sent six days earlier from a camp in Litzmannstadt. The name, address, and camp number were on the back of the envelope. Litzmannstadt was the name the Nazis had given to Łódź. The letter was from Hermann Maschewski, his former deputy at Lietuvos Philips:

Lieber Herr Zwartendijk!
I am delighted to inform you that my family and I were rehoused on
13 March. Since 16 March, we have been staying in a transit camp in
Litzmannstadt-Waldborn. I am truly glad to breathe freely at last and
no longer to fear the worst. Now that I can think normally again, my
first thought is of the business – that is, our business – and I am sure
you understand that I would like to be in personal contact with our
firm as soon as possible to pass on information about the latest events
and developments. You see, it has been completely impossible in recent
times to carry on any business correspondence, and after our company
was nationalised, it would even have been dangerous, because the
Russians searched for ill intent behind every word, even the most
insignificant.

Zwartendijk had often been surprised by how cheerful Hermann
Maschewski remained under all circumstances. In 1917, at the age of
twelve, he had seen his place of birth, Kybartai, destroyed, but the
experience had not turned him into a fatalist.

Despite his Polish name, Maschewski was a German-speaking
Prussian Lithuanian, a *Volksdeutsche*. His broad smile made him
a phenomenal salesman. He was a magnet for female attention,
which he clearly enjoyed, even though he was married to the sublime
Eugène, a former ballet dancer. Although he was faithful to her, he
loved to flirt with the ladies, including Erni.

The fact was, you could always count on him. When the
nationalisations began in July 1940, Lietuvos Philips had been spared
for a couple of weeks. According to Maschewski, that was because
the Russians hadn't yet figured out who really owned the company,
and suspected that the German companies Telefunken and AEG
were involved behind the scenes. The orders from Moscow were to
spare German companies in order not to upset Hitler. It had taken
the Russians a long time to figure out who the shareholders were.
Zwartendijk had not been forthcoming, and after his unavoidable
departure, Maschewski had maintained for quite a while that he didn't

know the true situation because the Dutch managers had run off with the crucial papers. So although Lietuvos Philips had been assigned a commissar who supervised the company, Maschewski remained the main Philips representative in Kaunas and the actual head of the company.

The letter, a copy of which Zwartendijk placed in the Philips archives, shows that Maschewski had gone on sending confidential business information to other Philips divisions. He had got rid of contracts and licensing agreements, and fiddled with the accounts so that the people's commissar could not gain a grip on the company. Lietuvos Philips had not been nationalised until 13 January 1941; after that, there was no more place for Maschewski there. He no longer had a shred of authority at the office, and the entire sales division had been moved to Leningrad. He expected to be arrested at any moment, and he feared that his wife and only daughter would waste away in the gulag.

In early 1941, the Soviet Union and Nazi Germany concluded a treaty on repatriation from Lithuania for *Volksdeutsche* who were citizens of the Reich. The Germans called that *Umsiedlung*, resettlement. The Soviets still feared that the *Volksdeutsche* would rise up against them, and that Hitler would seize the opportunity to invade Lithuania. It was Dekanozov, the Russian ambassador in Berlin, who signed the treaty on behalf of the Soviet Union. The *Volksdeutsche* were to be accommodated in a camp in Łódz´.

Maschewski saw this as his one and only chance to escape the Soviets. That was not unreasonable; on 14 June 1941, the Soviet Union cracked down, deporting some 20,000 Lithuanians to Siberia in twenty-four hours. Maschewski, sensing the danger, had left Lithuania with his wife and daughter three months earlier. He wrote to Zwartendijk from Litzmannstadt-Waldborn on 18 March. He had not been allowed to bring anything with him when he crossed the border, and asked Zwartendijk to send a little money.

I assume Zwartendijk did so, because eleven months later, Hermann Maschewski showed up at his door in Eindhoven.

Operation Barbarossa put an abrupt, if unsurprising, end to the non-aggression pact between Hitler and Stalin. The Führer feared the Red Army would become too strong. The attack on the Baltic countries and the Soviet Union, which began on 22 June 1941, was a reprise of the *Blitzkrieg* in the West. Within less than a month, the Wehrmacht's Army Group North was one hundred kilometres from Leningrad, and the Army Group Centre reached Smolensk. From August onwards, the Germans made slower progress, because the Russians kept sending new, fresh troops. Winter came, and the Wehrmacht still had not reached Moscow.

But in the summer of 1942, the Nazis chased the Russians out of the Baltics, and occupied Lithuania. This made it still more important to keep 'the secret of Kaunas' than it had been during the Russian occupation.

What Maschewski liked least about his life in Poland was being assigned a number: *Umsiedlungsnummer* OB 1, 10/53/89. Never had he felt so much like a second-class citizen as he did in that camp in Litzmannstadt. It turned out to be not far from the Jewish ghetto, where the men in Maschewski's camp who were waiting for permanent housing had to do forced labour. The woman and girls were assigned to the soup kitchen; that included Maschewski's wife and daughter.

Once the Germans had driven away the Soviets from Lithuania, he wanted to return as quickly as possible to rescue Lietuvos Philips. He must have heard in Poland that the Reichskommissariat Ostland had issued a decree reinstating private property. The Nazis regarded the Baltic countries, eastern Poland, and western Russia as forming a single colony, and had set up the Reichskommissariat Ostland (RO) as its civil administration. The RO's first act was to confiscate all Soviet property. An additional decree, issued on 27 October, gave the head of the RO, the Reichskommissar, the power to appoint interim administrators of confiscated businesses and estates for the purpose of returning them to their previous owners.

On 12 November 1941, Hermann Maschewski was appointed the

interim administrator of Lietuvos Philips. His role was to oversee the restoration of the ownership and management structures that had existed at Lietuvos Philips before the Soviet invasion.

At Philips headquarters in Eindhoven, his appointment was welcomed. There they had been dismayed to see authority over the Philips branches in the two other Baltic states, Estonia and Latvia, assigned to Philips Valvo in Berlin, a Nazi-controlled German company whose wartime operations were completely independent of Eindhoven headquarters. That ruse didn't work in Lithuania, thanks to Maschewski.

In January 1942, Hermann Maschewski lugged his heavy suitcase from the Eindhoven station to Goorstraat 2. Edith couldn't believe her eyes:

He embraced my father as if he had seen him the day before in Kaunas. He went up to my mother with a beaming smile and kissed her on both cheeks. He put his suitcase on the dining room table and, to everyone's delight, opened it to reveal a fat goose. He had also brought two jars of goose fat. The next day, my mother used the fat to fry cracklings. They tasted good. But not as good as a year later, because in 1943 Maschewski came back. He had another fat goose and another two jars of goose fat. Even in early 1944, when we had almost nothing left to eat, he turned up at our door again. He had travelled from Kaunas to bombed-out Berlin and from there by way of half-demolished Osnabrück to Eindhoven. Each time he brought a fattened goose from Lithuania and jars of fat. The cracklings in 1944 were the most delicious thing I've ever eaten. We had just sold *Grossmaman*'s grand piano in exchange for a little food. And suddenly we had a feast, thanks to Maschewski.

He came to Eindhoven to arrange for the delivery of parts to the radio factory in Kaunas. The Philips company lawyer, Jan Schaafsma, wrote in an evaluation of Maschewski just as Eindhoven was liberated on 18 September 1944:

After Germany occupied Lithuania, the former director Maschewski returned to Kaunas and was able to obtain management authority over the Philips company there from the official German organisations. The company was removed from the Soviet trust in its entirety. Maschewski became its 'Verwalter' [administrator assigned by the occupying regime]. Throughout the German occupation, he did a fine job of managing our affairs, and as a result the Philips Ostland company, established by Berlin in order to take over all business in all three Baltic states, failed to do so in Lithuania. Even though when given a choice between Russia and Germany he opted for the latter, his attitude is good. A hard-working Philips employee, he has always acted in accordance with the policies made here for the company as a whole.

In July 1944, Maschewski and his wife and daughter fled Kaunas for the second time, a few days before the Red Army's Baltic offensive. As during their first flight, they could bring nothing with them. Berlin was not safe; a few weeks later, they travelled on to Hamburg.

After the German capitulation, Maschewski visited Philips in Eindhoven again. Of all the company's subsidiaries, the German ones had been the most subservient to the Nazis. That may come as no surprise, but even in Austria, for instance, the situation had been quite different: the Philips subsidiary, Radiowerk Horny A.G. in Vienna, had managed, despite many intrigues and accusations, to retain all its Jewish employees until the end of the war. But in the German subsidiaries, everyone at every level had marched in step with the Nazis. The Philips medical-equipment factory in Hamburg had gone to the greatest extremes.

Philips gave Maschewski a job in the German lighting division. Almost nothing remained of the company's activities in Hamburg and Cologne. He rebuilt the business there from the ground up, and remained a general manager at Philips until his retirement in December 1970.

He was active and enjoyed the limelight. But in all the interviews he gave, he never said a word about the long queues of Jewish refugees at the Philips office in his birth country of Lithuania, waiting for visas.

Hermann Maschewski died long after Jan Zwartendijk, in 1990. He took the secret of Kaunas with him to his grave.

32

Mauthausen

In the Zwartendijk home, one Saturday afternoon in the autumn of 1942, the doorbell rang. Edith opened the door. On the doorstep were two German officers. *Arrest* – that was the first word that shot through her mind.

The Germans wanted to speak to her father. Before Edith even had time to call his name, he was at the door.

The Gestapo, Zwartendijk saw.

It's all over, he thought. *They've figured it out: more than 2,000 visas issued to Jews. And now they're looking for the list of names …*

His legs were trembling. He stepped outside, and walked a short distance away from the house. He didn't want Edith and Jan to see their father arrested and dragged off.

'Are you Jan Zwartendijk?' asked the elder of the two officers.

He nodded.

'Does the name Aletrino mean anything to you?'

He narrowed his eyes, as if deep in thought.

The officer pressed the point: '*Herr* Louis Aletrino.'

He had always called his friend from Prague 'Aletrino', without any first name.

'Why do you ask?'

'We found a slip of paper in his breast pocket with your name and address. It said, "Warn in case of emergency."'

'I hope nothing serious has happened to him?'

'He fled and was shot down. In Romania.'

'I think there's been some mistake.'

The officer hesitated, but then pressed on.

'Arrested in Romania. Shot in Austria. In Mauthausen.'

Mauthausen. The concentration camp for political prisoners.

'So you do know him?'

There was no point in denying it. Aletrino had his name and address in his breast pocket. Telling the truth was his best chance of saving himself.

'He was my oldest friend.'

'When was the last time you were in touch with him?'

'Years ago. Before the war. But please, don't get me wrong ...' He looked the officers in the eye – first the younger one, then the older. 'Do you have friends?'

The older one nodded, but his smile was a little distrustful.

'Really good friends?'

'One.'

'Louis Aletrino was the only friend I could count on. I'm moved to hear he had my name and address in his breast pocket. I hope you have such a friend, *Herr Oberleutnant*.'

'Papers, please.'

Edith was eavesdropping from the kitchen. The thought made her head pound: Uncle Louis, shot dead. And what would she do without her father?

The younger officer examined Zwartendijk's papers, took a long look at him, and said with a sniff, '*Kein Jude*.' ['Not a Jew.']

The papers were returned to him.

As he went back inside, his knees were shaking and his teeth were chattering. If they had taken him into custody, the whole operation would have come to light. The Gestapo tortured you until you confessed.

'Are you OK, Pa?'

The question came from Jan, who had tiptoed down the stairs.

'Did you hear what …'
'Don't say a word, Pa.'
'Shot as he tried to escape. In the back …'
'Don't say a word, Pa.'

It was not until years later that Zwartendijk learned exactly what had happened to his friend.

On 23 January 1942, Louis Aletrino had been arrested in Bucharest by the Iron Guard, a violently anti-Semitic fascist militia. Aletrino was then a *New York Times* correspondent in Romania. After the occupation of the Netherlands, he had no longer received work from Dutch newspapers, but the *New York Times* had offered him a steady job. The Iron Guard arrested him on suspicion of political activities.

Aletrino was arrested at the same time as Ludovicus (Lou) Doorman, a Dutch rear admiral. Lou was the brother of the most renowned Dutch rear admiral, Karel Doorman. Like Aletrino, Lou Doorman was suspected by Ion Antonescu's government, which had Hitler's full backing, of being a spy.

Antonescu's greatest enemy was the Soviet Union; he sent fifteen Romanian divisions to the eastern front in the campaign against the Red Army. Aletrino and Doorman may have tried to contact the leader of a communist Resistance cell.

After months of imprisonment in the dreaded Siguranţa (secret police) prison, Aletrino was transferred to a camp for political prisoners in Târgu Jiu. From there was deported to Mauthausen, where he died on 29 August 1942 under circumstances that have never become clear. 'Shot dead while fleeing,' the Gestapo officers had told Zwartendijk. Maybe he really had tried to escape.

Doorman was transferred to the German prisoner-of-war camp Stanislau in Poland. He escaped on 11 January 1944, and made it to London via Bucharest.

Decades later, a plaque commemorating Louis Aletrino, 'editor and international journalist', was placed in Mauthausen, with two lines of poetry by Friedrich Hölderlin:

Ach, töten könnt ihr,
aber nicht lebendig machen.
Oh, you can kill,
but not bring to life.

By then, Zwartendijk was dead.

I wonder if he ever learned what had happened to Aletrino's wives. I don't think so, and I hope not; after the news of his friend's death, it would have come as another blow. He had known Trude well in Prague; Eliska had often visited Rotterdam with Aletrino in the 1930s; and he had met Bertha several times.

Trude Kisch would have liked to have children. Two years after divorcing Aletrino, she married Otto Zweigenthal. In 1930, she gave birth to twins, a boy and a girl.

Trude, Otto, and their twelve-year-old children, Viktor and Suzana, died of exhaustion in 1942 on transport N, No. 725 from Prague to Terezín (Theresienstadt) and the onward transport Ar.No. 963 from Theresienstadt to Zamość in eastern Poland. They were headed for the extermination camp in Sobibór or Bełżec.

Elisabeth Eliska Eckstein married Louis Aletrino in Prague in December 1929 and became a Dutch national under section 5 of the Nationality Act of 1892. They were also divorced in Prague, in 1935, but thanks to her Dutch passport, Eliska escaped to the Netherlands in September 1939. In Haarlem, she registered under the name of Ellen Emilia. How she survived the war is an open question. In 1946, she returned to Prague; in February 1951, she came back to live in the Netherlands, in Amsterdam, and two months later she was dead at the age of fifty-two. A life cloaked in mystery.

The place where Aletrino's third wife, Bertha Haase, died remains unknown, but she did not survive the Holocaust.

Edith was still sitting at the kitchen table when her mother came home with the groceries. She briefly described what had happened.

Erni asked, 'Where is Pa?' He had gone out for a walk.

Aletrino was Erni's 'special friend from home'. Summer after summer, the two of them had gone out dancing together in Prague. Winter after winter, they'd had long conversations in Rotterdam about the political situation in Czechoslovakia. No one else could make her laugh the way he could.

Erni sat down at the kitchen table, nodded a couple of times, bit her lower lip, but would not shed a tear in front of her daughter.

Edith says, 'That's how people were in her generation.'

33

A secret burial

Ineke, Piet Zwartendijk's eldest daughter, was seventeen years old when her relatives returned from Lithuania to Eindhoven. To her, Uncle Jan and Aunt Erni seemed very happy and relieved to have put the whole thing behind them. She and her cousin Edith, who was four years younger, rarely discussed Kaunas. 'She refused to say anything about it.'

Later in the war, she suspected that Uncle Jan had always played it very safe and wasn't especially courageous. When she heard about the Curaçao visas after his death, she concluded that a few casual impressions don't tell you a thing about how people will act in wartime.

In the late 1940s, her father happened to hear a rumour about the false visas his brother had issued to thousands of Jewish refugees. He was furious with Jan for not taking him into his confidence, and let him know that right away. 'I'm your twin brother, damn it! Don't tell me you thought I'd turn you in!' No, Jan hadn't thought that for a moment. But Piet made no secret of his own opinions, and in defying the occupiers, he took serious risks. So the chance that one day he would be arrested was considerable. And in the Gestapo torture chambers, everyone confessed sooner or later.

Or almost everyone. Jan was wrong about his twin brother; Piet knew how to keep his mouth shut, even in the face of the Gestapo or SD, as he proved in 1943.

A year earlier, Piet and Mary had taken in a close Jewish friend of Mary's from Rotterdam, who had escaped a roundup and was searching for a hiding place. The children were told to call her Aunt Bertie. She stayed with them for the whole year of 1942. In January 1943, she fell ill, seriously ill. It turned out to be cancer. A doctor who was a friend of the family gave her morphine for the worst pain, but she couldn't go to the hospital because she would be arrested at once and deported to a concentration camp. For weeks, she lay in Piet and Mary's guest room, wasting away.

One Saturday afternoon, she died. That left the family with a huge problem. How do you go about an illegal burial? A Resistance group gave them the address of two young men who buried bodies in secret. They hid the remains in a delivery bicycle and took them to a dump outside Eindhoven just before the evening curfew. On their way back into town, they were arrested.

That same Saturday evening, three shouting Germans in uniform barged into the Zwartendijk home. Mary and the three daughters were made to leave the living room and stand in the corridor while Piet was interrogated, beaten, and tortured. But they got nothing out of him. In the corridor, his wife and daughter could hear him denying, after every blow, that there had been a Jew in hiding in his house.

Encouraged by his example, Mary and the children also denied every accusation. They were led into the living room one by one. Ineke, the eldest, a tall, skinny girl, often stared at the ground to give the impression that she was slow. Marijke, nearly eighteen and still far from grown up, bit her lower lip. Josien, fifteen years old, lisped even worse than usual – an impediment that had earned her the nickname Slos. Ineke was the calmest, Slos the best liar. Meanwhile, the Germans were searching the house. They had left Aunt Bertie's bed as it had been when she was removed from it, and a few of her things were still lying around, although most of them had been cleared away when the two young men took the body downstairs.

In the living room, Piet, Mary, Ineke, Marijke, and Slos had the incredible luck to all come up with the same story. Even though they had never discussed it, each one of them said that Aunt Cootje from Rotterdam had come to stay with them and then returned home. She was old and sick, they explained, and her house had sustained heavy damage in the bombing, so she came to Eindhoven for a few days at regular intervals, mostly keeping to her bed.

Aunt Cootje was a real person: Cootje Montijn, Jan and Piet's aunt. Didi had taken her in before the war. After Didi's death, she had moved to an old-age home not far from the centre of Rotterdam. The windows there had been broken, like so many windows in the city, as a result of the German bombing attack on 14 May 1940. But she had visited Eindhoven only two or three times. On the last occasion, 6 December 1942, the train had stopped about ten kilometres away from the city because, at that very moment, the RAF was bombing the Philips factories near the station.

The interrogations seemed endless. Each of the daughters had to tell the same story again and again, in German, and each of them talked about Aunt Cootje. They didn't change a single detail of the original version – not even Marijke, who bit her lower lip so hard that she needed a handkerchief to stop the bleeding.

The Germans stayed until well after midnight. They must have gone through the house twenty-five times, turning everything upside down, but they found nothing significant. By the time they left, it was three in the morning.

More than seventy years later, Ineke could still hardly believe it. 'Suddenly they were gone, and we never heard another word about it.'

That insane Saturday, the Jewish woman in hiding, the secret burial, the interrogations, the violence of the German officers, and the story each family member made up separately – Piet said nothing about any of this to his brother, Jan, even though Piet and Mary lived less than three minutes' walk from Jan and Erni, in Villapark, at the corner of Uiverlaan and Lijsterlaan. The neighbours must have noticed, and half the street must have heard something about it, but not Jan and Erni. Edith, Jan, and Robbie didn't find out either, not until long after the war. The first time Rob heard the story was from me. For Edith, it did bring back a memory: 'Aunt Bertie. I saw her a number of times, and thought she really was an aunt.'

Ineke Zwartendijk wanted to be an interior designer. In 1943, she began her studies at the Institute for Applied Arts (Instituut voor Kunstnijverheid) in Amsterdam. She moved into a room in De Lairessestraat, and went home once a week by way of Utrecht or Rotterdam. Either way it was a long trip, because the railway bridges over the major rivers had been bombed. Every week she spent half a day going home, and another half day returning to Amsterdam. That made her an ideal courier.

A boy she knew from secondary school asked her to 'take a few things with her', and said his parents would pay for all her railway travel. She didn't feel like she was joining the underground; in fact, she didn't quite know what she was doing, even though she was given a kind of corset in which to hide letters, coded messages, and illegal newspapers. In any case, she didn't know what papers and messages she was transporting; their contents were deliberately kept secret from her. She travelled to Utrecht, Zwolle, and Zutphen, and from Amsterdam to The Hague and Rotterdam.

One afternoon, she rang the doorbell of an apartment in the centre of Utrecht. Someone upstairs pulled a cord, and the front door swung open. She mounted the long staircase, stepped into the apartment, and knew something was wrong.

The living room was full of men and women with blank stares, all refusing to speak. One of them indicated with a nod that she should sit down in the only vacant chair. She realised they had been betrayed and that the traitors were holding them in the room, waiting patiently to see if yet another courier would show up. After a while, a man said, 'Follow us to the *Ortskommandantur*.' The city's German headquarters. The whole group had to go along.

Ineke was shut up in a cellar alone in the offices of the Gestapo, SS, or SD. No one had frisked her; her corset was still crammed full

Ineke Zwartendijk, 1943, a few weeks before her arrest.

of papers and illegal newspapers. She ate them all. Looking through the peephole now and then to see if anyone was spying on her, she went on chewing until it all turned into wet pulp in her mouth and she could swallow it.

The next day, German soldiers took her on the train to Amsterdam, to the prison in Amstelveenseweg. She shared a tiny cell with six other women. They couldn't even lie side by side; two women had to be standing at any time. She was bashful about anything related to the body; the women were older than she was, and told all sorts of scary stories. She was interrogated daily, but gave away nothing, feigning not understanding why she was being held and trying to look as slow-witted as possible. She had a whole series of interrogators, most of whom thought she was touched in the head.

After a few months, she was transferred to the prison in 's-Hertogenbosch. There, too, she was interrogated daily, this time by a friendly German who kept his hands to himself and did not beat her. By then it was 1944 and the Allies were approaching. She could hear the bombs landing and the jingle of keys as the guards raced down the corridors, but she couldn't leave her cell. During every bombing, she worried about whether to sit on the left or right side of the cell. That kept her mind occupied much of the time.

One day, the prison director came into her cell. She had been held prisoner for around six months by then. He asked if she had relatives in 's-Hertogenbosch.

'No.'

'Too bad. In that case, I would have let you go.'

OInke told me, 'You think, *I'll remember this for the rest of my life, until my dying breath.* But you won't. If you live to be old enough, you'll forget most of it.'

She was not released until October 1944, as the 53rd (Welsh) Infantry Division neared 's-Hertogenbosch. But she didn't see more than a scrap of blue sky before taking shelter again, because there was heavy combat in and around the city. A gynaecologist let her stay in the cellar of his home for two weeks.

For her, the war ended with an enormous bang. Near the station and the gynaecologist's house, a bridge was blown up. The explosion blew the windows, doors, and everything out of the house. She crawled out of the cellar; it was a beautiful sunny day. A Jeep was parked out in front; a man rose to his feet and stepped out. She beat the grime off her clothes and called out to him, 'Over here, Pa.'

Her father had been making daily attempts to reach 's-Hertogenbosch. After weeks without a sign of life from her, Piet Zwartendijk had gone to the German administrator at Philips. 'You people have arrested my daughter. I want to know where she's being held, or else I'll do some very stupid things.' It took a while, but then he heard that Ineke had been arrested in Utrecht, imprisoned in Amstelveen, and later transferred to 's-Hertogenbosch. But no one knew where exactly in 's-Hertogenbosch he could find her.

Back in Eindhoven, which became one of the first Dutch cities liberated by the Allies on 18 September 1944, Ineke experienced a strange phenomenon. She found herself among people who had already been living in freedom for six weeks, to whom the German occupation already seemed like a distant memory. She, on the other hand, was stuck in the war, still a prisoner in her mind. She had the feeling she was stuck in the past and didn't fit in among those happy, relieved people.

Ineke signed up for the Dutch women's naval service, established on 31 October 1944. Queen Wilhelmina wanted women in the navy, and Ineke was one of the first six to be trained in Mill Hill. Her war went on until 31 August 1945, when she returned to the Netherlands as a sergeant. She remained in uniform until 1950, when she went to work for the Red Cross.

Piet Zwartendijk kept it secret from his brother, Jan, until long after the war that his eldest daughter had taken huge risks as a courier and been trapped in Utrecht. Ineke herself never spoke of it; that would feel like bragging, she told me.

I visited Ineke in her flat in Bathmen, not far from Deventer. She is ninety-three years old, and still lives independently. When I ask her what beliefs motivated her wartime actions, she shrugs; she has never seen the inside of a church, or belonged to a political party. But when I ask whether she had a role model, she answers, without a second's hesitation, 'Aunt Didi.'

When she lived in Rotterdam, she spent every Saturday afternoon with Aunt Didi. She was not yet twelve when Aunt Didi started taking her to exhibitions in museums and galleries – 'salons', as they called them before the war. Aunt Didi had to write about them for her newspaper, and she would let her niece go her own way among the visitors and the paintings. But Ineke learned to observe everything carefully, because on the way home, Aunt Didi would ask her, 'Did you see such-and-such? And that other one?'

After Didi's death, Ineke kept all the articles her aunt had written in a blanket chest, pasted neatly into albums, and whenever she was mulling over important issues in her life, she would pick up one of those scrapbooks and start reading. Everything Aunt Didi had written sharpened her intellect and improved her judgement.

She still has the blanket chest in her home in Bathmen, and gives me a couple of scrapbooks to take with me so that I can form an impression of Didi's style and opinions. When I tell her that her uncle Jan was also inspired by Didi, right away she adds, 'So was his brother, Piet. When Aunt Didi died, my father was so upset that he spent a month sailing in the Mediterranean. His first plan had been simply to go on holiday in Zoutelande. But his sister's death had left him badly shaken.'

When I conclude the interview by asking what Aunt Didi's greatest lesson was, again she replies without a moment's pause.

'Make sure you'll never have to feel ashamed of using your family name.'

That was the Zwartendijk code.

34

Mister Frits

That Frits Philips – or 'Mister Frits', as everyone called him, inside and outside the company – knew about the Curaçao visas during the war is beyond my ability to prove. I can make a strong case, but nothing was put in writing.

In the autumn of 1941, the German occupiers urged companies to dismiss their Jewish employees, giving them three months' notice and a tiny sum in compensation. This was a first step towards the later measure forcing all businesses to fire their Jewish employees without any notice. After consulting with a few Jewish managers, the Philips directors decided to set up a separate division for Jewish staff. This discriminatory measure was taken in the hope 'that going on the attack would be the best defence', as one director put it, and that the German authorities would then leave the Jewish employees in peace. They felt anything was preferable to cutting the employees' ties with Philips.

The decision wasn't made overnight; everyone understood the great risks involved. After days of meetings, Frits settled on a plan that seemed like it just might work. He set up a division where Jewish employees would do highly specialised development and manufacturing work that was crucial to the war effort – *kriegswichtig*, as the Germans liked to say. On 24 December 1941, the Special Development Office (Speciaal Ontwikkelingsbureau; SOBU) began work. Besides an assembly workshop for measuring equipment, the SOBU included chemical and electric laboratories, a drafting room, and a number of administrative units. All Jewish employees from all levels of the organisation were together there, working on the same products, *kriegswichtig* products, to show how indispensable they were.

Sixty-six men and women worked in the division. This figure would rise to over one hundred when the Jewish employees of the Dutch Transmitter Factory (Nederlandse Seintoestellen Fabriek), a Philips subsidiary in Hilversum, were also reassigned to the SOBU in Eindhoven.

The SOBU employees were in a delicate position, partly because of the new German administrator, Dr Ludwig Nolte, who had come from the competitor AEG to Philips in February 1942. Nolte, an experienced factory director, had been personally instructed by minister Albert Speer – the same man who had overseen the construction of the Nazi regime's iconic buildings – to put Philips's manufacturing capacity to the most effective possible use for the war effort. It started to become clear that Philips employees were purposely causing delays. An order for receiver installations that Telefunken placed with Philips in June 1940 had not been fulfilled by February 1943, despite the 200,000 man-hours devoted to it. Nolte was determined to make the company more efficient and increase its contribution to the war industry, and SOBU would have a part to play in that.

Frits felt the situation was becoming too risky; in a *razzia*, all the Jewish employees could be arrested. When he heard a rumour that Unilever, the second-largest Dutch multinational, was trying to send its Jewish employees out of the Netherlands, he sent a message via Switzerland to his father and his brother-in-law in New York. His emphatic request to headquarters was to budget at least two million guilders for 'saving the lives' of the Jews in the company 'by obtaining exit visas out of the occupied areas'. Frits wanted to arrange for the entire SOBU group and their families to emigrate to South America.

His brother-in-law, Frans Otten, refused to cooperate. 'The main question is certainly not how much money should be budgeted,'

Frits Philips at company headquarters.

the Philips director in New York declared through a messenger in Geneva, 'but in whose pockets it would end up.' Nazi pockets – that was obvious. But wasn't that an acceptable price for the lives of one hundred to two hundred people?

The Dutch government in exile agreed with Otten. On 24 November 1942, they announced on Radio Oranje – the Dutch programme broadcast on the BBC to the occupied Netherlands – that buying Jews' freedom with foreign currency was prohibited. But Frits Philips couldn't be stopped that easily. In the spring of 1943, he approved a new plan to make it possible for Jewish employees to emigrate to Curaçao and Suriname with their families. I suspect he discussed this with Jan Zwartendijk. In the new plan, the earlier, more general destination of 'South America' was replaced with 'emigration to Curaçao and Suriname', the same phrase used on the visas that Zwartendijk had issued in Kaunas.

The head of the Philips travel office, W.J. van Wershoven, mapped out a route – and there, too, I see signs that Zwartendijk was involved.

He had sent all the refugees in Kaunas on a route leading through Japan; the idea was for the SOBU group to pass through Spain, so they would need transit visas, like the ones issued by consul Sugihara.

To obtain the required Spanish travel documents, Van Wershoven left for Barcelona and Madrid in March 1943. Oddly enough, the German administrator and the German authorities gave permission for this trip, taken on a business pretext. In Madrid, Van Wershoven negotiated with Spanish and Dutch organisations, and called on the assistance of the director of Philips Portuguesa to smooth the way for the emigration of the people on the Philips list – 194 by this stage. He also explained the plan to Otten, the company president, who told the Dutch embassy in Washington that the directors were willing to pay the full cost of emigration to Curaçao or Suriname, and do whatever else was required to make the plan work.

After Van Wershoven returned to Eindhoven with the news that the Spanish transit visas were ready at the Spanish embassy in Brussels, the only thing the SOBU group was waiting for was permission from Berlin. Meanwhile, they prepared for departure, not only mentally but also by 'practise packing'; stickers for suitcases were printed and filled in, the railway journey was discussed, and the employees were assigned seats on the train.

On the last day of June, the commander of the Vught concentration camp visited Eindhoven; he was thought to be there to check the speed and efficiency with which the SOBU group could be transported to the camp. And on 1 July 1943, the German administrator informed them that the emigration plan was *kaputt*. Philips then advised the SOBU group to go into hiding as fast as they could. By 5 July, only eight of them were still at work.

But most group members returned after hearing from a 'trusted source' that the emigration plan was still alive and kicking. Two weeks later, an SD officer in civilian clothes came to the company to inform the SOBU employees personally that their emigration could go ahead entirely according to plan. The emigrants (the 'Philips Jews') and their families were told to gather in one place, namely the camp in

Vught, so that everything would go smoothly. Some of them believed the SD officer and reported to Vught voluntarily. On 18 August 1943, vans drove onto the Philips site in Eindhoven to take the remaining members of the SOBU group to the camp in Vught.

Again, they were told they had been brought there so they could emigrate. Most of the family members who had remained in hiding, some fifty in total, believed this lie and reported to the camp. But the whole thing was a German plot to capture as many Jews as possible.

In Vught, the SOBU group was merged with the Philips-Kommando, a group of well-educated men and women who had been assigned to the Philips workshop there since February 1943. The Kommando members were being held in Kamp Vught as political prisoners. At first, Frits Philips had brushed off the urgent request from Berlin to supply prisoners with work. But at the insistence of the German administrators assigned to Philips, he had given in, mainly because it was an opportunity to demand certain improvements in the prisoners' lives, such as a hot meal every day – which soon became known as the Philips mash – and a small payment for their work. Frits also made sure 'his' prisoners would no longer have to participate in the humiliating roll calls. The Kommando was to be headed by a Philips employee, and Mister Frits chose an old university friend: R.E. Laman Trip.

The post-war accusation that Philips, like all the major German companies, had used concentration camp inmates as cheap labour in the pursuit of profit – as BMW did in Dachau, for example – was unfounded. Over the two-year existence of the SOBU group, Philips had an operating loss of one million guilders. The intentions were good and sincere, but it was naïve to try to make a deal with an utterly untrustworthy and criminal regime.

The Philips-Kommando grew to more than one thousand members. More and more women joined the radio tube division, but their safety could no longer be guaranteed. The Jewish inmates were taken away from Vught on one transport after another; it no longer made any difference whether they belonged to the Philips-Kommando.

Sooner or later, all the Jews in Kamp Vught were deported. On 2 June 1944, the final group left the camp: 391 women, ninety men, and fifteen children under the age of fourteen. Four days and nights later, they arrived in Auschwitz-Birkenau.

A few days later, more than 200 women from the Philips group were transferred to Reichenbach concentration camp near Breslau, where they were put to work at a branch of Telefunken. In July, the other women from Philips, except for mothers with children, were sent to join the group in Reichenbach. Soon afterwards, the men were also transferred to Reichenbach, where they were forced to work in a labour camp for the Hagenuk company. Ultimately, 382 Jews from the Philips-Kommando came out of the war alive because they had been assigned to work in Reichenbach. But among the members of the original SOBU group who were sent to Auschwitz, only thirty-nine survived.

Immediately after the liberation of Eindhoven, the Philips directors set up an investigating commission to purge the company of employees who, in the words of its mission statement, 'had acted as traitors to their country or had emphatically collaborated with the occupying regime'. This commission did its job thoroughly, looking into almost 1,900 complaints and accusations, interviewing managers and co-workers, demanding written statements, and sifting through contracts and files for evidence. The investigation went on until 31 December 1946, but by late 1944, the commission already had so much work it had to form sub-commissions. Jan Zwartendijk became the secretary of one of those sub-commissions.

Jan Paulussen, the Philips company historian, wrote to me, 'That job was a great honour, but above all a huge responsibility, and I believe it shows that by that stage Zwartendijk's actions in Lithuania must have been known to a larger group.' Or, at the very least, to the top man, Frits Philips, who insisted that all members of the investigating commissions had to have had an unblemished wartime record.

Zwartendijk must have taken 'Mr Frits' into his confidence in February and March 1943, while working on the emigration plan. That wouldn't have been possible any later. On 30 April 1943, Frits Philips and a few other directors were arrested. From that moment until the country was liberated, there was no way of communicating with them.

The reason for the arrests was the large number of Philips employees participating in the national strike against the occupying regime. The plan was to release the directors when work was resumed, but the strikers refused to give in to this form of blackmail and return to work. They gave in only after seven randomly selected hostages were executed on the company grounds.

All the directors were then released – except Frits. He remained in the custody of the occupiers for five months, first in Haaren, near Kamp Vught, and later in an internment camp for prominent Dutch hostages in Sint-Michielsgestel. The Germans tried to break down his resistance in the hope that he would resign as director and turn over full control of the company to its German administrators.

When Frits returned to Eindhoven on 30 September 1943, there was no longer any role for him to play as director. The German regime became more severe, and almost everything manufactured at Philips was intended for the war industry. The historian Loe de Jong later calculated that, in the first half of 1944, 70 to 80 per cent of the output of the Dutch Philips factories went to the Luftwaffe, the German air force. But in his history of the Philips corporation under German management, Dr Ivo Blanken is sceptical of this figure; Loe de Jong saw every light bulb supplied to Germany as a contribution to the war industry. Blanken's own estimate is that deliveries of a military nature to the Wehrmacht amounted to 24 per cent of revenue – and that was after total production had been sharply reduced by the bombing of the main factory complexes in Eindhoven. But by 1944, despite all the attempted sabotage and foot-dragging, Philips was entirely under German control.

On 20 July 1944, a couple of employees went to Mr Frits to warn him that SD agents were on their way to his office. He slipped out through his window and went into hiding, where he remained until the liberation of Eindhoven.

During the final months of the war, the Germans plundered the company, picking it bare. Like thousands of other Philips managers, Piet and Jan Zwartendijk looked on, powerless, as machines, raw materials, and stocks, along with thousands of radios, were carried off to the Ruhr region.

When the post-war investigative committee released its final report, on 31 December 1946, 788 employees were dismissed, 536 placed on long-term suspension, and 104 reprimanded.

But whatever the impact of this news in Eindhoven, Jan Zwartendijk was no longer there to see it. He had gone to Athens – without his wife or children for the time being – where he had been appointed director of Philips S.A. Hellenique. It was another difficult assignment. Even before the Germans had well and truly retreated from the Balkans, civil war had broken out in Greece.

In Athens, he was reunited with an old acquaintance – one he had spoken to many times on the telephone but had met only once, for a moment, in person. At the Dutch embassy, he shook the hand of the newly appointed envoy, who had just arrived from London: L.P.J. de Decker.

De Decker adopted a formal attitude, as if they barely knew each other and had never worked together on an ingenious rescue plan. It wasn't until their second meeting that he murmured to Zwartendijk on the embassy steps, 'I need your help.'

35

Hey! Blow! Scream! Bang!

In August 1941, Benjamin Fishoff was sent from Kobe to Shanghai. 'A forced evacuation' – that was his term for it. It was a change of country but not of regime – both when he left Japan and when he arrived in Shanghai, he had to show his papers to Japanese soldiers.

Ever since the bloody Battle of Shanghai from August to late November 1937, with 200,000 Chinese and 70,000 Japanese dead, the Chinese port had been occupied by the Japanese army. Shanghai would remain in Japanese hands until Japan's surrender on 2 September 1945. Benjamin Fishoff spent the entire rest of the war in the city, at first in the International Settlement and later in the Jewish ghetto. Not until 1946, after the American army had captured the city, could he board a ship to New York.

Benjamin looked back on Kobe as a paradise compared to Shanghai. Kobe was civilisation; Shanghai, a disorderly mess. He was not the only one to feel homesick for Kobe after disembarking in Shanghai.

In *Cafe Scheherazade*, a novel based entirely on historical fact, Arnold Zable describes the seven-year flight of two Polish Jews with Curaçao visas from Kaunas to Australia:

This is what struck Zalman [about Kobe and Japan]: the efficiency, the precision, the politeness; and cleanliness. More than ever he felt as though he was moving in a dream … And he thought, 'I am entering the land of *Madame Butterfly.*'

Shanghai was the complete opposite: a bitter reality.

What stands out? What impressions come to mind? The confusion. Where Kobe was symmetry, Shanghai was chaos. Where Kobe was an idyllic interlude, Shanghai was a rat's maze, a dead-end.

In the Shanghai ghetto, some twenty-five thousand Polish, German, and Austrian Jews were clumped together, amid constant shouting, screeching, and cacophony:

If I were a painter trying to depict Shanghai in the war years, I would plunge my brush into all the colours of the palette and splash them on thick, at random. Or if I were a musician I would take all the instruments from all over the world, put them together, and say, 'Hey! Blow! Scream! Bang! Play as loud as you can! All of you!'

Still more overwhelming was their disillusionment. After the attack on Pearl Harbor, all overseas connections to Europe, the Americas, and the Middle East had been severed.

Intense disappointment took hold of the refugees, the Polish ambassador's daughter Teresa Romer recalls. They said things like, 'This will go on for years. I can't take any more. Maybe we'll never have a home of our own.'

With each passing month, they grew more fearful that their journey – which for most had begun almost two years earlier, in the autumn of 1939 – would prove to have been utterly pointless. This was an understandable fear, in view of the relentless efforts by Josef Meisinger, 'the butcher of Warsaw,' to massacre the Polish, German, and Australian Jews who had escaped the atrocities in Europe and fled to Shanghai.

Meisinger had been sent to Japan by submarine in 1941, after

Josef Meisinger in 1937.

Poland became too hot for him. As the commander of the death squad Einsatzgruppe IV, SS Standartenführer Josef Albert Meisinger had presided over a reign of terror, authorising the execution of 1,700 Jews, Polish intellectuals, politicians, and athletes in the forests of Palmiry. He had ordered the execution of fifty-five Jews on 22 November 1939 in reprisal for the murder of a Polish policeman, and the execution of 107 Poles on 20 December in retaliation for the murder of two Germans. All the reprisals and other Nazi horrors inflicted on the Netherlands in 1942, 1943, and 1944 had been tested in Poland in the autumn of 1939 – under Meisinger's authority.

In the early months of 1940, Meisinger was involved in creating the Warsaw ghetto, erecting a wall around it, and patiently starving the prisoners inside. All this was his idea. But he had to make a hasty exit when his past in Germany came back to haunt him. In the 1930s, he had harassed large numbers of senior military officers, shadowing them, blackmailing them, threatening them, and accusing them of homosexuality. He was hated by everyone in the military leadership and SS, except for Heydrich, who had known Meisinger as his right-hand man. He knew too much; even Hitler started to worry. Meisinger was about to face a court martial when Heydrich rushed to his aid – not for the first time – by whisking him away to Tokyo with Himmler's approval.

In Japan, Meisinger became a Gestapo liaison and the coordinator of SD activities at the German embassy. He was dismayed to witness the arrival of the thousands of Jews with Curaçao visas, and tried to stop the Polish ambassador and Dutch consul from offering them further assistance by asking the Japanese government to shut down the Polish embassy and Dutch consulates at once.

He was even more vexed by the twenty thousand Jews from Austria and Germany who had travelled to Shanghai in 1938 and 1939 on ships of the Lloyd Triestino Line: the *Conte Rosso* and *Conte Verde* from Trieste, and the *Conte Biancamano* from Genoa. Norddeutscher Lloyd's *Potsdam* had also continued to operate a service between Bremen and Shanghai. The Jews who chose that route had paid a heavy price; when they left Germany and Austria, their houses, possessions, and savings were taken into custody, and their bank accounts were frozen. They lost everything, and had only their jewellery with which to pay their way. Even that was often seized at the Austrian border by the Gestapo. Nonetheless, nearly twenty thousand people had found their way onto ships that carried them via the Suez Canal, Bombay, Colombo, Singapore, and Hong Kong to Shanghai. Later, when the Nazis refused to pay foreign currency for the Suez Canal toll, the route went by way of the Cape of Good Hope. The passengers were allowed to disembark anywhere but Port Said, because the British authorities feared that from there they might run off to Palestine.

These refugees, like the ones in Kaunas, had received assistance from a foreign consul. Ho Feng-Shan, in the Chinese consulate at

German and Austrian Jews disembarking from a ship of the
Lloyd Triestino Line in Shanghai.

Beethovenplatz 3 in Vienna, wrote visas for them from November
1938 until his return to China in May 1940. Those papers, like
Zwartendijk's, were technically invalid. The Republic of China had
lost its authority over Shanghai in 1937, when Japan occupied the city.
Nevertheless, the visas gave thousands of Jews the opportunity to
escape, because the Austrian authorities took them seriously.

Ho Feng-Shan defied the wishes of his immediate superior, the
Chinese ambassador in Berlin, who hoped to maintain good relations
with Hitler. But Ho had a strong will. He had grown up as a farm
boy in the province of Hunan and, after his father's premature death,
had received a helping hand from a group of Norwegian Lutheran
missionaries. Thanks to them, he completed school and eventually
went on to a university. Ho was motivated by Christian beliefs. 'Do
nothing you cannot justify in Heaven' – he had learned that motto

by heart at the Lutheran school in Hunan, and he put it up on the wall in Vienna. 'Speak only thoughts that contribute something to this world' was another motto that came to his mind on 15 March 1938, when he witnessed Hitler's triumphal procession through Vienna and heard two hundred thousand ecstatic onlookers shouting, '*Wir wollen unseren Führer sehen, wir wollen unseren Führer horen.* ['We want to see our Führer, we want to hear our Führer.'] *Sieg Heil! Sieg Heil! Sieg Heil!*' It is unknown how many visas Ho Feng-Shan issued, but they probably numbered in the thousands.

Hitler's annexation of Austria was immediately followed by an explosion of anti-Semitic hatred in Vienna. It started with insults and acts of humiliation. Gangs of thugs forced their way into the homes of Jewish families in prosperous areas of Vienna, forcing them to clean the streets on their knees with toothbrushes. A crowd gathered to watch and snigger.

Most of the German and Austrian Jews who went to Shanghai had spent several months, or in some cases even years, as prisoners in Dachau or Buchenwald. They were sent away to make room for the thousands of Jews taken captive on Kristallnacht, the Night of Broken Glass, a massive anti-Semitic pogrom that had taken place on 9–10 November 1938. In Germany, Austria, and the Sudetenland, 1,400 synagogues and 7,500 shops had been set on fire or demolished, and thirty thousand young Jewish men had been arrested and sent to concentration camps. The released Jews, mostly political prisoners, had to pledge to the Gestapo that they would leave Germany and Austria at once. They had seen enough of the concentration camps that they did not hesitate a single day. Aside from ten marks and a few personal effects, they were not allowed to take anything with them. Even so, the Lloyd Triestino Line could hardly handle the glut of passengers. The shipping company offices in Vienna and Berlin normally demanded from each passenger not only the price of the ticket but also a deposit of US$150 or more, for incidental expenses on the voyage. The company waived this required deposit for the Jewish passengers, because even their wedding rings were not safe when they crossed the Austrian–Italian border; Gestapo agents conducted thorough body searches, robbing the refugees of any remaining valuables.

Until mid-1941, the Japanese government had taken a clear stance on the Jewish question: despite its two treaties with Nazi Germany, concluded for political and military reasons – the Anti-Comintern Pact in November 1936 and the Tripartite Pact (to which Italy was also party) in September 1940 – Japan had no intention of adopting Hitler's anti-Semitic policies. At a press conference on 31 December 1940, Japanese foreign minister Yosuke Matsuoka expressed this position succinctly:

> I am the man responsible for the alliance with Hitler, but nowhere have I promised that we would carry out his anti-Semitic policies in Japan. This is not simply my personal opinion, it is the position of Japan, and I have no compunction about announcing it to the world.

These were not the words of a man of peace – far from it. Matsuoka was a far-right nationalist and a political bulldozer. Even after negotiating a neutrality pact with Stalin and Molotov in April 1941, he wanted Japan to take part in Operation Barbarossa, the Axis war against the Soviet Union. Hitler was an avid supporter of the plan; if Japan joined the attack on the Soviet Union, the Red Army was sure to be defeated. But Matsuoka could not win over prime minister Fumimaro Konoe or the leaders of the Japanese Imperial Army, who had previously striven to expand Japanese power and influence in the south of Asia. When he continued urging them to declare war on the United States, he was dismissed in July 1941. Six months later came the attack on Pearl Harbor; by then, Japan believed itself strong enough to challenge the United States. Matsuoka would have been better off biding his time; he was excluded from government for the rest of the war. But his policy on the Jewish question remained more or less intact.

In the autumn of 1941, Josef Meisinger visited Shanghai and, to his astonishment, saw that Jews were allowed to live in freedom throughout the city. He presented the Japanese authorities with a number of plans for making Shanghai *Judenfrei*. Chongming Island, at the mouth of the Yangtze, struck him as the ideal place for a concentration camp. On the other hand, it would be much cheaper simply to send the Jews out to sea on a couple of broken-down ships and let them starve there. He drafted that plan, too.

The Japanese authorities rejected these proposals, but did take a few measures to limit Jews' freedom of movement. In one respect, the butcher of Warsaw got his way: on 15 November 1942, the Japanese decided to establish a Shanghai ghetto. But not until 23 February 1943 were all the Jews sent to that ghetto, in the Hongkew area.

Until then, many refugees regarded life in Shanghai as an astonishing dream. In the words of Yossel, a character in *Cafe Scheherazade*, they led 'a Yiddish life', maybe even more Yiddish than in Warsaw:

> Of all the cities I have known, Shanghai was the best, the most beautiful. You cannot imagine it. My beloved Warsaw was burning. Krochmalna Street was circled by barbed walls. My loved ones were in *gehennim*, and in Shanghai I had a good life.
>
> A Yiddish life. With Yiddish theatre. First-class. With the best actors. From Warsaw and Vilna. From Odessa and Harbin. And Yiddish clubs. Yiddish radio. Yiddish newspapers: *Unzer Leben*, *Unzer Welt*, *Dos Wort* and *Der Yiddisher Almanach*. And the ghetto? The internment camps? The bombings?
>
> Of course, my dear Martin, after Pearl Harbor, it all changed. Of course we were squashed into Hongkew. Yes, it is true, we could be beaten up when we queued for a pass. Hundreds died of starvation. Of typhus. Of cholera. Of malaria and *meshugas*.
>
> Of course I saw the bombings. I was in the street at the time. I saw it all. I saw the planes swooping over Hongkew, and people diving into the gutters. I heard the bombs whistling as they hurtled down. I saw the corpses lying on the road, with flies crawling over their wounds. I could

smell the bloated bodies in the heat. I saw people frantically searching for their loved ones. I saw dismembered coolies slumped against their mangled rickshaws. I saw it all.

Yet somehow, for me, Shanghai was a beautiful life. That is how I remember it. What do you want me to say? That I am ashamed? That I should not have enjoyed myself when I had the chance?

What young men like Yossel may have liked best of all was that Shanghai had a Sephardic Jewish elite. Many Sephardic businessmen were millionaires. A Jew in Shanghai was not necessarily one of the wretched of the earth. The idea that Jews could succeed in life was especially inspiring to Polish Jews, who had pursued that dream in Warsaw or Łódź, but very often found it to be a mere illusion.

The Mizrahi Jews had come to the Chinese city in the mid-nineteenth century from Baghdad, Tehran, Bombay, Calcutta, and Thessaloniki. They believed Shanghai would one day outshine even the Iraqi, Persian, Indian, and Greek cities of their birth. They used the millions they earned in the opium trade to found banks and shipping companies, and to erect hotels and retail emporia. They gave carefully selected architects firm instructions to design Jugendstil buildings for them along the Bund, the promenade along the Huangpu River, giving the area a modern, European atmosphere. Even the customs house was a sight to see, with a clock tower that made it look like a modern commodity exchange in London or Amsterdam.

Yossel met the magnate Sir Victor Sassoon in the lobby of the Cathay Hotel. An Iraqi Jew by origin, he held sway over a vast financial empire. The hotel established by Sassoon still exists today and is called the Fairmont Peace Hotel. It's on the corner of the Bund and Nanjing Road, Shanghai's main shopping street. I go there every afternoon for tea to marvel at the grandeur of the marble lobby, with light fixtures and mirrors by Lalique. Yossel drank whisky there with Sir Vic, a great philanthropist who had survived a plane crash in the First World War while serving as a pilot in the Royal Flying Corps. He walked with a limp, and showered money left and right. Everyone who asked for

A Jewish family in a rickshaw in Shanghai.

his help left the hotel with a smile. To a refugee who had escaped the Warsaw ghetto by a whisker, this was the land of milk and honey.

In the 1920s, Sir Victor Sassoon had shown exceptional generosity to the Russian Jews who had settled in the Chinese seaport. He remained a willing donor when the German and Austrian refugees came down the gangplank and took their first steps on the Bund. In the year 1939 alone, he gave $170,000 to humanitarian aid organisations. As the owner of more than one thousand properties in Shanghai, he could afford to be magnanimous.

But after Pearl Harbor, he was no longer to be found in the city. He was in Bombay when the Japanese bombers attacked the US naval base. Only after the war, in December 1945, did he return to Shanghai

The Bund, Shanghai, late 1930s.

to see to his financial interests. The visit lasted less than two days, and he spent his twilight years in the Bahamas.

I am staying in the Astor House Hotel, which rose to greatness in the early twentieth century under the Kadoorie and Ezra families – Jews from Baghdad and Calcutta whose dream was to turn the originally British hotel into an institution. They succeeded. Einstein stayed in room 304, Charlie Chaplin in 404, Joseph Kessel in 410, and André

A Jewish refugee from Vienna posing with her son in front of the Broadway
Mansions Hotel and the Garden Bridge.

Malraux in 401. Directly above that is my room, 501. Through the
window, on the far side of the Russian embassy, I can see the ships
heading around the long bend in the river towards the sea. Before
the Second World War, this impressive embassy housed the Seamen's
Club. The sounds of the vessels – the long-drawn-out tones of the
freighter, the thinner, higher whistles of the towboats – must also
have reached the ears of André Malraux. He spent many weeks at
the Astor House in 1920, while working on *La Condition Humaine*
(translated into English as *Man's Fate*), his novel in which down-and-
out aristocrats and communist ascetics join forces to fight the fascistic
Shanghai regime. One sentence from Malraux's work has found a
permanent place in my memory: 'A man is what he hides.'

The Garden Bridge provided access to the ghetto.
On the far left is the Astor House Hotel.

If I lean out of the window and look to the right, I can see the
Broadway Mansions Hotel, a Chicago-style Art Deco edifice built in
1934 for an investment bank run by Victor Sassoon. It looks like the
set of an American gangster movie, especially at night, when it's lit
from all sides. The Broadway Mansions and the Astor are near the
Waibaidu, or Garden, Bridge, the first steel bridge in China, which
connects the Bund to the north-east of the city – the Hongkew district
(then Hongkew), where the Jewish ghetto was located.

Hongkew was known for its old lane houses. The buildings were
slated for demolition, but proved large enough to serve as *Heime*,
group homes for the refugees. These brownish-red brick buildings are
still there. The only change since 1943 is the dozens of air conditioners
protruding from the windows. One *Heim* accommodated twenty to
thirty families.

This district, formerly Japanese, was chosen for the Jews because
from 1937 onward the Japanese were allowed to live anywhere in the
city, and poured out of Hongkew by the thousands. The area changed
rapidly: the wooden geisha tearooms made way for Viennese coffee
houses, the Japanese kimono shops became Polish sewing workshops,

Overcrowded *Heime* in Hongkew.

and the Japanese-only restaurants and brothels became soup kitchens. In the space of a few weeks, Hongkew became an overcrowded Central European Jewish quarter.

Electricians, masons, carpenters, and plumbers set about transforming the area. They had no jobs, but to keep up their skills they built houses. Engineers went to work as roadmenders; architects, as plasterers. With the aid of the Komor Committee, to which Victor Sassoon had donated huge sums before his departure, bakers, barbers, and grocers returned to their former occupations, and shops opened up everywhere.

In the winter of 1943–1944, unusually cold weather and runaway inflation made life a good deal more difficult. Coal and food cost the ghetto residents thousands of yuan. A Red Cross report described conditions in the district as abominable, and warned that at least six thousand people were on the brink of starvation.

Yet music was still played there, and even in 1944 you could find Viennese cakes and pastries at the Wiener Café-Restaurant Delikat.

The refugees remained in Shanghai for at least six years. Many German and Austrian Jews stayed even longer; the first had come ashore on the Bund in December 1938.

From the very first moment Lisbeth Loewenberg arrived in 1939, everything was different:

> When we got off that ship on the Bund and on Nanking Road, I saw these masses of people. And they were all Chinese and there was a different odour in the air. I thought that I would never be able to breathe again in my whole life. A mixture of cooking oil and incense, and masses and masses of people. And I thought that there has to be an accident or something going on, there cannot be that many people always, always, like ants, constantly, but you get used to it.

The Poles, who had come to Shanghai in the autumn of 1941 in the belief that they would travel on to the United States in a matter of weeks, were among the greatest optimists in the refugee community. Michèle Kahn vividly describes their attitude:

> They decided to make the best of it. They founded their own aid organisations and literary and artistic clubs, and they organised plays and concerts. They also had Hebrew movable type made for them, and when the books they printed began to fall apart in the damp air, they would reprint them. For example, they published the Babylonian Talmud – a corpus of almost six thousand pages! – and a whole arsenal of sacred writings and prayer books. They created a library of Hebrew and Yiddish works, and works that people had brought with them from Europe were collected for reproduction.

The Polish rabbis and rabbinical students regarded themselves as the Hongkew elite, and were not always well liked. The yeshiva students refused to stay in the *Heime*, four-to-six-storey buildings in which as many as ten people might sleep in a single room, stacked one on top of the other. They wanted a place of their own, and, in the

Yeshiva students in Shanghai.

course of 1943, were assigned a housing block on Wayside Road. The students refused the food from the collective kitchen because much of it was not kosher, and prepared their own food instead. This kosher food was said to be so much more expensive that they received an extra stipend from the Joint Distribution Committee. According to a joke told in Hongkew, if you wanted to eat well, it was best to let your *payot* (sideburns) grow. After their long, exhausting Torah studies, the students could be heavy drinkers. These rabbis-to-be, who preached moral lessons and regarded secular Jews as apostates, also threw wild parties and danced far into the night. This apparent inconsistency bewildered other, more cosmopolitan groups of Jews in Shanghai, such as the those from Berlin who were known as *Piefkes*, and the *Jekkes* from Vienna.

The rabbinical students had frequent run-ins with Japanese soldiers, who felt little sympathy for men with long beards, corkscrew curls, and black hats. According to Ernest G. Heppner's account of life in Hongkew, such incidents even led to the death of some Haredim, strictly religious Jews. But I have not found any confirmation of this.

Marcel Wejland thought Shanghai was the best place to spend the Second World War. He waxed lyrical about the city: 'It was exciting there. Sensual. Free. Even freer than pre-war Europe.' Of course, some parts of the city were best avoided. Marcel never went into the walled Chinese city to the south of the International Settlement, close to the river, because of its reputation as a sink of gambling halls, opium dens, and brothels. The police took down your name when you entered the area, and if you hadn't reported back to the guard post by nightfall, they started dragging the river. But Marcel was a schoolboy with a pass that made it easy for him to leave Hongkew. The adults had to stay there all day, and work. Marcel suspected the only thing keeping them going was the Polish ambassador.

The Polish Jews felt profound respect for Count Tadeusz Romer. 'Romer paved the way for our exodus to Shanghai,' Marcel wrote in his memoirs, 'and was the first to take measures to accommodate the large groups in which we arrived.' Romer feared that the voice of the Polish Jews would be drowned out by the Austrian and German Jewish choir; the gap between the Polish shopkeepers and the intellectuals and artists from Vienna and Berlin was considerable. Most of the Austrian and German Jews were secularised, while the majority of Polish Jews were Orthodox. Romer saw to it that they could remain true to their identity in every way. He helped the refugees find jobs and organised vocational training for both children and adults. One day the war would be over, and they would embark on new lives in new countries. So they needed to be able to start work right away as electricians and auto mechanics.

Hala, Marcel's sister, learned to design clothes. She turned out to be such a gifted seamstress that she was soon working for Chinese fashion shops in the French concession and earning a pretty penny. It didn't take her long to find work in Australia.

Marcel's mother learned how to run a mega-kitchen. She was soon in charge of Kitchen No. 1, where she and a team of Chinese cooks prepared two hundred meals a day. To the disappointment of the yeshiva students, she refused to use garlic. Back in Poland, garlic stood for poverty, and she hated the stuff.

The most important thing in Marcel's life was learning – just as it had been in Kobe, Vilnius, and Łódź. The Shanghai Jewish School was modelled on the British educational system, but most of the teachers were Russian Jews. Mrs Margaleff taught George Eliot's *Silas Marner*, which was much heavier going for Marcel than *Pan Tadeusz*. But if he wanted to be able to translate Adam Mickiewicz's verse epic into English one day, he would have to learn the subtleties of the language, so he pressed on.

English literature and biology were taught by Joe Gershevitch, a Renaissance man. He didn't give lessons, but swept his students up in his enthusiasm. Science, Art, and Literature – 'always write those words with capital letters' – were to him the different facets of the diamond called knowledge. In class, he would race from Chaucer, Marlowe, Jonson, and Shakespeare to Swift, Fielding, and Defoe, and then plunge into the great Victorian novelists. To his delight, Marcel observed that while on the other side of the world, in accursed Europe, every form of civilisation was being trampled, the Shanghai

Jewish School was awakening an insatiable thirst for knowledge in its students, along with a great respect for the arts and an overwhelming desire to succeed in life.

Teresa Romer, who to all appearances led a quiet life in the sheltered neighbourhood around the Polish legation, remembers a very different side of Shanghai. What struck the ambassador's daughter was the abject poverty. Every night, hundreds of Chinese people starved to death. On her morning walk to the Lycée du Sacre Coeur with her sisters, she would see the corpses by the roadside, wrapped in newspaper. Adults. Children. Babies.

This made it all the more surprising that her governess, Miss Hubisz, managed to return from the market with fresh vegetables and a little meat each day. To go shopping for groceries, Miss Hubisz would take a rickshaw, while Teresa looked on, a little shocked to see that the coolie who pulled the two-wheeled cart had bare feet:

> They were battered and broken from walking, not red or brown like calloused skin but purple or lavender. I hated the idea of people being used as beasts of burden, and refused to go with Miss Hubisz when she took the rickshaw.

Teresa left Shanghai on 15 August 1942, with her parents, her sisters, and Miss Hubisz. At that stage, the city was still in much better shape than it would be in 1943, 1944, or, above all, 1945. After an accidental American bombing, the situation in Hongkew became truly desperate. The target of the air attack was the Japanese naval base where warships were prepared for the conflict in the Pacific. The B-29 bombers flew at an altitude of 15,000 metres. The thick cloud cover made it impossible for the pilots to see exactly what they were bombing. On 17 July 1945, most of the bombs landed in the Hongkew ghetto, where the houses had no cellars.

One boy was on his bicycle when he heard the whistling of the falling bombs. He tried to make a dash for it, but a Japanese soldier with his rifle at the ready commanded him to stop, seized his bicycle, and took off like a rocket. The boy dived into a ditch, and survived the violent explosions; the soldier was hurled into the air, bicycle and all.

The bombing led to the death of thirty-one of the refugees, a figure that could have been much higher, with twenty-five thousand of them – men, women, and children – living in houses that were much too small. Even so, the houses were severely damaged. To make matters worse, it started to rain, during a monsoon that went on for days and transformed Hongkew into a filthy den of disease.

By the final weeks of the war, the district resembled an internment camp with overcrowded infirmaries and famished prisoners. When Shanghai was liberated, in September, American aid organisations had their work cut out for them.

36

From Avenue Joffre to the ghetto

February 2016. Eight degrees Celsius. Tentative sunlight pokes through the morning mist. The plane trees are leafless, their trunks a pale colour, and for an instant I'm reminded of a French provincial town in winter. But the traffic contradicts me, worming its noisy way down the broad boulevard, honking, growling, rattling, screeching.

I walk along a pavement almost as wide as the street passing through the former French concession, in search of the avenue that in 1942 was known as Avenue Joffre. Finding it is no trouble at all, even though Shanghai is a city that transforms itself twice a year.

Nina Wertans lived with her parents on what is now Huaihai Road, number 925. I see an opening between two tall buildings connected from the fourth floor up, giving the impression of a gate. The stone crosspiece, which bears the inscription 925, gives access to a warren of narrow streets and alleys. The tall buildings along the boulevard were erected recently, but the houses along the side streets are the same ones that Nina Wertans passed daily. The building where she lived with her parents is still there; it is tiny and narrow, but then again, there are almost no large dwellings in this city, which already had four million inhabitants in 1941. The brickwork makes the house look European, but the red-lacquered doors are as Chinese as a lantern.

The Japanese occupation of Shanghai in 1937 had led to a hard-fought victory over the Chinese. To avoid dragging the major powers into the conflict, Japan had guaranteed the neutrality of the foreign concessions: neither the army nor the city authorities would interfere in affairs in the French concession or in the International Settlement, a merger of the British and American concessions. Those concessions were autonomous, miniature states. The peace treaties of 1860, which had put an end to the Opium Wars, had ceded control of large parts of Shanghai to Western powers. It was a kind of colonialism by stealth: French law applied in the French concession, and British law in the International Settlement. On Avenue Joffre, gendarmes with capes on their shoulders and flat-topped kepis on their heads directed traffic; in the International Settlement, the constables were turbaned Sikhs. But it was in the Old City next to the French concession that the real China began.

The day after the Japanese attack on Pearl Harbor, the Imperial Japanese Army took control of Shanghai. At first, this was a mere formality; until 23 February 1943, the concessions were still administered by French, British, and American officials. One thorny issue for the occupying power was that the Vichy regime had submitted to the authority of Nazi Germany and that France was therefore, in theory, an ally of Japan. As a result, the French – unlike the British and the Americans – were not sent to internment camps outside the city.

On Avenue Joffre, you heard equal measures of French and Russian. After the Russian Revolution of 1917 and the defeat of the White Army, around one hundred thousand Russians had fled to Manchuria, and many had later sought refuge in Shanghai. Despite their privileged background, they had trouble finding employment other than as waiters, taxi drivers, and security guards. Young, blonde Russian women worked as hostesses in gambling houses for wealthy Chinese patrons, or in the better restaurants. Otherwise, their only options were the cabarets and brothels.

In 1942, Nina Wertans was ten years old and on her way to school. She slowed her step when she heard the soft conversation of Russian women. She liked to try to pick up as many languages as she could.

A Jewish girl in Kobe, photographed by Tetsu Kono for
the exhibition *Wandering Jew*.

The more languages, the more freedom – that was the lesson Shanghai
had taught her.

Nina had come into the world in a Warsaw shrouded in darkness.
The sun did not break through until three days after she was born,
her father had told her. She was the only child of Jakub Wertans from
Warsaw and Judzif Szeskin, born in Vilnius. Her parents differed in
age by seventeen years. Her father had earned his reputation as an
engineer and as the owner of a number of warehouses. He'd had the
good sense to gather an emergency fund of dollars and gold coins.

Still, Nina's parents must have led a life that was somewhat divorced
from reality. On 1 September 1939, as they were listening to the radio,
they heard explosions outside and thought it was a drill. When the
bombing grew more intense, they realised that Hitler's Luftwaffe was
engaged in a large-scale attack on the city. The family took shelter in the
cellar with other residents of their flat block; the children spent a couple
of nights there. Nina's parents were unhappy with this arrangement,
and decided to take their seven-year-old daughter away to Vilnius with

them. It was a 487-kilometre trip, she heard her father say. The roads that led to Vilnius were narrow. Above them, one Messerschmitt after another flew past, bombing and strafing. Every time they attacked, Nina and her parents would run for cover in the deep ditches along the road. The many burned-out vehicles brought traffic to a standstill. The long lines of stopped cars were like sitting ducks – easy prey for the German fighter planes. The journey took days.

In Vilnius, there was a strange calm, even as refugees poured into the city. In the narrow streets of the Jewish district, you had to use your elbows to avoid being crushed flat. When they first arrived, they stayed with her maternal grandmother; then her parents rented part of a flat. Ten months passed. Nina's life was not very different than it had been in Warsaw; she went to a Polish-language school.

But the arrival of the Red Army made the atmosphere grimmer. Her uncle, Miron Szeskin, was taken prisoner; the Soviets feared the influence of Zionist leaders. Their flat was searched several times by the NKVD. Nina's parents were looking for an opportunity to flee Europe, and heard about the Curaçao visas. Grandma Szeskin announced right away that she wouldn't be joining them; at her advanced age, she was certain no one would harm a hair of her head if she stayed behind in Vilnius. She felt that starting a new life elsewhere was the prerogative of the young. Nina's father was not so young himself, but his first thought was for his daughter's welfare. He had no intention of exposing her to any more danger.

So Nina's parents obtained the visas and left with their daughter. The railway journey from Moscow to Vladivostok took twelve days. What made the most lasting impression on Nina was the anxiety and excitement among the passengers, as if the carriages of the train were wrapped in a cloud of unease and suspicion. Nina hardly dared to look outside. When the train had to stop at a red signal, starving women and children would bang on the windows, pleading for food.

On the *Amakusa Maru*, the boatswain pointed the refugees to their spot between the chalk lines, on a mat that covered the whole steerage deck. Each rectangle drawn on the mat indicated the space for a bed.

Their ship departed in a storm; everything on deck was groaning and creaking. Her parents were seasick, and so were all the other adults around her. Nina made it through the voyage by pulling up her knees and putting her fingers in her ears. If you can't hear anything, you won't get seasick; that was her experience.

In Kobe, the Wertanses moved into a hotel with a rock garden. Nina spent many hours staring at the goldfish, which were always bumping into each other in their crowded pool. The hotel almost seemed designed to allow her to slowly adjust to the Far East. The rooms were separated by screens and sliding doors made of rice paper. It looked serene, but you could hear the neighbours' slightest whisper.

She went to a school called St. Marie's, where the nuns turned English lessons into a game. They had the Polish girls in the class sing out the words, syllable by syllable: 'es pee ee cee (spec) tee aye (ta) cee el ee es (cles) – spectacles'. The other girls – some Japanese, others the daughters of Western diplomats – would clap or sing along.

She was sad to have to leave Japan six months later; she had made friends there, and Kobe was a pleasant place. The people there were friendly and seemed to like children, although she had to admit she had never been able to communicate with them, because in Japan even the gestures were different.

In August 1941, she left for Shanghai with her parents and hundreds of other Polish Jews. They found a little flat off Avenue Joffre where they had one room, a hot plate, and a bathroom not much bigger than a toilet. They would live there for more than two years. To get some fresh air, Nina would play hopscotch with Chinese friends on the street that led to Avenue Joffre.

On her walk to her school, she saw not only Russians but also distinguished French gentlemen, always deep in debate with each other, and Chinese people in Western dress, smoking cigarettes in ivory holders. She giggled to hear their mishmash of English and Chinese words. Somehow, whenever anyone spoke pidgin, she felt they must be joking.

The hardest thing about those years was crossing the street without injury. She was always jumping out of the way of traffic. The coolie-driven rickshaws would reach dizzying speeds as they zigzagged between the cars and bicycles. The cyclists rang their bells constantly and never used their brakes.

Towards the end of the year, she would stop every afternoon to gaze into the window of Tchakalian, an Armenian bakery on Avenue Joffre. She wasn't sure what most impressed her: the *Bûches de Noël*, sponge cake Yule logs with thick chocolate bark and green marzipan leaves, or the silver paper stars with the words 'Joyeux Noël', 'Merry Christmas', and, in Cyrillic script, 'Rozhdestvo'.

It all looked so peaceful, even after the Japanese attack on Pearl Harbor. That same month of December, the British had surrendered Hong Kong to the Japanese. In January and February 1942, the Japanese army had occupied Borneo, Java, Sumatra, and the other islands of the Dutch East Indies. The war soon spread to Burma, Malacca, the Philippines, and British India.

On the streets, Nina could see who was a friend of Japan and who an enemy. All Westerners from enemy states had to wear armbands with letters for their nationalities: A for Americans, B for the British, H for Holland, and X for other hostile powers. The French were exempt, because of the Vichy regime. Jews weren't required to wear armbands either, since most of them came from Germany and Austria, countries allied with Japan.

One day, there was no sign of the people with armbands. As it turned out, they had been sent to internment camps north of the city.

Not until the summer of 1943 were the Wertans family moved to Hongkew. Jakub Wertans had won a delay of many months by making himself useful at an engineering office, but their time had finally come. The term 'ghetto' was stringently avoided. The authorities called the district 'the designated area for stateless refugees in a small section of the Chinese city across the Whangpoo River'. That had a nicer ring to it, even though it was an overcrowded district surrounding the Ohel Moshe Synagogue, with a soup kitchen where long queues of

Nina Wertans in front of the house in MacGregor Road, 1945.

German, Austrian, and Polish Jews would stand waiting for a bowl. It was really just a ghetto, of course, and the adults held there were not allowed to leave. But the twenty-five thousand Jewish refugees were safe there. The district once known as Little Tokyo became Little Vienna.

The Wertans family had a seven-square-metre room at 266 MacGregor Road, now 266 Ling Tong Lu. Again, I have no trouble finding the building. Over the alley, which is so narrow two people can't walk side by side, clothes are hanging out to dry. Above the quilted coats and the trousers, telephone cables cross electrical wires. Air conditioners and satellite dishes mark the passage of seventy years. But even today, it's no place for the claustrophobic; the Wertans were in the middle of an anthill.

Nina had started grammar school a few months earlier, at the Shanghai Jewish School in the International Settlement, and was allowed to remain enrolled there. Whenever her parents wanted to leave Hongkew, they needed a special pass. Applying for one was time consuming, and there were long waits at the checkpoints. In practice, they could do no more than take a quick look around outside the district a couple of times a year. Nina didn't have to queue. She says she would walk the length of Changyang Road, take the Garden Bridge across the canal, and stroll down the Bund. I retrace her steps, crossing the bridge; it takes me nearly an hour of vigorous walking to reach the Bund. From there, it's still some distance to 500 Seymour Road, now Shaanxi Bei Lu. All in all, it takes me an hour and a half.

Did Nina – like Marcel Wejland, another student at the Shanghai Jewish School – ride her bicycle? Marcel remembered being given a map with a red line indicating what route they had to take to school. The map also stated how much time, at most, they were allowed to spend outside Hongkew. At the checkpoints, their times of departure and return were recorded.

Nina can't remember any of this. What has stuck in her mind is that, from the age of twelve to fourteen, she was allowed to go to school on her own, and no one in Shanghai appeared to think anything of it.

Sometimes the news from Europe drifted her way from a crackling radio. Jews there had to wear yellow stars. It seemed to Nina like a daily miracle that she could move around freely without an armband or any other markings. One day, her British teachers did not come to school. She heard they'd been taken prisoner. But she was even allowed to visit her Chinese friends in the French concession after school.

For other children at the Shanghai Jewish School, it wasn't so easy to enter and leave Hongkew. Peter Schattner, a friend of Marcel Wejland's, had constant run-ins with Mr Goya, the Japanese deputy commander of the Shanghai Stateless Refugees Affairs Bureau, who issued passes and was often present at the checkpoint – no one really

School photograph, Shanghai Jewish School. Nina is in the front row, fourth from the left.

understood why. Peter was a *Jekke*, a Viennese Jew. Every time he passed, Mr Goya singled him out, maybe because he had blond hair and was a head taller than the other students. Or maybe Mr Goya just didn't like the look in Peter's blue eyes. The hot-tempered Japanese official, who was as skinny as a rail, more than once gave Peter a black eye or bloody nose.

Mr Goya targeted certain adults, too. Kano Goya, who liked to joke that he was the King of the Jews, became such a hated figure that a pamphlet published in September 1945 was entitled *Good-bye Mr. Ghoya*. It contained seven cartoons by Friedrich Melchior summing up the complaints about the former deputy commander. According to Marcel Wejland, Mr Goya was lynched by an angry mob soon after the city was liberated. That's not entirely true. It is true that he was attacked and beaten by a group of young people after most of the Japanese had left. But Mr Goya died long after the war in his own bed in Tokyo.

Nina was an overzealous student, always first or second in her class. After school, she never neglected her homework. Her father would wait impatiently for her to come home; he had been unable to find work in the ghetto, because everyone there was looking for something to do. In the ghetto, you were better off being a barber than an engineer – then at least you had something to do. At ten each morning, he had coffee at the Wiener Kaffee; at eleven, he wondered how he would get through the day. As soon as Nina got home, he would have long conversations with her or throw himself into her homework, quizzing her until she thought she would lose her mind. Or he would talk politics with her, discussing big issues like communism, capitalism, and Zionism. Nina couldn't have been more pleased to be taken seriously by her father – an adult, and a man at that.

Jakub Wertans would pore over every word in the *Shanghai Woche*, the *Yiddish Almanach*, the *Shanghai Jewish Chronicle* – a German-language publication despite the English title – the *Unser Leben–Nasha Jhisni*, and the *Israel's Messenger*. Jewish newspapers were flourishing in Shanghai as never before, thanks to the arrival of so many intellectuals from Vienna, Berlin, Prague, and Warsaw. They fell under the authority of the Japanese censors, but quite a bit of information slipped through the net. The journalists received their news from the British, Australian, and Russian short-wave stations.

Using pins on the map, Mr Wertans tracked the Allied advance in the Pacific. When American B-29s started bombing Shanghai, he was anything but concerned. 'They're almost here,' he told Nina the day a bomb hit the Hongkew district. 'The war's as good as over.'

A surviving photograph shows how Nina celebrated the American liberation of Shanghai by dancing with her mother in their little room in Hongkew. They both look serious, even sad. Maybe they already suspect that terrible news is on the way, and that they won't be able to board a ship to America any time soon. There was a general understanding among the refugees that they had to be patient, wait and see what Washington would decide, address the most urgent needs, and tend to the sick and wounded. Nina's parents visited the American

Nina Wertans dancing with her mother.

consulate, bringing her along to interpret for them. They could get a visa for the United States or Ecuador right away – that wasn't the problem. The question was when they would find places on a ship.

The post brought scraps of information about the gas chambers, and about who had and hadn't made it through the war. Grandma Szeskin had died of hunger. Nina's uncle had been a prisoner in Siberia. Most relatives on her father's side had been murdered in Treblinka. Nina was almost ashamed to read those letters, because she had not gone hungry for even a day.

Eleven days after Nina's fifteenth birthday, they left Shanghai at last on the USS *General W.H. Gordon*. The ship visited Hong Kong, the Philippines, and Hawaii, and arrived in San Francisco on 17 December 1947.

The Displaced Persons Act proposed by President Truman had been passed by Congress. It was a step that should have been taken nine years earlier. The Wertans family were classified as DPs, Displaced Persons, a status that gave them the right to settle permanently in the United States.

Nina studied political science at New York University, and economics at the University of California in Berkeley. She married a fellow student, Nahum Admoni, born in Jerusalem, whose parents had been among the first Polish emigrants to British Mandatory Palestine. After a week-long honeymoon, Nina said farewell to her parents and boarded the MS *Shalom* with Nahum, arriving in Haifa on 14 April 1954.

In January 1961, she and her husband and two daughters took an aeroplane to Addis Ababa, where Nahum had been appointed consul and she had been appointed to a staff position at a United Nations economic aid organisation. From 1966 to 1970, Nahum was counsellor at the Paris embassy, and Nina worked for an investment company as an economic consultant. In 1971, they returned to Israel, where Nina became the director of the Israel-America Chamber of Commerce, and Nahum started working for the Mossad, the Israeli intelligence service.

From 1982 to 1989, Nahum Admoni was the director-general of the Mossad. Soon after taking on that role, he was sharply criticised for not giving the Israeli cabinet sufficient warning about the Christian militias in Lebanon. From 16 to 18 September 1982, Israeli troops looked on as these Christian extremists massacred Palestinian and Lebanese Shiites in the Sabra and Shatila refugee camps. Somewhere between 762 and 3,500 civilians were murdered. This must have been a very trying time for Nina, since she knew from her days in Hongkew what it was like to be a refugee. The criticism of Nahum Admoni did not lead to his dismissal, and he remained the head of the Mossad for seven years.

37

So many names on a wall

A thick fog descends on Hongkew as I study the names engraved in copper on the wall of the Ohel Moshe Synagogue and the Jewish Refugees Museum next door. I am bundled up, but still shivering with cold. The biting wind here by the river makes a temperature of −1 °C feel like −10.

In the winter of 1944, it snowed once in Hongkew. For the length of that day, the refugee district turned into a suburb of Vienna, Berlin, Warsaw, Poznań, Łódź, or Vilnius. Parents encouraged their children to scoop up snow from the gutter and knead it in their hands. It was a day of celebration in the ghetto.

That same year, 1944, the Japanese commander ordered three girls – fourteen, fifteen, and sixteen years old – to compile a list of the refugees in the Jewish district. They were each assigned a table, a chair, and a typewriter. Sonja Golombek, Eva Mannheim, and Helga Hirschel were selected because they had all taken a touch-typing course. They set to work. A long queue formed in front of the tables. All the residents of Hongkew were required to participate. Japanese soldiers looked on and kept the crowd under control.

As time went on, Sonja, Eva, and Helga began to slow down. They turned Jewish names into English ones like Arthur, Harry, and Dave, made deliberate errors, and 'forgot' to take note of some names – because they were suspicious. What did the Japanese mean to do with those lists? Was this a first step towards deportation? Would they soon be sent to a camp somewhere north of Shanghai?

The girls kept changing the spelling of the names in little ways, so that the person in question could say, 'That's not me.' They stopped when they had registered 14,795 refugees, probably because that was when the Americans started bombing the district.

For each refugee, Sonja, Eva, or Helga would type the last name (for example, Szmulewicz), first name (Hilde), sex (F), age (20), address in Hongkew (696/45 Tong), occupation (music teacher) and status (Polish refugee). They registered both adults and minors, and made note of whether the children were attending school. The occupation was frequently recorded as 'student' or 'Rabb. Student'.

The list, which paints a clear picture of the refugee community, was filed away in an archive. Seventy years later, all the data was digitised, and all the names were engraved into the black wall right next to the synagogue. Visitors to the Jewish Refugees Museum who had known or were related to the internees – in many cases, their children or grandchildren – were asked to check the names for accuracy. This made it possible to correct some five hundred errors.

On the wall, I find names such as Sigmund Kafka-Pollak, Freud, Portnoj (as in *Portnoy's Complaint*), Mendelssohn, Rubinsztein (the Polish spelling of Rubinstein), Barenboim, Frank, Marx, Ginzburg, Garfinkel, Lipszyc, Trotzki, and Glass, Glass, Glass (like the composer Philip Glass, whose parents came from Lithuania). Not to mention Bruskin. (Jakob Gershowitz's mother was named Rosa Bruskin. She came from the Vilnius ghetto, married Moishe Gershowitz from Saint Petersburg, and emigrated to the United States. Their sons, Jakob and Israel Gershowitz, Americanised their names, becoming George and Ira Gershwin.)

Dozens of names on the wall are also on Sugihara's list. Like Zwartendijk, the Japanese consul wrote down only the name of the visa applicant. The wall, in contrast, lists whole families: men, women, children, and often nieces, nephews, or cousins who were still minors.

Every morning, I return to scan the names again and take note of how many people with Curaçao visas made this journey. Now and then, when the cold is too much for me, I go into the synagogue. Or else I drink coffee across the street, at the Vienna Café. The original café, in the middle of Hongkew, was demolished to make way for a new metro line. The new one is a copy of the original Wiener Kaffee coffee house.

One morning, a Chinese student who gives tours of the synagogue comes up to me. He's seen me standing out in the cold with my notebook every morning. There's no need for that, he tells me. Do I know that the names on the wall have been digitised?

In the synagogue, he takes down my details and promises to e-mail the list to me. I don't expect anything more to come of it, but the next morning I receive a message in impeccable English. The list, he tells me, is on a CD-ROM published by Sonja Mühlberger in connection with the exhibition *Leben in Wartesaal: Exil in Shanghai, 1938–1947* (*Life in the Waiting Room: exile in Shanghai, 1938–1947*) at the Jewish Museum in Berlin. But the CD-ROM is under copyright. The most he can do is give me Sonja Mühlberger's address in Germany.

I send Ms Mühlberger a message right away. Even before leaving Shanghai, I receive a reply from Germany. Sonja Mühlberger tells me she'd be pleased to contribute to a book about consul Zwartendijk. His role, she writes, has been shamefully neglected. The e-mail comes with an attachment: the list.

Sonja was born in Shanghai on 26 October 1939. Her father, Hermann Krips, had been released from Dachau after Kristallnacht on condition that he leave the Reich immediately. Without a moment's hesitation, he and his wife, Ilse (née Herzfeld), took the train to Trieste, where they boarded the SS *Conte Biancamano*. This ship of the Lloyd Triestino Line was white, had two yellow funnels with black bands, could carry 3,450 passengers, and was packed with Jewish refugees.

From Shanghai, Hermann Krips planned to go on to Birobidzhan, the Jewish Autonomous Oblast founded by Stalin, but Ilse was pregnant and could go into labour any day. He had no choice but to remain in Shanghai, where he soon set up an anti-fascist committee with other left-wing radicals.

When Hermann went to Shanghai City Hall to register the birth of his daughter, he was handed a list of permissible German names. He wanted to call his daughter Sonja, but that name wasn't on the list. The city official refused to register her under the name he had chosen and instead wrote 'BABY KRIPS'. Three months had passed by the time her father persuaded the municipal council to change 'baby' to 'Sonja'. There was no ill will involved, but the Chinese bureaucrats had the same mentality as the Germans: rules were rules. Besides, they were nervous about the Japanese occupiers, who were peering over their shoulders.

Sonja spent the entire war in Shanghai with her parents. She was at a German private school at first and then, starting in 1945, at the Kadoorie School in Hongkew. Her father, who had been a merchant in his former life, earned his living by selling eggs door to door; her mother worked as a seamstress in return for one meal a day.

In July 1947, Sonja returned to Germany with her parents and her brother, Peter, who had been born in the last year of the war. They were among the exceptions. As soon as the war ended, 70 per cent or more of the Jewish refugees tried to emigrate to the United States. But not all of them could find a place on a ship to New York or San Francisco. In 1946, many went by train to Canton and on to Hong Kong, hoping to find help more quickly there. Often, no help was forthcoming, and many others decided to sit it out in Shanghai. They stamped on the letters they sent to the United States and Australia: 'OPEN THE DOORS FOR 15000 SHANGHAI REFUGEES'.

So even though most of the refugees came from Germany and Austria, few returned to those countries. One ship, the troop transport USNS *Marine Lynx*, took 650 remigrants from Shanghai to Naples; 295 planned to travel on to Berlin by freight train. Their decision to return to Germany was so exceptional that, fifty years later, this group of Jews from Shanghai became the subject of an exhibition at Berlin's Jewish Museum. The other remigrants spread out across Central

Europe. The train journeys to the north were reminiscent of wartime transports: the doors had been removed from the freight wagons, and parents had to cover the openings with tarpaulins so that their children wouldn't fall off the train.

Sonja was one of the passengers aboard the *Marine Lynx*. When she arrived in Berlin, she was almost eight years old and spoke better English than German. In a sense, she was lucky; the contempt and derision that she encountered often went over her head. In the eyes of the Berliners, she had taken a pleasant trip to China while they were crouching in the sewers like rats to escape the bombs – that was the general idea.

Sonja became an English teacher, and kept trying to gather information about the Shanghai Jews all her life. She tracked down the list made by Sonja, Eva, and Helga, checked all the names, made corrections, and added others.

According to Sonja, the list includes only 60 per cent of the Jewish refugees in Hongkew. That would mean there were many more than was long believed – at least twenty-five thousand.

The list includes a strikingly large number of German Jews (8,557) and stateless people with German names (1,090). The number of Jews from Austria (1,182) is not much greater than the number from the USSR (1,101). But what stands out most is the small number of registered Polish Jews: 883. Many, many names are missing; no one at all from Lithuania is listed. I suspect that many Polish and Lithuanian Jews did not show up to register, perhaps because they spoke no German and had missed the announcement.

Among the names on the wall next to the synagogue, I find four hundred people from Sugihara's list and the list compiled by the Holocaust Memorial Museum in Washington, which is a reconstruction of Zwartendijk's list of people with Curaçao visas. On the wall, they are listed with their wives and children. What I learn from my study of the names on the wall is that between two to seven people travelled on a single visa. The average is almost four. Around 1,500 to 1,600 made it to Shanghai thanks to Curaçao visas.

That doesn't include the seventy-four visas written by consul De Voogd, used by another two-hundred-odd people. And then there were the refugees with visas issued by consul De Jong in Stockholm. They cannot be found on any list. The highest serial number I have found on any of these Stockholm visas is 472. Multiplied by four, this makes 1,888. About half of them were probably able to travel on from Japan to their final destination.

There is also another group, whose exact size no one knows: the people who managed to obtain visas from Zwartendijk and Sugihara after the closure of the Dutch consulate in early August and the Japanese consulate in late August. A serial number that Zwartendijk wrote on a visa on 23 August 1940 suggests to me that this group had at least 180 members, but there may have been many more. The pamphlet 'Visas for Life' produced by the Israeli foreign ministry includes an illustration of a visa issued by Zwartendijk on 24 August 1940: it is numbered 981. At the railway station in Kaunas, Sugihara gave out transit visas that did not even include the names of the applicants. This may explain why, on websites and in memoirs, I have come across numerous survivors whose names are not on any list. Zwartendijk must have done the same as Sugihara; the visa of 24 August does not include a name.

According to my calculations, some 2,700 registered refugees in total went from Lithuania to Shanghai. If we assume a roughly equal number of unregistered refugees, then the true total must be around five thousand. About four thousand Jewish refugees were allowed to travel directly from Japan to their final destinations in 1941. In the long run, the escape plan devised by Zwartendijk enabled nine thousand to ten thousand men, women, and children to flee Poland and Lithuania. But once again, all these figures are shrouded in uncertainty, since many of the refugees aided by Zwartendijk and Sugihara were not registered anywhere.

I come into contact with Pan Guang, a professor at the Shanghai Academy of Social Sciences and the dean of the Centre of Jewish Studies Shanghai (CJSS). Professor Guang's long list of publications includes *Eternal Memories: the Jews in Shanghai*, which serves as my guide during my investigations in China.

Professor Pan sifted through Shanghai's civil registers, collecting much more information even than Sonja Mühlberger – especially on departure dates and countries of destination. Then he digitised all the data and compiled an alphabetical list of the Jews who stayed in Shanghai from 1938 to 1948. He gives me the opportunity to try out his digital list. I check the first four letters of the alphabet, compare the results to the earlier lists, and reach the conclusion that at least 600 Curaçao visa holders ended up in Shanghai, or around 2,400 people travelling on those visas.

But even Professor Pan's list is nowhere near complete. My impression is that the refugees who went from Japan to Shanghai in the autumn of 1941 were less carefully registered than the German and Austrian Jews who disembarked on the Bund in the late 1930s.

There are thousands upon thousands of names on the wall – nearly fifteen thousand in total. When I look at all those names of survivors engraved in copper, I fully appreciate for the first time the massive scale of the rescue operation. The wall of names was erected in a symbolic place: the square in front of the Ohel Moshe Synagogue. That was where, in the early months of 1946, bulletin boards displayed the names of Shoah survivors. Every few days, new names were added.

A photograph in the Jewish Refugees Museum shows a woman, six men, a rabbi, and a boy jostling to scan a billboard for signs of life from the relatives they left behind in Europe. The men are craning their necks, making their way through the lists, while the woman walks off, shaking her head. No news. That meant waiting for a letter with more names of people murdered in Treblinka or the gas chambers of Sobibór – or shot by an SS officer, like Marcel Wejland's grandmother as she lay sick in bed in the Warsaw ghetto.

Jewish refugees in Shanghai jostling to see the lists of
Holocaust survivors, 1946.

38

Everything's fine in Psychiko

From Athens, Zwartendijk would tuck packs of gum into his letters to his second son. Robbie still had incredibly blue eyes, but the red spot on his nose had fortunately faded. He had begun primary school in Eindhoven by then, and whenever he was out in the schoolyard could be found softly smacking his lips as he chewed on a stick of gum from his father. You could buy chewing gum at every newsstand in Greece; Athens and its surrounding area was teeming with GIs. The Americans had rushed to the aid of the British in their struggle against the communist revolutionaries.

Zwartendijk found himself in the midst of his third war in row; the Greek Civil War would continue until the end of the 1940s. The war was one of the reasons his wife and children had stayed at home for the time being. The situation was as volatile as it had been in Lithuania after the Red Army invaded.

His earlier foreign postings had taught him that you should never rent a house or make other arrangements from a distance. He had become a seasoned expatriate, and still enjoyed the adventure of starting from scratch in a country that was utterly new to him. The one major downside was that Edith and Jan had told him they wouldn't accompany him to Athens – and they meant it. They were intent on leaving their childhood home and providing for themselves. He consoled himself with the thought that Greece wasn't a bad place for a holiday, so they were sure to visit every summer. Jan junior was going on eighteen, and Edith had not yet turned twenty; to their father, they were still children.

What Zwartendijk had forgotten was that he himself had just turned sixteen when he'd stepped ashore in England to finish secondary school in Reading. And he didn't realise that his eldest children saw him as quite strict and old-fashioned in his views. It wasn't that they had come to dislike him, but they wanted to lead their own lives, and the first stop was Amsterdam. The war had left them housebound too often, for too many years. Jan's first outing was to Casablanca on the Zeedijk, and his second to the Cotton Club in Nieuwmarkt. When he heard jazz, it was as if he was already in America. And he had no doubt that was his destiny: to spend the rest of his life on the far side of the ocean. He was sick of Europe.

Erni used the last months of 1946 on her own in Eindhoven to pick up the threads with her own family. She made a couple of trips to Friedrichshafen, where her sister, Ille, and brother-in-law, Bert, had ended up after being driven out of Prague, and finally heard the whole story of her eldest sister, Gretl's, death on a forced march to Germany. Gretl, whom Erni had loved with a fierce passion, had gone blind on the journey, and had eventually died of hunger and exhaustion. The end came more quickly because of her heart trouble, which had grown worse as the war continued. On that same march, Erni's other sister, Ille, had lost her six-week-old baby. She was breast-feeding Hänchen, but ran out of milk because she was malnourished and couldn't get powdered milk anywhere. She'd had to bury her child herself at the side of the road. Erni tried desperately to show her sister how much she sympathised with her.

Ille and Bert had been forced by Czech militias to flee their home in Prague, leaving everything behind – a fate that had befallen two-to-three million German speakers. After being driven out of their home, they'd had great difficulty in surviving. They remained destitute until Bert found a job at the *Schwäbische Zeitung* in Friedrichshafen. It was the start of a rapid and astonishing rise that would culminate in him occupying the position of editor-in-chief of the quality newspaper *Die Welt*, based in Hamburg. But Bert Komma's heart was still in Bohemia. Each morning after the editorial meeting, he would withdraw into his office, write the editorial for the day and a political opinion piece, and read historical studies. For the rest of his life, he would remain preoccupied with the story of the Sudeten Germans and German-speaking Jews who had inhabited adjacent parts of Bohemia and Moravia since the thirteenth century.

Before Erni left for Greece, she saw as much of her sister and brother-in-law as she could, usually with Edith, but she felt as though they no longer spoke quite the same language, even though they were all still conversing in German. From Ille and Bert's perspective, Erni had become part of a different world, and even though they never said it in so many words, they seemed to believe that they had suffered a great deal more in the war than Erni and Jan had. Sometimes Erni wanted to shout that she, too, had feared she would die, but she kept quiet about what had happened in Kaunas, because she believed that you can't ease other people's pain by relating your own misfortunes.

Erni felt boundless admiration for everything her sister and brother-in-law had done to climb out of the abyss and build a new future for their children. But she saw in their eyes that she could never share in the loss they had suffered when forced to leave Czechoslovakia.

Edith remembers her Uncle Bert as a reclusive scholar, doing his best to prove to himself, over and over again, that their expulsion from Prague had been historically inevitable. He would never recover from his grief, and his only consolation was that his children could go on to higher education. According to Edith, that was 'his last shred of pride'.

Uncle Bert resigned as editor-in-chief of *Die Welt* in 1953, when media magnate Axel Springer bought the newspaper and forced the editors to take a much more conservative line. Then he retreated once and for all into his study in Bad Godesberg, and no longer read about anything but Prague. Yet, as paradoxical as it may seem, not a word was spoken in the Komma home about their expulsion from Czechoslovakia. Their son, Georg,who became a lawyer for the

Westdeutscher Rundfunk, a public broadcaster headquartered in Cologne, never asked his parents about it, and his sister, Hanne, who married an atomic physicist and moved to Jülich Research Centre in North Rhine-Westphalia, did not even recall losing a little brother on the forced march to the West in 1945.

Still, Komma must have hoped that one day the truth about what had happened to him and his family would come to light. After his death, his daughter-in-law, Evi, found a complete family tree in a desk drawer, along with papers and documents dating from 1920 to 1945, irrefutable proof that his roots lay in Prague and Bohemia.

In July 1944, Edith had taken her school-leaving exam and found a job in the radiology department of the Diaconessenhuis, a hospital in Eindhoven. She wanted to go on to higher education, but all such options in the Netherlands were in the north, which remained under German occupation for many months longer than Eindhoven. After her father left for Greece in 1946, she moved to Amsterdam and studied to become a Montessori schoolteacher. Her first job was also her last; she had the chance to become a Montessori teacher in Amstelveen, but there, so close to Schiphol Airport, she met a KLM employee and married him. Hendrik Jes had just returned from the Dutch East Indies, where he had done his compulsory military duty. Jobs were scarce, and the best position he could find was as a tour guide for KLM. When the airline finally granted him a permanent contract, Edith was not allowed to accompany him to his posting in Singapore. They remained separated until years later, when he was transferred to Milan and Edith rejoined him. Their longest posting was in Manchester, which was then still a grimy industrial centre. Edith had to change her stockings twice a day. Whenever she could, she took the train to London to see old friends of her mother's, including Trude Polak from Prague.

Henk's last name, pronounced 'yes', was a never-ending source of silly jokes: 'Is Mr Jes really saying no?' That problem went away when they were transferred to Frankfurt, but by then Henk had had enough of working for a boss. He left KLM to set up his own business, a furniture factory. Back in the Netherlands, Henk and Edith adopted two boys: the elder boy was one year old; the other, still a baby.

Jan went to the technical institute in Delft to study mining engineering, soon switched to road engineering, grew tired of that, and decided to do geology at the University of Amsterdam. But he was unhappy there, too. University life went on in a stuffy 1930s atmosphere of bourgeois pettiness as if the war had never happened and the Allies had never liberated Europe. Jan emigrated to Canada and enrolled at McGill University in Montreal. The educational programme there was organised along modern lines; after a semester of theoretical background at the university, the rest of the year was dedicated to practical geological work in the wilderness of the Rocky Mountains. This field work even earned him a small salary, enough for Jan to support himself and pay for his studies.

He described his adventures in the mountains at length in his letters to Edith, who was overjoyed at this renewed intimacy between them. She became the first Zwartendijk to visit Jan in Canada. After earning his geology degree, Jan also studied economics and received a Ph.D. for his detailed study *Economic Aspects of Mining Subsidence*. He worked for the Canadian government, often accompanied ministers to conferences, acted as an adviser in international forums, and always kept Edith up to date on his adventures.

Jan was grateful to his sister for her sage advice – and not only on work issues. Before his career took off, she had given him careful, step-by-step instructions for informing their father of his plans to marry an American woman who was not yet divorced from her first husband. Both his intended bride and her husband were friends of his parents.

Jan had met Nancy Ellison in the summer of 1949, on his second visit to Greece. She lived a couple of houses up the street in Psychiko, a suburb of Athens. His father was not amused, to say the least, by the Olympian speed at which his son fell for her, head over heels. 'Couldn't you have picked someone else?' he grumbled at his son. Jan had just turned twenty; Nancy was almost five years older.

Jan, Robbie, and Edith in Greece, in front of their house in Psychiko.

Robbie was the only one of their three children to move to Greece with them. When he arrived there with his mother, he was seven years old. What Kaunas had been to Edith and Jan, Athens was to Rob.

Erni had a more difficult adjustment. She missed her two older children, and dreaded the Athens heat. Over the next ten years, her regular July and August routine was to stay in the cellar of their house in Psychiko day and night. But even when the thermometer rose to 40 °C, her husband was unfazed. To him, it was glorious to be so close to the sea.

Edith and Jan visited Greece every summer; Jan, because of his American flame. Nancy Ellison had decided to divorce her husband, but, not wanting to cause a scandal in the Athens expat community, she kept Jan at a distance, at least in public. Yet as soon as the divorce came through, she was off to Montreal, where Jan was just one exam away from graduating. They married in 1955.

Forty years later, on 7 December 1995, Jan wrote to his brother, Rob, from Tucson, Arizona, a city in the Sonora Desert where he spent his winters:

> Like most boys my age, I was in a kind of ecstasy after the country was liberated and couldn't help celebrating my newfound freedom. I thought Pa was strict and old-fashioned. You, Robbie – you couldn't imagine why I felt that way. To you, Pa was the very soul of reasonableness. Ma was very different. She always let us go our own way. We never even had the beginnings of a disagreement with her. Pa set a very high bar when it came to moral standards. The strange thing is that when I look back now, that's what I admire most about him. He was demanding, especially of himself. He wanted to teach us that you're 100 per cent responsible for your actions. In his eyes, any excuse was no better than a lie. By the way, have you held onto any of his personal effects from home? All I have is an inkwell with silver antlers that Pa used to keep on his desk. He had it in Kaunas, too.

Erni tried to bring about a swift reconciliation, suggesting to her husband that they go on a trip with Jan and Nancy in the United States. After she lost her temper with him a couple of times, calling him narrow-minded, he agreed to the plan. The trip was unexpectedly successful, and he and Erni would later visit the United States and Canada four more times to travel with Jan and Nancy.

None of the children were told that their father had seen De Decker again after so many years. Erni was the only one who knew, and she didn't say a word to Edith, Jan, or Robbie. Kaunas remained unmentionable in the family circle, and never once was De Decker's name spoken.

It must have been a strange moment for the two men when they shook hands in Athens. After leaving Kaunas, Zwartendijk had not once spoken to the former Dutch envoy in Riga, not even in 1944 and 1945, when Eindhoven was liberated and postal services resumed between the continent and Britain. Zwartendijk had been in Athens for a year and a half by the time he read in the newspaper that the new Dutch ambassador, L.P.J. de Decker, had presented his credentials to the King of Greece.

After 1942, De Decker had kept a remarkably low profile in Sweden. It was as if he hoped to be forgotten by his superiors and considered himself lucky to be overlooked by almost everyone. The reason he kept such a low profile must have been the close working relationship he'd had with the consul general in Stockholm. De Decker had been as fast and efficient in his work with Adriaan Mattheus de Jong as in his days in the Baltics with Jan Zwartendijk. Hundreds more Curaçao visas had been posted from Stockholm.

When De Jong came under fire for his headstrong actions, his far-reaching contacts with the British secret service, and his unconditional support for anyone who claimed to be a Resistance fighter, De Decker had started to avoid him. Embracing the solitude of his life as a widower, he turned down all invitations to receptions and other events.

He did not re-emerge from the shadows until he was in London – although his posts there were hardly the crowning glory of his diplomatic career. On 27 April 1944, he became the envoy to the Yugoslavian government in exile, which, like its Dutch counterpart, was in London. And a few weeks later, when the Kingdom of Yugoslavia was no more, he was appointed envoy to the government in exile of Greece. In Europe in the late 1940s, Greece was not a political heavyweight. In the summer of 1945, pending the return of the Greek government to Athens, De Decker was asked to make preparations for moving the Dutch foreign ministry from Stratton House in London to the Plein in The Hague. No one imagined he might ever have done anything heroic; his superior, Minister Van Kleffens, described him as 'earnest and conscientious', and his progress as 'slow but steady'. In late 1945 he left for Athens, but it was not until 1947 that he could finally present his credentials to the newly crowned King Paul.

He ran into Zwartendijk at receptions and the like, but they only had a few face-to-face conversations, and said little or nothing about Lithuania. De Decker, on the verge of retirement, began to worry about his return to the Netherlands, and pleaded with Zwartendijk to ask Philips to arrange for a place for him to live. In the post-war years, housing was in very short supply, and De Decker was no longer a man of means. Zwartendijk made a vague promise to put in a good word for him in his correspondence with Eindhoven. But on an official visit to the Netherlands, De Decker buttonholed the head of the Philips housing office and claimed that the former Dutch consul in Lithuania had told him the company could provide him with housing. Zwartendijk received a severe letter from the board member A.J. Guépin, a copy of which has been preserved in the Philips archives. Guépin, the number two in the company, asked him how he could have been so presumptuous as to promise De Decker a new home when hundreds of employees were on the waiting list.

Zwartendijk had to tie himself in knots to placate his furious boss. In his reply, he wrote that De Decker had evidently 'sounded a somewhat strident note' during his conversation in Eindhoven, and explained that he had never made any promises or raised any expectations. But the rest of the letter does show that he had been trying for around six months to help De Decker find a home somewhere in the Netherlands, and that he had sought help from other housing specialists in the Philips organisation.

When De Decker left Athens in early 1948, Zwartendijk must not have been sorry to see him go. For months, the ambassador had been turning up his nose at Zwartendijk for failing to help him find a decent place to live. De Decker, who had never recovered from the death of his wife in Riga, had become a bitter, lonely man in the course of the war. He eventually contacted a distant relative, and was able to rent a terraced house in Nunspeet, a very insular town in the rural Veluwe region. He did not live there for more than a few months. In that same year, 1948, following a brief illness, he died, two weeks before Christmas, at the age of sixty-four.

His early death at least spared him from a reprimand or reproach for his wartime actions, and he never had to undergo a single investigation. Unlike A.M. de Jong, he would never have to appear before a commission; De Decker had heard all about it when the consul general in Stockholm had resigned from his office on 1 January 1947, outraged by the post-war politicians who could not begin to understand the difficulties of being a consul in wartime. Not only did De Decker escape the scrutiny of the Van Rappard Commission that investigated De Jong, but he was also never questioned under oath by the parliamentary committee of inquiry that began looking into wartime government policy in November 1947, which interviewed not only ministers but also senior officials and diplomats. He never had to account for his actions to anyone but God. For if De Decker had lost his faith in humanity, he had never lost his religion.

Zwartendijk did not say anything to Edith about his meetings with De Decker either. But during his daughter's third trip to Greece, he did tell her about Frits Philips visiting Athens. The two men had finally had a chance to talk at length then, for days at a stretch. 'The idealist,' Zwartendijk called Mr Frits. But he said it with a smile. He liked him all the more for his enthusiasm. 'He never finishes a sentence,' he told Edith. 'Every idea makes way for a new and better one; the words fight for space in his mouth. No two ways about it: he's a remarkable man.'

Edith was taken by surprise; her father was not often so full of praise for the management at Philips. He had an especially vocal dislike of Othon Loupart, a Belgian who headed the radio sales department before the war and the television-set department after the war. Loupart ran the foreign offices with an iron fist, never satisfied with their results. 'What a skunk,' Zwartendijk would often complain over dinner, both in Kaunas and in Athens.

Meanwhile, the Greek Civil War raged on. Robbie noticed how unruffled his father was. When the maid's man friend came to the house, he would take the hand grenades out of his pockets and put them on the kitchen table. When he left, he would put them back in his pockets. Without his hand grenades, he wouldn't have dared to go over the hill, because on the other side were the communists. The thought of showing the maid's friend the door never crossed Jan Zwartendijk's mind. Nor did he ever ask him not to bring weapons or ammunition.

Until late 1949, they could hear gunfire and the occasional loud boom every evening on the other side of the hill. Was it the sound of mortars? Or grenades going off? Their house was halfway down the hillside. Pa said to Robbie, 'Let's agree that we'll never stick our heads up over the hilltop.' They had a good laugh about that.

The rumour went around that the communists were stealing children. According to this story, they sent them to Bulgaria and Romania, and they returned to Greece as fully trained revolutionary fighters. The question was whether Robbie could go to school on his own. His parents said, 'Just don't go off with any strangers.' He was about the only child in the neighbourhood allowed to go to school on his own. But he wasn't scared in the least. He knew that as long as he didn't go off with any strangers, nothing could go wrong.

His father's attitude was always that everything was fine. Meanwhile, the Greek Civil War claimed 160,000 lives, and they learned afterwards that 28,000 children really had been kidnapped.

Robbie was sent to an unusual school, the Anavryta Lyceum, that had only thirty-three pupils, and where everything revolved around the children from the royal family. Three special classes had been formed for the education of Crown Prince Constantine and Princesses Sophia and Irene. The classes comprised a cross-section of Greek society: shipowners' children, but also a boy from a shack with a corrugated-iron roof at the foot of the Acropolis; the son of a communist leader alongside the children of military officers; the daughter of a teacher; and the son of a foreign businessman – that one was Robbie. He was

Erni, Jan, and Rob Zwartendijk at the Acropolis, Athens, 1950.

in the boys' class with Constantine, with whom he got along well from the start.

At first, the little school was in the wealthy suburb of Psychiko. Robbie could ride his push scooter there and back. During the second year, the boys' class moved to a castle on an estate in Kifisia, about fifteen kilometres away. Robbie would receive the remainder of his primary education there, in Constantine's class.

It was a boarding school, and a fairly strict one. Robbie stayed there from Sunday before dinner to Saturday after breakfast. His father would pick him up at the end of the morning on Saturday, and make him sit in the back of the car because he 'reeked to high heaven of garlic'. By Sunday evening, he was back among his friends, gabbing in Greek again. It became his first language.

When Robbie turned twelve, his parents sent him to the Netherlands for his secondary schooling, because he was having more and more trouble expressing himself in Dutch. He went to the Lorentz Lyceum in Eindhoven, like his brother and sister before him, and lived with teachers. But he spent the Christmas, Easter, and Whitsun holidays and the whole summer in Greece, helping out his father as an interpreter.

Whenever conflict was brewing at the factory, his father would bring in Robbie, who would find out exactly what was wrong. Rob Zwartendijk's success years later on the board of the complex Ahold corporation can be traced back to those formative years in Greece, when he learned the fundamentals of management from his father.

According to his youngest son, Zwartendijk was constantly asking himself, *What is good? What is evil?* His thinking was never black and white. People less tied to their conceptual schemes are more considerate of others, Rob believes. When his father had a hard time with an employee, his first response was never dismissal. Instead, he would ask himself how he could have a serious conversation with that person. Then he would make a plan for the two of them to resolve their differences:

> My father always wondered what that was: a good person. Others could rattle off an explanation, but not him. To him, there was nothing so complicated as a good person. A bad person, a thief or collaborator, is easy enough to figure out. But a good person? Gentle people can be cowards, and sharp thinkers can be so ambitious that they give no

thought to anyone else. At the radio-tube factory in Athens, there was a new employee who soon turned out to be a communist. You should fire him, the factory manager said to my father. He asked, Why? Is he a bad person? Well, no, it wasn't that … What, then? That man never left his job at the factory.

Many, many years later, Frits Philips, who lived to be one hundred, would tell Rob Zwartendijk that he had tried many times to persuade his father to come to Eindhoven and become a company director. In fact, that had been the main reason for Frits's visit to Athens; he had hoped to persuade Zwartendijk, in a series of conversations, to join the Presidium, the core group within the board of management.

Of all the Zwartendijk children, Rob had the most illustrious career. He studied economics in Manchester, staying with Edith and her husband, Henk, and became involved with the only Dutch girl in the city, an au pair, Marijke, with whom he would spend the rest of his life. His career got off to a flying start at Unilever: he and Marijke were sent to Milan, the first of many foreign postings. He worked for Polaroid in Belgium and the Swedish firm of Molnlycke in France, and ended his working life as an Ahold executive board member for nineteen years, and the president and CEO of Ahold USA. Rob Zwartendijk earned great respect in business circles by leading Ahold through uncertain waters after the kidnapping and murder of his fellow board member Gerrit Jan Heijn. When he retired, twelve companies asked him to join their supervisory boards, and he said yes to all twelve.

When Frits Philips asked why Jan Zwartendijk had not aimed for an equally illustrious career, Rob told him that his father would have preferred to remain in Greece. According to Rob, Jan felt that he had taken enough risks in his lifetime, and lacked the boundless ambition of people who consider their lives a failure unless they attain the absolute summit of achievement. He believed truly intelligent people are contented with less. His brother, Jan, he said, was also too intelligent to have much ambition – just like his father.

In 1956, at the age of sixty, Jan Zwartendijk retired – reluctantly. In fact, he blamed his brother, Piet, and told Rob that his uncle had been such a troublemaker over the years that Philips had been eager to dump him. And if they pensioned off one of the Zwartendijk brothers, then wouldn't they have to do the same to the other? But that was a misunderstanding. In the final years of his career, Piet had pleased everyone at the company and earned high praise by putting in place a well-functioning signal system along the Nieuwe Waterweg ship canal. The brothers' compulsory retirement was simply part of a general measure at Philips. To keep the company alert and innovative, senior executives were asked to leave by the age of sixty at the latest, and neither Piet nor Jan could do anything about that.

Having to retire may not have mattered much to Zwartendijk, but it was hard for him to say goodbye to Greece. Less than six months after returning to the Netherlands, he drove back to Greece for a few weeks' holiday with his brother and Rob in Piet's brand-spanking-new Peugeot 203.

The brothers took turns at the wheel, driving for two hours at a stretch. Somewhere in Yugoslavia, Jan drove much too fast over a pothole, and the chassis banged into the cobblestones. Piet swore at Jan, and Jan got so angry he wouldn't say another word to his brother. Rob, almost seventeen by then, looked on from the back seat in growing astonishment at the two retirees' behaviour. For three days, the brothers gave each other the silent treatment, even during a late-night card game at a roadside inn.

There was only one place where Jan Zwartendijk wanted to grow old: his hometown of Rotterdam. He bought a home in the Kralingen district, near where he had grown up. Erni didn't object, even though her memories of Kralingen were less sunny. But of all the gloomy corners of the Netherlands, the elegant home at Oranjelaan 24a was far from the worst, and her husband claimed he could smell the Maas River from there. In fact, they were much closer to a pond, the Kralingse Plas.

Never before had Jan led such a calm life. It went on until 1963, when

Jan and Erni on the balcony of their home in Rotterdam.

he received a telephone call from a woman at the foreign ministry in The Hague, who asked whether he was the Angel of Curaçao.

39

The reprimand

The letter Zwartendijk received from the archivist at the foreign ministry on 4 April 1963, sent on behalf of the minister, was not very friendly in tone. With no salutation, L.J. Ruys wrote:

> Please find enclosed a photocopy of a letter with an enclosure that I received from the consul general in Los Angeles. I have learned from studying the ministry records that, after Dr Tillmanns was discharged in 1940, you were temporarily assigned the role of acting consul in Kaunas. I was given your address by the Stichting tot Behartiging van de Belangen van de Beambten der N.V. Philips' Gloeilampenfabrieken.

This was the Philips pension fund. Zwartendijk's details must have no longer been in the foreign ministry's system:

> Following your confirmation on the telephone that you are the individual known as the 'Angel of Curaçao', I hereby request that you draw up a report on the assistance you offered at that time. It is rather peculiar that this tale is still in circulation after so many years, and it strikes me as worthwhile to hear the true story from you yourself. I will subsequently send the report to the consul general in Los Angeles with the request to forward it to the weekly newspaper *B'nai B'rith Messenger*.

Miss Ruys was requesting this information on behalf of her boss, the foreign minister, Joseph Luns. He had held that office since 1952, and would remain there for many years more, until 1971. At the time the letter was sent, Luns was part of the De Quay government.

Both Luns and prime minister Jan De Quay had serious stains on their wartime records: Luns had belonged to the Dutch Nazi party, the NSB, from 1933 to 1936 (he later falsely claimed that his brother had signed him up without his knowledge), and De Quay had, in 1940 and 1941, been part of the triumvirate that led the Nederlandsche Unie (Dutch Union), a political movement that sought closer cooperation between the German occupying regime and the Dutch authorities to prevent the NSB from gaining complete political control. The Unie took it as a given that Germany had won the war, and had no compunction about discussing the 'Jewish problem' with the occupiers. In December 1941, the occupying regime banned the Nederlandsche Unie, because the group had not supported Operation Barbarossa wholeheartedly enough. By then, the Unie had 600,000 members.

The De Quay government fell on 15 May 1963, but the correspondence with Zwartendijk continued, and Luns remained the foreign minister in the next government under prime minister Victor Marijnen.

The brief article in the *B'nai B'rith Messenger of Los Angeles* asked just one question: who was the 'Angel of Curaçao'? One refugee believed he remembered the name of the man who had written the note in French in his passport, the man who had saved the lives of thousands of Polish Jews: Philip Reyda. This was probably a blurred memory of 'Mr Radio Philips'. The refugee also claimed that the man had been the Dutch consul; that was why the Dutch consul general in Los Angeles had requested clarification.

In a typed letter sent to The Hague on 9 April 1963, Zwartendijk explained. The contents of the article and the title 'Angel of Curaçao' had left him 'extremely surprised'. 'I do not deserve such credit. It should go to Her Majesty's Envoy, His Excellency L.P.J. de Decker.' He explained that he had acted on De Decker's instructions.

Zwartendijk went on to write that, to his regret, he no longer recalled the exact words he had written in French in the visas. Nor could he look them up, since he had seen to it that all the consular paraphernalia were destroyed when he left Lithuania in September 1940. It had not been a true entry visa in any case, he explained, but something more like a note to officials in the Dutch West Indies. The provision of the note had led to an unanticipated chain reaction; many Lithuanians and, most of all, Poles had then asked for an identical note in their travel documents. But Zwartendijk rejected the estimate of 'thousands' in the *B'nai B'rith Messenger*. 'As far as I remember, the figure was 1,200 to 1,400.'

Zwartendijk sensed trouble; that much is clear. He played down his own role, making it seem almost insignificant. All credit was due to the envoy, he wrote, because De Decker was fifteen years dead by then and beyond the reach of official reproach. He spoke of the note in the passports in hazy terms, claiming he hadn't realised it was incompatible with consular regulations. The words he had written in more than two thousand passports were etched indelibly into his brain, but he hoped to let sleeping dogs lie. Furthermore, he knew perfectly well that he had issued more than 2,000 'pseudo-visas' (his own term), because, with the help of Van Prattenburg and De Haan, he had kept a numbered list. But, no, 'as far as he remembered', there were only 1,200 to 1,400. He wanted to avoid the impression of a mass exodus. Finally, he described the recipients as Lithuanians and Poles rather than as Jews, and avoided mentioning that some had come from the Netherlands or at least had Dutch nationality.

But at the end of his two-page letter he could not resist adding how much he would appreciate it if the consul general in Los Angeles could tell him how many Lithuanians and Poles had taken the Curaçao route to the United States and made a new home there.

On 23 April 1963, Zwartendijk received a note from the archivist thanking him for his reply. Miss Ruys's tone was considerably friendlier than in her first letter. 'The fact that so much work was done in the brief period when you were acting consul and so many people were saved, even if you were hardly aware of that at the time, must give you great satisfaction in retrospect. It is good for these matters not to be forgotten, but to be entered into the record in a timely fashion, so that the true story is known.'

Zwartendijk would later say that this brief letter had 'thrown dust in his eyes'.

The foreign ministry passed on the information to Dr Louis (Loe) de Jong, director of the Netherlands Institute for War Documentation (NIOD). De Jong and his wife had escaped to England in May 1940. For the rest of the war he had worked there for Radio Oranje, the Dutch-language program broadcast to the Netherlands by the government in exile. His parents, sister, and twin brother, who had stayed in the Netherlands, had been sent to an extermination camp and murdered.

De Jong was then engrossed in organising the overabundance of source materials for the first part of his authoritative history of the Second World War in the Netherlands, which would be published almost six years later. The complete work would consist of fourteen parts in twenty-seven volumes. It was a mammoth undertaking, too huge for one man, or even for one research institute for war documentation.

De Jong responded to Miss Ruys's letter by return of post, and later contacted Zwartendijk himself to shed light on the 'affair'.

As far as either I or Zwartendijk's children know, De Jong never made an appointment with him. To call this a missed opportunity would be a gross understatement. In 1963, De Jong was, of course, inundated with requests to look into all sorts of matters more deeply and to contact the surviving eyewitnesses and key actors. He couldn't do it all, although he did have the option of sending an assistant to interview an important witness.

In the end, De Jong devoted only a few lines to the Dutch consul in Kaunas, in volume nine of his magnum opus, which relates to the

Dutch government in exile in London.

This version of the story begins with the Dutch *chargé d'affaires* in the Baltic republics (by which De Jong meant De Decker) going to Stockholm after the Russian occupation of the Baltics in June 1940. From Sweden, he grants permission to the acting consul in Lithuania, J. Zwartendijk, to issue declarations to Polish-Jewish refugees stating that they will be admitted to Curaçao without a visa.

This story is only half true.

L.P.J. de Decker granted permission not from Stockholm but a month earlier, from Riga, while still the Dutch envoy to the Baltics. In fact, besides giving permission, he also composed the French declaration.

In De Jong's version, the declarations are issued at the urging of a young Orthodox Jew from Scheveningen, Nathan Gutwirth, a student at the Talmud school in Lithuania since 1935. With assistance from his Japanese counterpart, Zwartendijk sends more than a thousand Polish Jews, who are *able to furnish dollars*, to Japan by way of the Soviet Union.

Again, this version of the story shows how a few small changes can convey a completely different picture of the situation. First of all, it remains unclear whether Nathan Gutwirth or Peppy Sternheim was the first to go to Zwartendijk; but, in any case, the consul did not require much *urging*. Gutwirth and Zwartendijk had known each other for years. It would be more accurate to say that they looked at the situation together and discussed what should be done – with help from De Decker in Riga.

De Jong, who had never made any secret of his socialist views, then emphasised the dollars the Polish Jews *were able to furnish*, without revealing the actual sums involved. A casual reader might well think that the cost was in the thousands and that this route was therefore available only to the wealthy. If the historian had spoken to Zwartendijk, he would have learned that most of the refugees who came to the consulate had little money and that a Jewish-American organisation had assisted those who could not afford the $400 fee. The relatively small number given by De Jong – more than a thousand Polish Jews – reinforces the impression that only a select group of prosperous refugees were able to flee, with 'help from the Lithuanian representative of Philips-Eindhoven' – a company whose wartime actions had made a very poor impression on De Jong.

Stranger still is the role that Dr Loe de Jong attributed to the Dutch consul general in Stockholm, his namesake De Jong. As he tells it, Zwartendijk is expelled from Lithuania in September and then, in January 1941, the consul general in Stockholm, Adriaan Mattheus de Jong, receives 'a number of letters with photographs from Jews in the former Baltic republics requesting the visas for Curaçao'. De Jong draws up very official-looking visa declarations, pastes the photographs alongside them, and sends the declarations to the applicants, who are then granted exit visas by the Russian authorities and can, with support from funding organisations in Sweden, reach Stockholm and travel on through the Soviet Union to Shanghai or Japan.

True, consul De Jong did receive visa applications from Latvia and Lithuania. De Jong then asked De Decker what to do with them, and De Decker supplied his magic French formula. De Jong did then send the completed visas to Vilnius. But not one Jewish refugee used Russian papers and Swedish funds to travel to Stockholm and from there to the Soviet Union, Shanghai, or Japan. No travel was possible between Lithuania and Sweden, or between Sweden and the Soviet Union. Likewise, it was impossible to travel directly from the USSR to Shanghai. Not one Jewish refugee set out on the Moscow–Vladivostok–Tsuruga–Kobe–Shanghai escape route from Stockholm.

From April 1941 onward, there was no postal service between Stockholm and the former Baltic republics, De Jong continued.

'Exactly how many people were rescued by the consul general in Stockholm is unknown; he issued declarations for use by more than two thousand Jews, and it is possible that many hundreds, perhaps around one thousand, escaped.'

'More than two thousand' visas issued by A.M. de Jong. 'Many hundreds, perhaps around one thousand' who travelled on those visas. No source for these figures is provided, not even in a footnote.

In 1966, Dr Loe de Jong asked the former consul general in Stockholm if he had acted on his own initiative. Adriaan Mattheus de Jong made the following reply, 'I was never in communication with the governors in the Netherlands West Indies or with the Dutch foreign ministry about it, not at all ... Immediate action was required. The end justified the means.'

Although Loe de Jong did not contact Zwartendijk in 1963, he did ask Adriaan Mattheus de Jong a few questions in 1966. Considering Dr De Jong's role as an official historian in the employ of the Dutch government, one might be inclined to accept his version: Zwartendijk issued visas to just over a thousand Jews, and A.M. de Jong to more than two thousand. The opposite is closer to the truth, though still not right.

Fortunately, by the time volume nine of Dr De Jong's history was published, Zwartendijk was no longer around to hear about it. Still, until the very end, he tried to protect De Jong from embarrassing mistakes. In the 1970s, the historian received more and more information about Jews in Japan. On 24 June 1976, he asked Zwartendijk for clarification. How had the Jews travelled there? With what documents? Zwartendijk replied by return of post, sending along several letters with more information. He also made an urgent request:

> I want to point out that the whole business of Jews in Japan from 1940 onwards came about because of the so-called Curaçao visas, and that makes it crucial to present the relevant people and circumstances in an accurate way. I have heard many versions, many incorrect. Although the enclosed letters paint a picture of what happened, I would still suggest that I meet in person with you or one of your assistants.

De Jong did not reply.

Back to 1963. For the sake of the historical record, the foreign ministry asked Zwartendijk to agree to an interview, so that the truth could come out 'in a somewhat casual way'.

The ministry proposed to select a reliable journalist from a reputable newspaper, to whom Zwartendijk could explain how he had 'saved a large number of Jews from the gas chambers', and insisted that the facts stated in the interview must correspond to the information that Zwartendijk had provided in his letter. The officials wanted to keep control of the story.

It took them eight months to decide that the correspondent in The Hague for the *Leeuwarder Courant* (a provincial Dutch daily) was the most suitable candidate. The article had no byline, but according to a note in the foreign ministry file, the author was one Van Overbeeke. This must have been Fred van Overbeeke, who worked at the *Haagsche Courant* and took occasional assignments for provincial papers. The article, '"Angel of Curaçao" tracked down after 23 years' appeared in the newspaper on 27 December 1963. The opening is suspenseful:

It happened in Lithuania in July 1940, when the Germans had already trampled the West but were thus far contented to have occupied Poland in the East. In the little statelet on the Baltic where the Nazis were at the gates, tensions had risen to the boiling point. The thousands of Polish Jews who had crossed the border illegally, fleeing the German advance, found themselves caught in Lithuania like rats in a trap. There was no way left of escaping to a free country, because no foreign consul dared to help them. And without a visa, escape was impossible.

The refugees, packed together in sweltering hotel rooms, guesthouses, or slums, drifted from one consul to the next in desperation, but to no avail. Then one day, they heard a snatch of a rumour: 'a Curaçao visa, the Dutch consul will give them out for free if he has to …' This is the start of a unique episode in Dutch consular history, of which even the Ministry of Foreign Affairs was unaware until recently. The truth did not surface until earlier this year, when a Jewish weekly in America published a story about 'the Angel of Curaçao', the unknown consul who saved so many Jews from the gas chambers.

The story told by this Philips man – now 67, retired after a long international career, and residing in Rotterdam – may be grim, but it speaks volumes about the helpless fear in which the Jews were living. He himself was surprised by the article the foreign ministry had sent him and had to dig deep into his memories to untangle the tumultuous events of those days.

Zwartendijk summed up what had happened, again claiming to have forgotten the French words of the note. 'But in any case, it wasn't a fully fledged entry visa to what were then our Western colonies.' No one else could track down the words either, because when he had left Lithuania, he had destroyed all the consular paraphernalia.

The entire rescue operation had unfolded in July 1940, he told the journalist. In that one month, he had written 'twelve to fourteen hundred notes of that kind' in passports.

Not a word about August. But he did mention that the Japanese consul had called him a number of times and asked him not to work so fast, because Sugihara was using brush and ink, and couldn't keep up. And he described the street outside his office, full of applicants.

But instead of acknowledging that he and the Japanese consul had issued at least 2,139 visas, he gave a much smaller figure.

At the end of the interview, he expressed his fervent wish to find out how many Jews had ultimately escaped by this 'Curaçao route'.

You might think that all the newspapers and weeklies would have jumped on this story, asking Zwartendijk to recount his experiences again at greater length and in plenty of detail, and sketching the exact historical context. You might also think that radio and TV reporters would have spared no effort to find Jews who had escaped by way of Curaçao. Instead, the silence was deafening. The article appeared in the *Leeuwarder Courant* between Christmas and New Year's Eve, and not one newspaper picked up on it – not even the *NRC* in Rotterdam, which still counted Zwartendijk among its loyal readers, because he still associated it with his sister, Didi, and his friend Aletrino.

In February 1964, Zwartendijk was invited to the foreign ministry. He put on his best suit, expecting a conversation prompted by the interview in the *Leeuwarder Courant*. He didn't give much thought to the question of who might want to speak to him until he was driving from Rotterdam to The Hague. Minister Luns? A deputy minister? Or the ministry's secretary-general?

At the end of the afternoon, he returned home, defeated. The look on his face startled Edith, who had stopped by to see her mother. Her father had said nothing to her beforehand about the trip to The Hague, and he didn't explain exactly what had happened when he came home. He had a cup of tea, and went off to take a nap. Only later did she find out her father had been reprimanded, and she recalled the sight of his pale face.

Edith describes what the ministry official said to him: 'He should never have done what he did in Lithuania. He had broken the rules, so he would never be eligible for a decoration. The medal meant nothing to him, but being scolded felt humiliating.'

Many good deeds are done in the shadows. 'Do good and don't look back,' Didi had often said. Zwartendijk had no need for a medal or a newspaper article. But a reprimand was a different story: holding his actions against him, accusing him of breaking the rules. He was outraged.

Nothing was put down in writing. 'It was and is customary here to handle such matters through a conversation,' the foreign ministry historian, Bert van der Zwan, told me. 'Not a tongue-lashing, but a brief statement. I assume it was made clear to Zwartendijk that his actions had been inconsistent with the consular guidelines, and that he was therefore ineligible for a decoration, despite all his accomplishments.' And that was that.

40

The need to know

After his rap on the knuckles in The Hague – that was how he saw it, as an undeserved rap on the knuckles – Zwartendijk's daily life was tainted with chronic dissatisfaction. Normally so cheerful, he became a fretful grouch. And as he knew perfectly well what had caused the problem, he went in search of the only effective remedy: the true story of what had happened to 'his' Jews.

Ever since leaving Kaunas, he had been afraid that none of the refugees would make it. During the war, their prospects had looked very bleak indeed, and right after the war ended, the full scale of the Holocaust had come to light. He couldn't imagine that even a single one of the Jews he had rescued had escaped the killing machine – although he still secretly hoped for a miracle.

He often said to Erni, 'What I wonder is how they could have made it through the Soviet Union. They must have been interned somewhere in Siberia.'

And Erni would reply, 'Who knows? Maybe they're still there.'

In the late 1950s, it became an obsession. He had still heard no news – from anyone. What had become of Peppy Sternheim? Her mother, Rachel? Her brother, Levie? And her husband, Dr Isaac Lewin from Łódź, who had sat on the other side of his desk for half an hour, but whose face he could no longer remember, because it was the first time he was writing the French words in a travel document and he was worried he'd leave out an accent? Where had Nathan Gutwirth ended up? Had he managed to escape with his Lithuanian fiancée? No, of course he hadn't. After all, if anyone would have got in touch with Zwartendijk, it was Nathan.

The weekly *B'nai B'rith Messenger* published the information provided by the Dutch foreign ministry about the 'Angel of Curaçao'. Less than a week later, the Dutch consulate general in Los Angeles received another letter from a survivor.

Benjamin Grey, who lived in California, still treasured the visa he had received from the Dutch consul in Kaunas. He was hard at work, in cooperation with the Institute for the Righteous Acts founded not long before in Berkeley, 'trying to establish all the facts pertaining to the issuance of the so-called visas to Curaçao during the summer of 1940 in Kaunas'. He planned to try to track down the former Japanese consul in Kaunas and find out what he knew. He also hoped to get in touch with Zwartendijk, so that he could determine how many Lithuanians and Poles had reached the United States.

The consulate general passed on the request, and the foreign ministry informed Zwartendijk. On 21 August, he received a copy of Benjamin Grey's letter, and that very day he sent a detailed reply. He told the whole story, explaining that he'd had the full cooperation of the Japanese consul and that the two of them had known that applicants with Curaçao visas and Japanese transit visas could count on receiving Russian transit visas. Grey also asked specifically whether he had continued issuing visas after the consulate closed, but Zwartendijk said no. In fact, Grey himself had a visa issued in August, but he didn't mention that in his letter. Zwartendijk's denial was categorical: 'I did not issue any at all "unofficially" after the consulate had been closed formally. He kept on insisting that he had issued 1,200 to 1,400 visas between late June and late July 1940.

For the rest of his life, he would never admit to anyone – not even his wife and children – that he had continued to issue visas for the entire month of August.

He was obviously happy to have found a survivor at last, and wrote that he had heard only recently that a number of people with his note in their passports had escaped Lithuania and 'reached California by way of Curaçao'.

So, as late as 1963, Zwartendijk must have still believed that the refugees with Curaçao visas really did travel to Curaçao, and that they went on to the United States from there. Benjamin Grey did not set him straight, but did send a brief reply stating that he was honoured to be embarking on his research. In the course of that research, Grey was in communication not only with the Institute for the Righteous Acts in California, but also with the International Institute for Holocaust Research in Jerusalem. He proceeded with skill, at a measured pace – far too measured. It would take years before his research yielded any results.

From the Dutch embassy in Washington, Zwartendijk received a letter from Chaim Shapiro, a rabbi from Baltimore who was planning to write a book about his escape across the breadth of the Soviet Union with a Curaçao visa in his pocket. He had made it.

Zwartendijk was overjoyed at first, but in the days that followed this gave way to sadness. By then, he had heard from three survivors: two in Los Angeles and one in Baltimore. This had to mean that more than 2,000 men, women, and children had *not* made it. Otherwise they would have shown signs of life, like Samuel Schreig, who had tipped off the *B'nai B'rith Messenger* in Los Angeles, or like Benjamin Grey and Chaim Shapiro, who had asked the embassy in Washington for information.

What made him even gloomier was that Shapiro's visa had been issued in Stockholm and signed by the Dutch consul general to Sweden, A.M. de Jong. In other words, Shapiro wasn't even one of 'his' Jews.

Zwartendijk sent Shapiro a brief reply. As his son Jan later wrote to his brother, Rob, 'In his response, Pa seems to do his best to remember as little as possible.'

In the autumn of 1996, thirty-three years later, Jan junior gave a talk at the Baltimore Synagogue. There he met Shapiro, who gave him a copy of his correspondence with his father. Shapiro admitted then that he had been a little surprised by the morose reply from the former Dutch consul in Kaunas, because, as he put it, 'For years I have been screaming and beating the drums about your father.'

Jan junior and Rob eventually realised that their Pa was shouldering a tremendous guilt complex. He believed that instead of giving thousands of people the papers that would ensure their future safety, he had sent them to their doom. In his mind, this idea became increasingly vivid.

It was Jan junior who suggested that, alongside Benjamin Grey's research, they should also turn to Simon Wiesenthal's Jewish Documentation Centre in Vienna for assistance. Right away, Wiesenthal promised to help, but he felt it was more a matter for the new research centre he was establishing in Los Angeles. That centre did not open until 1977 – too late for Zwartendijk. Aware that his health was failing, he suggested to his wife that they move to an assisted-living facility in Soest. Even though Erni was nine years younger, she was worn out as well and only too happy to make the move. Besides, Soest was in the forest, and as far as she was concerned that was always a plus.

When Jan Zwartendijk was fitted with a pacemaker, he recovered some of his old flair. He began to make jokes again, wondering aloud whether, with that device in his chest, he would ever kick the bucket. It would keep working until the battery ran out, and as an old Philips man, he knew that could take a while.

Until the age of seventy-five, he had smoked – pipes, but also cigarettes, around a pack a day. In Greece, his favourite brand had been Karelia. After returning to the Netherlands, he would always ask visitors from Greece to bring Karelias with them by the carton. They had a wonderful, spicy scent. According to Rob, Pa never stopped smelling like Athens; he gave off that scent like a tangible memory. When out of Karelias, he would smoke Egyptian cigarettes, the skinny, oval kind. And he'd always say, 'Oh well, with a glass of ouzo, you'd never know the difference.'

In the summer of 1976, he fell ill. He had to stay in bed at home, to his frustration, because his son Jan and daughter-in-law Nancy were visiting from Canada for a few weeks. Just after they boarded the plane for the return trip, his doctor told him he had only a few weeks to live. Zwartendijk had lung cancer.

Rob returned from France, and he and Edith came to stay in Soest. For a whole week they slept on mattresses on the floor, so that they could be there with their mother for their father's final days.

As death approached, the past resurfaced; they shared old memories from Greece, Eindhoven, and even further back. Jan's thoughts were often in Prague, where he had met the love of his life, or in Kaunas, because that was where Erni had proved he could always count on her. He relived his swim across the Memel with his eldest son one last time, and rowed down the Rotte and Maas again with his brother. They were days of profound beauty.

By the time they had gone through almost his whole life story, Zwartendijk could no longer speak. He had used up his energy, but he could understand what other people were saying and point at what he needed. On the morning of 14 September 1976, he made it clear with a gesture that he wanted to stand up. Rob took him by the underarms and hoisted him to his feet. At that moment, he died.

Rob took a step back, wondering if he was imagining things, but there it was, plain as day on his father's face – a smile. He called out to Edith and Ma and, when they came in, asked if they saw it, too. Yes, Pa had died with a smile on his lips.

Rob – who was an old man, too, by then, with skin cancer in the very spot on his nose where he'd had his strawberry mark – wondered what that smile could mean. Was it resignation? Or the realisation that, despite all the mistakes, the misunderstandings, the partial and total failures, life was worth living after all?

No, Rob didn't think that was it. His father had simply been glad that his death would put an end to the doubts and uncertainties that had tormented him, especially since the reprimand at the foreign ministry. He would finally be free of all his worries. What a relief! What a consolation!

Or was it something entirely different? In that final moment, had he seen Erni disembark from the train with her bawling baby, Robbie? And there, on the platform of the Kaunas station, had he taken them into his arms? Crossing the bedlam of Germany to cure her son – now *that* was an act of heroism.

The funeral procession left from Soest. Zwartendijk was laid to rest in the family grave in Rotterdam-Hillegersberg. That was how he had wanted it, and he had put his wishes in writing in his will. Just before the coffin was carried out of the house, a letter arrived with news from the Holocaust Research Center.

A report from Rabbi Marvin Tokayer in Japan had settled the matter. The centre had concluded, in part from the Kobe figures, that 95 per cent of the Jewish refugees with visas from the Dutch consul in Kaunas had survived the war.

When Rob read this conclusion aloud, Edith clapped her hand to her mouth and cried, 'Oh, no.'

If the message had reached the Zwartendijk home a week earlier, their father would have died not only with a smile on his face, but in peace. After wondering for so long about the fate of the thousands of people he'd tried to help, he could finally have put those cares behind him.

41

Under a spruce or pine tree

Rabbi Marvin Tokayer, from New York, had been sent to Japan in 1962 as a United States Air Force chaplain. He had decided to stay, or as he put it, 'I forgot to leave.' Tokayer served the Jewish community in Japan from 1967 to 1975, and spent the rest of his life studying the history of the Jews in Japan and China, and the role of the Japanese in assisting Jewish refugees.

At the request of the Holocaust Center, and above all with the encouragement of Jan Zwartendijk junior, who had stumbled across his name, Rabbi Tokayer did research in the Kobe city archives and the Jewcom archives. He traced the journey of 2,178 Jewish refugees from Kaunas to Japan, and supplied an abundance of information on the numbers of men and women, their ages (although he overlooked many children, he did learn of niniety-nine boys and 114 girls aged one to fifteen), and their occupations: fifteen physicians, sixty-two engineers, sixty-one lawyers, 233 officials, seventy-nine rabbis, and 341 rabbinical students. The large number of Jewish rabbis and religious teachers in training led *The Jerusalem Post*, which covered the story on 29 June 1996, to run a hyperbolic headline: 'Jan Zwartendijk, The Man Who Saved Judaism'.

Rabbi Tokayer combed the archives for the destinations of the refugees when they left Japan: the United States (532), Mexico (17), Cuba (27, a surprising number after the *St. Louis* tragedy), Panama (2),

Argentina (40), Brazil (17), Canada (186), Burma (28), Australia (81), New Zealand (29), Palestine (59), Manchuria (15), and Shanghai (860).

Tokayer estimated that 800 of the 860 Jews who had gone to Shanghai travelled on to the United States after the war.

His figures later had to be adjusted upwards. Rabbi Tokayer didn't know about either the refugees who had received visas from consul De Voogd or the Jews sent on to the Dutch East Indies by the Dutch consul general in Kobe. He also left out the Jews who were temporarily housed in Yokohama and Tokyo. Nonetheless, he was the first to engage in serious archival research.

On 12 September 1976, the Holocaust Center sent its findings to Zwartendijk. The report arrived in Rotterdam on 18 September, four days after his death.

Even so, Jan Zwartendijk junior went to see Rabbi Tokayer in New York and thank him profusely for his efforts. Without his detective work, the Zwartendijk family would have remained in uncertainty much longer.

Jan junior had been unable to attend his father's funeral. Soon after their return home to Canada, his wife, Nancy, had been plunged into a fog from which she would never re-emerge. This was the heartbreaking sequel to a brain operation she'd had in 1973. In removing the tumour, the surgeons had done irreparable damage. Over several years, Nancy became mentally and physically handicapped.

Jan remained her loyal caregiver, even though she barely recognised him anymore. She lost control of her behaviour, used rude words, ranted, moaned, and made rude comments to strangers. Dozens of extra pounds and a swollen face made her look nothing like the woman he had met in Athens.

Jan kept up the appearance of control for as long as he could, but he was running himself ragged. He eventually had no choice but to have Nancy admitted to the secure ward of a psychiatric clinic. He went on visiting regularly, even though she didn't recognise him and, on top of everything else, had lost her ability to speak.

After every visit, it took him days to return to his usual self. In 1984, he was diagnosed with cancer. He would never have survived, but for a new woman in his life: Anne Bowden, an old friend of Nancy's, who left her home in Washington, DC, to live in Ottawa with Jan. Jan didn't want to marry Anne until Nancy was dead. But his lawyer explained to him that he could remarry without any special legal proceedings if his previous wife had been in a coma or without any mental faculties for twenty years. Jan, who had retired by that time, moved to the United States with Anne. They spent their summers in a small apartment in Salem, Oregon, and their winters in Tucson, Arizona. In May 1994, they were married. Exactly one month later, Nancy died.

Jan devoted himself to restoring his father's reputation, writing to one organisation after another. 'It keeps me busy,' he told Edith, when she showed her concern about whether her brother could handle it all. Jan had to nag and insist. No one seemed to want to learn the whole story of the rescue operation.

The news from the Simon Wiesenthal Center took ten years to arrive. The result of the investigation was that the visas issued by Zwartendijk and Sugihara had enabled at least six thousand people to escape the Holocaust. The centre's calculations suggested that an average of 2.8 people had travelled on each visa.

At first, Jan couldn't believe this conclusion; he feared it was a gross exaggeration and therefore a crass form of hero worship. He maintained his belief in 2,139 visas issued and a roughly equal number of survivors. 'Let's not make more of it than it is,' he wrote to Rob. As for the consul general in Stockholm who, according to the historian De Jong, had saved two thousand Jews from the gas chambers, he wrote, 'What a braggart.'

During my own investigation in Shanghai, I arrived at a still larger figure, nearly ten thousand. But I must make one reservation. I was able to verify how many visas Zwartendijk and Sugihara issued, more or less, and the average number of people to use each one. But I do not know how many families with visas actually went on the journey. Some gave up on the idea at the last minute; others, like Solly Ganor's parents, put off their departure too long. Almost everyone who hesitated was sent to an extermination camp and died there, or else was murdered in Lithuania. Solly Ganor is an exception – he survived the war. But his brother disappeared without a trace, and his mother and sister died in Stutthof concentration camp.

Hillel Levine, Sugihara's biographer, fears that many people left too late, but nonetheless shares my belief that around 10,000 people survived, thanks to Curaçao visas. Sugihara's widow gave the same figure. The exact number will always remain unknown. We do not know the names of the applicants either for the Stockholm visas or for the ones that Sugihara and Zwartendijk issued on loose sheets of paper in August 1940. What we do know is that, thanks to this smart and simple plan, one of the largest rescue operations of the Second World War succeeded.

Erni's later years were soured by the lack of due recognition for Jan's deeds. She could not discuss her sense of injustice with anyone. Her sister and brother-in-law had passed away, one of her sons went back and forth between Canada and the United States, and although her other son had returned to the Netherlands, he spent more time on aeroplanes than at home. Her son-in-law had said farewell to the KLM and started a furniture company that made bookcases. He and Edith had moved to Bussum, not far from Soest, but they spent almost as much time in the Dordogne, where he bought the wood for the bookcases. The only time Erni could shake off her troubles was when she saw her grandchildren. She was pleased that the youngest, David Zwartendijk, was named after the brave little king who stood up to Goliath.

Her sunny disposition had helped her through all the difficult times. She had always been more active and energetic than her husband, or, as her niece Ineke put it, 'Aunt Erni always took the initiative.' But Jan's death put out the spark. She struggled with her health, aged fast, and couldn't keep track of when to get up and when to go to bed. She forgot Dutch words, and couldn't remember the German ones either. Her mind went dark, dull, and vacant.

When she hardly recognised anyone, Edith took her in. She died on 26 September 1979 in the Bussum hospital, near Edith and Henk's home. The doctors wanted to perform an autopsy to determine the cause of death, but Edith, Jan, and Rob decided that was unnecessary. They already knew the cause: Erni had strayed into the vast and barren land called loneliness. At the time of her death, she was only seventy-four years old.

Not long before she died, one of her early admirers had come out of the woodwork. Carel de Neeve visited her in the hospital. He'd been nineteen or twenty, and she'd been twenty-six or twenty-seven back in the days when they'd hit the dance halls of Hamburg. They'd gone out swing dancing together at least once a week. Jan preferred to watch the ships go down the Elbe. Even by night, the lights of a passenger liner on the river sent him into a strange ecstasy.

After Hamburg, Carel de Neeve had gone to work for Unilever in the Belgian Congo. He returned to Rotterdam just before the war broke out. More than once, he had invited Erni for a cup of coffee, and she had sent him a yearly Christmas card from Eindhoven and later from Athens.

He came to the hospital to say farewell; they'd had so much fun together. But she refused to see him. 'That'll never do,' she told Edith. 'I look dreadful. Send him away.'

Erni's last wish was not to be laid in the family grave in Rotterdam-Hillegersberg with a lot of uncles and aunts she'd hardly known, or never even met. She wanted to be cremated.

Her instructions were for her ashes to remain in Soest, the last place she had lived. She asked that the urn be left under a tree, a beautiful spruce or pine like the ones around Prague in Bohemia, or in Lithuania.

42

No news from the survivors

With only a few exceptions, the survivors never contacted their rescuers. The question is why. It wouldn't have taken so much effort to send a note, some sign of life, to the people who had saved them in their hour of need. You might even feel that Zwartendijk, De Jong, De Voogd, and Romer had a moral right to information. In the absence of any news, they were burdened with questions and guilt feelings for many years. Not all of them were equally troubled, but Zwartendijk, De Jong, De Voogd, and Romer often wondered when and how they had fallen short. I haven't mentioned De Decker here because he died in 1948. Nor do I include Sugihara, because before his death in 1986, he was the only rescuer to learn the outcome of the investigation by the Institute for Holocaust Research and the Simon Wiesenthal Center. The other four received no news from the survivors.

At first, Sugihara was not as lucky as Zwartendijk. He and his wife and their three sons were arrested at his last diplomatic post, Bucharest, when Soviet troops invaded Romania in 1944. They spent eighteen months interned in a prisoner-of-war camp.

When Sugihara returned to Japan, he was informed that there was no longer a place for him in the diplomatic service. His dismissal had a great deal to do with what his wife, in her memoirs, called 'that incident in Lithuania'. That same year, 1947, his son Haruki died of leukemia. To Sugihara's mind, it was no coincidence that his only child born in Kaunas died at the age of seven. The city had brought him nothing but misery; he was inconsolable.

The family moved into a house in Fujisawa, in the province of Kanagawa. This was the period when Sugihara sold light bulbs door to door, not earning enough to support his wife and children.

In 1949, Yukiko gave birth to a son, Nobuki. They had three children again. Their upbringing was largely in Yukiko's hands. Sugihara was going back and forth between Japan and the Soviet Union, where he worked as a migrant labourer in and around Vladivostok for sixteen years. It was seasonal work; between jobs, he usually had a couple of weeks to visit Japan.

In 1968, Jehoshua Nishri took charge of the economic affairs department of the Israeli embassy in Tokyo. His first act in Japan was to go in search of the man who had signed the slip of paper inserted into his father's Polish passport when Jehoshua was ten years old. Mr Nishri's name is not on any of the lists of visas, but his son could explain that: he'd been one of the boys on the platform who begged for Sugihara's signature – and got it, on a blank sheet of paper from the Japanese consulate. He had been the second-to-last boy to receive a visa. So it's easy to see why he never forgot. His father had later told him, 'You saved our lives.'

Nishri tracked down the ex-consul in the port of Fujisawa. Sugihara had just put his Vladivostok days behind him and decided to limit himself to an occasional job in Japan. By this time he was sixty-eight years old. Nishri invited him to visit Israel the following year, and Sugihara accepted the offer, mainly in the hope of finding a place at a university for his youngest son, since he lacked the means to pay for his studies in Japan. His plan was successful: Nobuki was admitted to the Hebrew University in Jerusalem.

Sugihara, grey-haired but as energetic as ever, gave interviews from morning to night for a full week, to not only Israeli but also American media. It was then that the Japanese government finally realised what an asset Chiune Sugihara could be to them. Imagine – a Japanese diplomat had saved thousands of lives in the Second World

Reunion of Chiune Sugihara and Zorach Warhaftig during Sugihara's visit to Israel, Jerusalem, 1968.

War! It was the best possible proof that not everyone in Japan above the age of fifty was a war criminal. Back in Tokyo, the former consul was welcomed to the foreign ministry as a dignitary. He was awarded a state pension and later rehabilitated.

More than that – he was hailed as a hero, so that everyone could forget as fast as possible that Japan had been allied with Nazi Germany and never made the slightest protest against the extermination of the Jews. The Japanese threw themselves into a strange sort of *Vergangenheitsbewältigung,* to borrow the German term for efforts to cope with the national legacy of the Holocaust. They embraced the Sugihara exception and turned their backs on the country's wartime record. On the rare occasions when the subject did come up, it tended to derail the conversation – in essence, it was still taboo. Sugihara, in contrast, was idolised. A senior Dutch diplomat I spoke to in Tokyo called it 'a kind of false romanticism without any awareness of who was really responsible for what' – and hastened to add that this was 'a personal opinion'. 'We' – Western countries, including the United

States and Canada – 'never want to offend the Japanese, of course.'

In 1985, Sugihara – still of sound mind – became the only Japanese person recognised by Yad Vashem as one of the Righteous Among the Nations. His name was added to the Wall of Honour in the Garden of the Righteous in Jerusalem. He was too old and sick by then to travel to Israel, but his wife and his youngest son did attend the ceremony. Chiune Sugihara died on 31 July 1986. He had become a household name.

The same cannot be said of the other diplomats.

Adriaan Mattheus de Jong died in 1972, Nicolaas de Voogd in 1976, and Tadeusz Romer in 1978. Like Jan Zwartendijk, none of them ever heard what had become of the refugees, even though they had put their careers and their lives on the line to save them.

Was it ingratitude on the part of the survivors? Or were they suppressing their trauma, trying never again to think of the war and its human cost, even in their own family circles?

The answer is probably much simpler: they had to build new lives in new countries, a difficult process with many setbacks. Some failed; others succeeded, only with great effort. They never had the time or the money to go searching for their rescuers.

Yet there was one other exception: a single survivor, in the case of Adriaan Mattheus de Jong. The former consul general in Stockholm *did* receive one piece of news.

I found out about this while in search of something else. I had often asked Magnus, De Jong's grandson, if he would browse through the papers in the attic of the family home in Stockholm, where his grandfather had died in 1972. My hope was that there he would find the list of visas issued, a list of at least 472 names. But Magnus de Jong could not read a word of Dutch, and besides, all of his grandfather's business papers were up in that damned attic. Heaps of them. Opa Adriaan had saved everything, including KLM tickets from just after the war. This was doubtless because De Jong had been reprimanded by the parliamentary committee of inquiry in 1949 for not saving all his receipts in wartime.

Magnus never did find that list, but there was a letter from Samuel Orlansky, written on 28 July 1966 and sent from Bnei Brak in Israel (a city near Tel Aviv that later became a bulwark of Orthodoxy), addressed to 'The Honourable A.M. DeYoung' in Stockholm. By some miracle, it had reached De Jong.

Magnus scanned it and sent me the file. It was a letter in English, with an enclosed copy in Hebrew so that the contents could be used 'for writing the history of our new state' of Israel.

Samuel Orlansky had left Kaunas with a Curaçao visa. He had received visas from both the Dutch and Japanese consuls on 5 August 1940. Sugihara had spelled his name Szmul Ela Orlanski.

Samuel was one of a large number of students who had set out from Mir Yeshiva together. I haven't been able to figure out why he needed a visa from A.M. de Jong in Stockholm anyway. Maybe it was intended for other Mir Yeshiva students who had waited too long to apply. In any case, they had departed as a group. They reached Vladivostok, then Kobe, and finally Shanghai.

I check this story against Sonja Mühlberger's list. Sure enough, number 11,601 is Szmul Orlanski, Rabb. Student, M, 22 years old, place of residence 340/32 Zang Rd.

Life had been hard in the Hongkew ghetto, Orlansky reported, and they'd had 'to put up with a whole lot from Hitler's cronies' – meaning the Japanese camp commander and the Japanese guards. But with God's help, the group had stayed together and made it through the war. In 1947, they had left China, in a difficult, dangerous journey through the Far East and Liberia that had taken them years. Many had ended up in the United States and Canada, and many others in Israel – all thanks to the consul in Stockholm and 'your friend in Lithuania'.

Samuel Orlansky suspected that Adriaan Mattheus de Jong and Jan Zwartendijk had been in constant communication and worked hand in glove:

It is no doubt a great source of joy and satisfaction to you and your friend to know not only that your deeds led to the actual survival of thousands of souls in the world, but also that they sparked a spiritual, immortal creative urge in hundreds of people among the Jews.

De Jong must certainly have felt gratified, but Zwartendijk never heard the news. De Jong never forwarded the letter or tried to get in touch with him. Nor did he send a copy to the foreign ministry in The Hague or to the Netherlands Institute for War Documentation (NIOD). That's because he was angry.

Angry at everyone who had thwarted him in the Netherlands: the government, the yes-men in the diplomatic service, and the politicians who had reprimanded him. When they had handed out medals, they'd made a point of passing him over. And how could he forget what his former boss – Willem Constantijn, Count of Rechteren-Limpurg, the envoy in Stockholm – had told the committee of inquiry about him on 19 August 1949? 'He was a very difficult man, who quite often caused trouble … He did much too much and was not always so tactful.' Meanwhile, the count himself had not done a thing.

De Jong was sick and tired of the war. He had seen how narrow-mindedness worked together with incompetence, how caution and going by the book had served as covers for cowardice.

Samuel Orlansky ended his two-page letter with some exceptionally warm words:

May you, together with your family, be granted happiness for the rest of your lives. There is no doubt that you and your friend deserve a place in the history book of our people, together with the state that you helped to found.

A heartwarming tribute. But De Jong left the letter lying among the receipts in a basket of papers, where it would go unread until exactly fifty years later.

43

The exodus from Egypt

In 1939, Leo Adler left Bavaria to continue his rabbinical studies in Mir. The fame of the local yeshiva extended far across the borders. Mir, then in Poland and now in Belarus, is some eighty kilometres southwest of Minsk. After the German invasion of Poland, the yeshiva was moved to Vilnius and later to Keidan (now Kėdainiai) in Lithuania.

Friends in Kaunas introduced Leo to the teacher Bella Hamburg. One handshake, one look, and a five-minute conversation were enough to merge their two lives into one. In retrospect, Leo was never certain what had been decisive – was it her eyes or her voice? To Bella, it was even more mysterious – after their first meeting, she couldn't have said how Leo looked, or even if he was tall, short, or middling. All she remembered after that first meeting was the almost religious attention he paid to her.

Bella had studied German, Lithuanian, and history at the University of Kaunas. She taught at a secondary school, and intended to remain there all her life. The daughter of a respected merchant, she had been born and raised in Kaunas, and loved the city on the Memel. If war hadn't broken out, she would never have dreamed of leaving – aside from an occasional jaunt to Vilnius, because they spoke Yiddish there and you could buy a Hebrew paper at every newsstand.

Bella and Leo came from different streams of Judaism. She was Orthodox in name only, except on traditional holidays, while Leo led his entire life in conformity with his strict religious beliefs. Before moving to Mir, he had earned a degree from the Jewish teacher-training institute at the University of Würzburg.

A week after their first meeting, Leo asked Bella to marry him. They were both twenty-four years old. From the yeshiva, Leo wrote to his future bride: 'I don't know what other people will think and say about our marriage. Don't be fooled by other people regarding as crazy that to which you and I have dedicated our whole lives. I suspect that we will face many painful experiences.'

They married in the early spring of 1940.

After the Russian invasion, Zorach Warhaftig advised Leo (who was not so concerned) to obtain visas for himself and his new bride as soon as possible. On 1 August 1940, two days before the Dutch consulate was closed, Zwartendijk stamped Leo's German passport; a day later, Sugihara gave him a transit visa for Japan. Leo then waited almost five months before boarding the train to Vladivostok. This was because Bella was pregnant; Leo wanted his wife and child with him when he left.

Warhaftig departed in September. In December, one of his confidants persuaded Leo that it was now or never. The Soviets would leave Jews in peace a while longer, but not men of the cloth, including rabbis in training. On top of that, the probability that Hitler would cancel the treaty with Stalin and the Baltic states was growing by the month. On 25 October 1940, the Reich Main Security Office in Kraków had issued a decree forbidding Jews to emigrate, even if they had tickets for the journey and could present visas from foreign consulates. SS Oberführer I.A. Eckhardt had stated the exact reason:

> The mass departure of Jews from Eastern Europe implies a continuous spiritual renewal of global Judaism, since it is primarily these Jews from Eastern Europe who, on account of their Orthodox religious attitude, furnish a large proportion of the rabbis, Talmud teachers, and so forth that are in demand among Jewish organisations working in the US. Furthermore, for these Jewish organisations in the US, every

Orthodox Jew from Eastern Europe is a valuable fellow participant in their unflagging efforts to promote the spiritual revival of American Judaism.

Leo Adler was one of a group of yeshiva students who decided to take the Trans-Siberian Express. The plan was for Bella to follow as soon as the child was born. Just before Leo left, Bella took the precaution of writing her post office box number in his address book – who knew, the strain of the journey might erase it from his memory. She also noted the address of her cousin, Soroh Berman, in America: 200 Windsor Street, Hartford, Connecticut.

At the Kaunas station, Bella kept trying to delay her husband's departure. In the station hall and on the platform, she planted herself right in front of him so that he couldn't leave. Before he boarded the train, Bella whispered her parting words into Leo's ear: 'Don't forget me, and get me out of here as soon as you can.' He pretended he hadn't heard and tried not to look at her swollen belly.

Once Leo reached Japan, he sent his passport back to Kaunas with the two visas, so that Bella could leave right after their child was born. The passport reached Kaunas by post, but without the Japanese visa, which Sugihara had generally brushed onto a loose piece of paper.

By the final weeks of spring, staying in Lithuania had become too risky for Bella. Not only was a German invasion in the works, but anti-Semitism was reaching fever pitch, without much interference from the Soviets. Bella witnessed a hostile act towards a Jewish family. That very day, she fled, thinking she could obtain a Japanese transit visa in Moscow.

In Moscow, she gave birth to a son. When she went to the civil registry five days later, she was arrested. After all, her husband was a German, wasn't he? No, she said, a Jew. But she had a German passport, didn't she, and German nationality? She couldn't deny it.

But she grasped the reason for her arrest only when she heard that German tank divisions had invaded the Baltics and the Soviet Union, and were advancing at a speed of two hundred kilometres a day.

Operation Barbarossa had begun. By order of the Supreme Soviet, all German nationals had to be interned in prison camps. Moscow feared a fifth column.

Bella and her newborn, whom she had named Marek, were transferred from camp to camp. She was eventually sent in a cattle truck to the Kazakhstan steppes, 2,000 kilometres south-east of Moscow. The camp – intended for German prisoners of war, Russian-Germans, German-speaking Estonians and Latvians, and Finns taken prisoner during the Winter War of 1939–1940 – was near Karaganda, and larger than the city itself. The prisoners made up 70 per cent of the local population. They had to do forced labour, chopping straw, kneading clay, and baking bricks.

Bella washed Marek's diapers in the snow. She came down with typhoid dysentery, and Marek with diphtheria. Bella didn't want her son admitted to the clinic in the city, because she was certain that, if he were, she would never see him again.

After two years of toiling in the fields and in the heat of the kilns, Bella convinced the Soviet political supervisor to allow her to open a school for the ninety-nine children in the camp aged four to eight. Without paper or a blackboard, Bella taught the children to read and write by scratching letters into bark with a needle.

Her greatest fear was that, if she died, Marek would no longer remember that he was a Jew. She made him a tiny kippa out of rags and went on repeating the prayer 'Shema Yisrael' ('Hear, O Israel') each morning and evening until he knew the opening words by heart.

The German capitulation did not put an end to Bella and Marek's captivity. Hitler was dead and the Nazis defeated, but inmates with German passports had to remain in the Karaganda prisoner-of-war camp.

In 1946, as Passover approached, Bella decided to hold a seder for Jewish children in her classroom, a ritual meal on the first evening of Passover in remembrance of the exodus from Egypt. The religious Jews in the camp were eager to make unleavened matzo bread, and urged Bella to do her best to obtain permission from the camp commander.

'You, too, really believe in this?' the Soviet officer asked. It was inconceivable to him that a teacher who spoke four languages and could teach mathematics and physics would voluntarily submit to religious laws and rituals. But he gave permission for the use of the camp kitchen for two hours.

Bella had the honour of baking the first matzo for the prescribed eighteen minutes so that it would be *kosher l'Pesach*, kosher for Passover. On the day of the seder, they covered the windows of the classroom with white sheets. They made water look like wine by dyeing it with juice squeezed from beets. But they left out the bitter herbs that commemorate the bitterness of slavery in Egypt. After more than five years in a prison camp, they had swallowed plenty of bitterness, and needed no ritual to remind them how it tasted.

During the meal, the five-year-old Marek listened to a reading from Exodus. It didn't seem to interest him much, but the next day he pointed to the barbed wire and said to his mother, 'We here are like the slaves in Egypt.'

In the autumn of 1946, the Finnish prisoners were released. One woman, grateful to Bella for teaching her daughter to read, offered to take a letter to Finland for her and to post it. Bella gratefully accepted the offer, but wondered who to write to. She had no know way of knowing where Leo might be – it seemed unlikely that he had stayed in Japan for long, and if he had, he would surely have died in the war. She had heard a vague story about Hiroshima. She knew at least ten addresses of relatives in Lithuania, but there was no doubt in her mind that they no longer lived there. She had also heard a few things about deportations and concentration camps. She really had only one address to write to, her cousin Soroh's in Connecticut.

The letter took a long time to arrive. The Finnish woman first had to travel back to Helsinki, straight across the Soviet Union – and in the winter of 1946–1947, that was no easy task. Sea mail to Connecticut also took weeks. The postman couldn't find a Berman in Windsor

Street. Soroh had moved. But just as he turned to leave, a neighbour came out of the building and asked who he was looking for. 'Oh, what a coincidence! I'd planned to visit the Bermans this afternoon!'

Soroh had given up hope of receiving a sign of life from any close relative. Images of the concentration camps had spread around the world by then, and the few survivors had contacted their relatives long before. On 16 October 1946, the Nuremberg trials had been completed and the death sentences carried out. She tore open the letter: 'Dear Sorohle ...' Through her tears, she read that Bella was alive, had a son, and really just wanted to know two things: whether Leo was still alive, and where he was.

Leo was in Shanghai. His friends had declared him meshuga to go on believing he would one day be reunited with the woman he loved and their child. Bella and his child had to be dead, they told him. How could he be such a fool? 'Then I'm mad,' he always told them. 'I know they're alive.' After the United States troops had arrived in Shanghai, Leo had sent a letter to 200 Windsor Street to inform Bella's cousin that he had survived the war. Knowing it might take a while before he and the other twenty-five thousand Jews could leave Shanghai, he sent her his address there.

On 17 May 1947, Leo, still in Shanghai, received a telegram from Soroh. He was surprised to learn, not that Bella was still alive, but that she had spent the entire war in a camp in northern Kazakhstan.

It took five more months before Leo could board a ship to New York, and a little longer before his wife and son were released from the camp and travelled by way of Odessa to Vienna.

On 14 January 1948, Bella and Marek arrived on Pan Am Flight 115 at LaGuardia Airport in New York. Seven years and three weeks had passed since Bella had planted herself in front of Leo at the station in Kaunas to stop him from going.

While Bella waited in the long queue at passport control, it didn't take her long to spot her husband. She lifted Marek high above her head.

'There's your daddy.'

'Where?'

'You'll recognise him.'

A New York policeman took pity on the pale little boy, and let him through while his mother stayed in the queue. Without a moment's hesitation, he ran up to a man who spread his arms wide – his father.

In Brooklyn, it wasn't long before Marek had two brothers: Samuel and David. But their father felt out of place in the New World. Even after Leo Adler was appointed youth rabbi at the Shaarey Tikvah (Gates of Hope) Synagogue, every step he took in New York made him all the more homesick for Europe. He struggled with the language, and longed to hear German again – not the barking Nazis of pre-war Bavaria, but the German of Schubert's *Winterreise*. That winter journey begins with a word that is more intriguing and ominous in German than in any other language: *Fremd*. Foreign. Unfamiliar. Strange.

> *Fremd bin ich eingezogen,*
> *Fremd zieh' ich wieder aus.*
> As a stranger I came here,
> As a stranger I move on.

His lucky day arrived in 1956, when he had the chance to become the rabbi of the Jewish community in Basel. It didn't take him long to decide, and his wife and children were just as eager to leave. What mattered to them was the chance to live in a nicer house at last. Their home in Brooklyn was a real hovel.

Bella helped her husband to found the first Jewish primary school in Basel, and put her energy into raising her children. Leo did what was expected of a rabbi, but spent more and more time in his study. In 1976, he received a doctoral degree from the University of Basel for his thesis on the Jewish aspects of the philosophy of Ludwig Wittgenstein.

His sons all had passports from an early age. Leo often said to them, 'You have only twelve hours to leave the Kingdom of Egypt. What toys will you take with you?' On a string in the entrance hall hung two passports, his and Bella's. The stamps and transit visas told the whole story of their exodus: Ansbach, Mir, Keidan, Vilnius, Kaunas, Kobe, Shanghai, Aktyubinsk, Gorki, Karaganda, Kok Uzed, Odessa, Vienna, Brooklyn, New Jersey, and Basel.

Leo Adler died of a heart attack at the age of sixty-three – in 1978, two years after Jan Zwartendijk. He'd never had the time or leisure to get in touch with the consul who had made it possible for him and Bella to escape the Holocaust. Or else he'd chosen not to. He and Bella had struggled to survive for so long that they were in the habit of keeping their minds on the present and future.

Bella survived her husband by only a few years. None of the children stayed in Switzerland; Marek, Samuel, and David all settled in Jerusalem.

I stumbled across Leo and Bella's life story in the papers of Jan Zwartendijk junior after his death. The journalist Barbara Sofer reported on the main events after interviewing the Adler grandchildren. Jan received the report from Jerusalem in April 2003, and wrote to his brother, Rob, 'I wish I could find out the full story of every survivor. It would be one big book of Exodus.'

44

Whoever saves one life
saves a whole world

For the majority of refugees, the road to safety was long. The lucky ones who had the chance to travel from Japan to Australia, New Zealand, Canada, or the United States without delay numbered barely in the double digits. Most of the refugees had to wait in Kobe for months, and many then embarked on a new odyssey. After their long sojourn in Japan, they found themselves stuck in the Dutch East Indies or Shanghai. New hope dawned for them only years later: in the final months of 1945, or, in American-occupied Shanghai, in the autumn of 1946.

From Shanghai, they travelled on to their final destination. For the ardent Zionists, that was Palestine. No sooner had they arrived there in 1947–1948 than they were plunged into a bitter struggle. The Israeli declaration of independence in 1948 was followed by the Pan-Arab invasion; the new state negotiated the first ceasefires with the Arab countries in 1949, and it was not until 1950 that the immigrants could start thinking about leading normal lives with jobs, houses, and families.

In 1948, the first Israeli consul, Moshe Yuval, arrived in Shanghai. He would issue seven thousand visas for Israel in total. Until late 1950, emigrants went by ship to Haifa. But in 1952, 570 of the refugees were still lingering in Shanghai. Wrestling with serious illness or deep despair, they could not yet stomach the idea of making a new life elsewhere. Though they'd adapted well enough to life in Japan and Shanghai, the thought of adjusting to yet another new country, a new climate, a new language, and a new culture was too much for them. This group was evacuated in the spring of 1953, with financial support from the American Joint Distribution Committee. By then, Shanghai had been under the authority of the Communist Party, under its first chairman, Mao Zedong, for almost four years.

Only a few refugees remained in Shanghai, young men who thought, *Well, why not here?* They married Chinese women or descendants of the first, nineteenth-century wave of Jewish immigrants. Max Leibovich was part of this small group. He died in Shanghai on 15 January 1982, at the age of seventy-five. In his last years, he no longer remembered his place of birth. Parkinson's disease had demolished his memory; he thought at first that he came from Russia and later from Lithuania. But his name is not on any list, including Sonja Mühlberger's comprehensive database – still more evidence that many refugees were not registered anywhere.

To all appearances, the Polish Jews admitted to the United States, Australia, and New Zealand made an easy adjustment, but their individual stories show that it took a long time for most to make a place for themselves in their new homeland. It took years to integrate into society, and even longer to find suitable work.

After a long series of odd jobs, Avram and Masha Zeleznikow opened the Cafe Scheherazade in a suburb of Melbourne in 1958. Although the writer Arnold Zable made them characters in a novel, he told the story of their flight a good deal more accurately than historians have, and his author's note makes it clear that Avram, Masha, and Cafe Scheherazade are all called by their true names. Avram and Masha came from the socialist vanguard among Eastern European Jews; their parents had been devoted members of the Bund, and they could tell countless tales at the bar about the organisation. None of those stories were exaggerated, and in the 1950s and 1960s, there were quite a few Avrams and Mashas in Melbourne, Sydney, and Wellington. And they all had a hard time adjusting to the rhythms of a normal life.

Benjamin Fishoff – the young man who had arrived in Tsuruga at the age of eighteen without a Curaçao visa, been sent back to Vladivostok, and readmitted to Japan only after consul De Voogd issued him a visa – had to remain in Shanghai until 1947. By November, he had valid papers and secured passage on a ship to New York. The first thing he heard when he arrived was that his parents had died in a concentration camp and that none of his relatives who had remained in Europe had survived the war. After eight years of wandering the world, he knew for certain that he was truly alone.

He needed to learn the language first, and then to pick a line of work in which he could succeed. Fishoff started out as an errand boy for the Metropolitan National Bank, and considered it a big step up when he was promoted to teller. He married and started a family. At that stage, his main concern was to find a good home and earn enough money to pay for his children's education. He became the branch director of the Metropolitan National Bank at 99 Park Avenue. His entire working life was spent in an office just a stone's throw from Grand Central Station. Every day, he was aware that he had escaped through the needle's eye. Not a day passed that he didn't think back, amid commonplace worries, to that frigid February morning at Moscow's Yaroslavsky Station when he had boarded the Trans-Siberian Express.

But contacting the consuls who had saved his life? No, he never found the time. One day, Fishoff received an invitation from the Zwartendijk children to a fundraising dinner in New York. He wondered where they could have found his name. Fishoff later learned he was on a list made by consul De Voogd at the Dutch embassy in Japan, which had eventually made its way to the United States National Archives and Records Administration. By 2004 or 2005, Benjamin Fishoff could no longer remember exactly when that dinner had taken place. In any case, he had told Edith, Jan, and Rob Zwartendijk that he was blessed with five children, twenty-eight grandchildren, and fifteen great-grandchildren, and that by his reckoning the two thousand men with Curaçao visas had brought hundreds of thousands of lives into the world. Yet it wasn't the figures that mattered most to him, but the Laws of Noah:

> To save one life is to save humanity, as is written in the Talmud. Or, more exactly, he who saves one soul, it is as though he saved the world.

Some became disappointed in their new homelands, and moved on again. Zorach Warhaftig arrived in Canada in 1941, and left Vancouver with his wife and daughter in 1947. He did not arrive at his final destination until he set foot on the soil of Palestine. The Shoah had turned him into a radical Zionist. Having escaped the murder machine, he blamed every goy in Canada, the United States, and Europe for what had happened in the war. He could no longer put down roots anywhere – save Israel.

In June 1948, he flew over Jerusalem in the open cockpit of a two-seater aircraft. He felt like a modern Isaiah entering the Promised Land. After landing, he rushed to David Ben-Gurion's office to sign the Israeli declaration of independence. He had contributed to the drafting of that historic document, but missed the announcement because of the fighting in and around Jerusalem. Three more weeks passed before he could arrange a flight on a small airplane to Tel Aviv.

45

The Holland 977 Case

Jan junior's search for the refugees became an obsession. It was as if he wanted to track down every man who had queued in front of his father's office on Laisvės Alėja. He wrote letter after letter, and often instructed his brother or sister to look into one thing or another. He criss-crossed the United States in search of witnesses. And he began an archive, in which he planned to organise all his findings, but which for years consisted of boxes filled with notes, letters, and photocopies.

Direct family members – parents, brothers, sisters, and children – cannot submit nominations for the title of Righteous Among the Nations. Jan urged survivors to put their stories in writing and send them to Yad Vashem, the Holocaust Martyrs' and Heroes' Remembrance Authority in Jerusalem. He had gradually come to see it as his sacred mission to win the recognition internationally that his father had never received in the Netherlands.

In 1994, Zwartendijk's nomination for the title of Righteous Among the Nations was rejected. Jan was thunderstruck. How was that possible? Was it a conspiracy to smother his father's deeds in silence?

Jan turned to Ernest Heppner in Indianapolis for help. Heppner had been born in Breslau, one of three children of a master matzo baker. After the destruction of the city's synagogue in 1938, his parents decided it was time to flee. But they could only get their hands on two exit visas. They decided to send seventeen-year-old Ernest and his mother out ahead on the *Potsdam* from Genoa to Shanghai. His father, sister, and eldest brother intended to follow as soon as they could. But they couldn't. His brother escaped to England, but his father and sister were murdered in Auschwitz. In Shanghai, Ernest married Illo Koratkowski. She and her father came from Berlin, and had taken the Trans-Siberian Express using visas issued in Kaunas. Ernest and Illo remained in Shanghai until 1947. The first time Jan Zwartendijk junior met the couple, they had a wealth of stories to tell. By then, Ernest was hard at work on his history of the Jewish refugees in Shanghai, published in 1994 under the title of *Shanghai Refuge*.

Jan also called on the assistance of the historian Jonathan Goldstein at Harvard University, who was just as much of an expert as Heppner on the history of the Jews in the Far East.

The two scholars protested Yad Vashem's decision. Goldstein applied for the 'Holland 977 Case' to be reconsidered, submitting proof that Zwartendijk 'had put the lives, liberty, and security of himself and his immediate family on the line', and therefore deserved recognition by Yad Vashem. This was a response to the remembrance authority's initial conclusion that, since consul Zwartendijk had carried out his rescue operation before Lithuania and the Netherlands were occupied by the Nazis, he had not run exceptional risks.

Hogwash, thought Jan. And he was right. His father had begun issuing visas two months after 10 May 1940, by which stage the Netherlands was already under the regime of Reichskommissar Seyss-Inquart. After his return to the Netherlands, the consul had good reason to fear for his life and the lives of his family. Furthermore, Lithuania had been occupied by the Soviet Union in June 1940, so the brand-new consul had been taking a double risk. But what frustrated Jan most was that the title of Righteous Among the Nations had been awarded to Sugihara as far back as 1985, for risking his life to save Jews in the Second World War.

'Why him and not our Pa?' Jan wrote to Edith and Rob.

His indignation only grew when, defying the thrombosis in his leg and his poor health, he travelled to Japan and saw the Chiune Sugihara Memorial Hall in Yaotsu: a museum set in a stunning garden high in the hills just a few kilometres from Sugihara's birthplace. In a traditional Japanese building made in large part from cypress wood, which is known for its unbending nature, the diplomat's life and courage are presented as a model for future generations. While the museum does place Sugihara's story in the much larger context of racism and the Holocaust, it is dedicated to one man, and he is represented in every room.

In the Sugihara House in Kaunas, which Jan visited a few months later, Jan became so irritated by the idolisation of the Japanese consul that his own return to the city of his childhood gave him no pleasure at all. The museum in Kaunas is housed in the former Japanese consulate. Everything there is at is was in 1940, or has been recreated with great care. The large, sturdy desk is the same one at which Sugihara sat when he wrote his transit visas; the Underwood is the same typewriter on which his Lithuanian secretary typed the names. The museum tells the whole story of the rescue operation, but again with one central character: the Japanese consul with the winning smile. For Jan, this was the last straw. When the two Japanese museums contacted him to request a portrait of his father (since they hadn't had one on display), he sent a picture of his Uncle Piet. The man in the dress suit now proudly displayed on the walls of both the Sugihara House in Kaunas and the Sugihara Memorial Hall in Yaotsu is not Jan Zwartendijk, but his twin brother.

Jonathan Goldstein contested Yad Vashem's decision, placing great emphasis on the document drawn up by Nathan Gutwirth that proves Zwartendijk put his personal safety on the line. His ingenious plan had pointed the way to freedom for Jewish refugees who had walked into a trap. Without Zwartendijk's deliberate and courageous omission of the reference to the need for permission from the governor of Curaçao, there would have been no point in Sugihara issuing transit visas. So Goldstein requested that the Holland 977 Case be reopened.

Ernest Heppner made the same request on 17 January 1996. A fierce controversy ensued: Heppner was said to have falsely accused Sugihara's widow of lying and to have tried to discredit Sugihara with the claim that the Japanese consul had spied for the Polish secret service. It cannot be denied that Jan junior had contributed those points without looking into the details, let alone understanding them. Jan was becoming overwrought and was trying to cast Sugihara's widow as the evil mastermind. Heppner had to rectify this mistake, and he found the right words:

As a Holocaust survivor I have a deep respect for every person who saved even one life, Jewish or otherwise, under any circumstances whatsoever. No attempt of any kind has been made to discredit the actions of Chiune Sugihara, but merely to emphasise that Jan Zwartendijk, no less than Sugihara, deserves a place of honour and will receive the posthumous recognition he truly deserves.

It is clear from the whole correspondence that Yad Vashem had seen Zwartendijk as a candidate as early as 1968 – but rejected him in 1969, after Zorach Warhaftig testified that the Dutch consul had 'not risked his life through his actions'.

That may have been true in Lithuania, Heppner argued in his written application, 'but it is unlikely Warhaftig knew that Zwartendijk would have to return to the Nazi-occupied Netherlands'. That is correct: Warhaftig didn't know that, nor did he realise that Zwartendijk was still alive.

Warhaftig clearly showed more respect for Sugihara than for Zwartendijk. Heppner explained: 'That is because Warhaftig met the Japanese consul in 1940 and personally urged him to issue transit visas to people with Curaçao visas.' Whatever recognition was granted to Sugihara reflected on him. Warhaftig later claimed in his biography that *he* had come up with a clever plan for getting Jews out of Lithuania, that *he* had first presented the Curaçao idea, and that *he* had gone to the Japanese consul for assistance.

So Zwartendijk's candidacy had been rejected twice, in 1969 and in 1994. The correspondence grew more vehement by the month, with numerous accusations made by both sides. Almost everyone seemed to have forgotten what the whole discussion was about: a rescue operation that had saved thousands of lives.

Zwartendijk could have met the same fate as the Swedish diplomat Raoul Wallenberg in Hungary. True, Stalin had consented to the evacuation of the Polish Jews via Moscow and Vladivostok (a fact unknown to Zwartendijk and Sugihara). But whenever he liked, he could change his mind from one moment to the next. Wallenberg was arrested by the Russians in January 1945, and even today it remains unknown in what Siberian camp or Moscow prison he died or was eliminated, and in what year (though the general assumption is now 1947). In September 1944, Sugihara was interned in a Russian prisoner-of-war camp with his wife and three children. Every day of the eighteen months they spent behind barbed wire, they thought they wouldn't make it out alive. Is that what you'd call not taking risks? According to decrees issued in Kraków, the Nazis were already aware by October 1940 of the 'escape' of large numbers of Jews from Eastern Europe. Both Sugihara in Königsberg and Prague, and Zwartendijk in Eindhoven knew throughout the war that the Gestapo might make them pay for their choices.

Nathan Gutwirth, fed up, made a written appeal to everyone involved in the case to separate the wheat from the chaff. The chaff was the cowards, and the wheat was the people who, in 1940, had the courage to lend a helping hand.

Help came from an unexpected quarter. Rabbi Ronald Gray ('call me Ronnie') from the Jewish Orthodox boarding school Boys Town in Jerusalem, founded in 1949, threw his weight behind the recognition of Zwartendijk by Yad Vashem. In 1997, he invited Jan junior, Anne, Edith, Henk, Rob, and Rob's eldest son, Bas, to Jerusalem for a memorial service on the school's sprawling campus. He put them up in the King David Hotel, and took them along to see the Yad Vashem directors. Jan and Rob were uncomfortable with this plan at first, but

Ronnie Gray felt it was high time for a face-to-face meeting. Rob still vividly remembers the encounter:

> He'd been locking horns with those people for months. He swore a blue streak at them, in our presence, because they still hadn't made a decision. Even though they were speaking Hebrew, the raised voices and accompanying gestures were very clear, almost to the point of becoming embarrassing. But it worked.

On 29 October 1997, the directors sent the letter awarding the title. 'We are really pleased that we were able to bring this case to a favorable conclusion,' Dr Mordecai Paldiel wrote to the Zwartendijk children. But he was the only one truly satisfied with how it had gone.

Not one Dutch minister or state secretary was present at the presentation of the Yad Vashem medal and certificate at the historic Beurs van Berlage building in the heart of Amsterdam. Even the secretary general of the foreign ministry was otherwise engaged.

In retrospect, Jan Zwartendijk had received the greatest recognition – at least, of the official kind that you might ordinarily imagine when you think of honour and recognition – a year earlier. It took the form of a letter from the White House in Washington, written and signed by the president of the United States. In connection with a charity dinner organised by Ronnie Gray, Bill Clinton wrote:

> At a time in human history when too many people turned their heads and looked away, Jan Zwartendijk showed the world the power of compassion in the face of injustice. The courage he demonstrated as Dutch consul in Kovno, Lithuania, during World War II serves as an example of moral integrity and selflessness that continues to inspire all of us today. He filled desperate lives with hope during a period of great darkness, and his actions will remain a beacon of decency and righteousness for generations to come. I join you in paying tribute to the memory of this great man.

From right to left, Edith Jes-Zwartendijk, Dr Mordecai Paldiel, director of the
Department of the Righteous Among the Nations, and Martijn Jes, Edith's
youngest son, at the Wall of Honour in the Garden of the Righteous Among
the Nations, Jerusalem, 1998.

I found this letter in a book that Jan Zwartendijk sent to Rob, well
preserved in a plastic sleeve, with a simple letterhead in blue ink: The
White House.

Seeing Zwartendijk's name on the Wall of Honor in the Garden of
the Righteous gave his children a sense of vindication. In 1998, all
three of them travelled to Jerusalem (a hard, painful journey for Jan
because of his thrombosis). All three were impressed by the ceremony
there, although they would never forget that the recognition had come
twenty-one years too late for their father, and seventeen years too late
for their mother.

In Lithuania, too, the acknowledgement of Zwartendijk's deeds was
a difficult process.

In 2003, there were plans to place a plaque on the façade of Laisvės Alėja 29. By then, the former Philips showroom had become a bookshop carrying Lithuanian and English-language literature. The plaque was inscribed, 'This is where the Dutch consul Jan Zwartendijk issued more than two thousand visas to Jewish refugees in the summer of 1940.'

One surprising fact was that the interior of the bookshop was still very much like the Philips sales room, with the same panelled walls and the same grand stairway to the upper floor where Jan Zwartendijk had issued the visas.

On the morning of the unveiling, the owner of the building announced that he didn't want a 'plaque for Jews' on his building front, throwing the plans for the ceremony into confusion. His excuse was that it would be 'architecturally unjustifiable' to mount a bronze plaque on the granite-coloured stone.

At the last minute, the Dutch ambassador and the deputy mayor of Kaunas decided to place the plaque on the building that had housed the Dutch consulate in the 1930s. This was a strange choice of location, because it had been the bank that housed the office of Dr Tillmanns, the consul who'd had to be dismissed because of his German nationality and Nazi sympathies.

In 2015, it took me a lot of searching to find the commemorative plaque in Kaunas, and without Rob and Edith's help I could never have done it. It was hidden behind a shutter. But, in any case, it was much too modest a tribute.

The Dutch ambassador to Lithuania, Bert van der Lingen, felt the same way. In 2016 and 2017, he made a fresh attempt to have a monument erected in front of Laisvės Alėja 29 with an inscription commemorating consul Zwartendijk. The bookshop still had the same owner: Arunas Povilas Paliulis, the son of an emigrant, born and raised in New York, who had moved to Lithuania in 1991. A fierce nationalist, he spoke out against globalisation in every interview, and never failed to stress that the Lithuanian language is the oldest in Europe and should be sheltered from all foreign influences.

Paliulis didn't want a monument. In a letter to the Dutch ambassador, he pointed out that 'one of your predecessors previously conspired with a local architect and the Kaunas municipality to place a bronze plaque on our façade some years back without our knowledge and consent'. He'd been staunchly opposed then, and that hadn't changed. 'Place your statue near the Jewish synagogue or the Sugihara Museum,' he wrote.

Van der Lingen refused to give up, instead finding an argument in Paliulis's hostile words to persuade the Kaunas authorities and the Lithuanian government that the monument should refer not only to the past but also to the present, and include a warning for the future.

The monument was erected: a magnificent and, above all, sensitive memorial, designed by the Amsterdam artist Giny Vos. Her light sculpture is a spiral of synthetic material that swirls around four trees in front of the former consulate on Laisvės Alėja. Thin lines of light reveal that the spiral is made up of 2,139 passports in a row. As darkness falls, the lights of the ring stand out in the gentle colours of hope: pink, sky blue, and spring green.

On 15 June 2018, seventy-eight years to the day after Zwartendijk's appointment as consul, the memorial was unveiled by his children, Edith and Rob. Guests at the ceremony included President Dalia Grybauskaitė of the Lithuanian Republic and King Willem-Alexander of the Netherlands, who was on a state visit to the three Baltic countries.

A couple of steps back, leaning on his cane, the ninety-one-year-old Marcel Wejland looked on. He had insisted on attending, even though he was sorry to miss the presentation at the same time in Melbourne of an anthology of Polish poetry that he had edited and translated. Without consul Zwartendijk, he would never have reached Australia and would never have been able to translate a Polish poem into English. Instead, his final destination would probably have been Auschwitz-Birkenau, where, at the age of fifteen or sixteen, he would have been sent to the gas chambers.

The monument to Jan Zwartendijk in Kaunas.

46

A wedding in Antwerp

Nathan Gutwirth didn't let anything keep him down, but he was held up in Batavia until late 1946 by a multitude of readers. After he was liberated from the Japanese internment camp, he came up with a plan to start libraries in each district of the city. Most Dutch nationals wanted to leave the Indies as soon as possible, but they had to wait ten, twelve, fourteen, or even sixteen months before they could board a ship that would take them home. What better way to kill time than by reading?

But establishing libraries was more than a question of providing entertainment. In the camps, the children suffered from a terrible lack of education, and it would take at least another year before the schools were reopened. In the public reading rooms that Nathan envisaged, they could start hitting the books right away. He began to carry out the plan on his own, renting a room here and a former barracks there, asking people to donate their books before leaving, and buying second-hand books for next to nothing at little Chinese bookshops. The reading rooms were soon mobbed.

The social affairs ministry hired Nathan, paid him the astronomical salary of a thousand guilders a month, and asked him to set up a similar project in Bandung. Scrambling to find enough books, Nathan appealed to American and Dutch readers, who sent them by the shipload. He was starting to enjoy the challenge, offering people a simple, pleasant way to pass the time, and encouraging children to read. During their three-and-a-half years behind barbed wire, some little boys and girls had forgotten that books even existed.

Then Nathan had another idea. In the camps, the children had hardly had anything to call their own. To celebrate the first post-war St Nicholas' Eve – the traditional Dutch gift-giving holiday in early December – Nathan decided to find enough little presents for all of them. He even managed to get the military authorities excited about the plan. Since there were no toys left on Java, he flew to Singapore with three officers and two Red Cross nurses. There, the six of them scoured the toyshops for days, loading up on all the dolls and Dinky Toys they could find. Back in Batavia, Nathan organised St Nicholas' Eve celebrations in his temporary libraries.

In his memoirs, he dismissed any suggestion that his motives were selfless. He had always been timid and shy, lacking in self-confidence. The post-war years in Batavia changed his life. He had people working for him, and they accepted his authority. He thought up plans, and other people were happy to carry them out. He was the linchpin of the organisation, and he loved it. Lithuania, the long escape route, the Japanese internment camp, the hunger, the dysentery – he could put it all behind him. He blossomed, because he still believed in goodness.

Nechama gave birth to Faigy, and once she had recovered, she said she wanted to go to New York by way of Holland. Nechama had thirteen brothers and sisters, who had all stayed in Lithuania, except for one sister who was living in New York.

'I'll drop in on the consul one of these days,' Nathan said.

And, sure enough, the United States consul in Batavia issued a visa for the whole family – after Nathan had explained to him that not one of Nechama's twelve brothers and sisters who had remained in Lithuania had survived the war.

Before they emigrated to America, Nathan wanted to visit his family. After thirty days at sea, they arrived in Amsterdam and took

Nathan and Nechama Gutwirth before their departure for Batavia.

the train to Antwerp. Nathan's father was at a loss:

> He was still hoping to hear something from my mother and four sisters.
> Europe was in chaos. People were living in a trauma, still hoping that
> in this Tohu Va'Vohu some relatives would turn up, from Poland or
> Russia or from the German ... camps. For most it was a vain dream, but
> some did turn up, giving false hope to others.

Tohu Va'Vohu comes from Genesis 1, and is Hebrew for 'waste and
empty'. Or, in the words of the King James Version, 'And the earth
was without form, and void.'

Nathan and his wife and child spent three months in Antwerp.
Then he started to feel hemmed in there, so the three of them set out
for New York. Seven days of uninterrupted storms at sea struck him

as a bad omen. Nechama's sister, Sima, and her husband, Abie, stood waiting for them at the dock. They gave the new immigrants a warm welcome, sharing their home in Brooklyn with them for a year.

Nathan was soon offered a job by a distant relative importing and exporting goods to Singapore. He and his wife found a place of their own, where their second child, Shoshana, was born. But she died at the age of just sixteen months. Their third daughter, Chana, arrived with a smile on her face to console them. A year and a half later, Pinchas was born, and Nathan was happy to have a son under his roof. He had a pet name for the boy: Pinny.

But his heart remained in Europe, with his father, his sisters, and his brother.

Every summer, he took Nechama and the children across the ocean. He had to empty his savings account to do it, because he refused to board just any old rust bucket. Instead, he travelled in style on the *Queen Elizabeth*, the *Queen Mary*, the *Nieuw Amsterdam*, or the *Statendam*, and told Nechama to bring her entire wardrobe. They'd pinched their pennies long enough.

His second home in Europe was always Scheveningen, the traditional holiday resort for Jews from Antwerp. There he was surrounded by old friends and family: his father, sisters, brother, uncle and aunts, cousins, nephews, and nieces. On his last summer visits to Scheveningen, he spent a full two months there. But it wasn't enough to ease the gnawing sensation that some call homesickness. To him, it was a longing – for a city, a time, an atmosphere he'd once known.

After ten years in New York, Nathan went back to Antwerp with his family. He returned to his former occupation as a diamond worker, settled into a house at Charlottalei 60, and moved to the much broader Belgiëlei in 1960. All the families in his new building, number 44, were Orthodox Jewish, and all the children attended the Jesode-Hatora Beth-Jacob, the oldest Jewish school in Belgium. Nathan was finally home again.

At this stage, he could have got in touch with Zwartendijk. But he

Nathan Gutwirth in his later years.

had other things on his mind. His father had died, and Nathan was the new head of the family. In the diamond business, a new market had opened up. And when you have a chance like that, you have to act fast. Diamonds were in demand in Bombay. So every other month, Nathan and his brother went to India.

The 1960s passed in a blur; the 1970s began. Then the worst event of Nathan's life happened. Nechama became gravely ill. He took her to the world's best specialists for treatment – in Brussels, in Paris, and at a clinic in New York. But nothing helped; she slipped out of his life. He was shattered, more shattered than he'd ever felt during the war years, and it took him a long time to pick up the pieces. In 1978, he heard that consul De Voogd had died. He placed a death notice in the *Nieuw Israëlietisch Weekblad*, the main Dutch-language Jewish weekly, signed 'the Gutwirth family'. Then he said to himself, *I wonder how old Mr Radio Philips is getting on?*

Too late. Zwartendijk was dead. What could Nathan do to make up for his thoughtlessness? For years, he couldn't find a solution. Of course, he wrote to Zwartendijk's children and learned about their father's life, but that wasn't enough.

Why hadn't he invited the Zwartendijks to Faigy's wedding, or Chana's, or Pinchas's? So many missed opportunities, he said to his son. Pinny told his father the time would soon come when he could make things right.

The wedding of Pinchas's eldest daughter came too late for Nathan, who had passed away not long before. But Pinny seized the opportunity to make up for his father's omissions, inviting the Zwartendijk children to the wedding in Antwerp.

Jan sent his apologies; he could no longer manage long flights. Rob and Marijke could attend only the start of the ceremony. But Edith was present for the whole event. She had never been to a Jewish wedding before, and her account of the day shows that nothing escaped her attention:

> Some parts were hushed and solemn and others happy and festive. Like a spellbinding performance – almost too much to take in. When the dancing started, everyone's heart swelled with joy. The bride stood in the middle of the room, surrounded by women; her husband-to-be stood in another room, surrounded by men. One at a time, the people around them left the circle and asked them to dance. The music grew ever louder, the dancing more riotous, until everyone was panting and blissfully happy and looking for a place to catch their breath.

Edith sat next to a distinguished lady who turned out to be the matchmaker responsible for the couple:

> The parents engage a matchmaker like her because they believe a young man and woman in love lack the insight into human nature to make a good choice. The role of the intermediary is to check the background of the potential spouse, and to find out whether there are

any hereditary illnesses in the family. In Orthodox circles they always marry very young, so that makes some sense.

They were having a friendly conversation – chit-chatting, Edith says – when a sudden silence fell. A woman tapped the two women on the shoulder and pointed at the stage, where an old rabbi with a long beard stood. As he spoke to the guests, he fixed Edith with a piercing gaze.

'It is a miracle,' said Rabbi Moron Hora Kreiswirth, 'that your father was living in Lithuania in 1940 and, in his role as consul, was able to help so many yeshiva students and Jewish refugees from Poland. This wedding celebration is only possible thanks to your father. Nathan, the bride's grandfather, was one of the first to receive a lifesaving visa from his hands. Nechama, her grandmother, was able to follow her husband thanks to such a visa.'

The rabbi then turned to the bride's parents. 'Your daughter would not have put on her beautiful wedding dress early this morning, and she would not have taken her place under the chuppah today, if there had not been a man with the courage to place a note in her grandfather's passport – for the simple reason that she would never have been born. Let us honour this man. And let us promise his daughter, here among us today, that we will never forget him.'

He made a bow and left the stage.

Edith was surrounded in no time by people who wanted to shake her hand or voice their admiration for her father.

Before they all went down to dinner, she met Nathan's sisters, who had spent the war in hiding near Antwerp. They told her, 'We couldn't leave, we couldn't go anywhere.' And Edith repeated those words to herself: *We couldn't leave, we couldn't go anywhere.*

During the wedding feast, seven blessings were recited. It was a copious and exquisite meal; the drinks were sweet and non-alcoholic, the speeches filled with humour but a little long for the non-Yiddish-speaking guests. Afterwards, the music summoned them to dance again. The clarinet laughed and cried, both at once, and the special dance around the bride and bridegroom started all over, the couple once again separated by a matte glass sliding door between the men's and women's rooms. All the guests knew the steps. They involved a funny little skip, a kind of hesitation, which confirmed Edith's sense of a constant back and forth between exuberance and introspection.

At the climax of the ceremony, the bridegroom broke a glass wrapped in a cloth by crushing it under his foot. This ritual is a reminder that joy can never be complete because of the destruction of the Temple and the Fall of Jerusalem. The guests cried out, 'Mazel tov!' ('Good fortune!')

The bride and groom withdrew into a separate room, where they were together for the first time. When they returned, the men danced around the groom, and the women danced around the bride once more. During the last dance, the bride and groom were lifted on chairs like a king and queen. Only after that were they finally allowed to present themselves to the guests together. The celebration went on until deep in the night.

When most of the guests had left, the immediate family gathered in a separate room. Edith was asked to join them so that she could witness the moment when the bride and groom embraced and danced the first dance of their married life:

> Crying happy tears and laden with gifts and good wishes, the couple said farewell to their family and to me, as if I were an inseparable part of the family.

Day was already dawning when one of Nathan's sisters gave Edith a gentle pinch on the arm. She had something to tell her.

Nathan had called Edith's father in 1971. Edith leaned in and asked if she had heard the year right. Yes, 1971.

Nathan opened with, 'Mr Zwartendijk, this is Nathan Gutwirth.'

'From Lithuania?'

'That's right, Mr Zwartendijk, *your* Nathan Gutwirth. The one who used to pick up your *NRC* to read the football pages.'

Edith shook her head in surprise. Her father had never mentioned this.

'You're the fourth to contact me,' her father had said on the phone.

'Only the fourth?'

'Yes, and that can't mean anything good about what happened to the others.'

Then Nathan Gutwirth understood why Mr Zwartendijk didn't sound happy. He had hoped for his phone to ring more than a thousand times.

Nathan decided to write down the whole story of his escape. But then Nechama fell ill. For years, he had no time for anything else.

Then finally, he managed to put a few things down on paper – the first step in the procedure that would eventually lead to recognition by Yad Vashem.

47

Pebbles on a grave

What is denied to the living is granted to the dead. One spring day, I visit the Rotterdam-Hillegersberg cemetery. Under the first warm sunshine of the year, the Japanese cherry tree is in blossom, an exquisite sight against the gnarled oaks and ashes. It reminds me of the white tree in front of the Dutch consul's former home in Kaunas, where three years ago I began my detective work.

Nothing stays the same, not even the memory of the dead. We find wisdom only when we search, but we often don't take the trouble. 'I know so much more now about the old days,' Edith said to me, just over a year after our first trip to Kaunas. 'Even about the things I saw with my own eyes, smelled with my own nose. I didn't know the background, and then you can't feel the impact of the events.'

Jan Zwartendijk lies buried in a spot that surprises me. The graveyard is on a small strip of land between the two lakes known as the Bergse Plassen, on which Jan and Piet Zwartendijk rowed with their father in their clinker-built canoe. To the east was the Rotte River, the final destination of their Sunday outings. After a little more strenuous paddling, the boys would dive into the peat-brown water. It's as if I can hear the distant splash.

To the Zwartendijks, Hillegersberg was an integral part of Rotterdam. But when I look around, I see a village. A peaceful village that the big city has forgotten. The Protestant cemetery is behind the

Hillegondakerk, which – just like all the other Protestant churches in the area – was built on a sandbar in the river-streaked landscape, a first step in the quintessential Dutch practice of land reclamation. It was not until the early twentieth century that this community was absorbed into Rotterdam. The place is permeated with the smell of brackish water.

As I walk to his grave, I realise that Jan Zwartendijk strove all his life to be part of a tradition. He wanted to be buried in the family grave, above his father, Jan, and his mother, Johanna, and next to his sister, Didi. And he wanted to make sure that when he was laid to rest there he would have a clear conscience. A Zwartendijk was supposed to see to it that he would never have any reason to be ashamed of the family name.

His sister-in-law, Mary, and twin brother, Piet, were later placed in the same family grave. They, too, were loyal to the family tradition all their lives. Piet outlived his twin brother by ten years, which was a great comfort to Edith, Jan, and Rob. Whenever they saw Uncle Piet, it was as though their father was alive again. He had not only the same facial features, but also the same voice.

Piet lived to the age of ninety, and mourned his brother every day. There were so many things he'd have liked to ask him – about Kaunas, say, or Aletrino. One day, he admitted to Rob that he had underestimated his brother. Rob said, 'It was mutual, Uncle Piet.'

It is a very simple grave; a traditional flat, grey stone bearing only the family name. No personal names, no years of birth or death. Just 'Zwartendijk'. Like a brand. And, of course, it was a brand of pipe tobacco and tea.

On the dark-grey stone I see light-grey pebbles, not in the centre but against the lower edge, and I feel a lump in my throat. It's an old Jewish custom. Each pebble stands for a memory of the departed. Family and friends leave them as signs that they visited the grave, that they remember and honour the deceased.

One of many explanations for this ancient tradition is based on very early Jewish history, when the Jews were a desert people. To

The family grave.

protect a grave in the sea of sand from carrion-eating vultures, jackals, and hyenas, they laid as many stones on it as possible. Passing nomads would add to the pile in respect for the dead.

Stones can endure wind and weather, as unchanging as love, as eternal as faith. Flowers wilt, while pebbles remain.

Behind each pebble is a story. All those stories together form the vast edifice of history. Jewish graves are held in perpetuity. So is the Zwartendijk family grave.

The pebbles stand for permanence, everlasting respect, and our bond to the dead.

Zwartendijk would have appreciated this tribute. It's plain and simple, but impressive, because the people who left the pebbles had travelled so far.

He had given the refugees the chance to escape life-threatening danger. They had seized the opportunity. What awaited them was uncertain; their journey was a leap in the dark. But they had the courage to go.

I pick up a pebble from the grave. I don't know why. Maybe because I've investigated so much evil in my books that I've come to see good as a rare phenomenon. The pebble in my hand, with its sharp edge, gives me the courage to believe there will always be hope. Act when action is called for, Jan Zwartendijk reminded his loved ones. Don't shut your door, don't turn away. I put the pebble back on his grave.

Sources and Acknowledgements

In the late spring of 1983, I took the Trans-Mongolian Express from Beijing to Moscow. From Lake Baikal westwards, it follows the same route as the Trans-Siberian Express. I spent the seven-day, seven-night journey in a soft sleeper, the communist equivalent of a first-class compartment. I shared the washing facilities with the passengers next door, an Australian woman in her forties and her two sons, seven and eleven years old.

Mary was under severe strain. I ran into her in the corridor one night and looked into eyes that must have seen many dangers, maybe even horrors. I overheard her confused words to Josh and Job, as if she were trying to share some story too bitter to fathom and too wide-ranging to grasp. She seemed to be on an impossible mission.

As we approached Moscow, I realised that she was following the same route, in the opposite direction, that she had taken with her parents in 1941 to escape the Shoah. She wanted to show her sons where she had come from, how Poland looked, how far it was from Australia, and what route she and her parents had taken to escape. Her husband, who wasn't Jewish, had decided not to join them.

It was from Mary, whose full name was Miryam, that I first heard about the escape route from Kaunas to Moscow, the 9,287-kilometre railway journey to Vladivostok, the boat trip to Tsuruga, the stay in

Kobe, and the crossing to Shanghai. For Miryam and her parents, the final step led from Shanghai to Australia.

In 2007, I went to Lithuania in search of stories for my book *Baltische zielen* (*Baltic Souls*, Amsterdam, 2010). There I learned a great deal more about the thousands of Jews who had escaped, on the Trans-Siberian Express, from certain death in a concentration camp. What was news to me was the decisive role played in the rescue operation by the Dutch consul, Jan Zwartendijk. The professor of Yiddish at Vilnius University, Dovid Katz, took me to the Jewish Museum and showed me photographs of the consul and his family. I considered including the consul's life story in the book I was then writing, but Zwartendijk had grown up in Rotterdam and spent only three years in Lithuania – there was no way I could turn him into a Baltic soul.

I first met ambassador Bert van der Lingen in December 2013. He had bought the original of the cover illustration for *Baltische zielen*. Ever since then, that photograph by Antanas Sutkus has hung in the entrance hall of the Dutch ambassador's residence in Vilnius. Ambassador Van der Lingen invited me to come and stay with him, organised a concert-lecture about *Baltische zielen* in the former house of the composer K.M. čiurlionis in Vilnius, and asked me if I wouldn't like to write a book about consul Zwartendijk, a man he described as 'a true inspiration to me and countless other diplomats'. I realised he wasn't exaggerating when he put me in touch with the Dutch consul general in Shanghai, Anneke Adema; her assistant, Timo de Groot; the Dutch ambassador to Japan, Aart Jacobi; the cultural attaché in Tokyo, Ton van Zeeland; the consul general in Osaka and Kobe, Roderick Wols; his successor, Gerard Michels; the Dutch ambassador to the Russian Federation, Renée Jones-Bos; and the Dutch ambassador to Latvia, Pieter Langenberg. Zwartendijk was a shining example to all of them, and I could count on their help when gathering information.

Ambassador Van der Lingen told me that Zwartendijk's youngest son was still alive and that the two of them were on good terms. Back in the Netherlands, I made an appointment with Rob Zwartendijk in Blaricum. When I entered the house on the sandy, tree-shaded path,

I was struck by the tall form of an elderly woman standing by the window. 'I've asked my sister to join us. She's come up from France.' At the age of eighty-nine, she had hitched a ride with a lorry driver from Dordogne, just as I used to do in my hippie years.

In the summer of 1940, Edith was thirteen years old. I spent the whole day talking to her and Rob – 'Robbie' to Edith. A couple of weeks later, I looked through all the photographs from Lithuania with Rob; another time, I gathered together all the letters and documents that Rob had found among the belongings of his late father and his brother, Jan. In December, I visited Edith Jes-Zwartendijk in her home in the Dordogne, a remote farm where she has lived alone since the death of her husband, Henk. I had an overwhelming list of questions for her in preparation for my planned trip to Lithuania with Edith and Rob. In April 2016, we spent seven days visiting all the places in Kaunas and its surroundings that are mentioned in this book.

Ten months later, I travelled to Shanghai to see where the hundreds of refugees with visas issued by Zwartendijk had ended up. On the wall of the Jewish Museum, I hoped to find Miryam's maiden name. I had a vague feeling it was Wiener, but couldn't find it anywhere in my notes. I did find an Ascher Wiener on the wall, and later learned more about him, thanks to his daughter Deborah Wiener in Melbourne. But no Miryam Wiener.

I'm sure I'll find out more about her someday. Her visa had saved her from the Holocaust, but she had never shaken off her bewilderment at being such a rare exception. In her own way – diffident, but no less impressive for that – she wanted to share something of that perplexity with her sons.

Arlette Schellenbach-Pollet lived in Kaunas from July 1925 to July 1944, and, like Edith and Jan Zwartendijk, attended the German primary and secondary schools there. Arlette's parents – her Dutch mother and her Belgian father, who was building an electrical plant near Kaunas – were friends of Kees and Lenie Stoffel's. Arlette was never in contact with the Zwartendijk children, although she does have vague memories of consul Zwartendijk. But the information she gave me about Kaunas was crucial to my research. In September 1940, the Zwartendijks left Lithuania. Arlette stayed until the Red Army had reached the Lithuanian border once again. I spent a full day talking to Arlette Schellenbach in her home on Rooseveltlaan in Amsterdam.

The Stoffel family has a richly informative digital family archive. Engbert Stoffel showed me how to use it, and supplied important information about Kees Stoffel and Lenie Stoffel-Barnehl, who lived in Lithuania until the end of the Second World War. He even gave me a few photos of Kees and Lenie in their Lithuanian days, so that I would have an image of the couple and their children. Kees and Lenie were Jan and Erni Zwartendijk's best friends in Kaunas.

Ingrida Gustienė, the owner of the Perkūno Namai Hotel in Kaunas, and her mother, Gygaja Vidmantaitė Žekieni, a childhood friend of Edith Zwartendijk's, welcomed Edith, Rob, and me to Kaunas as if we were part of the family. The moment when Gygaja and Edith saw each other again after seventy-six years was one of the most moving experiences I've had in the Baltic countries.

In Vilnius, I received valuable assistance from Mantvydas Bekešius, the deputy minister of foreign affairs; Faina Kukliansky, the leader of the Jewish community in Lithuania; Emanuelis Zingeris, a member of parliament; and Linas Venclauskas, the chairman of the Sugihara Diplomat for Life Foundation. Faina Kukliansky saw to it that I received copies of all documents about Zwartendijk in the Lithuanian state archives, including the KGB files and documents from the Soviet era – a very difficult task at times.

On 25 April 2016, Emanuelis Zingeris, who was then the only Jew in the Lithuanian parliament, Edith Jes-Zwartendijk, Rob Zwartendijk, and ambassador Bert van der Lingen laid a wreath at the stone in front of the Jewish Museum in Vilnius that is inscribed with Jan Zwartendijk's name. During the brief ceremony, Emanuelis Zingeris addressed the Zwartendijk children. 'Your father was the light in the Jewish darkness. He possessed the best qualities a person can have. Every Jew who survived the war has taken your father's name into his heart.' Sixty-four members of the Zingeris family were murdered. He added, 'In Lithuania, we have two hundred Jewish cemeteries and two hundred mass graves.'

The deputy mayor of Kaunas, Simonas Kairys, pointed me to a well-documented article by Modestas Kuodis, 'Kaunas, mid-June 1940, Lithuanian memories', published in the Kaunas Historical Yearbook, no 16 (Vytautas Magnus University, Kaunas, 2016), which contains eyewitness accounts of the Soviet occupation of Kaunas on the evening and night of 15 June and Sunday 16 June 1940. Kuodis confirms Edith and Jan junior's impressions.

The wife of the Dutch ambassador to Latvia, the historian Mieke Langenberg-Tissot van Patot, did archival research in Riga for me, and located the grave of Jenny Heyer, ambassador De Decker's wife, in the Great Cemetery in Riga. I also received help and support from her husband, ambassador Pieter Langenberg.

At the Dutch foreign ministry in The Hague, I benefited from the expertise, historical knowledge, interest, and assistance of Bert van der Zwan, the coordinator of the Historical Unit in the Office of the Secretary-General. It was Bert van der Zwan who made it clear to me that the Netherlands had not had ambassadors before the Second World War. After the Congress of Vienna in 1815, the Netherlands had the status of a minor power. The international diplomatic system established by that congress included rules of protocol under which the head diplomat at a minor power's mission was not an ambassador, but an envoy extraordinary and minister plenipotentiary. Like an ambassador, such an envoy was a direct, personal representative of one head of state to another. Smaller countries such as the Netherlands began appointing ambassadors only after the Second World War. This is why L.P.J. de

Decker was the envoy extraordinary and minister plenipotentiary of the Kingdom of the Netherlands to Estonia, Latvia, and Lithuania before the war, and the ambassador to Greece after the war.

Consuls are not diplomats in the strict sense, but representatives of a state (with official, protected status) charged with promoting the interests of its nationals and its economic interests. The distinction between consular and diplomatic status, which was never crystal clear, still exists in formal and functional terms, but has become vaguer over the past hundred years or so. But the nitpickers are unquestionably right to claim that Zwartendijk, Sugihara, De Jong, and De Voogd, as consuls, were not technically diplomats.

Bert van der Zwan pointed me to the international law handbook *Grondlijnen van het Volkenrecht* by Professor J.P.A. François, which explains these distinctions.

One important source of information about the Dutch foreign ministry during the Second World War is Albert Kersten's doctoral thesis *Buitenlandse Zaken in ballingschap, groei en verandering van een ministerie 1940–1945* (Alphen aan den Rijn, 1981). Strikingly, it does not mention the consular assistance to refugees in Lithuania, Japan, and Shanghai, and Zwartendijk's name is not mentioned, even though the thesis was published in 1981. But Kersten does offer an exceptionally clear account of the problems with which the ministry-in-exile wrestled, of minister Van Kleffens's policies, and of the problems at the Dutch embassies in Tokyo and Stockholm.

In *Jean Charles Pabst, Diplomaat en Generaal in Oost-Azie 1873–1942* (Zeist, 1997), Dr A.A.H. Stolk paints a more positive picture of the Dutch envoy to Japan. But, tellingly, consul De Voogd in Kobe is not mentioned in the book at all, and no attention whatsoever is devoted to the thousands of Jewish refugees who arrived in Japan with Curaçao visas.

Jan Paulussen, the Philips company historian, searched the corporate archives for me for all documents, letters, messages, and publications relating to Jan Zwartendijk, his twin brother, Piet Zwartendijk, and Robert van Prattenburg and Koen de Haan, Zwartendijk's assistants in Kaunas. He also gave me a great deal of insight into the complex and precarious circumstances in which Philips found itself during the war. Using documents from the archives, Jan Paulussen reconstructed Hermann Maschewski's attempts to save Lietuvos Philips as an independent enterprise. In one file, he found the desperate letter that Maschewski had written to Zwartendijk on 18 March 1941. Jan Paulussen also wrote *Philips, familie van ondernemers* (Zaltbommel, 2016), from which I took a few facts.

The interview with Robert van Prattenburg, the financial director of Philips Lithuania and the general director of Philips Norway after the war, was published in the *Philips Koerier* on 23 October 1969 under the revealing title of 'Werken als sport in een woelige wereld' ('Work as sport in a turbulent world'). Van Prattenburg creates the impression that he wrote a significant number of the visas himself, claiming to have replaced 'the preoccupied Zwartendijk' and 'confronted' him with his 'status as consul'. He then lays out the Curaçao route as if he had come up with it himself, saying Curaçao was chosen for its proximity to South America.

In my research, this version of events was not confirmed by anyone. After Van Prattenburg became the head of the Philips office in Norway, he had a penchant for exaggerating his role in wartime Lithuania, although in 1969 he still imagined that only a few people he 'had helped as consul' had 'managed to reach a freer world by that long and difficult route'.

Zwartendijk was never absent from Kaunas in the summer of 1940, nor did Van Prattenburg ever substitute for him.

I found information about Philips in the war in I.J. Blanken, *Geschiedenis van Philips Electronics N.V.*, vol. IV, *Onder Duits beheer* (Zaltbommel, 1997); L. de Jong, *Het Koninkrijk der Nederlanden in de Tweede Wereldoorlog*, vol. 7; F.J. Philips, *45 jaar met Philips* (Rotterdam,

1976); and Sanne van Heijst, *Philips-meisje van Kamp Vught* (Amsterdam, 2016).

In *Het Philips-Kommando in Kamp Vught* (Amsterdam, 2003), socioeconomic historian P.W. Klein and Justus van de Kamp try to answer the question of whether Frits Philips (1905–2005) collaborated with the Germans during the occupation of the Netherlands. They concluded that Frits 'played along' in the interest of protecting as many Jewish Philips employees as possible. The survivors unanimously agreed that if it were not for Frits, they would all inevitably have been murdered. In 1995, Yad Vashem awarded Frits J. Philips the title of Righteous Among the Nations.

Jan Kamp assisted me in my research. He spent half his working life at Philips. After retiring, he gave tours of the Philips Museum in Eindhoven. He tracked down survivors for me, contacted numerous sources, unearthed an abundance of facts and details, and protected me from major errors. My working relationship with him was exceptionally pleasant and enlightening.

The children of Albert and Ille Komma are no longer living. Edith Zwartendijk put me in touch with their daughter-in-law, Evi Komma. She searched for answers for me in her late father-in-law's papers, and gave me a wealth of information about Albert and Ille Komma, and their forced departure from Prague.

John de Jonge gave me a clearer picture of Lithuanian politics and the struggle for independence with his biographical portrait *Antanas Smetona (1874–1944): van vrijheidsstrijder tot Litouwse president*, available as a pdf from the website of the Nederlands Baltische Vereniging.

The escape of Peppy Sternheim Lewin and her husband, Isaac Lewin, was described by their granddaughter Alyza D. Lewinon the website pillaroffire.nl on 26 April 2016: 'Hoe het lef van mijn oma hielp om duizenden Joden te redden'. Unfortunately, Alyza Lewin did not respond to my written request for more information about the Lewin and Sternheim families.

She firmly believes that it was her grandmother's initiative and perseverance that opened up the escape route to Vladivostok, Kobe, and Shanghai, and that today there 'may be 100,000 living descendants of those who survived thanks to the visas issued by Zwartendijk and Sugihara'.

Her surviving grandfather, Isaac Lewin, published his memoirs in 1994, under the title of *Remember the Days of Old: historical essays*. Her father, Nathan Lewin, described the flight of the Lewin and Sternheim families at length in a speech he gave in Potomac, Maryland on 1 May 2011, entitled 'Where were you 70 years ago?'. The entire speech can be found online: Address by Nathan Lewin, Yom Ha-Shoah Commemoration – 2011, Bnai Tzedek Congregation, Potomac, Maryland.

Jan Kamp obtained factual information about Naftali and Rachel Sternheim, their daughter, Pessla, and their son, Levie, from the Stichting Joods Monument, the Stichting Oorlogsgraven, the list of naturalisations after 1850, the Amsterdam City Archives 'Save a portrait' project, and the civil registry of the City of Amsterdam.

Nathan Gutwirth (1916–1999) recorded his memories in writing for his own children and Jan Zwartendijk's. His 'Memoirs of Nathan Gutwirth' is an English-language document just twelve pages long. I owe him a great debt of gratitude for his lively account and the clear light he throws on the events of 1940 in Lithuania.

Perla Frankel-Shalev and her daughter, Miriam Don, described the Frankel family's escape in *Memoir: a true story of a family's escape*, privately published in Israel in 2006. 'In addition to all the people who remained in Europe when the Nazis invaded, there were those who managed to escape and their stories as survivors are of equal importance to the collective memory of the Holocaust,' they wrote in the introduction. This does not alter the fact that their approach to the facts is quite careless. They call the Polish ambassador Rommel instead of Romer, and joke about him having the same name as the German general.

The Frankel family obtained a visa for Burma. Count Tadeusz Romer strongly advised them not to accept it. Three months later, Burma was occupied by the Japanese army. Mr Frankel and his sons would have had to work on the Burma railway if they had gone. In retrospect, they were deeply grateful to 'Ambassador Rommel'.

Asher Sarfati collected the information about his grandfather Abram Marber. He also checked all the documents from the Second World War still in the family's possession. Jan Kamp tracked down Asher Sarfati, and exchanged information with Sonja Mühlberger.

Sonja Mühlberger, born in Shanghai, has written a great deal about life in the city's Jewish ghetto. She had the answers to all my questions about Hongkew. The assistance she offered me was nothing short of exemplary, and I cannot thank her enough for her contribution to this book.

A great deal of information about the German and Austrian Jews in Shanghai has been brought together in *Leben im Wartesaal, Exil in Shanghai, 1938–1947* (Berlin, 1997), a publication of the Jewish Museum Berlin that accompanied the 1997 exhibition of the same name.

The twelve-year-old Hannelore Klein was one of the 937 passengers on the *St. Louis*. She went on that voyage with her parents and grandparents, her aunt Rosi, and her niece Ruth.Hannelore Grünberg-Klein published her memoirs under the title of *Zolang er nog tranen zijn* (Amsterdam, 2015). The afterword is by her son, the writer Arnon Grunberg.

The voyage of the *St. Louis* was the subject of Hans Herlin's documentary *Kein gelobtes Land. Die Irrfahrt der St. Louis* (Hamburg,

1961). Jan de Hartog's novel, *Schipper naast God*, was reissued (in the original Dutch) in 2008 by Atlas Contact.

Yukiko Sugihara wrote her memoirs after the death of her husband, Chiune, in 1986. The American edition, *Visas for Life*, was published in San Francisco in 1995. Linas Venclauskas wrote the short biographical sketch *Chiune Sugihara: visas for life* (Vilnius, 2009) for the Sugihara House in Kaunas. The director of that museum, Simonas Dovidavicius, led me on a tour, and was a mine of supplemental information on consul Sugihara. The historian Linas Venclauskas also provided me with facts about Vladimir Dekanozov.

Michinosuke Kayaba, the head of the Moscow office of Fuji Television, interviewed Sugihara in a Moscow hotel on 4 August 1977. What the seventy-seven-year-old Sugihara was doing there has never become clear to me. Sugihara sometimes confuses dates; for example, he claims that he left Kaunas on 1 September 1940 (three days before the Zwartendijk family), but I believe he left the day after the Dutch consul. Nonetheless, Sugihara's account is entertaining; for instance, he admits that he had to look up Curaçao's location in an atlas. I obtained a typed version of the interview in the Port of Humanity Museum in Tsuruga. Sugihara says in that interview that he provided 'around 4,500' transit visas to Jewish refugees.

Light One Candle: a survivor's tale from Lithuania to Jerusalem (Tokyo, 1995) by Solly Ganor is generally seen as one of the finest books about the Holocaust. There is also a German edition: *Das andere Leben: Kindheit im Holocaust* (Frankfurt am Main, 1997). Anonymous online Holocaust deniers have tried to discredit the book, claiming that Ganor did not spent a single day in Dachau. An open letter from his fellow camp inmates has proved them wrong.

Hillel Levine wrote the first study of Sugihara to meet rigorous standards of historical scholarship: *In Search of Sugihara: the elusive Japanese diplomat who risked his life to rescue 10,000 Jews from the Holocaust* (New York, 1995).

Bert van der Zwan and Jan Kamp aided me in my search for L.P.J. de Decker. I was able to reconstruct his career from the Dutch foreign ministry's database Persoonsgegevens Diplomatieke en Consulaire Dienst ('Personal Details, Diplomatic and Consular Service'). The most remarkable facts were discovered by Jan Kamp in newspaper advertisements.

Chaim Shapiro described his flight, which went on for seven long years, in the breathtaking epic *Go, My Son: a young Jewish refugee's story of survival* (Jerusalem and New York, 1989). Jan Zwartendijk junior saved the correspondence between Shapiro and his father, and added a few clarifying notes. Jan also spoke to Chaim Shapiro at length in Baltimore.

I found information about consul General Adriaan Mattheus de Jong in the foreign ministry archive kept in the Dutch National Archives under 'consulaat-generaal Stockholm 1896–1946 (2.05.221)'. The wartime Dutch community in Sweden is described by Dr L. de Jong in *Het Koninkrijk der Nederlanden in de Tweede Wereldoorlog*, part 6, vol. 1, in the chapter 'Contact met Londen'.

Information about the Resistance group 't Zwaantje is taken from J. Klatter, *De verzetsgroep Zwaantje: oorlogsbelevenissen van dr. Allard Oosterhuis* (Amsterdam, 1968). No one has better described Anton van der Waals, a man of a thousand faces, than Auke Kok in *De verrader, leven en dood van Anton van der Waals* (Amsterdam, 1995).

From Sweden, A.M. de Jong's grandson Magnus de Jong sent valuable information that he found in his grandfather's papers, as well as the letter of thanks from Samuel Orlansky and around ten photographs. It was Jan Kamp, yet again, who tracked down Magnus de Jong.

I found information about Louis Aletrino and his three wives on the website joodsmonument.nl, the Jewish Monument, which commemorates the Jews who died in the Holocaust in the Netherlands.

Jan Kamp helped me to look into all the details.

Lucas Bruijn wrote a gripping portrait of Louis Aletrino in *Tijdschrift nr-be*, 2008/3, the magazine of the Vereniging voor Nederlandse en Vlaamse cultuur Ne-Be.

The long and difficult road to diplomatic relations between the Netherlands and the Soviet Union forms the topic of a master's dissertation by H. P. M. Knapen, *Nederland en het andere Rusland* (Nijmegen, 1975). Alexander Munninghoff contributed the article 'Queen Wilhelmina and the Romanovs: an uneasy relationship' to the exhibition catalogue *1917: Romanovs & Revolution* for the Hermitage Amsterdam (2017).

Karl Schlögel's *Moscow 1937* (Cambridge, UK, and Malden, Massachusetts, 2012, original German edition 2008) offers a penetrating look at the Soviet Union at its historical nadir. Amy Knight wrote a biography of Beria: *Stalin's First Lieutenant* (Princeton, 1994). Unlike Stalin, who called him 'our Himmler', Amy Knight compares him to Göring. *Stalin: the court of the Red Tsar* (London, 2003) is a chilling depiction by Simon Sebag Montefiore of how the clique surrounding Stalin supported his tyranny and how high-ranking Party members such as Beria and Molotov played politics, interacted, and assassinated each other. It also gives a detailed and enlightening answer to the question of whether Stalin was an anti-Semite.

Victor Israelyan, who had a long conversation with Jan Zwartendijk junior on 4 June 1996, published his memoirs *On the Battlefields of the Cold War* (Pennsylvania, 2003). I received Zwartendijk's notes on the conversation from his brother, Rob. Professor Ilja Altman published his report *The issuance of visa to war refugees by Chiune Sugihara as reflected in the documents of Russian archives* as a digital publication of the Russian Research and Educational Holocaust Centre in Moscow in 2017. This research centre was established in 2012, a year after the collapse of the Soviet Union.

The decree signed by Stalin regarding 'Jewish refugees from Poland now residing in Poland' can be found in the archives of the Politburo under TsVKP31/7/1940. The letter from Vladimir Dekanozov to the foreign minister, Molotov, is dated 21 April 1940 and can be found in the 1940 archives of the international department of the NKVD.

Jan Kamp located the sons of the Dutch consul in Kobe for me: Jan J.N. de Voogd in Sydney and Egbert (Bert) C. de Voogd in Bairnsdale, Victoria. They gave me written information about their father and sent me copies of letters, including the letter from Nathan Gutwirth dated 22 August 1992. Jan and Bert also told me their parents received a bouquet every year in the last week of December, no matter where in the world they were. The sender was always 'someone from Antwerp'. Shortly before he left for Japan, where he had been appointed as ambassador, N.A.J. de Voogd was interviewed for the Dutch national newspaper *De Telegraaf* (11 January 1960). I took a couple of interesting anecdotes from there. Japan was to be his final post. He took his church organ to Tokyo with him.

Zerach (Zorach) Warhaftig incorporated his personal experiences into the much broader-ranging study *Refugee and Survivor: rescue efforts during the Holocaust* (University of Michigan, 1988), digitised in 2006. I drew some telling details from the obituary published by Lawrence Joffe in *The Guardian* on 8 October 2002, 'Zerah Warhaftig: a founding father of modern Israel'.

Abraham Liwer gave his children and grandchildren a brief written account of his escape and of how he gained his wife and daughter's release from a camp in Siberia. His daughter, Johevet (Joan) Liwer-Wren, supplied some supplementary information. His granddaughter, Arlette Liwer, married a Dutch national and moved to The Hague. In May 2018, Arlette Liwer-Stuip sent her family's story to Rob Zwartendijk, who sent it on to me. Arlette also generously answered all my follow-up questions.

The Japanese journalist Akira Kitade looked into the role played by the shipping company NYK in the war years, and wrote up the experiences of a few Jewish refugees in Japan. His book *Visas of Life and the Epic Journey: how the Sugihara survivors reached Japan* (Tokyo, 2014) is fairly unstructured, but served as an important source of information for me. The photographs collected by Kitade say at least as much as the orally transmitted stories.

Akira Kitade was able to track down both Jan Krukowski and Benjamin Fishoff, both in New York.

Cultural attaché Ton van Zeeland put me in touch with Kitade, and the two of us met in Tokyo. He was a rich source of information about the Japanese side of the story. Using the Sugihara list, Akira Kitade investigated where in Japan the refugees had stayed and what ships they took to Los Angeles, Vancouver, and Shanghai. Kitade could produce documents supporting the claim that 3,080 men, women, and children had been saved by visas from Zwartendijk and Sugihara. He had the professional courtesy to send copies of all the evidence that he had collected. This showed me that even such an exceptionally conscientious journalist and researcher could make an occasional error: he traced only the father and one child in the Wejland family, not the mother or Marcel's two sisters.

Akinori Nishikawa at the Port of Humanity Museum in Tsuruga offered up an entire weekend for me (Easter 2018), guided me through the museum with the assistance of an interpreter, and supplied me with the eyewitness accounts that the Tsuruga archivist gathered around the year 2000. I remained in contact with Nishikawa by email, and he found answers to all my questions. Erika Nishiura, the director of Tsuruga's historical museum Red Brick Warehouse, was also very helpful.

Tamar Engel's *The Jews of Kobe* (Stanford, 1995) filled in the historical background of the Jewish community in Kobe.

Masja Bernstein, using her husband Leon's personal name as a surname and an 'h' instead of a 'j' in her own first name, became one of New York's best-known society columnists, writing for the English edition of the world's oldest Yiddish newspaper, *The Forward*. All her life, she went on contributing colourful columns filled with fascinating facts about Polish-Jewish history and culture. Akira Kitade interviewed her in New York. Masha Leon died at the age of eighty-six. I drew much of my information about her from the detailed obituary published in the *New York Times* on 7 April 2017.

Chaim Nussbaum published his memoirs, *Chaplain on the River Kwai*, in New York in 1988. The stories of Leo Adler and Bella Hamburg are related in Barbara Sofer's brief account 'Passport to freedom', published on a website in Jerusalem on 10 April 2003.

My Polish translator, Alicja Oczko, was especially helpful to me as I searched for information about Count Tadeusz Ludwik Romer and his wife, Zofia Romerowa Wańkowicz. She sent me the link to Jerzy Wójcik's film *Wrota Europy* (*The Gateway of Europe*), and as I kept returning to it for another look at the Polish nurse, I began to understand Zofia a little. Andrzej Guryn is the only journalist and Ewa Pałasz-Rutkowska the only historian who have written about the assistance that the Polish ambassador to Japan and his wife and children provided to the Polish-Jewish refugees in Japan and Shanghai. (Andrzej Guryn, 'Tadeusz Romer's Help to the Polish Jews in the Far East', in *Newsletter Canadian Polish Research Institute, Toronto*, X, 1993.) Ewa Pałasz-Rutkowska's study of Tadeusz Romer was published by the University of Warsaw and has been online since 2017; this Polish historian had access to the archives of the Polish government in exile (1939–1945).

With the help of the Polish foreign ministry, Jan Kamp located the ambassador's eldest daughter in Canada. I sent Teresa Romer twenty questions, which she answered by email in the summer of 2017, two questions a week. I am exceptionally grateful to Teresa Romer for sharing her poignant memories with me.

I. Michel-Michalewitz paints a superb picture of the Jewish

community in Obeliai, the village where Tadeusz Romer was born. Her sketch of Abel, as the village is called in Yiddish, can be found on the website JewishGen.

Marcel Weyland's *The Boy on the Tricycle* (Blackheath, Australia, 2016) is a buoyant lesson in survival. After arriving in Sydney, Wejland changed the spelling of his name to Weyland. I learned a lot from this book, and not only facts. Marcel Weyland's English translation of *Pan Tadeusz* (New Zealand, 2006) is dedicated to 'emigrants and refugees from tyranny all over the world and to the children and grandchildren of those refugees'. That epic poem by Adam Mickiewicz (who was born in Zaosie, now Zavosse in Belarus, in 1798, and studied at the renowned University of Vilnius) begins with an ode to his lost country of birth. In Weyland's translation:

> Lithuania, my country! You are as good health:
> How much one should prize you, he only can tell
> Who has lost you. Your beauty and splendour I view
> And describe here today, for I long after you.

After the unveiling of the monument to Jan Zwartendijk in Kaunas, Marcel Wejland told me a few anecdotes that are not in his book, including the trip to the border in the Ford Eifel. He also had this to say:

> To survive, you have to be lucky. Not just once. No, once a day, once a week, a month, a year. If you don't have that good fortune, it doesn't make you a failure. You've simply had bad luck in life.

Although the wartime Jewish community in Shanghai is little known, much has been written about it. Every study emphasises the good relationship between the Jewish refugees and the Chinese people. The exodus to Shanghai began after the October Revolution in 1917, when many Jewish intellectuals emigrated to Harbin and from there to Shanghai. I have made grateful use of all the published memoirs, many of which I found during my stay in Shanghai. For example, I stumbled across Rena Krasno's wonderful book *Once Upon a Time in Shanghai: a Jewish woman's journey through twentieth-century China*, published in China in 2008. Wang Jian's *Shanghai Jewish Cultural Map* (Shanghai, 2003) was also very useful.

Finding other books about the Jews in Shanghai was not hard; I had the opportunity to borrow them from Ellen Schalker, my publisher from 1991 to 2009, who has a remarkable collection in her bookcase in Amsterdam. On Ellen's initiative, the Dutch publishing house of Atlas published Dutch editions of works such as Michèle Kahn's *Shanghaï-la-Juive* (Paris, 1st ed. 1997).

The main character of this novel is a young Jewish journalist from Vienna who, after being interned in Buchenwald, sets out from Trieste for Shanghai. Michèle Kahn offers a penetrating look at Jewish life under the Chinese sun from 1939 to 1948. The novel hews very closely to historical fact; for example, Benjamin Fishoff (see Chapter 44) appears under his own name. When I corresponded with Michèle Kahn, she was so kind as to tell me what sources she used.

One of the best first-hand accounts is *Shanghai Refugee: a memoir of the World War II Jewish Ghetto* by Ernest G. Heppner (University of Nebraska Press, 1993). Heppner was one of the first authors to focus on Zwartendijk. He befriended Jan Zwartendijk junior, who showed Heppner all the historical source materials he had found, and discussed them with him. After his death in 2004, Heppner left his archive to the United States Holocaust Memorial Museum in Washington, D.C. It can be consulted online in digital form.

Leben im Wartesaal. Exil in Shanghai 1938–1947 (Berlin, 1997) contains interviews with Sonja Mühlberger, Renate Gutschke, Peter Konicki, and others.

Even though *Cafe Scheherazade* (Melbourne, Australia, 2001) by Arnold Zable is a novel, I gleaned a great deal of information from it, especially about the atmosphere in the Polish-Jewish immigrant community in Kobe and Shanghai. Avram and Masha Zeleznikow presided over Cafe Scheherazade in St Kilda, a suburb of Melbourne, for forty-one years. All the historical facts mentioned by Zable are accurate.

Joan Veldkamp's *Vrijhaven Shanghai: Hoe duizenden Joodse vluchtelingen in China aan de Holocaust ontkwamen* (Amsterdam, 2017) was published after my visit to Shanghai, but I was nonetheless able to draw a few facts from it.

The Chinese consul general in Vienna, Ho Feng-Shan, published his memoirs, *My Forty Years as Diplomat* (Pittsburgh, Pennsylvania, 2010), but revealed little about the events of 1938–1940. He remained loyal to the Republic of China, and continued his diplomatic career in the service of the Taiwanese government. Recognition came too late for him, too; Ho Feng-Shan was recognised by Yad Vashem in 2000, three years after his death.

Nina Admoni, née Wertans, sent her spoken testimony by Skype to the Sugihara House in Kaunas. Ambassador Bert van der Lingen supplied me with a transcript.

The Dutch consul general in Shanghai, Anneke Adema, put me in touch with Professor Pan Guang at the Academy of Social Sciences. After I left Shanghai, the consul visited Professor Pan two more times to discuss all my questions with him. I am very grateful to her for that and, of course, to Professor Pan himself, an independent scholar who regards 'the experience of Jews in Shanghai' as 'an unforgettable chapter in history'. He published the first edition of his study *Eternal Memories: the Jews in Shanghai* in 1995, and the thoroughly revised and expanded second edition in 2015. The bibliography lists 156 publications, including works in Chinese.

Professor Kano Kenji researched the attitude of the Japanese authorities towards the Jewish refugees in Kobe and later in Shanghai. His was the first Japanese voice to give Zwartendijk more credit and to not focus on Sugihara exclusively.

Professor Kenji gave me information about the deputy commander of Hongkew, Sergeant Kano Goya (whose name is spelled Ghoya in all the Chinese documents). He interviewed the son of Sergeant Goya, who died in 1983, and debunked the myth that the deputy commander had been lynched.

Marvin Tokayer and Mary Swartz published *The Fugu Plan: the untold story of the Japanese and the Jews during World War II* in New York in 1979. Jan Zwartendijk junior received much information from Rabbi Tokayer.

The eldest daughter of Piet and Mary Zwartendijk, Ineke, provided me with all available information about their wartime experiences. Ineke Zwartendijk's courage and cool head are celebrated in a history of the Dutch Resistance: *Het grote gebod, de geschiedenis van het verzet, de Landelijke Organisatie Hulp aan Onderduikers en de Landelijke Knokploegen* (Kampen, 1979). But she herself looks back on her wartime actions with humility and humour. I spent an entire day talking to her on 1 February 2016; she was ninety-three years old, and I was struck by the clarity of her mind. Ineke lent me her Aunt Didi's scrapbooks. Jo Zwartendijk's article about George Grosz was published in the *Nieuwe Rotterdamsche Courant* on 17 December 1932. Ineke also explained to me how to tell Jan and Piet Zwartendijk apart in photographs; because her father Piet had a mild form of asthma, his mouth was always slightly open.

It was not only Edith Jes-Zwartendijk and Rob Zwartendijk who combed through vast quantities of photographs, letters, notes, and clippings for me, and helped me find my way through a thicket of facts, details, and anecdotes. Anne Bowden, the second wife of Jan Zwartendijk junior, also laid out numerous facts for me, and sent me a great deal of information from her home in Salem, Oregon.

I found all the information about the foreign ministry's response to consul Zwartendijk's actions in Kaunas in the ministry archives, under 'periode 1955–64, inv.nr. 2257 Zwartendijk, J.: onderzoek door het ministerie naar de 'Angel of Curaçao' die in 1941 [*sic*] aan Poolse joden visa zou hebben uitgereikt om zo aan de nazivervolgingen te ontkomen, 1963, in 2.05.118'. My thanks to Bert van der Zwan, coordinator of the Historical Unit in the Office of the Secretary-General (BSG) at the foreign ministry, for allowing me to consult this file, which is kept in the National Archives in The Hague.

Dr L. de Jong's standard reference work on the history of the Netherlands in the Second World War, *Het Koninkrijk der Nederlanden in de Tweede Wereldoorlog,* was published in fourteen parts (twenty-nine volumes) from 1969 to 1994. The two volumes of part 9 date from 1979.

After his father's death, Jan Zwartendijk junior collected all the materials he could find about Kaunas, the Curaçao visas, the Soviet regime in Lithuania, consul Sugihara and his wife, and the personal experiences of the Jewish refugees. He sent copies of almost all these documents and interview notes to his sister and brother. A year after Jan's death in 2014, I began my research. Edith and Rob gave me all the information that Jan had gathered. Without his preliminary work, I would have had to spend much more time searching for many events and individuals.

The only serious historical study of the rescue operation organised by Jan Zwartendijk and Chiune Sugihara was conducted by the United States Holocaust Memorial Museum in Washington, D.C., for the exhibition *Flight and Rescue,* held there from 4 May 2000 to 21 October 2001. The accompanying catalogue, *Flight and Rescue* (2001), edited by Sara J. Bloomfield, contains countless documents, letters, telegrams, first-hand accounts, and photographs. The picture it paints of the historical background is clear and nearly always accurate, and I have put the abundance of information it contains to grateful use.

Jan Zwartendijk junior was involved in the making of the book and exhibition. A few months before he died, he sent a copy of *Flight and Rescue* to his brother, Rob, from the United States, placing a sticker on the inside cover with these words:

Death is but the turning of a page of life
To the eyes of others it is death
But to those who die it is life.

These lines are from the sayings of Hazrat Inayat Khan, translated by H.J. Witteveen.

Marie-Claude Hamonic experienced the making of this book from day to day, provided constant advice, and organised my trips to Lithuania, Shanghai, and Japan, as well as my long-ago journey on the Trans-Mongolian Express. She accompanied me, helped me with my research there, and took hundreds of photographs that jogged my memory as I wrote. Without her, I would have lost the thread of the story somewhere in the middle.

Emile Brugman guided me through turbulent times in the world of publishing, and made sure I would still have the peace and quiet to concentrate on this book. He edited the first, second, and third drafts of the manuscript with close attention and a critical eye. As always, he got much more out of the story (and of me) than could ever have been suspected from the first draft. My thanks to him for his unfailing encouragement and valuable advice. Anita Roeland was once again responsible for the final editing, and Fieke Janse for the copyediting; they pointed out all the mistakes, inaccuracies, and flaws in my writing, down to the last comma. Marre van Dantzig read the first draft and suggested the first cuts. Karin Beernink yet again took up the thankless yet vital task of questioning everything that was open to question. In the production stage, I relied on the assistance, support, expertise, and enthusiasm of Leonoor Broeder, Rick van Geest, and Marcella van der Kruk. After years in which I'd had to do without her, Marjet Knake returned as my publicity manager – and more than that, as my adviser and media whisperer. She worked with Yvette Cramer (publicity), Joyce in 't Zandt (sales), Ellen van Dalsem (marketing), Carmen Carnier (Belgian publicity), and Vé Bobelyn (at VBK in Belgium) to promote this book. Many thanks, as well, to publishing director Chris Herschdorfer, rights manager Hayo Deinum, and Mireille Berman of the Dutch Foundation for Literature for generating international interest.

Illustration credits

Alyza D. Lewin and Nathan Lewin, photograph © Na'ama B. Lewin:
p. 86, p. 94

Andries de Marez Oijens: p. 439

Arlette Stuip-Liwer: p. 272

American Jewish Joint Distribution Committee Photo Archives:
p. 128, p. 165

Bibliothèque historique de la Ville de Paris, France-Soir collection:
p. 132

Brandl & Schlesinger Book Publishers, Australia: p. 183

Bundesarchiv, photographer unknown: p. 155

Deborah Wiener: p. 211, p. 213

Delpher: p. 125

De Voogd family archive: p. 247

Dutch Ministry of Foreign Affairs: London archive (access number
2.05.80), via the Dutch National Archives: p. 123

Dutch National Archives: p. 250

Flight and Rescue, a publication of the United States Holocaust
Memorial Museum, Washington, D.C., 2001: p. 119, p. 218

Furusato Tsuruga no Kaiso / Port of Humanity Tsuruga Museum,
'old scenery of Tsugura' photograph collection: p. 233

Getty Images / Bob Landry/ The LIFE Picture Collection: p. 296

Historic Collection / Alamy Stock Photo: p. 269

Hollandse Hoogte / Süddeutsche Zeitung Photo, photograph by Scherl: p. 175

Hyōgo Prefectural Museum of Modern Art, Kobe, photograph by Nakaji Yasui: p. 264

Ivanov, Vsevolod Viacheslavovich. *The Trans-Siberian Express*. Moscow: Intourist, 1922. Special Collections, Claremont Colleges Library, Claremont, California: p. 163

Jan Brokken: p. 110, p. 451

Japanese Foreign Ministry Diplomatic Record Office: p. 97

The Jewish Museum / Art Resource / Scala, Florence. Photograph by Arthur Rothstein (1915–1985). © The Jewish Museum, New York. Gift of Arthur Rothstein Family, 1999–51: p. 374

Marcel Wejland: p. 182

Masha Bernstein-Leon family archive ©, included by permission of the copyright holders: p. 284, p. 286

Nathan Gutwirth Institution, Belgium: p. 442, p. 444

National Digital Archives, Poland: p. 277

Nina Wertans: p. 361, p. 363, p. 365

Philips Company Archives: p. 300, p. 306, p. 329

Romer family archive: p. 275, p. 282, p. 293

Rotterdam City Archives: p. 29

Shanghai Jewish Refugees Museum: p. 348

Sputnik: p. 173

Sugihara House: p. 153

Tetsu Kono, with thanks to the Osaka City Museum of Modern Art: p. 243, p. 259, p. 357

United States Holocaust Memorial Museum collection: p. 3 (Jan Zwartendijk), p. 77 (National Archives and Records Administration), p. 82 (National Archives and Records Administration), p. 91 (Lucille Szepsenwol Camhi), p. 136 (Hiroki Sugihara), p. 143 (Hiroki Sugihara), p. 198 (Hiroki Sugihara), p. 240 (Akira Kitade), p. 303 (Jan Zwartendijk), p. 339, p. 344 (Eric Goldstaub), p. 345 (Ralph Harpuder), p. 346 (Harry Fiedler), p. 347 (Ralph Harpuder), p. 350, p. 390 (Jan Zwartendijk)